# BEING MUSLIM THE BOSNIAN WAY

# BEING MUSLIM
# THE BOSNIAN WAY,

## IDENTITY AND COMMUNITY
## IN A CENTRAL BOSNIAN VILLAGE

*Tone Bringa*

PRINCETON UNIVERSITY PRESS    PRINCETON, NEW JERSEY

**Copyright © 1995 by Princeton University Press**
Published by Princeton University Press, 41 William Street,
Princeton, New Jersey 08540
In the United Kingdom: Princeton University Press,
Chichester, West Sussex
All Rights Reserved

*Library of Congress Cataloging-in-Publication Data*

Bringa, Tone, 1960–
Being Muslim the Bosnian way : identity and community
in a central Bosnian village / Tone Bringa
p.  cm.
Includes bibliographical references and index.
ISBN 0-691-03453-2 (alk. paper). — ISBN 0-691-00175-8 (pbk.: alk. paper)
1. Muslims—Bosnia and Hercegovina—Ethnic identity.   2. Bosnia and
Hercegovina—Ethnic relations.   3. Nationalism—Bosnia and Hercegovina.
I. Title.
DR1674.M87B75   1995
305.6′971049742—dc20      95-18059

This book has been composed in Galliard

Princeton University Press books are printed
on acid-free paper and meet the guidelines
for permanence and durability of the Committee
on Production Guidelines for Book Longevity
of the Council on Library Resources

Printed in the United States of America
by Princeton Academic Press

10  9  8  7  6  5  4  3  2  1

10  9  8  7  6  5  4  3  2  1
(pbk.)

To Nusreta and Jasna

---

# Contents

# Illustrations

# Foreword

IN THE ATTEMPT to understand politics in Muslim societies, observers have tended to place excessive emphasis on the formal resources and institutions of state and society. They have thereby often overlooked the more subtle forces which have provided the basis for civic order—and often the reasons for its collapse. If this has been the case in analyzing societies caught in the common processes of transition, the tendency has been magnified in examinations of major, even seismic, social and political upheaval. In such instances, focus is almost exclusively trained on the failures of state institutions and the destruction of centralized authority.

Tone Bringa's *Being Muslim*, by way of contrast, presents the more complex calculus of forces at work in the run-up to the disintegration of the Yugoslav state. She offers a fascinating and persuasive account of how Muslim religious and ethnic identity was sustained and experienced in Bosnia prior to the collapse of the Yugoslav state and how the politics of gender and household inextricably shaped and constrained wider political and ethnoreligious identities. In 1987–88, Bringa became the first foreign scholar granted permission to conduct long-term field research in "Dolina," her pseudonym for a mixed Muslim-Catholic village in central Bosnia, two hours' north of Sarajevo by road. Because Bringa has maintained ties with the Muslim villagers, all of whom are now refugees, her book includes an account of the disintegration of the local civic order.

Dolina was spared direct experience of the war until April 1992. Most Dolina Muslims thought that only outsiders (*ljudi sa strane*) would provoke incidents. When these "outside" forces arrived, villagers were dismayed that some of their neighbors joined in killing Muslims and burning their houses, turning the war into one in which "neighbor was pitted against neighbor" and "the familiar person next door had been made into a depersonalized alien." Through the voices of eyewitnesses from the village—whom we come to know through Bringa's richly textured ethnography—this book depicts the collapse of the fragile civic pluralism which had previously prevailed.

Bringa offers an evocative account of how the Yugoslav state sought to define identity in terms of *narod*, "people" or nation. Villagers defined themselves principally in terms of *nacija*, or ethnoreligious groups. The interplay between official discourse on identity and political responsibility, which men took seriously as they negotiated the gray zone between state authority and local opportunities, and the more complex village understandings of community and collective identity—especially as sustained by women—form the backbone of this book.

Bringa's focus on gender differences in defining and sustaining social and political identity is a major contribution to understanding what "being Muslim" means. She argues for the pivotal role of women and households in defining Bosnian ethnoreligious identities and traces how they have been sustained in the changed economic conditions and rising educational levels of recent decades. By the late 1980s, wage labor, education, and migration diminished the cohesiveness of extended kin groups, altered residence patterns, and allowed young people a greater degree of autonomy than they had enjoyed in the past. Clothing styles, festivals, language, names, and even house types subtly contributed to defining and redefining moral boundaries. The book explores how the nascent fault lines between Muslims and their non-Muslim neighbors became barriers to shared civic life.

Bringa's analysis is particularly suggestive for the study of what we call Muslim politics—the competition and context over symbolic production and control of the institutions, both formal and informal, which serve as symbolic or normative arbiters of society. Bringa argues that Muslim identity "cannot be understood fully with reference to Islam only, but has to be considered in terms of a specific Bosnian dimension which implied sharing history with Bosnians of other non-Islamic religious traditions." Not many years ago, Muslims in Dolina joined their Catholic neighbors in building churches, and Catholics helped their neighbors build mosques. The two communities were morally bounded and separate, but they shared a generalized reciprocity on feast days and important family occasions such as births, marriages, and deaths. The lavishly textured fabric of such exchanges, centered on households and land, gave value to religious and ethnic identities. Both as self-ascription and as ascription, "being Muslim" is not determined by Islamic doctrine or distinctively "religious" values. For both Catholics and Muslims in this Bosnian village, land, household, and family were inextricably linked to questions of personal and community identity.

Bringa demonstrates how family, marriage, and kinship networks emerge as the repository of social values in Bosnian Muslim society, shaping and constraining wider political and social identities. As with other ethnoreligious groups, including the Catholic Croats in Dolina (and Orthodox Serbs elsewhere), religious and ethnic identities shaped and constrained choices of marriage partners, residential patterns, and dress—especially for women—but they did not preclude educational and employment opportunities. These were not religiously defined in the former Yugoslav state, and even within rural households, resistance to women continuing to higher education had gradually eroded. The lines between Muslim and non-Muslim moral communities had become redefined to the point where younger women and men could consider breaching boundaries of social intimacy to include marriage partners and friendships from different religious groups. In the end, however, most villagers (as opposed to townspeople, for whom mixed marriages had become common) felt that such mixed marriages would disrupt the orderly running of households, a primary focus for personal and social identity.

Bosnian Muslims in Dolina were aware of debates about what constituted "proper" Islamic doctrine and conduct. For a few religious scholars, "being Muslim" was defined by an "improved" understanding of Islamic doctrine and ritual. For most Bosnian Muslims, however, "being Muslim" was defined principally in contrast to the non-Muslim groups closest to them. As Bringa demonstrates, the usual dichotomized distinctions between public and private, above and below—tenuous at best in analyses of politics—are unhelpful in understanding the struggle for the control of resources and opportunities in Dolina. Politics is as much a struggle for people's imaginations as it is a struggle for control over resources and the defense of "interests." As such, it involves cooperation in and contest over what people think is right, just, or religiously ordained. Muslim politics, like all politics, can be seen as the setting of boundaries between decision-making units in society and the enforceable rules for resolving jurisdictional disputes among them. Bringa's account depicts a contest in which a local understanding and practice of moral and civic pluralism have collapsed; indirectly it offers suggestions for how the civic ties that bind might one day be restored.

*Dale F. Eickelman*
*James Piscatori*

IN NOVEMBER 1988 my anthropological field research (which had started in September the previous year) in the mainly Muslim community of a mixed Muslim/Catholic village in central Bosnia was drawing toward an end. I had just been to visit some learned Muslims at a sufi sanctuary, and back in the village I was calling in on eighty-year-old Atif to report on who I had met and what they had taught me. I had seen the old man every day for more than a year now as I was living in his house with his son, daughter-in-law, and their children. When I first arrived he had been skeptical of my presence. He, like many other villagers, had not wanted to accommodate me. They had worried about who I was, what I wanted, whether I would stir things up, whether as a foreigner they could trust me—could I not be all sorts of things, including a spy? In addition, as I was a Christian, the women worried that they would have to cook me pork. The Catholics in the village were puzzled that I was staying with the Muslims: Did I not find them "backward," and how could I live without pork and wine? Surely, I thought their religion was better than the Muslims'?

Having visited the village for the fifth time over a period of three weeks, and through the mediation of the local Imam and my mentor from the Ethnographic Museum in Sarajevo, Atif's family decided to offer me a place in their house. Atif had been against his son and daughter-in-law's decision, but his skepticism was not apparent since he was treating me according to the renowned Bosnian code of hospitality. It later transpired that he was worried that I too would tell lies about Islam and the Muslims as, he said, was so common in the West.

But it was not only the villagers; the authorities too were uneasy about my presence. I started specializing in the former Yugoslavia and Bosnia in 1986 as part of my Ph.D. program. In 1987 I went to Sarajevo where I spent three months at the ethnographic department at the Zemaljski Muzej before I was granted a research permit to do extended field research in a Muslim community in a mixed Muslim-Catholic village in central Bosnia. Such a permit had never before been granted to a foreign researcher. Although, on the advice of local colleagues, I avoided all mention of ethnicity or Islam in my research proposals to the authorities and instead focused on women and modernization, the local authorities kept a close eye on my whereabouts.

The villagers' distrust of the foreigner, however, slowly turned into trust and warm friendships. That day in November 1988, only two weeks before I was to return to London, old Atif told me: "When you go back among those people, tell them about us and what you have learned among us. But when you are here among people who know better than you, do not speak but listen." While later trying to write this book in the midst of the horrors of the war and the tremendous sufferings of most of the people who appear in it, I have kept the old man's words in my heart. I can only strive, given my limitations, to be worthy of the trust of old Atif. As an outsider there is a limit to my understanding of his community. In advising how to avoid being drawn into village intrigues, the local *hodža* (Islamic instructor) reminded me that there was a limit to my friendship with and understanding of the Muslims. Ultimately I was not one of them, I was not Muslim. Furthermore, he warned, always remember that people do one thing, say another, and think a third. Since the anthropologist rarely gets access to all three versions from the same person, the above warning is also valid for the reader of this ethnographic account.

In the summer of 1991 the Yugoslav People's Army (JNA) and their tanks were rolling into Slovenia. This was only the beginning of much worse to come. Ethnically homogeneous Slovenia without any significant minority population did not, however, become the scene of war. The situation turned out very differently in the two republics to the south with large Serbian minorities. When the war broke out in Croatia some months later, people in Bosnia-Hercegovina hoped and believed that they could avoid war, but the unthinkable (and from the attackers' point of view, the inevitable) finally happened in April 1992. The war had raged for exactly a year before it engulfed the village which is the focus of this study. It was in one of the last regions of Bosnia-Hercegovina to be pulled into the horrors. During most of that year, people in the village believed that the only way they could be directly involved in the war was if "outsiders" (*ljudi sa strane*) entered and start provoking them. Even when Bosnian Croat (HVO) and Croat army forces clashed with Bosnian government forces (mainly Muslim) elsewhere in central Bosnia, the Muslims and Catholic Croats in our village continued to live together side by side in peace. In the end what was so painful to most Muslim villagers and to many of their Croat neighbors was that the attackers were not only "outsiders." When HVO started shelling and killing Muslims and burning their houses in the village, some of the Muslims' Catholic Croat neighbors joined in, although the attack had been planned and initiated by people far from the village. Starting out as a war waged by outsiders it developed into one where neighbor was pitted against neighbor after the familiar person next door had been made into a depersonalized alien, a member of the enemy ranks.

After I had revisited the village in May 1993 and had seen almost every Muslim house destroyed and all the Muslims gone, it was very difficult to sit down in peaceful Cambridge and continue writing this book. Nothing of what I had earlier said seemed real or to matter. At the same time, however, it became even more important to write about the community and the lives that had once, not very long ago, existed. It had been a community where people treated each other with dignity and respect, and understood how to accommodate each other's cultural differences.

One of the major difficulties I had to face while writing was the choice of tense. The original manuscript had been written in the ethnographic present, but it became impossible to write in the present when such dramatic changes had taken place, particularly since the Muslims did not live in the village any more. Nevertheless, it also felt wrong to use the past tense consistently, for several reasons. First, much of what is described in the book is still a part of Bosnian Muslims' lives, and of who they are. Second, the military and political situation in Bosnia-Hercegovina keeps changing and therefore where and how people live does too. Third, and perhaps most important, when I talked to Muslims who had fled the village in April 1993 I found that they themselves were mixing tenses in a striking manner, infusing both the past and present with a sense of unreality though also of open-endedness; they were living in a time, a dramatically and constantly changing time, which was neither in the past, the present, nor the future. My own use of tense partly reflects this open-endedness. Yet, there are descriptions of places and events which I know have disappeared or have been destroyed. Here I use the past tense.

In addition to the dilemma concerning the use of tense, I had to make decisions about the use of names on country and language. Before 1992, the period with which this book deals, Bosnians were citizens of the Socialist Federal Republic of Yugoslavia (SFRY) or Yugoslavia. I have chosen to use the adjective "Yugoslav" within quotes to indicate a past identification, while referring to this former federation by its historical name. Before the dissolution of the Yugoslav Socialist Federal Republic the official language used in Serbia, Croatia, and Bosnia-Hercegovina was Serbo-Croat. When the federation split, the language split too. In Serbia, the official language is called Serbian and in Croatia it is called Croatian. There was a slight difference in vocabulary and in accent between Serbian and Croatian, however. This difference has been carefully noticed by philologists in Belgrade and Zagreb, and in addition as part of the nation-state building project they are searching for new words to replace earlier ones that were shared between the two. In

Bosnia the spoken language was a mixture of the Croatian and the Serbian versions of the language, but it also contained a vocabulary specific to Bosnia; some of these words and expressions were mainly used by Muslims. An obvious solution left to the Bosnians was to call their language Bosnian (although in Croat-administered councils in central Bosnia in 1993, the official language was said to be Croatian and children's schoolbooks were printed in Zagreb in the "Croatian language"). Bosnian Muslim philologists on their part are returning to an old Bosnian vocabulary which was common currency in villages and among older Muslims, but before the war was perceived as archaic by the urban, educated elites. When I refer to the language spoken by people in the village I will use the term Bosnian. When referring to the official language before 1992 I will, however, use the term "Serbo-Croat." The village where I worked is situated in the Bosnian part of Bosnia-Hercegovina. I will therefore mainly refer to Bosnia, but will use the full official name of the country in some instances where this seems more appropriate. Because of the volatile political situation in Bosnia-Hercegovina I have chosen not to refer to the village by its real name, using the fictive name Dolina instead. To protect the identities of individuals I have used pseudonyms.

My anthropological training had not prepared me to deal with the very rapid and total disintegration of the community I was studying. Although our theoretical models do allow for social change, these are slow changes that the anthropologist can study by returning to the field at intervals, registering modifications and integrating them into a neat model, which demonstrates for example how people themselves make sense of such changes in a more or less coherent way. In short, it all seems to make sense both to the "locals" and to the anthropologist. This war has made sense neither to the anthropologist nor to the people who taught her about their way of life.

I have been able to follow a Bosnian community over a period of six years during which it has undergone dramatic changes and events. In the late eighties people were working hard against the odds of hyperinflation and economic crisis to improve their lives materially. In 1990 they were full of optimism about the future under the new economic reforms and the political and religious freedoms introduced under the premiership of Ante Marković. In January 1993 it was a village in fear surrounded by war on all sides. Relationships between Muslim and Croat neighbors had come under strain, but people still held on to the hope that they could preserve peace in their village. In April 1993 the village was attacked by Croat forces. In October 1993 none of the four hundred Muslims in the village remained. They had either fled, been placed in detention camps, or been killed. (In June 1994 the detention camp was closed and its Muslim prisoners released. They and other Muslims from Dolina, who are internal refugees in Bosnia, are waiting to return to their village.) During the winter of 1993 several Muslims from Dolina died of cold, hunger, and exhaustion. Throughout that winter the fighting between Croat and Bosnian forces was ferocious and many of the Muslims from Dolina who had been forced from the village in April kept fleeing—it wasn't safe anywhere any more. Many of the people in the photographs in this book were killed. Among them were twenty-year-old Fatima pictured six years earlier, at age fourteen, cleaning the mosque with her friend. She was killed by a shell as she ran out of a building in the town where she was a refugee. Fatima had tried to assist a young woman who had been hit moments earlier. Her dream before the war had been to study economics in Sarajevo. She was her parents' only daughter and youngest child. This war has claimed the lives of many young Bosnians like Fatima. So many voices have been silenced.

In May 1993 I returned for the second time to central Bosnia after the war had started with a Granada film crew in connection with the making of the "Disappearing World" series documentary, "We are all Neighbours" (our first visit had been in January). We wanted to try and find my friends who had fled the village after the attack by HVO forces two weeks earlier. We found the parents of one of my best friends in their sons' house five kilometers from the village. Their house had been shelled to rubble and two close relatives had been shot while trying to flee. Mehmed, my friend's father, was in deep shock. This particular meeting has remained a powerful image for me both because of its sadness and pain, and because of what it symbolized. I believe the episode sums up thousands of Bosnians' lives in this war. It also echoes my own feelings as I try to grapple with what has happened.

Mehmed took a key out of his pocket and held it in his hand, looking at it as if at a loss for what to do. Then he asked me to go to his house and lock the door, but could I take out some things for him first? He described to me exactly where I would find what he wanted. I knew the house well. Then he said that after I had locked the door I should hand the key over to his neighbor for safekeeping. What was the point, his wife asked. Maybe someone might want to go in there and steal something, he said. We both stared at the key in his hand in silence. I wondered whether he really did not know what had happened to his house. Or did he need me to tell him, to confirm the unspeakable? I could not tell him, he did not hand me the key; we both knew. We were left with a key with no door to fit it. Then I realized that the key and the missing house were not the most significant things in this encounter. Rather it was the silences about what we both knew, the words we did not speak. This book is also about what has been left unsaid.

Ethnographic accounts draw on the activities, experiences, and thoughts of the people they claim to present. This account is no exception and my greatest debt is to those people in Bosnia who lent their voices to this particular account. Bosnia treated me to her renowned hospitality and there are many to whom I am grateful. I have nevertheless made the difficult decision not to acknowledge by name any of the individuals in the village and beyond who made particular contributions to this book. Those people to whom I am indebted for their assistance and knowledge will know and I hope they will accept my thanks. I should add that the arguments and interpretations put forward here are entirely mine.

My field research in 1987–88 was made possible by a Yugoslav state scholarship awarded through the Norwegian Research Council (NRC) and the generous assistance of the Zemaljski Muzej in Sarajevo. My mentor there was Miroslav Niškanović who, apart from practical assistance, also contributed his ethnographic knowledge. My colleague Gordana Ljuboja encouraged my ethnographic work in Bosnia and provided the initial contacts. In London I am above all indebted to Dr. Peter Loizos at the London School of Economics (LSE) who supervised the doctoral work upon which this study is based. He also commented on a late version of this manuscript. His firm belief in my project was an encouragement throughout. When the war broke out in Bosnia, and after my return visits there in the spring of 1993, his own background from a village which became ethnically divided by war and intercommunal violence enabled him to lend me unique support based on his own insight and understanding. My research at the LSE was partly supported by a British Council Scholarship and a grant from the Radcliffe-Brown Memorial Fund.

In writing the book I was greatly helped by the rigorous comments and suggestions of Princeton University Press's two anonymous readers. I would also like to thank the Press's editor Mary Murrell for supporting the book and for her patience. During the last five months of my writing I have been employed as a lecturer at the Department of Social Anthropology at Bergen University. I am grateful to the department and my colleagues for making sure I was not allocated a heavy workload until I had finished the book. In Bergen, I would also like to thank Reidar Grønhaug for reading and commenting on an earlier draft of the manuscript, and Moslih Kanaaneh who commented on parts of my writing and from whose suggestions I have benefited. Karin Ask read several drafts of chapters five and six and made useful suggestions. Dzemal Sokolovic made helpful comments about chapter one.

Most of the book, however, was written while I was affiliated with the Department of Social Anthropology in Cambridge. The department provided me with an office and a good and inspiring work atmosphere. While in Cambridge I was also affiliated with King's College. Without the support of a two-year postdoctoral fellowship from the Norwegian Research Council, neither the Cambridge stay nor the book project would have been possible. In Cambridge Susan Ducker-Brown read and made useful comments to chapter four. Figure 2 is a modification of a map made for me by the Zemaljski Muzej in Sarajevo. Zlatan Pilipović made figure 3 and gave encouragement throughout the difficult last year of writing. Lastly, Deema Kaneff read and commented extensively on several chapter drafts. Without her help and support this book would have been considerably more difficult to complete.

# A Note on Language and Pronunciation _____

BOSNIAN (Serbian and Croatian spelling) is phonetic, that is each letter of the alphabet always represents the same sound. Serbian is written in the Cyrillic script, while Croatian uses the Latin script. The scripts' geographical distribution reflects the historical division of the South Slav lands between the Orthodox and Catholic spheres of influence. In Bosnia-Hercegovina before the war, typically enough, both scripts were used, although the Latin script was more widespread and popular. For example, the Sarajevo newspaper *Oslobođenje* conscientiously printed one article in the Cyrillic script and the next in Latin (while Zagreb newspapers used the Latin script and Serbian newspapers the Cyrillic). Present-day Bosnian uses the Latin script. The following brief guide to pronunciation includes only those letters whose pronunciation is significantly different from English. It is based on the Croatian and Bosnian alphabets (which have been modified for the Croatian and Bosnian phonetic system).

| | | | |
|---|---|---|---|
| A | a in *father* | J | y in *yes* |
| C | ts in *cats* | Lj | ll in *million* |
| Č | ch in *church* | Nj | n in *news* |
| Ć | a soft 'tch' | O | o in *not* |
| Dž | j in *John* | R | rolled |
| Đ | roughly 'dj' | Š | sh in *she* |
| E | e in *let* | U | u in *rule* |
| H | ch in *loch* | Ž | s in *pleasure* |
| I | e in *he* | | |

# BEING MUSLIM THE BOSNIAN WAY

# Introduction

WHEN I returned from Bosnia-Hercegovina after my first field trip in 1988, I was asked by colleagues in Britain, "Where is Bosnia?" Today very few Europeans would have to ask that question. For more than three years now (1995) Bosnia has been making front-page headlines in European newspapers. Even names of villages and small market towns have entered the daily newspaper vocabulary. The first war on European soil in almost fifty years has produced an enormous interest in the region both on the part of the media and that of the academy. Many researchers, historians, social scientists, and others have turned their interests toward the former Yugoslavia. The questions these experts ask themselves relate to the "whys" and "hows" of the war: the fall of communism, the role of the old communist establishment, the Yugoslav army, the historical competition between the Serb and Croat national movements for hegemony in the northwestern Balkans, and the interests of the greater European powers. The more qualitative data-oriented social sciences such as sociology, social anthropology, and social psychology have particularly turned their interest toward refugees and the victims of different forms of systematic violence (such as mass rape). The media has been focusing on the "age-old hatreds" in the Balkans of which Bosnia-Hercegovina is assumed to be the prime example. In the media coverage of the war there seem to be two approaches. The first is that the people in Bosnia-Hercegovina have always hated each other and whatever tolerance and coexistence there was had been imposed by the communist regime. The other is the idealized approach that Bosnia-Hercegovina, with its potent symbol Sarajevo, was the ideal example of a harmonious and tolerant multicultural society, where people did not classify each other in terms of "Serb," "Muslim," or "Croat."

Neither of these approaches reflects the Bosnia I experienced during the five years before war broke out in April 1992. There was both coexistence and conflict, tolerance and prejudice, suspicion and friendship. To some a person's name (which usually indicates a person's ethno-religious affiliation) was important and implied a barrier to social intimacy and trust; to others, however, it did not matter. Attitudes depended on age and the sociocultural environment in which a person had grown up. To the generations who grew up in the fifties and sixties it was usually not an issue, while to pre-World War II generations it often was, and it was starting to become important among young people in the eighties. In 1987, when I visited a primary school in the region where I worked, the teacher of one class asked me whether I wanted to know the "nationality" of the children, that is, how many Muslims, Serbs, and Croats there were. He then asked his ten-year-old pupils to identify themselves by raising their hands. Most of the children were confident in their knowledge of whether they were Serbs, Croats, or Muslims, but some hesitated or got it wrong and had to be instructed by their friends.

When I related this story to a friend of mine in Sarajevo, she was surprised and said this question would never even have been posed when she went to primary school in the sixties. She claimed that even if the question had been posed most children would not have known the answer, and they certainly would not have known, or been interested in, whether a person's family background was Serb, Croat, or Muslim. Other Sarajevan friends of the same generation confirmed that children's knowledge of the "nationality" of their schoolmates was a new development. This change in awareness among young Bosnians in the late eighties should be seen in relation to the change in official policy toward the "nationality question" in Yugoslavia during the 1970s, and will be discussed at greater length in chapter one. In Bosnia-Hercegovina consciousness of a "Yugoslav" identity was strongest among the generations who had been educated in the 1950s and 1960s.

Nevertheless, in rural areas, such as the village which is the locus for the present study, it was different. There people did know the ethnoreligious family background and affiliation of their neighbors and schoolmates from the village or neighboring villages. Yet, this is not to say that people resented each other or could not live together. Again and again when I visited the village in January 1993 I was told by Muslims and Croats alike that "We always lived together and got along well; what is happening now has been created by something stronger than us."

In Bosnia there were many different ways in which people from different ethnic, religious, and socioeconomic backgrounds would live together and side by side. These varied between town and country, sometimes from one village to the next, from neighborhood to neighborhood, and from family to family. While in the village people of different ethnoreligious backgrounds would live side by side and often have close friendships, they would rarely intermarry. In some neighborhoods they would not even live side by side and would know little about each other. And while some families would have a long tradition of friendships across ethnoreligious communities others would not. In towns, especially among the urban-educated class, intermarriage would be quite common, and would sometimes go back several generations in a single family. Here the socioeconomic strata a person belonged to was more important than was his or her "nationality."

Since the war started I have often been asked whether any of the material I gathered during the late eighties can explain the current war. My answer is no. Neither my material nor this book can or intends to explain the war for the simple reason that the war was not created by those villagers who are the focus of this account. This war has been orchestrated from places where the people I lived and worked among were not represented, and where their voices were not heard. In the end, after resisting for almost a year, these villagers too became part of the war, initially becoming involved in order to defend their own homes and families. The story of how this happened is, however, beyond the scope of this book. Suffice it to say that war changes people in profound ways. It changes their perceptions of themselves and who they are, and it changes their perceptions of others and who they are. This book is concerned with the voices behind the headlines, the lived lives behind the images of endless rows of refugees and war victims, deprived of past and future, defined by others solely in terms of what they have lost— as refugees. These people used to belong to communities, which they valued and which provided them with a sense of belonging and identity. This is the account of some of these peoples' lives, and aspects of the community in which they lived. It is set in a particular time in history, and focuses on the lives of some specific people in one specific village community at that time. It does not pretend to be an account of all of Bosnia or its people, but is the detailed study of one of the yarns that made up the Bosnian weave.

The book is about how one community of people lived their lives before the war, but it is also about how a foreigner and anthropologist put her own words and understandings to what she saw, heard, and learned in this one community. Furthermore, before all of this became filtered through anthropological theory, it had been colored by the experiences and perceptions of the people I had easiest access to, and closest contact with. During my first fieldwork visit in 1987–88 I stayed in an entirely Muslim neighborhood although the village as a whole was mixed Muslim and Catholic/Croat. This was not a choice I made but rather a coincidence. Inevitably, which household, neighborhood, and even village I lived in did delimit what I was able to observe and learn and also colored and directed my research in specific ways. My own status in the village as a young, unmarried woman simultaneously restricted me to the world of women and excluded me from the world of men. Living in an all-Muslim neighborhood meant that I had less contact with Catholics in the village than did some Muslims who had Catholics as their first neighbors. As a member of one particular household and neighborhood it was important for reasons of loyalty (which will be clearer in subsequent chapters) that I socialize with people who were part of my house-

eighborhood's social network. The Catholic households I
l a female family member who was a good friend of my
bors. This is, in other words, the study of a Muslim com-
lage of Muslim and Catholic inhabitants, as seen mainly
ough the eyes of women.

## Muslim Europeans

All academic disciplines divide themselves into subdisciplines and sub-
fields of special interest and competence. Social anthropologists often
categorize themselves according to geographical regions of interest. Regions are defined by geography but ultimately often by certain common
ethnographic traits established through cross-cultural studies. This has
led to more or less arbitrarily delineated "ethnographic regions." One of
these is "the Mediterranean" which is geographically defined as the
countries surrounding the Mediterranean Sea.[1] This region, in other
words, includes European, North African, and Middle Eastern countries. The ultimate defining characteristics have therefore been ethnographic, particularly the so-called honor-shame complex (for a discussion of such common traits, see Gilmore 1987). Although this concept,
and with it the whole idea of a Mediterranean ethnographic region
(Pina-Cabral 1989), has since been challenged, anthropologists working
within this so-called ethnographic region have been divided into two
more or less separate fields of scholarship—the Europeanists and the Islamicists—each with little knowledge of the other's field. But while the
latter have at times studied aspects of the former's field, Europeanists
have dealt exclusively with Christianity or its influences. Thus anthropology has contributed to reinforcing an image of Europe as exclusively
Greco-Latin Christian.

In recent years the increased presence of Muslim immigrants in Europe and a growing awareness that the idea of "Europe" was part of the
same tradition which created "orientalism"—that is, an image of the
"orient" as Europe's "other" which Europe ruled culturally and economically, and negated (Said 1978)—have been reflected in anthropological research. Europeanists have increasingly also had to become Islamicists, or Islamicists have moved to Europe (Gerholm and Lithman
1988; Mandel 1990). But European academics' "orientalist" baggage
still travels with them. This has become apparent in the writing on the
Balkans and the war in the former Yugoslavia. In Europe today, people
in the Balkans have been assigned the role of the oriental other (Hayden
and Hayden 1992). Yet, as early as 1975, William Lockwood had published an ethnography with the remarkable title "European Moslems,"

subtitled "Economy and Ethnicity in Western Bosnia." Within the field of "Mediterranean anthropology," which operated with a southern non-European Islamic shore, and a northern, Christian and European one, this title must have seemed like a contradiction in terms (Davis 1977).

That the Bosnian Muslims themselves became a contradiction in relation to these cultural area definitions was of course more serious. Lockwood's European Muslims were Bosnians living in Bosnia-Hercegovina, and at the time of study, in Yugoslavia. Whether or not Bosnia could be reckoned as part of the "Mediterranean area" is beside the point here. What is essential is that the case of the European (indigenous) Bosnian Muslims challenges the rigid definitions of Europe (and the northern shore of the Mediterranean) as "Christian" and, I would think, many Europeans' perceptions of "European."

The Bosnian Muslims are, however, not the only European Muslims in the Balkans given that there are Muslims in Serbia, Montenegro, Albania, and Bulgaria, for example. In his now classic *People of the Mediterranean*, Davis (1977) argued for "an anthropology of the Mediterranean" that takes into account comparative considerations of empirical data from both the northern and southern shores of the area. This implied, as Gilmore points out, that the academic barriers between the Europeanists and Islamicists had to be dissolved (1982:176). However, his argument rests on the assumption that the "Islamic ethnography" was to be found on the southern, non-European shore (unless the "Europeanist" dealt with immigrants). In my view, academic barriers based on false assumptions about what "Europe" implies, which pervade much of the northern European dominant discourse about "Europe," need first of all to be dissolved within the field of European studies itself (i.e., the northern shore). The only other alternative is either to define people like the Bosnian Muslims as not European, or as European but not really Muslim. Both definitions have been and are being attempted by various commentators on Bosnia-Hercegovina. In his ethnography, by putting the Bosnian Muslims on the European ethnographic map Lockwood established their "Europeanness," but almost totally ignored the Islamic dimension and the role of Islam as a set of religious beliefs and practices (Lockwood 1975a).[2]

Yet Islam is the moral system on which a Muslim collective identity is based. Islam as a practiced and lived religion has to be understood in terms of its specific role in the Bosnian context, where it forms the main constitutive factor in a collective identity that distinguishes Bosnian Muslims from Catholic Croat Bosnians and Bosnian Orthodox Serbs. Such understanding is best gained by an anthropological study of (practiced) Islam which makes a distinction between Islam as a social identity, as a set of formal doctrines, and as actual beliefs and practices, and accounts for the interrelationship between these elements (Joseph 1978:11). However, as Gross has noted, "the understanding of religiously based identities is only one aspect of a complex of identities which are not closed, unidimensional, unchanging" (Gross 1985:16). The present study explores both the Bosnian and the Islamic dimensions of Bosnian Muslim identity immediately preceding the dissolution of communist Yugoslavia and the war in Croatia and Bosnia-Hercegovina.

## "Yugoslav" and Muslim

In September 1987 when I first arrived in the then-mixed Muslim and Catholic (Croat) village which was the location for this study, I noticed in almost every house I visited a picture of Tito, the leader of post-1945 communist Yugoslavia. It had a prominent place either on the wall in the kitchen-cum-living room where people would spend most of their time when at home, or else was hung on the wall in the foyer, which everyone passed through when entering the house. This was specific to village households. In the larger towns and in Sarajevo it was rare for people to have a picture of Tito on the wall at home, this being a practice restricted to public buildings and offices.[3] In addition to the former Yugoslav leader, most village households had family pictures and the official school photographs of their children, the child sitting at a school desk with an open book in front of him or her. In both Muslim and Catholic houses, there were the same kinds of pictures, symbolic of the similarity of these families' relationship with the state, through the educational system and the communist leadership. But the walls also spoke about another dimension of villagers' identities, since a third motif often joined those of Tito, the family, and children learning to read and write. Religious pictures were different in Muslim and Catholic households; while in Muslim houses the images were of a girl in a headscarf praying, or of the Kaaba, the Catholics had images of the Virgin Mary with the child Jesus, and a crucifix. Through these pictures on the walls in the central room in their houses, the room where guests were received and which thus was open to the outside world, the villagers told me about important defining dimensions of their identity.

Although Tito symbolized a unifying state and ideology for all "Yugoslav" citizens, he was also the architect behind a diversifying nationality policy which had ascribed nationality status to the Catholic and Muslim communities in this Bosnian village as Croat and Muslim respectively. Tito's Yugoslav state defined these two communities as two *narodi* ("people" and "nation") sharing the territory of Bosnia-Hercegovina, together with the Serb *narod* (the Orthodox Christian commu-

1. Map of Bosnia-Hercegovina and the former Yugoslavia. Map courtesy of Kjell-Helge Sjøstrøm.

nity). Yet adherence to different religions was perceived as the difference which separated the village population into two *nacije*: Muslims and Catholics. Aside from the fact that Tito was a much respected leader for having brought Bosnia-Hercegovina (and Yugoslavia) peace and relative prosperity, he had supported the rights of the Bosnian Muslims to claim status as a *narod* equal to that of the Bosnian-Hercegovinian Catholics and Orthodox Christians, who held *narod* status as Croats and Serbs respectively. This meant that any governmental body, council, or committee had to be made up of an equal number of representatives from all three *narodi*. Thus, from 1971 onward (when Muslims gained *narod* status) Muslims were guaranteed numerically equal political and administrative representation with Serbs and Croats. Therefore to many Muslims Tito symbolized not communism or communist party membership, but rather their Muslim *narod* identity. However, officially this Muslim *narod* was defined (historically and culturally) in secular rather than religious terms.

But in the village the expression of a religious (Islamic) identity was an integrated part of the expression of a Muslim secular (cultural) identity, symbolized by a second picture, of Islamic inspiration. That this picture symbolizing the Bosnian Muslims' Islamic religious identity was often that of a girl praying is very apt, since women rather than men were the key performers of religious rituals in the village. It was a girl and not a boy who thus represented Islam as the moral and ideological counterpart to areligious "Yugoslavism." The picture places women (and girls) at the center of the Muslims' Islamic identity. It was particularly important that a girl be brought up in accordance with Islamic values. Indeed a girl would probably also be able to hold on to that education more successfully in adulthood as she would not have to compromise herself to the same degree as would a boy later in life when he entered the public, secular, "Yugoslav" world (see chapter three). The villagers' anxieties about marriage between members of different ethno-religious communities (discussed in chapters three and four), which in Muslim families particularly focused on daughters marrying non-Muslims, were as we shall see in chapter five a key to understanding the pivotal role of women in the construction and maintenance of a collective Muslim identity anchored in Islam.

Prior to the war in Bosnia-Hercegovina (April 1992) its population officially consisted of three *narodi* distinct in terms of religious affiliation but not of geography, language, or social life. Affiliation with one of the three religious doctrines, Roman Catholic, Serbian Orthodox, and Sunni Islam, corresponds to membership in a Bosnian *nacija* or official *narod*. Thus Catholics are Croats, Serbs are Orthodox, and Muslims are members of the "Muslim" *narod*. In "Serbo-Croat" orthography (the official prewar Yugoslav language designation now split into Serbian and Croatian, while Bosnian Muslims increasingly refer to their language as Bosnian) the potential ambiguity of the term "Muslim" was avoided by writing the noun designating a person's national identity with an initial capital (*Muslimani*) and the member of the religious community with a small letter (*muslimani*), (Purivatra 1974:305). Hence in official discourse there were two kinds of Muslims: Muslims in the ethnic sense of the word and Muslims in the Islamic and religious sense of the word. Thus official socialist "Yugoslav" policy implicitly denied that the national category "Muslims" was dependent on religious identity. But as Irwin notes: "There is no basis for distinguishing 'Muslim' other than religious self-selection, from other indigenous speakers of Serbo-Croat in Bosnia" (1984:438). According to Joseph, religious identity can refer to theological issues as well as consciousness of group membership, or social identity, and is thus an ambiguous term (1978:4).

In the former Yugoslavia, this distinction was made explicit as part of the official discourse on the "nationality" status of the Bosnian Muslims. Contrary to Joseph's formula, however, in which Islam forms the building block for both types of identity, the Yugoslav communist party discourse consciously attempted to keep the relevance of Islam to the identity of the Bosnian Muslims to a minimum.[4] In Yugoslav Bosnia-

Hercegovina two official spheres governed by a communist and an Islamic body respectively presented different discourses about what a Bosnian Muslim is or should be. In socialist Yugoslavia, the *Muslimani* were
the subjects of the secular, areligious, Yugoslav Bosnian-Hercegovinian
republic, while the *muslimani* were the subjects of the Islamic community and its bureaucratized organization, the Islamic Association (see
chapter six).

Consequently, when talking about the Muslims of Bosnia-Hercegovina and the former Yugoslavia (including the Sandžak in southeastern
Serbia), it is important to remember that in the former Yugoslav official
context and within the present public discourse the term "Muslim" refers both to a "nation" (*narod*) and to a religious community. There
were an estimated 4 million Muslims in the former Yugoslavia when
they were classified as a religious group (1.1 million of whom are Albanian Muslims living in Kosovo), but less than 2 million of these
declared themselves as belonging to the officially designated Muslim nation. The overwhelming majority of these Muslims lived in Bosnia-
Hercegovina.[5] According to the 1981 national census there were for
instance 78,000 registered Muslims in Montenegro, and 151,000 in
Serbia (without Kosovo).[6] (These numbers do not include Muslims in
the religious sense who declared their nationality to be other than
"Muslim" such as Serbian, Albanian, or Yugoslav.)

This ambiguity of the term Muslim reflects the debate on the origin
and history of the Bosnian Muslims and their contested status as a *narod*
within both the nationality hierarchy in the former Socialist Federal Republic of Yugoslavia, and the present nationalist fight for dominance in
Bosnia-Hercegovina which has had such tragic consequences. It is to a
discussion of these issues that I now turn.

# One

## History, Identity, and the Yugoslav Dream

> We live in the borderland between two worlds,
> on the border between nations, within
> everyone's reach, always someone's scapegoat.
> Against us the waves of history break, as if
> against a cliff.
>    Meša Selimović, *Dervish and Death*

### Contested History

The Balkans generally, and Bosnia-Hercegovina specifically, is the historical outcome of the various civilizations which have met on its soil. All influenced and left their imprint on the demographic, cultural, and political makeup of the region, kingdom, province, and later Republic of Bosnia-Hercegovina.

Throughout history Bosnia-Hercegovina has straddled some of the major political and ideological divisions on the European continent. It straddled the boundaries between Byzantium and Rome, those between eastern and western Christendom, and those between the Catholic Austro-Hungarian empire and the Islamic Ottoman empire. In recent times it was often described by Western observers as being behind the iron curtain (although after Tito broke with Stalin in 1948, Yugoslavia was a nonaligned state and not part of Moscow's sphere of influence). Migration followed in the aftermath of military conquests by the various imperial powers (particularly the Austro-Hungarian and the Ottoman), as a consequence of shifting economic policies, or because the various rulers discriminated against one community or segment of the population while favoring another.[2] The main dividing line in historical times was between the Latin western and the Greek eastern churches' areas of influence and later between these and Ottoman Islam. With the exception of Slovenia, Croatia, and Vojvodina (today in northern Serbia) which were part of the Habsburg empire, most of Yugoslavia's (SFRY) territories had until the nineteenth century been part of the Ottoman empire. But while Croatia was conquered by the Austrians in the seventeenth century, and Serbia received its independence in 1830, Bosnia-Hercegovina remained under Ottoman rule until taken over by the Austro-Hungarian dual kingdom in 1878. The competing claims of the Catholic central Europeans on the one hand, and the Orthodox Byzantine empire on the other, as also of the Islamic Anatolian Ottomans, have left contrasting legacies and a lasting imprint on South Slav culture.

In modern times the line of conflict in Bosnia-Hercegovina has run mainly between (Catholic) Croatia and (Orthodox) Serbia with the Bosnians and Muslims caught in between. Historically, since the withdrawal of the Ottomans from the western Balkans, Bosnia-Hercegovina became the main arena for competing Serb and Croat nationalist claims (Bracewell 1993:154). These claims were part of wider Serbian and Croatian hegemonic aspirations in Bosnia-Hercegovina: making the Bosnian Muslims into Serbs or Croats—in other words, assimilating them— would strengthen one of the two contestants considerably. The pressure on the Muslim population to identify (or even assimilate) with either the Croat or the Serb *narod* has, as a consequence, at times been strong.

The historical aspirations of both Croatia and Serbia to parts of Bosnia-Hercegovina is reflected in the writing of history on Bosnia-Hercegovina by both sides. The history of the Bosnian Muslims has been contested by several South Slav and Balkan historians, and because their past is being contested so too is their ethnic origin and claim to status as a distinct *narod* (see discussion below). One prominent illustration of this contestation is Mehmed Paša Sokolović (1506–79), a vizier at the sultan's court in the mid-sixteenth century. A writer of Bosnian Croat origin claims that the famous Pasha was an Islamicized Croat (Tvrtković 1993) while a Serb historian claims that he was of Serb origin, and Orthodox before he became Muslim (Samardžić 1971). Nevertheless, both agree that the Pasha was a Muslim convert and from Bosnia.

Contesting the Muslims' past and questioning their distinctiveness, or alternatively emphasizing their historical "discontinuity" as a "people," has obstructed both Muslim and Bosnian efforts at establishing that they are a people with "historical continuity" (Saltaga 1991). The construction of a nation's historical continuity is of course essential to a nationalist discourse which seeks to establish a legitimate (that is, "natural") link between a people and a defined territory. For any nation to create a continuous past it has to be selective, ignoring the intermingling of peoples and their constant migratory movements, and playing down major changes in political, cultural, or religious allegiance. Although some influence of other cultures and peoples may be acknowledged, the backbone of the kind of ethnic nation-state with which we are concerned here has to be "one original source." In Serbian and Croatian historiography, in the former Yugoslavia the Bosnian Muslims as a "nation" were primarily defined as converts, that is, as people who had broken away from their original religious and ethnic roots (seen by

Croats to be Catholic and Croat, and by Serbs to be Orthodox and Serb), and had later denied it by refusing to accept that they are either Serbs or Croats. In the current conflict this debate is logically about who the legitimate owner of Bosnia-Hercegovina and its territory is. Nationalists are invoking different events and periods in the history of the peoples sharing the same territory, in order to support their nationalist cause and "prove" who owned the land by establishing "who was there first." Both groups can find support for their claims depending on what era and area of Bosnia-Hercegovina they focus on.

This chapter will seek to place the Bosnian Muslims as an ethnoreligious group in the cultural and political history of the region to which they belong, and examine the academic discourse about their identity, and the claims and counterclaims about "who they are." An introduction to the Bosnian Muslims' cultural, historical, and political background is particularly salient in terms of the current war in Bosnia-Hercegovina and the attempt by Bosnian scholars to establish a Muslim national history and identity.

## Heretical Bosnia

At the heart of the academic debate on the "origin" (and ethnicity) of the Muslims and their status as a *narod* is the Islamization of Bosnia-Hercegovina, for this is the critical point through which "historical discontinuity" might be established. Three main arguments have traditionally been dominant in the debate among Balkan scholars. First, it is argued that Bosnian nobles converted in order to retain their property and privileges; second, that conversions were forced (or at best coerced); and third, that those who converted were members of the medieval Bosnian Church persecuted as "heretics" by the established Christian churches and particularly by the Roman Catholic church. The link between the Bosnian Church and the Bosnians' conversion to Islam has become one of the most contested points in the history of the Bosnian peoples, lying at the heart of the nationalist discourse in Bosnia-Hercegovina.

Balkan scholars agree that the Bosnian Muslims are descendants of South Slavs who converted during the four-hundred-year reign of the Ottoman empire. They disagree, however, about who converted and why. During Ottoman rule conversion followed different patterns at different periods in time and varied from one region to another. The pattern in Bosnia-Hercegovina was thus different from that in Bulgaria, for instance. The main reason for this was that conversions were not necessarily forced, and were often the result of specific political and socioeconomic circumstances in the various Balkan countries and regions.[3] The often simplistic understanding of the Ottoman period reflected in much Balkan nationalist historiography has contributed to crude theorizing about the Islamic conversion process in Bosnia-Hercegovina. Indeed, the processual character of the conversions—inherent to all forms of social change—has often been lost. Among the most well-rehearsed arguments to explain the conversions is that the converts were either forced to do so by the Ottomans or that conversion was a strategy followed by the Bosnian-Hercegovinian gentry to allow them to retain their property and privileges. While some authors argue that before these landowners adopted Islam they were mainly Orthodox "Serbian," others claim they were mainly Catholic "Croats" (e.g., Eliot 1908 on the former, and Šidak 1940 on the latter).

Such arguments reflect a highly oversimplified view of the religious and socioeconomic structures prior to, and above all during, the Ottoman empire. What is clear is that Bosnia-Hercegovina represents a case which sets it apart from others in terms of a few key factors. First, nowhere else did the local population convert to Islam in such large numbers or so early on during the Ottoman conquest. Second, those who converted came from a broad cross section of society. Although the evidence suggests that the Bosnian gentry were among the first to embrace Islam—and the securing of property may have been a motivating factor—peasants followed suit.[4] Nevertheless the numerous, early, and broad based (in terms of social class) character of the conversions to Islam in Bosnia-Hercegovina has been an enigma to many Balkanist historians. The "Bogomil, and Bosnian Church theses have therefore seemed attractive ones. The Bosnian Church and the Bogomils have come to occupy a significant and mythical role in Bosnian history and have been critical in the academic discussion of the historical identity of the Muslims. This is not least the case because written sources and documentation about the Bosnian Church are few. The controversy about the Bosnian Church is closely linked to the debate on the Islamization of Bosnia-Hercegovina and the "ethnogenesis" of the Bosnian Muslims.

According to this thesis the Bosnians who converted to Islam had been members of the Bosnian Church. It seems the Bosnian Church was anticlerical and opposed to both the Greek and Latin Church hierarchies. Both churches condemned it as heretical; the Catholic Church was particularly antagonistic and persecuted its members through the Hungarians.[5] Its tenets are believed to have been influenced by Bogomilism, a Christian sect with a dualist world-view said to be a successor of the Manichees or Gnostics.[6] Both Catholic Croat and Serbian Orthodox historians have claimed that the Bosnian Church was not heretical but was indeed part of their own respective churches (Šidak 1940).[7]

Other evidence suggests, however, that the Bosnian Church had virtually disappeared by the time of the Ottoman conquest (Šidak 1940; Malcolm 1994). According to Šidak there is no reference either to the Bogomils or to the Bosnian Church after 1470. He does quote sources which claim to have come across Bogomils in parts of Bosnia-Hercegovina in the nineteenth century. Interestingly, these "Bogomils" are in one instance said to be Muslims and in another Catholics (Šidak 1940:151–52).

Fluid confessional definitions are widely reported in Bosnia far into the twentieth century. Ethnographic data show a nondoctrinal attitude toward religion by Bosnians of all three confessions. For-instance, certain shrines, whether a "Bogomil" tomb, a *šehit*'s grave, or a Christian saint's tomb, are used by all Bosnians irrespective of faith. Practices like these are often referred to as syncretistic. But such a term assumes that there is an original version. The examples from Bosnia show that no one original version existed. Rather there were several, and until the last part of the twentieth century many people were not that concerned with its religious source (see Filipović 1982; Hadžijahić 1977; Hasluck 1929; Šidak 1940).

Several authors have, however, suggested that the three "classical" arguments cited above concerning the Islamization of Bosnia is one-sided and of limited relevance (Banac 1984; Donia 1981; Fine Junior 1975; Malcolm 1994). Fine maintains, for instance, that there is no evidence that the Turks pressured people to convert in Bosnia (except for short and particularly fanatical periods). Nor did the Christians need to embrace Islam in order to retain their land (Fine 1975:382). He also suggests that although the so-called heretics or Bogomils converted in great numbers, the evidence points to a multidirectional change of religion—Catholics accepted Islam or Orthodoxy, Orthodox believers turned to Catholicism or converted to Islam—partly because of the absence of any strong church organization in this region. It has also been suggested that those Bosnians accused by the Roman Catholic Church of being heretics were seen as such because they were practicing their religion according to Orthodox tenets and traditions (Malcolm 1994:36). It is possible that the Bosnian Church—first persecuted by both the Catholic and Orthodox churches (though particularly by the former), and later claimed by both—given its independent position in relation to the established churches, combined elements from both these competing doctrinal churches. This is plausible considering the sharp competition and antagonism between the western and eastern churches in Bosnia at the time, which continued into the Ottoman conquest (Karpat 1982; Filipović 1982:158–59; Džaja 1984: 209–10). Since many in Bosnia and Hercegovina were persecuted as heretics, the new religion, Islam, which

may have had some similarities with the way religion was already practiced locally, may have been considered both attractive and liberating.
Islam, furthermore, had the advantage of being the religion of the con-
quering state, and as the local people were persecuted as "heretics" by
the established churches and their promoter states, Islam and the Turks
offered a new kind of identification free from the fear of persecution.[8]
The problem is, however, that there exists very little written evidence of
the Bosnian Church and its specific interpretation of Christianity, and of
practiced religion among Bosnians at the time.[9] Today the idiosyncratic
Bosnian and Hercegovinian tombstones called *stećci* are the most striking legacy of this almost mythical past.[10]

In his book on the Bosnian Church Šidak concludes that "the fate of
the 'Bosnian Church' and their Christians has been buried forever in the
silence of a past which is dead" (Šidak 1940:153). For Bosnian Muslim
scholars this "dead past" has become the stumbling block to the "ethnogenesis" of the Bosnian Muslims (and some would argue to a common
Bosnian heritage independent of confession). It is this silence which
bothers a Bosnian sociologist when he argues that the history of Bosnia-
Hercegovina was written by either Serb or Croat historians who had a
vested interest in constructing such a "dead past" and thereby a historical discontinuity for those of the Bosnian-Hercegovinian population
who were neither Catholic Croats nor Orthodox Serbs. Nationalist Bosnian scholars, however, sought such a link, stressing that this would include rather than exclude the Catholics and Orthodox Bosnians who
lived alongside the Muslims. Indeed, according to this view, Bosnia had
three religions even before the arrival of Islam, with heretics (Bogomils),
Catholics, and Orthodox Christians living within the same territory
(Saltaga 1991). At the core of the Bosnian historical self-perception
which included the "Bogomil" thesis was the notion of Bosnia and its
peoples as heretical. Indeed, during my stay in Bosnia an Islamic instructor concluded a discussion on the specifics of Islam as it was practiced in
Bosnia by saying: "Bosnia was always heretical."

There is a saying in Bosnia, *Do podne Ilija, od podne Alija* ("Until
midday Ilija [Elijah], from midday Alija"). This saying refers to the Muslim celebration of Aliđun and the Orthodox Serb celebration of Ilindan,
both events taking place on the second of August.[11] A Bosnian ethnologist reported in 1978 from a village in north Bosnia with a mixed Serb
Orthodox and Muslim population that *Aliđun/Ilindan* was celebrated
by both groups with a fair in front of a well-known *turbe* (allegedly of
the hero Đerzelez Alija, who, according to Muslim legend, was killed on
this spot while praying). Here, the literal meaning of the saying was
acted out in practice. Until the midday prayers Muslims prayed at the
*turbe*, while the Serbs were at a different place, said to be the site of a

church before the Turks arrived. After midday the Serbs joined in at the *turbe* for the general fair with music and dance, competitions, and food. It should be added, however, that the two groups celebrated side by side more or less separately, with the competitions, mainly in physical endurance, always being between a Serb and a Muslim (Niškanović 1978). This event illustrates the fact that although people in local communities acted out their continuity with their past, events can change people's identifications over a relatively short period of time. Differences arise but people continue to coexist, albeit in competition. People with different names and different religious affiliation share sites and events, but they also have their own sites and exclusive events. For people in these former mixed communities, past and present were a continuous whole and shared, but their communities were at times separate and at others they merged.

## The Ethnic Dimension

Bosnian families' present religiocultural affiliation to one of three religious traditions—Orthodox Christian, Catholic Christian, or Islam—was in most cases determined during a period of more than five hundred years of coexistence between these faiths on Bosnian soil. At some point in the past their forefathers would have decided to join one of these communities, Orthodox, Catholic, or Muslim. Adherence was communicated to others by practicing certain rituals specific to that faith, and not least for Muslims by changing their name. There are for instance several documented examples of brothers throughout the history of the Ottoman presence in Bosnia (and long into the nineteenth century) belonging to different religious communities. One brother might be an Orthodox Christian while the other declared his allegiance to Islam. Eliot (1908:344) claims that sometimes a family divided itself between Christianity and Islam so as to have friends on the right side no matter what happened. In such cases family members recognized each other as relatives, but generally used different names conveying the same meaning in Slavonic and Turkish respectively. (There are also examples of brothers who have declared their allegiance to different sides in the present war.)

The decision brothers in previous generations made to retain their allegiance to a certain religious community or to convert was motivated by several factors. In addition to personal conviction, religious affiliation was often a political statement and reflected identification with certain political, social, or economic interests. Religion could also reflect occupational identity. A Bosnian who made a career in the professions or

Ottoman administration was more likely to declare himself a Muslim. Bosnian last names are often a description of a profession or social status of the person who first adopted the name. It could reflect his trade or status, or an honorary title such as *beg* (bey; for Muslims such names often consist of a Turkish rather than a Slav word), with an added *-ić* at the end, a historical diminutive which indicates "descendant of." Or, as is typical in the Slavonic tradition, a person's last name might be made up of a patronym in the possessive form *-ov* plus the diminutive, such as Ahmedović. But there are also Muslims with a Muslim first name and a last name consisting of a Christian patronym, such as Ahmed Filipović. In Bosnia your name tells people who you are. Although many Bosnian Muslims have last names with a Turkish language component which sometimes also clearly indicate their Islamic heritage, there are other last names that are used by all three *nacije* and indicate a common cultural history and common descent.

First names, too, indicate ethnoreligious background. Muslim first names are of Turkish or Arabic (Islamic) origin. These names are, however, often transformed or shortened in everyday speech, and thus obtain their specifically Bosnian coloring. Thus Mehmed becomes Meho, Salih becomes Salko, Fatima becomes Fata, Emina becomes Mina, and so on. (Christians have their specific biblical or saints' names, with sometimes slight differences in form for Catholics and Orthodox.) For the Muslims themselves, however, personal names are not only important as identity markers vis-à-vis Christians, but closely linked to ideas about the person in Islamic etiology as described in more detail in chapter five.

In addition to typical Muslim or Christian names there are two other kinds of names. The first consists of typical Slav names, such as Miroslav or Čedomir. These names were used by Croats and Serbs alike, but never by Muslims. The other kind consists of so-called *narodni* or "folk" names which were not specific to any ethnoreligious group, such as Zlata, Jesenka, Zlatko, or Damir. These names were particularly popular during Tito's Yugoslavia and indicate either a person's parents' communist party membership or their outlook on Yugoslav nationality or the fact that they are of different *nacije*.[12] Other names which have come into the "Serbo-Croat" language from German, French, or English (such as Ilma or Denis), were becoming increasingly popular with Muslims in the late 1980s because they were seen as neutral names which did not immediately identify a child as Muslim. This was particularly true of parents who were not religious and wished to avoid the stigma which they felt "muslimness" carried among sections of the non-Muslim population.

The combination of first and last name therefore frequently signals to

Bosnians the ethnoreligious background of other Bosnians they meet
for the first time. If a person's first name does not tell the story his last
name usually will, or vice versa. Or in the rarer cases where neither indicates a person's exact background, the additional information about
that person's father's personal name and possibly the neighborhood or
area of Bosnia from which he or she comes will be decisive. When ethnoreligious identity (or "nationality") is not immediately clear from a person's name it is quite common to remark on that person's father's first
name, as for instance in "His father is Mehmed." In other words he is a
Muslim.

Through the generations religious affiliation has also become an ethnic identification. For Bosnian Muslims his or her last name is no longer
mainly an indication of social and occupational status, and religious
identity. It represents generations of cultural knowledge which has been
formed and transformed first by membership in a moral community
based on Islam (or its cultural heritage) and second, by the close coexistence with Bosnians defined by affiliation to other non-Islamic religious
traditions.

## The Muslims as a Bosnian *Nacija*

In addition to introducing their religion, Islam, the Ottomans also established an administrative scheme, the *millet* system, whereby membership in a "nation" was determined by religious affiliation and not for
example by shared language, a defined common territory, a perceived
common history, or ethnicity (that is, perceived common descent). According to Braude and Lewis (1982:12), *millet* was a term which originally meant a religious community and in the nineteenth century came
to mean a nation, although "nation" did not necessarily become integrated with "state" the way it is in western Europe.

The Ottoman state was organized in a series of self-contained non-
Muslim religious communities called *millet*, each with a spiritual leader
at its head.[13] Muslim subjects of the empire were under the imperial administration's direct jurisdiction, but like the *millet* it had designed in its
image, this administration was characterized by the integration of religious and political power in that religious laws and doctrines were the
basis for regulating rights and duties between persons. However, in contrast to the Christian *millet* in which all the governing posts were part of
the ecclesiastical church hierarchy, the Muslims participated in a vast
and influential military and civil service which recruited mainly Muslims,
either from different parts of the empire or locally. In Bosnia-Hercegovina, local Muslims predominated in the administration of their own
territory. In areas such as Bosnia where the local ("converted") Muslims

were particularly involved in the civil service, a well-educated secular Muslim community evolved as a consequence.[14]

In the Republic of Bosnia-Hercegovina this *millet* legacy is salient as there is a complete overlap between the notion of a separate nation and membership in a specific religious community or *nacija*. There is furthermore no overlap between state and nation. Thus in Bosnia-Hercegovina, in addition to the legacy of Tito's nationalities' policy, which I will discuss shortly, there was the historical legacy of the Ottoman *millet* system, which created collective cultural identities based on membership of a religious community. Here three ethnoreligious communities with status as a nation—Muslims, Catholic Croats, and Orthodox Serbs—speak the same language and until the war (1992– ) shared the same territory and economic life, even to the extent of sharing villages.

At the beginning of my stay in rural central Bosnia, when I was not known to people there, I was often asked, "What *nacija* are you?" I thought they were asking me about my citizenship and said Norwegian, but I was soon to learn that this was not what I was being asked (they already knew I came from Norway). The answer which made sense was not Norwegian, but Protestant. It was only when people asked additional questions to clarify such as, "Have you got churches or mosques where you come from?" "Do you cross yourself with three or five fingers?" that I understood.[15] All these questions related to characteristics of the known Bosnian *nacije* of Muslim, Catholic, or Orthodox. Filipović, among other scholars, has argued that the term "Muslim" understood as a "nationality" did not exist among rural people even as late as 1990 in several parts of Bosnia-Hercegovina (central Bosnia included) other than in its "only and original meaning, i.e., as a religious term" (Filipović 1990:66).[16] Filipović fails to mention, however, that a religious identity is also a social and cultural identity and in the Bosnian context has an ethnic aspect, since a person usually "inherits" his or her religious identity from his or her parents and, above all, from the father who passes on his surname to his children and thus establishes a child's ethnic identity. Moreover, the Muslims were not the only ones who understood their identity in this way; in the village where I worked before the war Catholics too referred to themselves (and were referred to by the Muslims) as Catholics rather than Croats. They, too, understood their identity primarily in terms of religious affiliation. This was, however, changing among the younger generations who used the official term Croat (which they had learned in school). I have been told that in northern Bosnia it was likewise common to refer to a Bosnian of Orthodox Serbian background as *pravoslav* (Orthodox) rather than as "Serb." To refer to people of a different ethnoreligious background, villagers themselves use interchangeably "someone of a different faith," and "someone from a different *nacija*." Throughout the remaining chapters

of this book I will use the term *nacija*, which accorded with local usage
and understanding, or alternatively describe this as an ethnoreligious
identity.

The term *nacija* referred specifically to what I term ethnoreligious
identity and community. Indeed, as we have just seen, traditionally and
in some rural areas up until the war, the term was used to refer to affiliation with a religious community and its traditions and practices. The
three main *najica* thus were Orthodox (*pravoslav*), Catholic (*katolik*),
and Muslim (*musliman*). (At the national census [or for bureaucratic
purposes] members of these communities generally chose to declare
themselves under the corresponding *narod* status: Serb, Croat, and
Muslim. However, there was not always an overlap between membership in an ethnoreligious community locally and the selected census category as individuals could also choose "Yugoslav," "undeclared," or any
other available census designation.) The census term *narod*, on the
other hand, was used in everyday speech first, more generally to refer to
the "people" or a people (the French or the Germans, for instance) and
even sometimes to the Yugoslav population as a whole. Second, the
term implied a "national" collective such as Serb, Croat, or Slovene, and
was specifically associated with the people of one republic (Serbia,
Croatia, or Slovenia).

According to the predominantly western European conceptualization
of the terms "nation" and "ethnic group," the latter is a group of people
who share certain cultural traits, a past, and usually a territory . They are
either the group overlapping with the nation which defines the state, or
they are a minority people within the nation-state. Although the logic of
the legal international community avers that state and nation have to be
one and the same, ethnic pluralism is indeed the rule in the vast majority
of "nation-states" (for instance, the United States of America). Even in
the United States, however, there is only one official nation and there is
a complete overlap between nation, state, and citizenship. The Socialist
Federal Republic of Yugoslavia, by contrast, represented an alternative
to this relational definition of nation and state, which suggests that it
would be more useful to define nation as an ethnic group which either
aspires to or has obtained its own state. Furthermore, in Bosnia-Hercegovina applying the concept of either "ethnic group" or "nation" in the
western European sense stipulated above would mean ignoring and dis-
torting local conceptualization. Indeed, terms used officially and increasingly by non-Bosnian commentators such as nations and ethnic
groups were not used locally before the war. However, indigenous conceptualization and labeling may vary too, daily local discourse representing one usage while the state represents another, politicized one. In
Bosnia-Hercegovina as part of the communist-governed federal state of
Yugoslavia one set of classifications and definitions existed at the state

level (and as part of a political discourse), while another, which differed in some important aspects from the official ones, existed among the villagers in central Bosnia. Having discussed local everyday usage and categorizations, I turn to a discussion of the official Yugoslav nationalities' categories.

## Tito's Socialist Yugoslavia

The main field research on which this book is based was conducted in 1987–88 before the disintegration of the "Socialist Federal Republic of Yugoslavia" (SFRY). In order to comment on the political status of the Bosnian Muslims at the time, I start by giving a short outline of the pre-1991 Yugoslav federation, its history, and structure.

Yugoslavia was first founded as the Kingdom of Serbs, Croats, and Slovenes in 1918 under Alexandar Karađorđević, the Serbian prince regent, but after the Partisans led by Tito liberated the country from the Germans and their allies (Italy and a Croatian puppet regime led by the Ustaša) in 1945, Yugoslavia was declared a Federal Socialist Republic. World War II had seen the different peoples of the Yugoslav kingdom mobilized on opposite sides in the war. There were at least two other wars running parallel to World War II and the Partisan war of liberation: a Serb-Croat war and a Serbian civil war. Several hundred thousand Serbs died in Ustaša-run concentration camps and tens of thousands of Muslim civilians in eastern Bosnia, in particular, were massacred by Serbian nationalists or Četniks.[17] More people in Yugoslavia were killed by "fellow Yugoslavs" than by Italian and German occupational forces.

Tito's dream was to create a new Yugoslavia where the different groups who had fought each other could live together in peace and prosperity. He knew, however, that the major groups would not be able to agree on a version of the past, on a common "Yugoslav" history. He therefore decided it was better to "forget" the past and build a new Yugoslavia with a carefully constructed system for the balance of power between the largest "ethnic" groups so that no one people would dominate the other. However, in this he was only partly successful. Although in the 1960s and 1970s generations grew up in Yugoslavia who identified themselves with the future of Tito's federation, and as "Yugoslavs" rather than with the past antagonisms and lines of division, many people of the World War II generation had neither been able to forget nor been given the chance to forgive.

After Yugoslavia was expelled from the Cominform in 1948, and the Yugoslav communist party was no longer under the Soviet sphere of influence, Tito's policies continued for some years to be closely modeled on those of Stalin (Malcolm 1994:194). This was particularly true for his nationalities' policy. After the break with the Soviet Union, Yugoslavia presented itself as a nonaligned power characterized by its "distinctive creed of self-managing socialism" (Ramet 1985) and henceforth navigated its course between the communist central and eastern European states and the capitalist West.

The SFRY was a federation of six republics and lasted from 1945 to 1991. On 25 June 1991 both Croatia and Slovenia declared their independence and war broke out shortly thereafter. Bosnia-Hercegovina declared its independence on 3 March 1992 following a referendum. War broke out a month later. In May 1992, all three states were admitted to the UN. Macedonia voted for independence in September 1991, but was not admitted to the UN until April 1993. The remaining two republics, Serbia and Montenegro, adopted a new constitution for the "Federal Republic of Yugoslavia." This new federal republic consisting of Serbia and Montenegro claimed it was the successor state to the former Yugoslavia and should therefore legitimately "inherit" the latter's place in all international organizations. However, in the summer of 1992 both the CSCE (Conference on Security and Cooperation in Europe) and the EU (European Union) condemned Serbia for its role in the war in Bosnia-Hercegovina, and in September the same year Yugoslavia was excluded from the UN assembly, and as of 1994 has in effect no internationally recognized status as a state.

The Yugoslav (South Slav) federated state was with its 22.4 million inhabitants a complex mosaic of different cultures, languages, religions, nationalities, and ethnic minorities. As of 1981[18] the breakdown of the three largest nationalities in Yugoslavia was as follows: Serbs, 8.1 million (36.6 percent of the total population), Croats, 4.4 million (19.7 percent) and Muslims, 1.9 million (8.9 percent). Of the Muslims (who declared themselves as of Muslim nationality) about 86 percent lived in Bosnia-Hercegovina. Other large groups were the three remaining "nations" of Yugoslavia—the Slovenes, Macedonians, and the Montenegrins—as well as the Albanians and the "Yugoslavs." The two latter did not have a status as "nations." Their numbers were: Slovenes 1.7 million (7.8 percent), Albanians 1.7 million (7.7 percent), Macedonians 1.3 million (6.0 percent) and "Yugoslavs" 1.2 million (5.4 percent).

Yugoslav policies relating to the "nationality question" in the former Yugoslavia were influenced by the ideas of several Marxist-inspired writers on nationality, including the Austro-Marxists (mainly Karl Renner and Otto Bauer), Lenin, and Stalin. It has been argued that the Yugoslav nationalities' policy can only be understood as a reaction to, development of, and repudiation of ideas put forward by these theorists (Ramet 1992:43). Nevertheless, Stalin's writings on the "national question" formed the backbone in Tito's early nationalities' policy, and

"Stalin was credited with 'pointing the way,' and the Soviet Union was held out as 'the model' for solving Yugoslavia's national question" (Connor 1984:147). This model was similar to that pursued by other communist multinational or multiethnic states such as the former USSR and China. Its main characteristic was the prominent role of the state in defining nationalities within its borders, and "in objectifying that identity, through conferring nationality status, or contesting the group's ethnicity, by refusing recognition" (Gladney 1991:76). In the Yugoslav multiethnic and socialist federal state, "nationality policies" were the tool by which the federated state sought to secure peace and a balance of power between its constituent parts and to legitimate its structure and thus its existence.

A key concept within the socialist federated states' nationalities' policy is represented by the terms here given in "Serbo-Croat," *narod* and *nacionalnost*.[19] The former term has often been translated in Western literature as either "nation" or "ethnic group" and the latter as either "nationality" or "ethnicity." None of these translations conveys the accurate meaning in the original usage of the terms. Indeed, one scholar writing on ethnicity in the former Soviet Union refers to the Russian equivalent of the term (*nacionalnost*) as "the case of a missing term" in the English language (Shanin 1989:409). In the former Yugoslavia (as in the former Soviet Union, see Karklin 1986) there was a hierarchy of nationality categories where the Slav term closest to the Western sociological concept of "ethnic group" was *narodnost*. According to the Marxist definition *narodnosti* are smaller than *narodi*, do not have an industry or working class of their own, and exist only in relation to a larger nation (that is, a *narod*). However, a *narodnost* may gain political recognition as a *narod*, as did the Muslims in Bosnia-Hercegovina.

The concept of "nationality" in a socialist state differs significantly from that within western European discourse. While in western Europe citizenship and nationality are synonyms and nationality refers to the relation of a person to a particular state, in the multiethnic socialist state national identity was different from and additional to citizenship. Thus for instance, in the former Yugoslavia, everybody held "Yugoslav" citizenship but no one held Yugoslav nationality. Indeed for state administrative purposes "Yugoslav" was never an option as a nationality, but only as either an ethnic minority or as an "undeclared" category. On an individual level this allows for manipulation and choice, since self-ascription and self-identification are ultimately decisive. A person's state or place of residence may not necessarily matter. It is, in short, an identity a person can either inherit or adopt (Shanin 1989).

As part of their "nationalities' policy," these states had a hierarchy of categories within which they grouped different peoples and according to which they were granted national rights. Yugoslavia was a multinational federation with a three-tier system of national rights. The first category was the "nations of Yugoslavia" (*Jugoslovenski narodi*) in which there were six nations (Serb, Croat, Slovene, Macedonian, Montenegrin, and Muslim). Each had a national home based in one of the republics (except Serbs and Croats who had two; Serbia and Croatia respectively, plus Bosnia-Hercegovina) and a constitutional right to equal political representation. The constitution of each of the six republics stated that it was the republic of the particular nation concerned (Serb, Croat, Slovenian, or other). The republic of Bosnia-Hercegovina, which was constituted as the republic and national home of the Serb, Croat, and Muslim nations was, however, an exception.[20] The second category was the "nationalities of Yugoslavia" (*narodnosti*) which were legally allowed a variety of language and cultural rights. These were considered to have their "national home" outside the SFRY. There were ten groups officially recognized as *narodnosti*, the largest being the Albanians and Hungarians. The third category was "other nationalities and ethnic minorities"—such as Jews, Vlahs, Greeks, and Russians, including those who classified themselves as "Yugoslavs" (Petrović 1987; Poulton 1991).

The 1991 census for Bosnia-Hercegovina shows that Muslims made up 43.7 percent (or 1.9 million) of this Republic's total population of 4.3 million people; Serbs accounted for 31.3 percent (1.3 million), and Croats 17.3 percent (753.400).[21] Other groups were Montenegrins, Gypsies, Albanians, Ukranians, and "Yugoslavs." This last group was the most numerous at 239,845 people or 5.5 percent of Bosnia-Hercegovina's total population.

## When Others Tell You Who You Are

My country is called Bosnia. But I am not a Bosnian. I saw my dad's army card—in it is written: nationality—undeclared. In my birth certificate is written: *Musliman*. My dad is really my dad. I know that. When I asked my dad why he did not declare himself, he said: I did not exist. I cannot understand that my dad did not exist in 1960 when I was born. . . . Today I learnt about the birth of my country. My country was born 25 November 1943 in Mrkonjić-Grad. My dad was born in 1938. My dad is older that my country.
    Zilhad Ključanin[22]

As noted above, Bosnia-Hercegovina was the only republic in the former Socialist Federal Republic of Yugoslavia which was not defined as the "national home" of one particular *narod*. Instead it had three—Muslims, Serbs and Croats—and none of them carried an ethnonym which identified them with the Republic of Bosnia-Hercegovina (in the same way as Montenegrins were directly identified with Montenegro, Macedonians with Macedonia, Serbs with Serbia, and so on). In the passage quoted above the Bosnian poet Zilhad Ključanin reflects on the paradoxes of being Bosnian but not officially recognized as such, and on the changing state policies toward the Bosnian Muslim population.

The question of a person's national identity would turn up every ten years on the national census. National identity would never be written on a person's passport or identity card as was the practice in the former USSR (Karklins 1986), but it would be written on a man's Yugoslav People's Army identity card. In the national census people could choose from a range of different nationalities. For persons of "ethnically" mixed parentage it was common to choose "Yugoslav" when this was an option. Until 1971 when the Bosnian Muslims obtained the status of a *narod*, they had had various official categories from which to choose. In the population census of 1948, there was the option of "Muslims of undeclared nationality" in addition to Serb, Croat, and so on; in 1953 those who did not want to declare themselves as Serbs or Croats had the option of choosing "Yugoslavs of undeclared nationality." In 1961 the Bosnian Muslims were allowed to declare themselves as a *narodnost* (*Muslimani u smislu narodnosti*, Muslims in the sense of *narodnost*) and finally in the 1971 census they were able to declare themselves as "Muslim" under the category of *narod*.

Politicians and intellectuals in favor of Yugoslav nationalism in the decades immediately after World War II had long hoped that the Bosnia-Hercegovinian Muslims would become the first representatives of a new Yugoslav national identity. This hope did not materialize, however, and between 1967 and 1971 a series of amendments to the 1963 constitution was passed that marked a change in policy toward the "nationality question." These amendments transferred political authority from the central organs of the federation to its constituent republics. In fact, this marked a move away from the concept of a centralist Yugoslav federation ("Yugoslavism" and the attempt to form a Yugoslav national identity) toward one of Yugoslavia as a federation of national republics, sowing the seeds for heightened interrepublic rivalry and the cultivation of separate national and ethnic identities. (This development was strengthened in the 1974 constitution with the introduction of the principle of a collective leadership.) It was during this period that a Bosnia-Hercegovinian central committee communique "rejected Yugoslavism as an acceptable model for internationality relations and stated that: 'practice has shown the harm of different forms of pressure and instances from the earlier period when Muslims were determined to be Serbs or Croats from the national viewpoint. It has been shown and present socialist practice confirms that Muslims are a distinct nation'" (Irwin 1984:444). When the Muslims got the right to declare themselves a nationality in the 1971 census, the number of people who declared themselves as "Yugoslavs" in Bosnia-Hercegovina fell radically from 275,883 in the 1961 census to 43,796 in the 1971 census, while the total number of "Muslims" increased for the same period by approximately 200,000 from 842,247 in 1961 to 1,482,430 in 1971. Ten years earlier when Muslims were able to declare themselves as a *narodnost*, the number of declared Yugoslavs had likewise dropped dramatically (from 891,800 in 1953 to 275,883 in 1961).[23] The increase in Muslim numbers from 1961 to 1971 is demographically impossible and can only reflect the new option given Muslims to declare themselves as part of the Muslim *narod*. In 1961 80 percent of all declared Yugoslavs lived in Bosnia-Hercegovina, while in 1971 this number fell to 26.8 percent (see Petrović 1987:56). Thus the hope that the Bosnians (and primarily the Muslims) would spearhead a new Yugoslav nationality was revealed to have no basis in any popularly founded and experienced identity.

Some scholars argue that the recognition of a separate Muslim *narod* was a device initiated by Tito to secure a kind of "buffer" between the Croats and Serbs and thus "answer forever the Bosnian Question" (Rusinow 1981:11). It might also be argued that when the Muslims were recognized as a *narod* in 1971 the change was simply one of de facto to de jure status. For, as Banac notes, by the second half of the twentieth century the Bosnian Muslims lacked only a national name (1984:373). Indeed, it has been shown that Muslim group consciousness developed over time, and that political mobilization was initiated from within (see Donia 1978; Banac 1984).[24]

Over the last century the Bosnian Orthodox had increasingly identified with the Serbian *narod*, and started to associate their "national existence" with Serbia. The Bosnian Catholics had gradually come to identify themselves with the Croatian *narod*, and although this was a later and slower process than among the Bosnian Serbs, they too eventually associated their "national existence" with a geopolitical unit outside Bosnia-Hercegovina, though in their case it was Croatia. The process among the Muslims took a different direction in that they mobilized politically in order to transform the category "Muslim" from a merely religious identity into a "national identity" (Saltaga 1991:69). Prominent Muslim academics and members of the Yugoslav communist party played a central role in gaining political acceptance of the Bosnian Muslims as a separate *narod* under the ethnonym *Musliman* (Muslim)—rather than for instance *Bosnian* or *Bošnjak* (Bosniak). In retrospect, however, gaining acceptance for a separate Bosnian Muslim identity was less of a problem than agreeing under what ethnonym this identity could be made official.[25] Borneman has argued that "naming and categorizing are always contested acts because they are essential sources of power in the construction of local, national, and international loyalties" (1992:12). His argument seems particularly appropriate in the Bosnian case.

Owing to historical and sociopolitical factors, the national census was always unequivocal in stating Serb and Croat national identities.[26] But there was no official national identity of Bosnian, which would include all Bosnians whether Muslim, Catholic, or Orthodox, or of a Catholic or Orthodox nation for that matter. Yet the great variety in Muslim national and ethnic self-designation for administrative purposes before 1971 may itself be seen as an expression of the Bosnian Muslims' distinct identity (Purivatra 1974). When I asked my Bosnian Muslim friends how they identified themselves at censuses, the replies varied from person to person. Furthermore, the same person would have slotted into different categories at different times, particularly as census categories changed. Many would identify themselves as "Yugoslavs" when this was an option. Otherwise, they would identify themselves as Croat or Serb according to personal experience: if you had a good friend or neighbor who was a Serb, you would declare yourself a Serb. Atif, a sixty-year-old Muslim and former communist party member, was typical of many of his generation who for most of their lives did not have the choice of calling themselves Muslim for public and administrative purposes, that is, he could not identify with an official Muslim *narod*. Similarly, as a communist party member he was not allowed to practice his religion, and therefore had publicly to deny his Muslim religious identity as well. Atif had been through most of the categories: "Unspecified," "Croat," "Yugoslav," "Serb," and "Muslim." His choice was influenced first by official options, and next by sociocultural context, that is, by where he lived or where he worked. For instance, he told me that when he went to Belgrade to perform his military service, he categorized himself as a Serb, since he believed this would make life less complicated in that particular environment. This does not mean that the way he perceived and experienced his identity had changed; indeed, after giving me this list of official categories he added that in his heart he remained a Muslim throughout. He knew who he was. There were others, though, who did not know, or were not prepared to agree with him.

## Competing Nationalisms and the Denial of a
## Bosnian Identity

During the course of my research in Bosnia-Hercegovina I visited both
Zagreb and Belgrade. As I returned to Bosnia from these visits I was
puzzled. In Belgrade, when I had told a colleague that I was living in a
Bosnian village studying Muslim "customs," he told me: "The Muslims
will not tell you this, but they are really Serbs, they just say they are
Muslims." In Zagreb, the reaction was similar but with an important
difference. A Croat colleague told me: "They claim they are Muslims,
but they are really Croats." I asked myself how it could be that the Muslims themselves were the only people who did not tell me who they "really" were, and why both Serbs and Croats claimed them as "theirs."
Furthermore, in the village at that time the Muslims' immediate Catholic Bosnian (Croat) neighbors did not make similar claims.

This was not the first or the last time I would be confronted with such
claims, and as I later learned, they were particularly rife in Serbian and
Croatian historiography and academic literature on Bosnia-Hercegovina. In the run-up to the democratic elections in Bosnia-Hercegovina
in 1990, and amid the dissolution of communist Yugoslavia and the increasing nationalist rhetoric, such claims were often made by Serbian
and Croatian nationalists and academics in the media.[27] I will argue that
the Muslim Bosnians' collective identity could be contested because the
Muslims understood and communicated their identity in a different
idiom from both Serbs and Croats.

Contrary to what the above-mentioned academics seemed to believe,
for the Muslims with whom I lived it was not a question of not wanting
to admit who they really were—they knew very well who they were—but
rather that a myth of origins was neither a part of, nor necessary to,
knowing one's identity. This is where the nation-state aspiring, ethnically focused Serbs and Croats differed from the Bosnian Muslims.
Among the latter, shared collective identity was not perceived through
the idiom of shared blood and a myth of common origins, which is so
often invoked in discourses on ethnic or national identity by other European peoples. The symbol of blood referring to common descent is,
for example, used by Bosnian Serbs. The only Serb villager in Dolina,
the village where I did my field research, would teasingly tell his Muslim friends that they had Serbian blood in their veins. The Muslims,
on the other hand, referred to their collective identity in an idiom
which de-emphasized descent ("ethnicity") and focused instead on a
shared environment, cultural practices, a shared sentiment, and common experiences.

Ethnographers have for instance noted that Muslim villagers have little knowledge of or interest in their genealogies compared to Bosnian Serbs or Croats (Lockwood 1975a). To Muslims their identity derived primarily from the environment (*sredina*) in which they grew up and which they shared. This meant growing up in a household where morality was based on Islam, it meant giving a child a name which reminded it of this heritage, and as shown in chapter two it meant sharing a territory and village with others who adhered to different religions. I suggest that the Muslims' weaker emphasis on descent and "common blood" as defining their "ethnic identity" partly excluded them from a ethnonationalist discourse which revolves around such principles. In a sociopolitical climate where collective cultural identities based on such claims become the only valid ones, the Muslims' claim to nationality status on a different basis has been seen by those competing within such a discourse (here, Serbs and Croats) as illegitimate.

As part of the debate among Sarajevo intellectuals on Muslim national and Bosnian identity taking place in the main Sarajevo daily newspaper *Oslobođenje* in the summer of 1990, one author argued that while Serb, Croat, and Slovene nationhood was *natural* (my emphasis) because it was based on unambiguous and common ethnic origin, the national identity of the Muslims was merely based on a "psychological identification" subject to self-observation and, therefore by implication, less natural.[28] According to such a "natural" definition of a "nation" only groups who can claim that they originated from an ethnic group are legitimate nations. This would exclude the Bosnian Muslims, who would either be forced to assimilate or have to accept political (and cultural) minority status. The assumption is that all nations have developed from one ethnic group, and in the case of the Bosnian Muslims either from Serb or Croat ones. Alternatively, the argument is made that the Muslims cannot possibly be a nation. Croat and Serb nationalist politicians dismissed the Muslims as an "invented people," and claimed they were either Serbs or Croats respectively.[29]

Saltaga, a Bosnian sociologist, expressed concern that a definition which assumes that ethnicity, identity through blood ties, and descent—what the above-quoted commentator calls "natural"—are a more legitimate basis for a national identity than any other criterion, would exclude Bosnian Muslims. Since Bosnian Muslim national identity does not rest predominantly on a theory of ethnicity, he warns that it would be risky for Muslims to enter into any society which insists on "natural identification." For the Muslim population, he argued, this would imply assimilation, or should they refuse this, genocide. Perhaps with a premonition of what was to come, he argued: "If in the case of the disintegration of Yugoslavia there should emerge ethnically based states, such states in which democracy would not imply the right to [national] self-definition, Muslims whose identity rests on such a chosen declaration, would be exposed to permanent pressure to 'remember' their natural definition, i.e., to declare whether they were Serbs or Croats, before they became Muslims" (Saltaga 1991:16–17).

In Saltaga's view, Islam, to the extent that it has transformed local non-Islamic traditions, has become "the synthesis of a new ethnic community—the Muslims, where *kin relationships through blood give away to religious-cultural factors*" (1991:36; my emphasis). Yet although Bosnian Muslims conceptualize their common identity primarily through the knowledge that they share a particular moral environment, this moral environment has been shaped by the experience and common knowledge of generations of Bosnian Muslims. Its cultural historical continuity is reflected in a person's family name, which an individual usually inherits through his or her father; in the process an ethnic aspect (i.e., who a person is born as) is nevertheless added.[30]

Some scholars have argued that in order to create a collective identity individuals must submerge the heterogeneous sources of their identity, rather than just add these to one another (Strathern 1992:182). In Bosnia, however, Bosnians emphasized and added their heterogeneous sources of identity to one other, so that an overarching Bosnian homogeneous identity was never ideologically and institutionally constructed to supersede this. The superimposed Yugoslav collective identity, which was declared by only a minority of the Yugoslav population though by a much higher number in Bosnia-Hercegovina than in any other prewar Yugoslav republic, was inextricably linked to the Titoist Yugoslav state. Another prerequisite for perceiving collective identities is that this unit be elicited in turn by other social identities (Strathern 1993:183). A Bosnian collective identity was elicited by the non-Bosnian identities of peoples born outside the territory of Bosnia-Hercegovina. In prewar Yugoslavia *Bosanac* was constructed in opposition to others such as Slovene, Macedonian, Croat (from Croatia) and Serb (from Serbia). Thus, a Bosnian Croat when traveling in Croatia would be perceived and referred to as a *Bosanac*. Within Bosnia-Hercegovina itself people referred to themselves and were referred to by others in terms of their diversifying ethnoreligious identities as well as their unifying cultural and territorial identities which were often localized (i.e., primarily related to village, city, or region).[31]

The Bosnian dimension of people's identities embracing all three officially recognized "nationalities"—Muslim, Serb, and Croat—was never institutionalized during communist Yugoslavia or confirmed through any official rhetoric of nationality policy. In official population censuses "Bosnian" was defined as a regional identity, but never gained ideological backing or political status as a "nation" as did its territorially based counterparts Serb and Croat. Instead Bosnia-Hercegovina officially had three "nations": Muslim, Serb, and Croat. Although "Bosnian" was a unifying identity in the sense that it straddled ethnoreligious communities, it did not subsume these differences. Indeed, at its core was the tension between two opposing needs: on the one hand belonging to distinct but parallel ethnoreligious communities, and the need to communicate separateness, and on the other the awareness of sharing the same territory, social environment, and sets of cultural codes, and therefore of being interdependent and basically the same.

Although the collective identities "Bosnian" and "Muslim" referred to different categories, they shared one essential characteristic in the way they were constructed, as against "Serb" and "Croat." This was that their ethnic base related to descent and origin was contested, or not deemed relevant, or seen as multiplex. It is telling that after the Serb-Croat nationalist war for territory spread to Bosnia-Hercegovina the overwhelming number of those who continued to declare themselves as Bosnians and supportive of a multicultural (or multinational) Bosnian-Hercegovinian state were Muslims and those of an ethnically mixed origin. (There were also Bosnian Serbs and Croats who resisted the pressure to side with the nationalist causes of Serbia and Croatia.) Since being Bosnian was a synthesis of the historical and cultural experiences of all three *nacije* living on common territory where the different sources of people's identities were acknowledged and even emphasized, it represented a contradiction of the logic of nationalism which, after the defeat of the Yugoslav credo of "brotherhood and unity," seems to have been the only available recipe for political mobilization and state building. In a climate where the "logic of the ethnic nation-state" set the political agenda, the inclusive Bosnian collective identity could not, it seemed, form the basis for the building of a new state, nor does it seem likely to survive the campaigns of so-called "ethnic cleansing" promoted by its neighboring states.


### The Bošnjaštvo Debate

As already mentioned, a crucial element in the nation-building process is the establishment of the "historical continuity" between a people and a specific territory. While Croat and Serb nationalist historiography was busy establishing this "historical continuity" and coopting the Muslims into their own "national histories," Bosnian Muslim historiography was trying to establish its national identity as separate from Serbs and Croats and therefore against Serb and Croat claims. This "historical discontinu-

ity" was not conducive to an exclusive Bosnian Muslim nationalist rhetoric which could challenge Serb and Croat nationalism on the territory
of Bosnia-Hercegovina.

Prior to the war in Bosnia-Hercegovina, at the end of the 1980s and
particularly in the burst of public debate on nationality issues in 1990–
92, the national identity of the Bosnians generally, and of the Muslims
in particular, was heatedly discussed. The dissolution of communist
party rule had meant the breaking of the taboo issue of nationalism and
national loyalties. In Sarajevo newspapers and magazines many Bosnians
commented on the absence of an officially supported and politically
sanctioned Bosnian national identity. Reflecting on the upsurge in Serbian and Croatian nationalism next door, many worried about how Bosnia-Hercegovina would withstand the pressure. Attempting to counter
the increasingly menacing Serb and Croat nationalist rhetoric which
would be separatist and dangerously divisive given the complicated "nationality" mix in Bosnia-Hercegovina, Bosnian intellectuals revived the
historical concept of *Bošnjaętvo* ("Bosnianness" or "Bosnianhood") and
the category *Bošnjak*. Newspapers and magazines printed letters from
readers and articles by Bosnian intellectuals concerned with issues of
identity and nationality, and a lively debate evolved. One such letter
read: "Let's be *Bošnjak*s that Bosnia may secede." It continued: "Why
do they prevent us from strengthening our consciousness of our national belonging to Bosnia, and of the concept of *Bošnjaštvo*? The answer is simple—as long as we continue this way, without uniqueness,
without identity, as Yugoslav [meaning everybody's], everybody may
claim us as theirs. If we declare our independence [in a cultural and national sense] nobody will be able to attach Bosnia to themselves, nor
consider it theirs." The young author of this letter ended by saying that
her mother was Croat and her father Serb, but that she felt neither
Croatian nor Serbian for she had grown up in Bosnia.[32] The question
which concerned many Bosnians was: When Yugoslavia dissolved (and if
a demand arose for the division of Bosnia-Hercegovina into two), what
would happen to those who saw themselves as neither Croats nor Serbs?

Three main lines of argument developed. First, the concept of
*Bošnjak* was revived to replace the "regional" category *Bosanac* (in English both terms have been translated as "Bosnian"). Among those who
favored the *Bošnjak* concept were those who considered this a national
name term for everybody (whether Muslim, Serb, or Croat), and who
considered themselves primarily Bosnian and therefore supported a
united Bosnia-Hercegovina including all three *nacije*. This is close to
the historical meaning of *Bošnjak* associated with the Bosnian state in
the Middle Ages.[33] The most prominent attempt at reviving "Bosnianhood" in the past was that of Benjamin van Kallay, the Austro-Hungar-

ian governor of Bosnia-Hercegovina (1882–1903). He fostered the idea
of separate interconfessional Bosnian nationhood (Bošnjaštvo) to counteract growing Croat and Serb national movements and their decisive
claims to Bosnia-Hercegovina. The idea was supported by some Bosnian
Croats particularly the Franciscans, but was particularly taken on by the
Muslim gentry as a defensive vehicle against the Croat and Serb national
movements (Banac 1984:360–61).The second view equated *Bošnjak*
with "Muslim," in contrast to "Serb" and "Croat" which were already
established official national categories. Since Serb and Croat national
identification had won the day in Bosnia, *Bošnjak* had lost its meaning as
an inclusive term for Bosnians of all three confessions. Izetbegović, the
present president of the presidency of the Republic of Bosnia-Hercegovina (and leader of the Party for Democratic Action, SDA) supports this
view. To him *Bošnjak*s are "those whom we today call Muslims." He
feels that using the term *Bošnjak* to refer to the Bosnian Muslims would
put an end to the seemingly endless discussion of whether the Muslims
are Serbs or Croats, a question which the term "Muslim" seems to leave
open since it is primarily a confessional one. Furthermore, he argues,
reviving the concept of *Bošnjaštvo* would solve the ambiguities of the
term "Muslim" particularly since it causes confusion abroad.[34] It was
clear that *Bošnjak* as a term for the Muslim Bosnian people would also
establish the Muslims with a more obvious continuous historical link to
Bosnia-Hercegovina as a state and a territory.

A third position was to insist on continued use of Muslim as a "nationality" and "national identity," since this term had gained a secularized meaning as an ethnonym for the Muslim inhabitants of Bosnia who
differentiate themselves from the rest by perceiving themselves as neither Serbs nor Croats. Furthermore, the supporters of this option argued that the concept of *Bošnjaštvo* had similarities with the concept of
Yugoslavism, and that attempting to construct an identity category
which would include all three (Serbs, Croats, and Muslims) might eventually mean the dominance by one group and the attempted assimilation
of the Muslims into one of the other two (Saltaga 1991:95). One Muslim intellectual finally summarized the debate by giving one of his many
newspaper articles in the debate the title "Muslims know who they
are not."[35]

The debate reflected the old dilemma of fitting the Bosnian case into
the nationalist logic of the nation-state, and became highly politicized
during the runup to the first democratic elections in Bosnia-Hercegovina in 1990. It was acknowledged that if Bosnia-Hercegovina was to
survive as a state its subjects had to be identified as a nation directly
associated with its territory. The disagreement was about who should be
included, and whether it would be possible to have one state with three

"nations." Presently (1994) the term *Bošnjak* is gaining common currency in the Sarajevo media. It is being used mainly in contrast to "Serb" and "Croat" and as a synonym for Bosnian Muslim. The term *Bosanac* as a term for all the three former *nacije* in Bosnia-Hercegovina seems to be losing its meaning as a regional identity with the disintegration of a united and mixed three-nation Bosnia-Hercegovina. The Bosnians have apparently been organized into tidy, culturally and ethnically homogeneous categories, and the Muslims seem finally to have become a neat ethno-national category its neighbors and the international community can deal with and understand. They have been forced by the war and the logic of the creation of nation-states to search for their origins and establish a "legitimate" and continuous national history.

The rest of this book is about one village and how the Muslims in particular perceived and lived out their identity before this community was destroyed. It is an attempt to convey, not what everybody else claimed about what or who they were, but how they themselves lived their identity and claimed who they were by being Muslim the Bosnian way.

# Two

## A Bosnian Village

THIS CHAPTER will introduce the village of study and cover the main aspects of village life which were important in understanding the complexities of Bosnian Muslim identity. In it, I consider household life in terms of female-male and Muslim-Catholic relations and in relation to different social and territorial domains—household, neighborhood, village, and state—as these were the contexts within which perceptions of identity and belonging were expressed and acted out. Bosnian Muslim identity expressed itself in varying contexts within the village. For example, to understand this identity in some contexts, it is important to examine the Muslim-Catholic dichotomy. However, in other contexts this dichotomy is secondary to understanding the Bosnian Muslims as they shared a common village identity with the Catholic Croats against the outside world. Changes in household structure as a result of socioeconomic developments were shared by both Muslim and Catholic households, and so was occupational structure. Muslims and Catholics shared the experience of rural life, the educational system, and the state bureaucracy. However, they did not share kinship networks and therefore did not include each other in the most intimate rituals and relationships focused on the household. The first section of this chapter outlines the geographical and socioeconomic setting of the village that was the locus for this study.

## The Village

The central Bosnian village which I will refer to here as Dolina is situated in a valley about two hours' drive north of the Bosnian-Hercegovinian capital, Sarajevo. In the late eighties Dolina was a thriving village which the young did not necessarily leave for urban areas, as was the case in smaller and remoter villages, although they preferred to live on "flat land" in the modern neighborhoods in the lower part of the village.

Both geographically and sociologically, Dolina consisted of two major areas: the original settlements on higher ground and the newer ones further down the valley. The lower part of the valley is more open, with large flat fields on both sides of the river and the road running alongside it; the mountains are distant and unobtrusive. In this area in-

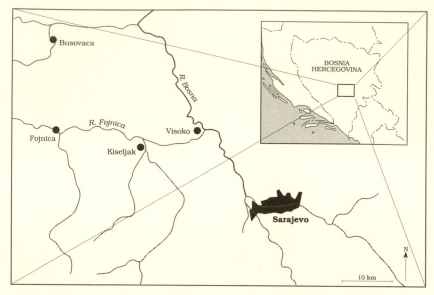

2. Map of the region within which reserarch was conducted. The main market towns and their position in relation to Sarajevo are indicated. Map courtesy of Kjell-Helge Sjøstrøm.

dividual houses were located at a distance from each other and there were relatively large areas of land between each one. Houses were bigger and more modern than in the upper part of the village, the architecture being clearly different. This part is easily accessible from the main road and therefore more open to the world, nearer to schools, shops, public offices, and buses. It was inhabited mainly by couples with children, the husband having grown up in one of the settlements in the upper part of the village. Halfway up the village there was a shop which marked the entrance into the second and upper part of Dolina. Here the hills on both sides become steeper and closer, the settlements were considerably denser, and there were two distinct house types. This part was also made up of clearly defined hamlets.

By the shop a path to the right led to hamlets which once, before the administrative unit of Dolina (as of 1987) was drawn up after World War II, were recognized as separate villages. On top of the hillside, not far from the Catholic churchyard, the forest has been cut down and the land, which used to be owned by the municipality, had been sold to young couples from Dolina's different hamlets, where until the war in Bosnia-Hercegovina they were building new houses and tilling the land. This settlement was the newest in Dolina, and the patrilineal kinship structure which was the organizing principle for other settlements had

3. Drawing of a village neighborhood, showing Muslim and Catholic houses

virtually disappeared, even if there were still examples of brothers building next to each other. It could no longer be assumed that close neighbors were kin.

On the stretch of land immediately beyond the shop and almost as far as the mosque, in the middle of the upper part, most houses were Catholic. A house inhabited by Catholics was easily distinguishable from one inhabited by Muslims by a marked difference in architecture. Muslim houses were square (as is the village mosque), while the Catholic ones were rectangular, with the longest side facing out toward the village.[1] In both cases the entrance was at the back or at the side. These architectural differences were characteristic throughout rural Bosnia. However, the differences were becoming increasingly blurred in the eighties in villages too, as both Muslims and Catholics were building their new houses in a style different from their respective traditional ones. These houses, in the style of large central European mountain chalets, consisted of two or even three stories. Judging from the style, I assume villagers were inspired by what they saw on labor migrations in Austria, and had adapted this to the needs and resources of their Bosnian village life. The area immediately surrounding the house was cleared for access to neighboring houses, with a bench to sit on where people gathered to drink coffee and comment on village life. There were also toolsheds, stables, piles of wood left out to dry, and the characteristic egg-shaped haystack. Physically, the house was an important delineation of the household, a concept which will be explained in more detail in later sections of this and the next chapter.

The mosque was situated in the middle of the upper part of Dolina. All the houses in the vicinity were Muslim. They were built in clusters, consisting of between two and four dwellings and a couple of outhouses. Such clusters, which I shall call settlements, were usually inhabited by brothers and their nuclear families, the youngest brother staying in the old house with his parents if they were still alive. Young couples considered this arrangement as less than ideal, but they often had no choice as they could not afford to build their own house. It was often only a temporary solution until a new and separate house could be built. Many managed to build their own house after years of saving and hard work, but some never succeeded. Another solution was to share the same house, but to keep separate household finances. During my long-term field research in the village I stayed in such a shared house with a family in one of the settlements across the mosque.

Some scholars have reported that in many villages in Bosnia which were mixed (either Muslim/Croat, or Muslim/Serb, or Muslim/Serb/Croat) the different groups often settled in separate and clearly defined areas of the village, such as each end of the village, or on opposite sides of a river (Lockwood 1975a). In Dolina this was not the case, as a Muslim settlement could be next door to a Catholic one, although the settlements near the mosque made up an entirely Muslim neighborhood. In the 1980s the village was composed of the patrilineal descendants of eleven Muslim families and three Catholic ones.[2] To the extent that Muslim families knew about their origins or had a myth about it, they said either that their family had lived in the village for as long as they knew, or that they had come there from other parts of Bosnia-Herce-govina. Catholic families had a traditional myth about their origin being in Dalmatia (Croatia) and their ancestors having moved to Dolina during Ottoman rule when there had been land to work.[3] About fifty years earlier, each of these families would have had its own settlement in the upper part of the village with between one and three communal houses and fifteen to twenty-five patrilineally related family members. According to the latest statistics available for the village, for 1981, the village administrative unit had 690 inhabitants divided into 158 households. My own estimates suggest that two-thirds of these were Muslim and the remaining third Catholic. Both the large population figures and the Muslim majority are consistent with statistics for 1889,[4] when the village, then as until April 1993, had a majority of Muslim households and the largest population of any village in the district. Unlike the Austrian governors who were in charge of the 1889 census, the compilers of the 1981 statistics do not specify the ethnic or religious composition of the village. There are, however, indications that the Catholic population had been steadily decreasing after 1945 as more Catholics moved out or went abroad as migrant workers (see chapter one, n. 2). By September 1993 none of the Muslims in the village remained. They had either fled during the attack by Croat defense forces (HVO) in the spring and summer of 1993, or were being held in Croat-run detention camps.

Only the most prosperous families in the upper part of the village had enough land and assets (often gained through migrant work abroad) to build houses further down the village. This was reflected in the marked difference in socioeconomic status between the households in the upper and lower parts, the lower being the more prosperous and urbanized of the two. These socioeconomic and class distinctions between the upper and the lower parts of the village had been manifested in reverse some decades earlier when those who owned much land lived in the upper part, and land was still a household's main source of income and subsistence. Wage labor offered villagers new opportunities and changed the organization and composition of the household and the socioeconomic layout of the village. The division of the village into a lower and an upper part with its accompanying socioeconomic stratification had taken place over a period of approximately fifty years, that is, within post–1945 Yugoslavia. This period also saw a transformation of the extended family household.

## Changes in Household Structure

A radical change in the composition and organization of the patrilineally-based household as a result of wage labor and modern education in the second half of the twentieth century is reported to have occurred in rural areas as far apart as in southeastern Europe and the Middle East.[5] In Dolina too, such changes were apparent. In the next sections we shall look at the structural and organizational changes within the patrilineal joint family household in the village over a period of three generations. These changes center on the relationship between the old and young conjugal couple, between the father and his adult son who through wage labor has become economically independent of his father's land, and between the mother and her daughter-in-law. Indeed, the changes in socioeconomic structure in the former Yugoslavia in the period after World War II most markedly affected women (and particularly women in rural areas), for their position as junior members of a patrilineally structured household was traditionally weak.

There are several terms in "Serbo-Croat" which are translated as household. However, they convey different organizational and membership patterns. *Domaćinstvo* or *dom* is the technical term used in official statistics and papers to refer to those who share a house, but, as we shall see, it did not always correspond to the local definition of what constituted a household, since kin who shared a house did not necessarily constitute one household.

In the village, *kuća* (house) referred both to the building and the unit which inhabited it. Generally, it is taken to mean those people who shared a household economy and the yield of the land, and who ate together. Only those people who ate together from the same pot were defined as a *kuća*. Nevertheless, there were inconsistencies within and exceptions to this general definition. This was due to a quite recent development wherein one household divided into two, yet continued to live under one roof so that in effect there were "two houses living in one house." A *kuća* could consist of several *porodice* (families), but the general pattern was a *kuća* or household being made up of a core family.

Most south Slav ethnography and historiography describes the extended family household as a *zadruga*. This is perhaps the most discussed and analyzed institution within Yugoslav (and Balkan) ethnology (see, e.g., St. Erlich 1966; Byrnes 1976). It is a term with a complicated history and multiple connotations. It is used for the most part in one of two different senses. First, in the sense of the communal living arrangements of more than two generations (or a group) of kin. This is how it is understood in the ethnographic literature. Second, in postwar Yugoslavia *zadruga* referred officially to a state collective. The only known meaning of *zadruga* in Dolina was that of a cooperative or "social property" run according to the Yugoslav self-management system. Thus the council (i.e., the communist party) ran a community house, situated outside the village (where among other events the Saturday dance attended by the village youth took place), which was referred to as a *zadruga*.[6]

The extended family household in Dolina was referred to as a *zajednica*. This usage is also reported by "Yugoslav" ethnographers for other areas of Bosnia (Stojaković 1987) while *velika kuća* (big house) or just *kuća* are also reported to have a wide distribution (Filipović 1976). *Zajednica* (community) would typically consist of a group of brothers, their parents, wives, and children. The expression used when describing this form of household organization is "to live in community" (*živjeti u zajednici*).

## The Decline of the Joint Family Household

The causes for the eventual disintegration of the communal household have been subject to much theorizing in the literature, ranging from the impact of industrialization and capitalism to a general change in traditional patriarchal values (St. Erlich 1966; Mosley 1976; Filipovic 1976). I suggest that it is not the division of the *zajednica* per se which demands an explanation, as the timing of the division, which has been occurring at a much earlier stage in the household's developmental cycle than in the past. Households would inevitably have divided into smaller units at some point (on the developmental cycle of the household and the inevitability of the short-term breakup of the joint family, see Parry 1979; and Stirling 1963). But over a three-generational period, the trend was clearly toward an earlier division of the communal household. For example, Rheubottom reported from his field research in Macedonia in the sixties that while in the previous generation it had been the custom for sons to continue living together after their father died, it was becoming common for brothers to split up when their father died (1976:217). In Dolina thirty years ago a son and his wife would start out living in *zajednica*, but would eventually build their own house and move out with their children, so that only the youngest son and his family would as a rule remain in his parents' house. During my stay in the village, however, the youngest son, too, increasingly tended to leave his father's house when he married, or at least started to build his own house as soon as possible after he had married. Consequently, often all the sons had moved out before their parents were dead. This meant that there was a development toward the domestic group being coterminous with the core family, namely the conjugal couple and their offspring. In the eighties, a division of the household was not a division of the group of brothers, but rather a division and reduction of the three-generation household, with married couples living separately.

Since the size of the joint family household was dependent on the quality and size of the landholding, the joint household in mountainous central Bosnia never reached the sizes that have been reported for areas of north Bosnia, Serbia and Croatia. Furthermore, both St. Erlich (1976) (whose data are from the 1930s) and Filipović (1976), who studied the communal household in Bosnia in the sixties, note that in Muslim districts the "*zadruga*" never flourished as it did in other areas.

In Dolina, the older generation remembered the biggest *zajednica* (a Catholic household) having up to twenty-five members.[7] Each house (dwelling) was called a *čardaklija* and had a particular layout adapted to communal living. It was a characteristically large wooden building with open hearths, in which every nuclear family occupied its own room. (The last house of this kind in the village had been uninhabited since 1986 and was falling down by 1988.) In the fifties and sixties when sons accompanied by their young wives and children broke away from the communal living in a *čardaklija*, they would not build a similar house with a view to creating a new household of the same size. Instead, they would build modern houses of concrete which were designed for much smaller household units. The changing composition of the household was aptly reflected in the change of architecture in the dwellings, and in the structural layout of the hamlets and of the village. Since most of the land immediately surrounding the original *čardaklija* had subsequently been built on, in the late eighties sons (and in some cases their fathers before them) had to build their house on their fathers' grazing fields further down the valley.

One patrigroup settlement in the center of the village consisted of two houses, here called A and B. House A was inhabited by eighty-year-old Latif, his wife, and youngest son with his wife and two children. Latif used to share a house with his four brothers and their families, but as his own family grew he had a separate house built in front of the original one. (His brother also had a house built next to this one, on the spot where house B was later built.) The old *čardaklija* had been demolished fifteen years before my stay in the village. After the son in house A got a regular job, his wife initiated the construction of the new house (with chimney and stove), and she insisted on having a separate kitchen from her mother-in-law. This was a radical move at the time and less common than fifteen years later. The new house consisted of three rooms: two kitchens and a third room which was used as a storage room, guest room, and in the summer as a bedroom. Latif and his wife lived in one room that served as a combined kitchen, living room, and bedroom, while his youngest son with his wife and two children lived in the other. They had separate finances, and produced, cooked, and ate their food separately. Since I was confused as to whether this constituted living in a *zajednica* or not, Fahra, the young daughter-in-law, gave me the following explanation: "When we live in the same house but do not eat together, we are two families (*porodice*, parents and their children). But when we all eat together and give the old man money, then it would be *zajednica*." In other words, Fahra emphasized commensality and a shared economy as the defining criteria of a household unit, and *zajednica* as a household unit consisting of more than one *porodica*.

Fahra was saying that her household was separate from her mother-in-law's and that, therefore, for guests to visit her parents-in-law next door was not the same as visiting her room, where she would be the hostess. Older people in particular did not see it the same way. They considered a visit to the old couple a visit to the house as a whole, although they might be persuaded by the daughter-in-law to stop by for a coffee in her kitchen as well. Or she might invite people who had visited the old couple, to come visit her the next time. Once an older man and his wife on their way out from a visit to Fahra's parents-in-law replied: "Your place and their place next door are one and the same thing." Younger people, however, accepted the daughter-in-law's as a separate household and would primarily come to visit her and her husband, while also paying the old couple a courtesy visit. Her mother-in-law, however, still liked to think of it as one household, with her as the head.

The disparity in their perceptions of the *kuća* manifested itself in recurring quarrels between the two women concerning the management of common property. To cite one example: the mother and daughter-in-law used to cooperate (though with difficulty) in milking and looking after a cow. After they had to sell the cow, the daughter-in-law refused to share the workload with her mother-in-law when a new one was bought, since all the money from the sale of the old cow and from the sale of excess cheese and milk went to the mother-in-law. The daughter-in-law had often confided to me that her greatest wish was for a place of her own. Eventually, the son and daughter-in-law started to build their own house in a different part of the village approximately fifteen minutes' walk away, and the old couple stayed behind.[8]

The second house, house B, was inhabited by Latif's youngest son but one, his wife, their daughter, and their son and his wife. In this household both the father and daughter had paid work and contributed to the household economy, whereas the son and daughter-in-law were unemployed. When this young couple first got married they were thus part of a communal household. But when the son and, somewhat later, his wife got regular jobs, a series of disputes about his financial contribution to the household led him and his wife to break away. The father had complained that the son should contribute a larger share of his wages toward the communal household. The quarrel ended with the young couple setting up a separate household in their room (situated on the first floor of the son's parents' house), which they turned into a traditional combined kitchen, bedroom, and lounge. The division meant that the daughter-in-law started cooking separately for herself and her husband. For house B the splitting up of the household was the most viable solution. This family was in possession neither of the land required nor of the financial means to build a new house. After the division the two couples in house B were considered to constitute two *kuća*. This was (among other things) evident in the visiting pattern of neighboring women. They considered coffee visits to the mother and daughter-in-law as separate occasions.[9]

Out of twenty households for which I have good data ten households consisted of a couple and their children (seven of which had children of school and preschool age; three with their children between the ages of 17 and 23); seven households consisted of a couple, their children, and a daughter-in-law (in four of them there were also grandchildren); three households consisted of a couple only (their children having moved out). In those cases where more than one son was married and where one son and his wife (and children) shared the house with his parents this was always the youngest son. However, this did not necessarily mean that the two generations lived in *zajednica*, since as we have just seen they could decide to share the house, but not the household, an arrangement made possible by the son's independent income.

Almost all the people in the village over the age of thirty had experienced living in *zajednica*, and what most seemed to associate with it was poverty, lack of space, and hard work. But talking about life in *zajednica* was also a way for people to reflect on what they had obtained in life and how much their living standards had improved. To thirty-six-year-old Kasim, living in *zajednica* in the fifties was associated with not being able to afford shoes so that he and his siblings had walked to school barefoot, even in winter. Sabina, who was forty, had left the village twenty years earlier when she married but came regularly to visit her parents. She told me that she had grown up in the old house where twelve people had lived in one room; mother, father, six children, her grandmother, and father's brother with his wife and their child. She added emphatically: "Father was working very hard, simply for us to be able to eat and drink." Women who had arrived as young brides to live in a communal household, emphasized the hard work, lack of rights, and the strict authority of their seniors. Kasim's wife, Aiša, often told me: "I don't think you can imagine what met me when I first arrived in this village. It was wretched. We didn't have anything, not even proper bed linen. And if I was hungry and wanted a piece of bread I had to ask my *svekrva* (mother-in-law) for permission. She never allowed me to eat of the freshly-made bread. You know we have a saying: *zajednica jadnica* (*zajednica* is poverty and misery)."

All these experiences belonged to the past. They had become memories of a time when living standards in rural Bosnia were much lower than in the nineteen eighties, but they were memories against which the social and economic progress of their own households as well as those of the larger village could be assessed. The frequent references villagers made to life in *zajednica* were a comment on their own economic and social achievements as well as on those of their society as a whole. Tito, the "father" of post–World War II Yugoslavia, was highly respected by the generations of villagers who had lived in *zajednica*. The oldest had also seen Tito bringing an end to a war in which more people had been killed by fellow "Yugoslavs" than by the German or Italian occupying forces, while the younger could point to the fact that their own children did not have to walk barefoot.[10] Indeed, after years of hard work they had even been able to build their own modern houses.

Younger women had primarily experienced life in *zajednica* from a junior position where they had no property rights or say in the running of the household or the management of its resources. The junior woman or daughter-in-law had the lowest and often the most difficult position within the *zajednica*, and had the most to gain in status from its breakup. The impact of socialist policies, encouraging education and wage labor for women, together with new values favoring the consumer society and the nuclear family, gave the junior woman a wider ideological legitimation for her demands and initiatives, and sometimes the economic power too. On the other hand, older women who had experienced life in a communal household in a senior role, would talk favorably about the labor organization in the house. These mutually opposed perspectives about what living in a communal household entailed, clearly reflect its hierarchical character and the different experiences of individuals in different positions in this hierarchy. While a senior couple would benefit from having power over the labor of sons and daughters-in-law, the latter aspired to control their own labor and household.

## Breaking Out of the Communal Household

Not surprisingly, it was often the young daughter-in-law who was pushing to break out of the two-generational household. Conflicts within households between a daughter-in-law and her mother-in-law were part of the drama of everyday village life, and a frequent topic of conversation between women during coffee-visits and evening visits (*sijelos*). Men were less interested and would rarely involve themselves in what they saw as women's talk (or even gossip), but if they joined in the discussion it would almost inevitably be to state that the bride was obliged to obey her mother-in-law. In particular cases, though, some men would agree that the mother-in-law was known to be a troublemaker. I heard of several cases of women in the village who had left during the early period of their marriage, only to return later after negotiations with their husband. Some of course did not return but eventually divorced their husband (if a legal marriage had taken place). These instances were commented on in detail by women in the neighborhood (who had not yet become mothers-in-law themselves), being welcome opportunities for them to relive their own experiences as low-status, young daughters-in-law. Unlike the young woman of the eighties, they did not have the means to break away. (It is said about a young woman who returns to her native household that *ona je se vratila*, "she has gone back." By comparison it is said that *ona je otišla*, "she has left," when a daughter leaves her native home to marry. In other words, it is the bride's return to her native household which is emphasized rather than her leaving her husband's household.)

During my stay in the village, the drama of one young bride's relationship with her mother-in-law preoccupied the women in my neighborhood for months. Mina was a beautiful, intelligent, and hardworking twenty-year-old. Amir, her husband, was a cheerful, kind, and hardworking young man. The two were very much in love with each other, but their relationship became strained because they were living with and sharing a small house with Amir's parents. His mother proved particularly difficult. Mina had to work extremely hard not only for herself, her husband, and child, but for her sisters-in-law too. She never heard a kind word and was getting close to breaking point. The neighborhood women were sympathetic and supportive of her but she was terrified that her mother-in-law, who made sure the same women heard how hopeless Mina was, would find out. She often cried, silently confiding in one trusted woman neighbor. In the end she decided to return to her native household and her neighbor confidante advised her to leave her nine-month-old baby behind. Her friend suggested it would be good for her husband and parents-in-law to see what she had to cope with, and besides, she told her, "the child is theirs." (Although the kinship structure has strong bilateral traits, a child is believed to belong to the husband's patrigroup. But women also take their child/children back to their native household with them if they divorce their husband.) I believe that by giving her this advice, Mina's neighbor thought it more likely that she would return to the village. Indeed, she stayed with her mother for two months, but said she could not bear it any longer because of the child. If it had not been for him, she insisted, she would never have returned.

This was also the outcome predicted by the women in the village. After she had left, they eagerly discussed the circumstances and reasons of her departure, what the mother-in-law had said or done, who was to blame, and the husband's reaction. Younger women were of the view that a conflict-ridden communal life with a mother-in-law was something a young woman did not have to tolerate. Depicting the difficulties of sharing a household with one's mother-in-law, women emphasized the lack of freedom under her authority. Older women agreed that young women today were more clever than they had been, as they did not put up with poor treatment. Most importantly, however, the economic standards and independence of young couples (and even of the wife) were much better than, say, twenty years earlier, and returning home to her parents was actually a viable alternative for a young woman. Her parents would have the economic means to support her, and the extra room to be able to welcome her back, and she could even support herself by taking on paid work.

A separation might not be permanent, and the woman might leave her husband for a variety of reasons, the most common being her relationship with his parents. While in the late eighties the husband would usually go and ask his estranged wife to come back to him, my neighbor Suada told me that when she had returned to her native household during the first year of her marriage when she lived in *zajednica* fifteen years earlier, her brother had sent her back saying, "You belong to your husband now, and your place is with him." Both men and women agreed that things had changed and that in those days "if her family was of any worth" they would send the young woman back to her husband and his family.

Although both men and women condemned the young bride's act as shameful in principle, I was carefully told that it used to be a really "big shame" (*velika sramota*) before. When I asked for whom it was a shame, I was told that it was shameful for both households but particularly so for the young woman's native household. In specific cases where the villagers knew the people and the circumstances concerned, however, there was less condemnation and more interested and lively discussion as to why she had left and who was ultimately to blame. In the above case women blamed Mina's mother-in-law for her difficult bossy nature and the husband for not standing up to her. They would never blame them directly to their faces but might indicate that they were also at fault.

The period during which a new member and stranger is in the process of being incorporated into a new household and made into a loyal member is critical for the household in question. Yet it seems that after the young woman has given birth and become a mother, and by implication fully a woman (*zena*), is most critical in a two-generational and patrilocal household, since the important change in the daughter-in-law's status can threaten the position of her mother-in-law. This is when a separation between the young woman, her husband, and his household is most likely to take place. The daughter-in-law now feels she has more rights and will more readily stand up for herself. She may also assume that her position and bargaining power with her husband are considerably strengthened. One young woman who to everybody's knowledge had very good relations with her mother-in-law and behaved respectfully toward her, allegedly changed after giving birth to a son. It was rumored that she was not respectful any more, but angry and rude (*bezobrazna*, without manners). Her change in behavior was ascribed to the fact that now that she had given birth to a son, she believed she could get away with anything, and that she could do no wrong toward her husband as the mother of his son. Whether this was true or not, this rumor reflected women's belief that their power within the household increased through their children and particularly through sons who, at least traditionally, would have stayed on in the household after their own marriage. On becoming a mother, a woman gained a higher status since she now had the responsibility for the successful socialization of new household members.

The increase in the availability of wage labor, education, and migration abroad from the 1960s onward secured the economic independence of sons, who became less dependent on income from agriculture and landowning fathers and allowed for a shift of authority from fathers to sons. This in turn resulted in the weakening of patrilineal ideology and shift from the extended family unit to the conjugal couple as the unit of reference (i.e., the unit around which both the moral and the organizational worlds of the household revolve) and represented a radical change in the situation of women and the way they perceived their own roles within the household.[11]

This change in the economic power within the household facilitated the realization of junior members' aspirations, particularly the desire of young women to have a separate household from their mothers-in-law. Their main incentives were the conflict inherent in the mother-in-law/daughter-in-law relationship, as well as junior women's increased sense of being justified in their demands for more say and control in the management of household resources. Since this often proved difficult within the traditional household structure (embodied in the mother-in-law), the ultimate aim became independence as a separate *kuća*.

## Women, Men, and Economic Life

Most households in the village did not own sufficient land to be economically viable, although most had plots of land where they grew vegetables, or, if they owned larger areas, hay. The majority of households were thus so-called "mixed households," that is, they drew their subsistence from both agriculture and industry. Those who had livestock, but not enough land to grow hay, could also enter into a contract of *kesim* (a lease which required repayment in kind, which in this case might be milk or cheese) with someone who did have surplus land. Only six households in the village (three Muslim and three Catholic) had viable landholdings and gained their income entirely from agriculture. Two households were completely landless. While I stayed in the village these two households had a contract of *kesim*. They were renting land from a widow to grow basic agricultural products, such as beans, onions, leeks, potatoes, and maize; they paid her by giving her a share of the crop which was negotiated for each product every cropping season. The adult male population consisted mainly of unskilled or skilled laborers (as bricklayer, welder, carpenter, electrician, car mechanic, warden, or lorry driver, to mention the most common) working in the nearby market towns or in the industrial suburbs of Sarajevo. There was no difference in occupational activity between Muslims and Catholics and they often worked together in the same factory or firm. Some men had been to Germany as migrant workers at some stage, but later returned to the village.

Contrary to the case in other European communist countries, there were no agricultural cooperatives in Yugoslavia at the time. However, so-called peasant working collectives or *zadruga*s had been introduced at the start of Tito's post–World War II regime, but they were an economic disaster. Reorganized in 1953, by 1965 they had ceased to exist. The 1945 agrarian reform had set a maximum of 25–35 hectares (depending on the quality of the land) allowed under private ownership. In 1953 the maximum was decreased to 10 hectares and was in the 1980s slightly increased again for mountain regions.[12]

As has happened in many rural areas where wage labor and labor migration have become significant sources of income, agriculture has been feminized.[13] Older villagers' accounts suggest, however, that in Dolina the change had taken place over a longer period of time than may be common in other villages (Jancar 1985). The switch from subsistence agriculture to wage labor was a process which took at least three generations (approximately sixty to eighty years) and may not therefore be as striking as in other, richer agricultural areas. I spoke to a few villagers in their seventies and eighties who told me that, like the majority of village households, they did not have viable landholdings when they started their own families, and had to seek wage labor as an additional source of income. At the turn of the century Dolina was a center for the production of ceramic water jugs (*bardak*) and cooking pots (*lonac*). As many as thirty men are said to have worked as potters at one time. Although they included both Muslims and Catholics, the majority were Muslims. Eighty-year-old Atif told me that when he was young, he worked as a potter and assisted one of the established ones to earn some money. In the 1930s there were six potters in the village while by the mid-1950s only one man and his son were still producing traditional pottery. This was based on an old Roman technique and pattern. (During the Roman period Dolina was near the route which went from Rome via Dubrovnik and eastward to Constantinople.) The jugs were sold on the market, or to villagers locally for household use and for use in the mosques during *abdest* (the ritual washing before prayers). After World War II production was drastically reduced, and in the late 1980s demand was poor since by then most households and mosques had installed water taps. In some older mosques, however, the *bardak* was still used and there was one Muslim man left in the village who practiced the skill, making miniature *bardak*s which he sold in the market as souvenirs and for decoration.

After World War II there was seasonal work in the forest, and at one time a majority of Dolina's adult male population was working in a factory about an hour's walk away, producing bricks. However, this factory closed down in the early seventies. (After the workers struck work for higher pay, the management found the factory unprofitable to run.) A few of these semiproletarian villagers had to put up with unemployment for long periods. Some migrated to the coast for seasonal work, mainly as builders. Some lived off social welfare for periods during which they saw their children poorly fed and poorly dressed and unable to go to school because they could not afford books, bus fares, and clothes. Some of the unskilled workers had great difficulty finding a new job, and if they were landless as well the outlook was bleak indeed. The two conditions often went together as they were self-perpetuating: a landless man was not able to send his children to secondary school, and the child would later have difficulties finding a job. The circle of poverty, landlessness, lack of education, and unemployment was thus difficult to break out of.

The situation for women, however, was different. They were vital to maintaining household agriculture, but they usually did not leave the household for employment. During my stay only three of the unmarried girls and one married woman (with no children) in the upper part of the village worked outside the household. (In the lower part there were a couple of younger married women who continued to work after maternity leave.) Some unmarried and young married women had at some point worked as seamstresses at the clothing factory in a nearby market town, but found it very demoralizing to do piecework at a very low wage. Some young girls worked there until they married or had a child. Married women who were not employed were able to earn some additional money by taking in sewing or knitting orders from other villagers. Some also knitted for a firm in a nearby market town which exported hand-knitted sweaters abroad, or made crocheted decorative items and tablecloths for private sale or for the market. In summer and autumn, the most industrious women took their children to pick berries in the forest which they then sold to the local cooperative shop. The money they earned would often be targeted for communal household projects

4. Wife and husband sifting white beans.

such as buying material and clothes for gift exchange in connection with a marriage.

The *bašča*, which is a garden or patch of land usually near the house (either at the back or next to it), was tended mainly by women. Here they grew all sorts of vegetables for household consumption, but were often joined by their husbands for physically more demanding tasks like clearing the fields, ploughing, or harvesting potatoes. If the household possessed additional land, the whole family would be engaged in clearing, planting, and bringing in the crop (the staple food was potatoes, which had replaced the more labor-intensive maize). This land was usually further away from the house, alongside the fields belonging to other households. If the land was on a slope, it was ploughed by a horse, but on flat land a tractor was used. Only a small number of households in Dolina proper, however, possessed a horse or tractor; two Muslim households owned a horse each and two Catholic households had a tractor each. Whenever major agricultural work like ploughing needed to be done, a household would pay the owner of the horse or tractor to do the job. Muslims and Catholics would work for each other.

Households with more land normally had several cows (the two households with the largest number of cows had five each). Villagers with a small landholding had to buy hay for winter feeding or arrange

for a *kesim*, a contract between a landowner and a tenant. The possession of one or several cows used to be a reflection of the economic
standing of the household and was still a source of pride and renown
even when agriculture was no longer the primary source of wealth. The
milking and processing of cheese was woman's work, traditionally allocated to the daughter-in-law where there was one. Surplus milk and sour
cream (*povlaka*), and more rarely cheese not consumed by the household, would be sold to households in the village that did not have a cow.
A woman running a household with no milk production would strike a
deal for the daily delivery of milk with the female head of a household
which had a surplus. The former would have to find new suppliers when
the production of the original one dropped, or if she decided to sell
cheeses and sour cream on the market, where she may obtain a better
price. To sell on the market she needed a permit issued by the council in
the market town. Every market town in the region had its market day
once a week when peasants from the surrounding villages came to sell
their dairy products, vegetables, or handicrafts. Since 1953 (when the
state-run *zadrugas* came to an end) farmers had been under no obligation in Yugoslavia to sell agricultural products to the state. They could
sign a contract to sell their products at a fixed price with a food-produc-
ing firm or a consumer cooperative, if they so chose. Some households
also kept sheep; this, I was told, was much more widespread some fifteen
to twenty years ago when living in *zajednica* was still common, and children and unmarried household members were available to herd the
sheep. Those who owned sheep but could not herd them themselves for
lack of labor, would leave them with the only full-time herdsmen, a
Muslim (the other, a Catholic, only herded his own sheep). It used to be
common for households to provide their own wool, and for women to
weave and knit. But in 1987 only two elderly women in the village knew
how to weave, and wool was generally purchased at the market or in one
of the shops in town.

## Social and Moral Geography of the Village

The inhabitants of Dolina described the village as consisting of several
*mahala*s (hamlets; in a city, quarters), some of which the older population considered to be different villages (*selo*). When traveling outside
Dolina people would say they were from Dolina, meaning the larger
unit. Within the village a villager would refer to his village (*selo*) or hamlet (*mahala*) depending on whether he was interacting within his *mahala* or outside it. Another important reference unit was the neighborhood (*komšiluk*), which sometimes overlapped with a *mahala*. The latter

was a defined geographical area. As a rule it consisted of households with the same last name (patrilineally related families), while the former was defined from the point of view of the individual household as those houses which immediately surrounded it, and with which it had relationships of mutual obligations, exchange, and support, reflected in the visiting patterns between them. Some households were part of more than one neighborhood. Seen from the point of view of the acting household, these neighborhoods were made up of concentric, partly overlapping circles of households which visited each other more frequently than they did others. They relied on each other for mutual help and support in times of need.

Muslims and Catholics visited each other over a more restricted area of the village than they did houses belonging to their own ethnoreligious communities, as each household's visiting circle also included kin and relatives who did not live in the *komšiluk*, but elsewhere in the village. This meant that while Muslim (or Catholic) neighbors shared concentric circles of visiting patterns, Muslims and Catholics did not. In other words, a Muslim woman could visit her Catholic next-door neighbor and find another Catholic woman there from another neighborhood in the village whom she herself would never visit. This would not be the case when she visited a Muslim next-door neighbor. If they were not "first neighbors," relationships between Muslims and Catholics often had the character of individual friendships, which sometimes extended to all members of the two households. These relations were, in other words, usually between individual members of households rather than between household units, and were consequently never formalized or reinforced through any communal rituals.

In some specific cases, Muslims and Catholics also paid each other formal visits beyond their neighborhoods. This occurred on ritual occasions in connection with a life-cycle event in one of the households, such as a son leaving or returning from national service in the army, the arrival of a bride, the departure of a daughter just married, a birth, death, or illness. It was considered particularly shameful not to pay one's respects by visiting "in sorrow" (*na žalost*). Muslims, however, often felt uneasy about visiting a Catholic household during a vigil, though as neighbors they would attend the funeral. These were occasions when co-villagers irrespective of religious affiliation came together to share in the sorrow or joy of a neighboring household. Religious celebrations, on the other hand, defined two communities within the village by including some neighbors in the village and excluding others.

Muslims and Catholics within the village greeted each other with the secular and standard *dobar dan* ("good day") and *doviđenja* ("goodbye"). These were also the greetings used in any public (and therefore

"nonethnic") or urban multicultural context. When Muslims greeted
each other they did so with specific Muslim greetings of Turkish, Arabic,
or Persian origin. There are several, some of which were seen by Muslims as more "religious" (*vjerski*) than others and therefore not used by
everybody or only used to greet older devout Muslims, *imam*s, or in the
context of religious ritual gatherings (such as *tevhid* or *mevlud* described
in a later chapter). This was the case, for instance, with *selam alejk.*
*Alahemanet* ("go with Allah") as a farewell greeting was the common
greeting for "goodbye" among Muslims in villages. However, many
younger people did not use it as they thought it old-fashioned and preferred the informal *zdravo* or *prijatno* or even the Italian-inspired *čiao*,
which would upset the older generation terribly if addressed to them.
While the "public" *dobro jutro* ("good morning") and *dobro veče* ("good
evening") was used between Muslims and Catholics, Muslims used
*sabah hajrola* and *akšam hajrola* ("I wish you a beautiful morning/eve-
ning") within their own community (both greetings required the reply
*alah razola*). Muslims in addition used the nonreligious informal greeting *merhaba* of Turkish origin ("You have arrived at a spacious place,"
meaning, "You are among friends"). It expresses friendship, acceptance,
trust, and hospitality, and was primarily used by and among men. While
some younger women might also use it the most common greeting
among them was *kako si/ste*? ("How are you?") which was also used by
Catholics. The Catholics have their own religious greetings such as *bog*
(or *bok*) and *hvaljen Isus* ("praise Jesus").

As a result of the nationalist rhetoric which fuels the ongoing war,
those greetings which were specific to one community and were never
used in public places in the late eighties, have become strong markers of
communal exclusivity and ethnoreligious ("national") territoriality. The
political significance of these terms was given new and painful force in
the spring of 1993 when the Catholic Croats (who by then controlled
the municipality to which Dolina belongs) used them in public places
and contexts (such as administrative offices, shops, or the police) which
earlier would have been defined as state-oriented and therefore nonethnic, the domain of nonspecific, intercommunal greetings. Thus in effect the language of exclusivity, which defines who belongs and who
does not, is being applied (in the context of political and military dominance by one group) in a sphere where earlier it would have been taboo,
because it was shared with members of other ethnoreligious communities to whom such greetings were alien. By expanding the accepted
sphere for the use of the language of exclusivity, the borders for cultural
supremacy are being redefined. Indeed, the Catholic Croats were redefining the whole area (market town and surrounding villages) as
"theirs" and transforming the local Muslims into outsiders, people who

did not belong. (This was one of many steps in a long series of more or less violent measures to squeeze the Muslims out of their villages and the municipality.)

Before the war, mutually acknowledged and accepted differences between the two village communities had been the basis for interaction and identity formation in the village. When the war with its accompanying nationalistic rhetoric had poisoned the minds of its target population long enough, such differences were no longer accepted. Indeed, they were no longer what informed and shaped a community's own identity, becoming instead an obstacle to the cohesion and unbounded expression of its collective ("national") identity. The desire to express such a collective identity necessarily implied that each group sought to establish its supremacy over any competing collective identities in the same area (such as Bosnian or Muslim).

The upper and older part of the village which lay beyond the mosque was referred to as "the village" by Dolina villagers who lived further down the valley toward the main road. This was the most densely populated part of the village, there being much less space between houses than elsewhere in the village. Here the Muslim and Catholic houses were also much closer to each other than elsewhere (where they often formed separate *mahala*s), and visits between Muslims and Catholics were more frequent. Except for one new house, all the houses in this part of the village were built in the traditional style which distinguished Muslim from Catholic houses (see Fig. 3). Because these houses were all older they had no water taps and water had to be fetched from the communal water fountain. People here were also seen as poorer, as they had not be able to afford to build a new house. When people who lived outside this more densely settled area visited it, they would say they were going "up in the village" (*gore u selu*). The opposite, "down in the village" was never used as this would have been a contradiction in terms. The newer settlements on open land were not "in the village," but seen rather as an intermediary link between village and urban suburb.

The upper part of the village, referred to not by a *mahala* name but simply as "the village" or "up in the village," was thought of as the real or true village (*pravo selo*). This expression alludes to certain ideas people have about living in a village. These ideas are as much a reflection of their own experiences as they are of nonvillagers' evaluations of villagers, influenced by the wider, urban, "modern," progressive society. While on the one hand this expression refers mainly to the practicalities of life in a "real village" (the absence of modern comforts such as hot water and proper bathrooms), on the other hand it also contains moral judgments and allusions to backwardness. Dolina "village" was not only the "true village" which embodied the critical characteristics of village and

village life as opposed to town and urban life, it was also the original
Dolina, where most of the families in the larger village had once had
their settlements. For people who no longer lived here it was associated
with their origins, and therefore with who they were. But it also held up
a mirror to who they had become, since it offered a reflection on socioeconomic change and on the past. Just where "up in the village" started
depended on where the speaker wanted to place him or herself, so that
for some "the village" always started beyond his or her own house (just
as the "Balkans" always seemed to begin south of one's own republic in
the former Yugoslavia). Indeed, the upper and lower part of the village
occupied different ends of what we can call a hierarchy of culturedness,
which is closely associated with the rural-urban divide.

### The Concept of Culturedness

In Bosnia, as in the former Yugoslavia as a whole and indeed in the Balkans, it is common practice to label people on a dichotomous scale of
"cultured" and "noncultured," distinguishing people who are "cultured" (*kulturni*) from those who are "noncultured" (*nekulturni*), or
those who have "culture" from those who do not. Being "cultured" or
"noncultured" refers to a whole set of ideas associated with other sociological oppositions such as town versus village, educated versus uneducated, poor versus rich, modern and Western versus backward and
Balkan. In the village the concepts of "culturedness" and "noncultured-
ness" were clearly associated with the dichotomies of village versus town
(rural versus urban), and education versus little or no education. People
were not necessarily labeled one or the other but rather were placed on
a sliding scale of culturedness assessed in relation to their behavior in
social interaction with others.

Being "cultured" was associated with having a formal education.
There was a clear correlation between the degree of a person's literacy
(or illiteracy) and his or her perceived degree of culturedness. But it was
also related to the way a person spoke, dressed, and to his or her de-
meanor generally, and ultimately to his or her socioeconomic status.
(For instance, I was told that someone who is *nekulturan* is someone
who does not know how to behave, is rude, has no manners, and no
education.) Overall, people in the upper part of Dolina were poorer, less
educated, and lived more "traditionally" than those in the lower part, so
that a villager from the upper part moving outside Dolina would more
readily earn the label "uncultured" than one from further down the
valley. I heard people in the lower ("modern") part describing the villagers further up as *bijeda*. This means poor, but also has the connota-

tion of being ignorant, uneducated, and miserable. Thus, when used in this context the term *bijeda* refers not only to material poverty, but also to a whole set of ideas associated with being "uncultured," such as lack of a formal education, unemployment, engaging in fights, cardplaying, promiscuity, and (for women) keeping a dirty and untidy home. It was said that the upper part of the village had people of "all sorts" (*ima svašta*) and that quarrel and gossip were endemic.

There was, in other words, a moral judgment. Young, upwardly mobile couples would always aim to move out of the upper part of the village and build a modern house further down the village and valley nearer the market town, where people were more urbanized and consequently more "cultured." Perceptions of "culturedness" stratified people in a moral hierarchy both within the village and between villages, though perhaps most markedly between village and city. To be a villager obviously meant different things to different people. However, there were some general ideas which pervaded all discourse on life in the village as opposed to life in the city. While one set of ideas which was projected by villagers themselves reflected city-dwellers' views of villagers, another reflected villagers' views on city life. I will deal with both in turn.

Two different words were used to refer to a villager: *seljak*, which was used by the villagers, and *seljačina*, a pejorative term used by city-dwellers with the connotation of country bumpkin.[14] But it was also used by people in the village to describe covillagers they did not like or whose behavior they found morally unacceptable. By describing a co-villager this way, the speaker could distance him or herself from "villageness," as this term more than any other implied "unculturedness." Sometimes when talking to me people made derogatory remarks such as, "People here are no good," (*narod ovdje ne valja*) which I took to be a gesture toward me as the Westerner, whom villagers saw as representative of that world which judges rural areas and places like Dolina as "backward," "primitive," and "uncultured." By pointing out the "unculturedness" and "villageness" in other people, individuals would simultaneously exclude themselves from such categorization, apparently identifying with the evaluations of the urbanized majority and, they imagined, with that of the anthropologist. At the same time, however, people often underscored the fact that it was difficult for a person who had "had no schooling" to be cultured. But as one of my proud and witty neighbors once pointed out, "Although you live in a village this does not necessarily mean you are a *seljačina*." Terms such as *nekulturni* and *seljačina* were used as individual value judgments and were neither categories with fixed content, nor, once conferred on a person, constantly used for that individual. Rather, these terms depended on the specific social contexts within which these individuals moved and on those with whom they interacted.

Villagers on their part constructed what it meant to be a villager in contrast to what it meant to be a city-dweller in terms of two major and interconnected behavioral and moral differences: first, the number and acceptability of marriages between members of different ethnoreligious communities, and second the presence or absence of religion or faith (*vjera*). A Muslim mother exemplified this when she told me she would never allow her daughter to marry "somebody from a different faith." She explained: "We are the way our social environment (*sredina*) is, and here we see things this way, although I know they see things differently in town . . . , there more people do marry those from different religions, but that is because in town this is not important; they have no religion."

This does not mean, however, that all villagers practice their religion consistently. Indeed I found that for many villagers religious observance was dependent on the social environment within which they were acting. Thus, as people moved between social settings or contexts, as from inside to outside the village, their practices and formal behavior also changed. There was often a switch in communication codes. Greetings, style of language, or dress, which did not carry strong moral implications, could change, as could behavior with strong moral and religious implications. Individuals who never drank alcohol with neighbors in the village might do so on special festive occasions with friends or family outside the village. A friend who in the village context was a devout practicing Muslim, commented when she heard that some neighbors (men and women) in the village had come together to celebrate the new year and got drunk, that they were stupid to do that in the village for everybody to see. So it was not so much what people did as where they did it that was important. Similarly, commenting about a man who was having an affair with a woman in the village, one of my neighbors said she thought his behavior shameful, but that if he absolutely had to have another woman he should have gone to Sarajevo. In other words, to many villagers, particularly women, the city represented a place with a different and often objectionable moral code.

### Muslims and Catholics: Perceptions of Villageness

The mosque, the focal point for the Muslims' consciousness of themselves as a community, was situated in the center of Dolina. The Catholics' focal point, the church, is outside the village, about three to four kilometers away toward one of the market towns, and their community feeling was directed as much outward as inward. (While the Catholics were in a minority in the village, they were in a small majority in the market town and in the overall *opština* or municipality.) And while the Catholics of Bosnia looked to Rome for their spiritual leadership, the rural Bosnian Muslims looked only occasionally beyond Bosnia: their religious leadership had its seat close at hand in Sarajevo. It could be argued that the Muslims' community identity was more strongly attached to Dolina, and their village particularism more pronounced. Thus, it was my impression that the Muslims were more ready than the Catholics to ascribe certain characteristics of village life to Dolina as a particular place. Catholics, on the other hand, would attribute the same characteristics to them as Muslims. Perhaps because the Catholics were a religious and cultural minority in the village, by symbolically constructing the Muslims as more "villagelike" and less "cultured," they were trying to reverse the power relationship between the two groups caused by the Muslims' stronger numerical and cultural presence.[15] The Catholics themselves identified more with the nearest market town which was their religious and numerical center.

That Catholics conceptually linked "Muslimness" with lack of "culture" became evident in the course of my conversations with them. Those who knew or learned that I was living in a Muslim household, asked me whether I had discovered the difference between Muslims and themselves [Catholics]? They were just like anybody else in the city, in the West. The Muslims, however, were different in the way they ate, dressed, and spoke. Young unmarried Catholic Croat girls compared themselves with their Muslim female friends and saw many differences. They mentioned what they thought was a stricter control of Muslim girls, as their parents often did not allow them to go to coffee-bars, fewer years spent at school, although they noted that this was now changing, and lastly the way they dressed (in the village). The Catholic girls felt they were less conspicuous than their Muslim counterparts, since both their dress and their speech were close to the urban and Western standard. Although Muslim girls and young women did not differ in dress from Catholic girls when they moved outside the village, the important point here is the perception of difference, and the fact that these differences were seen to be epitomized in women, not men. According to one of the Catholic girls, her best friend, who was a Muslim, used to ask her for advice on how to dress, and she would correct her whenever she used expressions that sounded "old-fashioned" and "villagelike" (these particular words are often of Turkish origin).

Diana, a young Catholic woman, told me: "Muslims dress differently, but as soon as they move outside the village they dress so that one cannot say if they are Muslims or something else. We generally dress the

same way both at home and when we go out. We could just as well
have been from town, nobody can tell that we are villagers." And she
added: "Earlier, when our parents were young, we were also different
from those in town, but we have left that behind and now there is
no difference. But Muslims keep more to their ways. I do not know
why this is so." She was thus equating Catholic (Croat) with modern,
urban, and cultured, and Muslim with rural and uncultured. At the
same time, however, she was constructing the Muslims as "the others"
in Yugoslav Bosnian society as a whole. Indeed, she indicated that, in
her view the Muslims seemed to refuse to become like her. While in the
village Muslim women (wives, not unmarried girls) could, and many
would, dress in a style which was considered "Muslim," that is primarily
*dimije* (traditional baggy trousers) or a long skirt and sometimes a
headscarf, this changed when they moved out of the village context and
into town.

Differences in clothing between Muslims and non-Muslims in rural
areas were thus becoming less apparent, particularly among the young.
A Muslim neighbor of mine in her thirties, who used to wear *dimije* in
the village (but never a headscarf, except when praying), would wear a
smart suit (the skirt above the knees) and high-heeled shoes into town.
She explained to me: "As a proper Muslim woman you should cover
yourself. However, when I go to Sarajevo I do not dress in *dimije* and
headscarf. It wouldn't look good, would it?" When in the village it was
both accepted and expected that women would express in their dress
styles who they were and which community they belonged to (i.e., Muslim and not Catholic). But in the city this was not an accepted (or necessary) way of expressing one's identity. To the Muslim women from
Dolina Sarajevo was primarily a secular, nonreligious (and nonethnic)
social space. They explained the different dress codes they followed in
terms of the village and the city being different social environments.
Since in the city the ethnoreligious dimension of the three official *nacije*
could only be actively expressed within a religiously defined sphere such
as the mosque or at religious gatherings in private houses, the village
and neighborhood became the focal point for expressing such ethnoreligious distinctiveness. Most Muslim girls and younger women changed
their form of dress markedly when they left the village, and they were
especially careful to dress according to urban standards when they went
to town. Generally, when moving outside the hamlet a young girl
wanted to look well-dressed and urban. I often overheard daughters instructing their mothers on how to dress when going into urban areas. In
the village the girls were primarily Muslim girls while outside the village
they were primarily Bosnian girls. However, while the two contexts may
have been more or less separate they were aspects of an integrative iden-

tity. Rather than excluding each other they were aspects of what it meant to be Muslim and Bosnian.

In the mixed Muslim and Catholic neighborhood in the uppermost part of the village Muslims and Catholics shared some practices which among the more urbanized Catholics in the lower part were associated with Muslims and "muslimness" and often perceived as agreeing with certain ideas of "unculturedness." Thus, the Muslim households—and a Catholic one—in this neighborhood served food on a cloth on the floor and ate seated on the floor from a common pot. Although this had been common practice in all households in the past, in the neighborhoods, and among the younger generation in the lower part of the village, this was no longer the case. In the new, modern neighborhoods, Muslims and Catholics would eat at table. Most Catholics, however, perceived it as a Muslim ("Turkish") custom. Not only was it associated with "muslimness," along with other practices which Muslims and Catholics had shared it was associated with "villageness" and therefore with the opposite of "urbanness" and all the labels—"modern," "educated," "cultured," and "civilized"—which being urban implied.

Older rural wives regardless of their ethnoreligious background used to wear a headscarf. Muslim women tended to tie their headscarf in several different ways, though, some specific to them, others indistinguishable from their Catholic or Orthodox Christian neighbors. The way they knotted it often depended on what they were doing. While praying they would usually tie it in the way specific to Muslim women, tucked in below the left cheek and brought low on the forehead to cover their hair. In the village Muslim and Catholic women would tie their headscarf under the chin, or they would tie it at the back when it was warm or they were working. Muslim women would also tie it at the back and then on the top, which I did not see Catholic women do. No Muslim woman wore the veil, and the headscarf was only worn by older women, or by all women when attending a mosque service or other religious ritual. Although it had never been the custom for unmarried women to wear a headscarf, some older women in the village felt a married woman should wear one. In practice, however, headscarves were rarely worn by women under the age of forty, even though a young woman's female senior (mother, grandmother, or aunt) would encourage her to wear it when she married and went to share a household with her mother-in-law. A young bride who was eager to please and who followed the advice of older women might do so for the first few weeks in her new home. (It was also supposed to be worn by women during their forty-day confinement after giving birth.)

It had also been common (and fashionable) for both Muslim and Catholic women to wear the *dimije* or baggy trousers, although they

5. Neighbors and best friends, Catholic and Muslim.

were distinguished from each other by color: the Catholics wore black ones, the Muslims various different colored patterned ones.[16] When I lived in the village, however, only one old Catholic woman living in the uppermost part of the village was wearing it, while it was still the rule among Muslim women. However, both Catholic and Muslim women were wearing long skirts. For older women, then, the differences in dress were not primarily between Muslim and Catholic, but between women living in the village and those living in the city. To non-Muslims the *dimije* had, nevertheless, become a Muslim identity marker, as it was worn by Muslim women of all ages at home and to some extent in the village. Women in their thirties and forties were reluctant to wear *dimije* outside the village as it was considered old-fashioned. Only older women wore them into town, while young girls were reluctant to wear them even in the village outside their house and neighborhood. It was becoming more common to wear a long skirt instead, even if this was definitely less practical, as you had to take more care as to how you sat or moved than when wearing *dimije*.[17] This was not true, however, for religious ceremonial occasions when the young women and girls wore their best *dimije* and headscarf with pride.

Increasingly associated exclusively with Muslim women, the *dimije* had been imbued with strong symbolic value; they epitomized "muslimness" and were seen as a sign of backwardness and "orientalism" in the minds of Christians and urbanized Muslims. The reason they had become such a powerful symbol of Muslim collective identity, I would argue, is that they were (at the time) the only conspicuous expression of "otherness" in Bosnia; and it is significant that women, not men, displayed their "muslimness" in this way. In this respect the *dimije* in Bosnia has played much the same role as the veil in Islamic Middle Eastern societies.[18]

During religious ceremonies or when attending *mekteb* (religious school) Muslim men would wear a black or dark-blue beret (French style). Some middle-aged men also wore it whenever they went for a social visit in the village or to the market town. *Hodžas* should always wear it; theirs is a bit different in style. Some young *hodžas*, though, did not wear it "off duty." This the older generation could find upsetting. There were a few old men who still wore the Turkish fez, but they were ridiculed by the young for being old-fashioned. The beret can be seen as the male equivalent of the *dimije*, as an expression of identity and a sense of belonging to a distinct community. But although it is less conspicuous, it is, as we have seen, rarely worn by younger men except during prayers in the mosque. The ways in which women often expressed their sense of belonging had become imbued with negative connotations which meant that women were less able than men to escape the prejudices of the westernized segments of the population in Bosnia—prejudices about Islam, "the East," and backwardness, in short the whole gamut of ideas covered by what Said (1978) has called "orientalism."

## A Village of Two Communities

In a previous section I noted that the neighborhood (*komšiluk*) was an important sociogeographical unit within the village, and that neighborhoods were usually mixed in that Muslim and Catholic families lived as next-door neighbors. Hospitality and related social exchange (such as women's coffee visiting and men's work parties) was the basis for neighborliness between them. These activities involved the two communities and in emphasizing a shared (and therefore nonreligious) identity acknowledged the existence of a village community beyond the ethnoreligious one. Socializing between villagers, Muslim and Catholic, provided an opportunity for identifying with one's ethnoreligious community and expressing this belonging to nonmembers. At the same time, however, it gave members of the two communities an opportunity to focus on shared experiences and other aspects of their identities that were common to both (being women, neighbors, villagers, Bosnians). Living in this Bosnian village meant, at one level, sharing certain characteristics with covillagers irrespective of *nacija*. At another, however, it meant belonging to an exclusive *nacija*. In this section we will first look at activities and institutions which emphasized similarities and therefore unified the two communities in the village, before turning to those that separated them by focusing on differences. It should be noted, however, that although the emphasis was on either similarities or differences in a given situation, no social context ever entirely excluded the other. It is precisely this tension between perceived similarities and difference which created the dynamic of social life.

The villagers thought of themselves as a specific village in opposition to other villages through the discourse of difference which took place both within the context of the village itself and outside it. At the village level, a common unifying Bosnian village identity was constructed through the assertion of common concepts, practices, and images about the village which were contrasted with what it and other villages were not, namely, the city. At the intravillage level, though, two ethnoreligious communities were constructed and sustained through parallel, oppositional, diversifying images and ideas about the village and its inhabitants. While the discourse on both similarities and difference between the two communities was part of what it meant to be Bosnian (*bosanac*), at the intravillage level the terms "Bosnian" and "Bosnia" were used as metaphors for what villagers perceived they had in common (an important part of which was the very fact of living in mixed communities) with other people (irrespective of *nacija*) throughout Bosnia (such as their particular food, music, greater hospitality, and love of socializing).

## Neighborliness

Although people in the village would always think about the abstract collectives "Muslims" and "Catholics" in terms of what separated them, on an individual basis when Muslims and Catholics actually interacted, they would refer to both differences and similarities between them.

Which of these was emphasized depended on context and could even change within the same interactional sequence, as for instance when Muslim and Catholic women drank coffee together. Coffee-visiting was not only the major social activity of married women but it was critical in integrating the Muslim and Catholic communities in the village. These visits enhanced Bosnian identity by the act of sharing the cultural value of hospitality and using a shared cultural code. Nevertheless, during such visits there were also frequent references to the perceived differences between the two groups, with some customs being described as practiced "among you" (*kod vas*) or "among us" (*kod nas*) or being "yours" or "ours." Such markers were not fixed, but varied with geographical and sociocultural context. (Similar comments were for instance made in mixed ethnoreligious company to refer to people in the city, the region, Bosnia, or even "Yugoslavia.") After having simultaneously situated themselves as members of an exclusive community and delineated their separateness from other such communities, people would often then conclude: "It is different among them, but we are used to our ways," or "This is the way they have learned it." They thereby expressed what they perceived as a fact of life: that different people have different customs, but what is primary is not that "we" are different from "them" but rather that we are "us."

On one occasion I accompanied three Muslim women on a visit to the home of a Catholic woman who had just returned from hospital. Other Catholic women in the neighborhood joined in to have a chat. (All the women were born in the village and had grown up as close neighbors.) We sat around a table and drank from cups; this was in contrast to the traditional Muslim custom of sitting on sofas or on mattresses on the floor and drinking coffee from *fildžans* (a small cup without a handle). The conversation revolved around issues common to any coffee-visit: the work the women had done in the house, the recent rise in prices, and so on. However, friendly acknowledgments of differences in customs between the hosts and the visitors were made throughout. Thus, a Catholic woman told her Muslim neighbors that she had been to the market and seen a good and reasonably priced material for making "your *bošća*" (the cloth which Muslims in older and more traditional houses spread on the floor when eating; although Catholics today eat at a table this was a fairly recent practice in Dolina). Furthermore, when setting out the coffee cups the hostess allotted one teaspoon for each guest. The Muslim women said they could share one, but the Catholic hostess answered that "Among us we have one teaspoon for each person." Since in both Muslim and Catholic households teaspoons may be shared or there may be one for each person, this woman's comment perhaps said more about what *she* did than about what Catholics as a group did. Nevertheless, from her perspective she was communicating who she was in terms of who (collectively) she identified with. To her Muslim guests, however, she sent the message that she perceived them as "not us." This remark was significant precisely because it was made in a context when shared experiences (as women, friends, and neighbors) were the basis for interaction.

Yet the women inevitably followed these statements up with jokes and humorous comments referring to their common experiences as women, thereby shifting the identity idioms and counterbalancing their statements of separateness. For such exchanges and social interaction to take place at all we have to assume that members of the two communities shared a considerable body of tacit cultural knowledge (and social skills). In other words, they shared a common frame of reference, experiences, and a past. When I was living in the village, the women in my neighborhood and a Catholic friend would sometimes meet in the evenings and sing in the traditional style (with one woman leading the tune and the others following) for entertainment. Both Catholics and Muslims take off their shoes before entering someone's house. Except for their religious symbols they decorated their houses in the same way and both Muslim and Catholic women pride themselves on keeping a clean and tidy house (although cleanliness is often seen as a particularly Muslim virtue). Expressions that (Christian) western Europeans often associate with Muslims and their "Islamic" attitude toward life, were used as frequently by Catholics, as by Muslims as in "If God wills" (*ako bog da*, "If god gives." Muslims may add inshallah, using both the "Serbo-Croat" and Arabic versions in the same sentence), or the use of fate and predetermination (*sudbina*) as an explanatory model for why certain things happen.[19] Their common identity and togetherness were couched in terms of shared surroundings and living together as neighbors in the village or in Bosnia.

Hospitality between neighbors is a form of social exchange. Such social exchange was most common in connection with women's daily coffee-visits, and also occurred less frequently during visits in connection with life-cycle events (dealt with in more detail in the next chapter), and cooperation in work tasks. Social exchange, entailing unspecified obligations, has been defined as "the voluntary actions of individuals that are motivated by the returns they are expected to bring" (Vinogradov 1974:2). These actions can take many forms, such as ceremonial gift-giving, voluntary work, ritualized hospitality, and institutionalized visiting patterns. The forms taken are often closely interrelated through the cultural ethos of honor and hospitality. As such, "hospitality is the central ritual of secular social relations" (Ortner 1978:62). In fact, "to refuse to give, or to fail to invite is like refusing to accept . . . it is to reject the bond of alliance and commonality" (Mauss 1990: 13). And in the "refusal to give" lies the seed of animosity and neighborhood quarreling. Muslims and Catholics were not involved in each others' neighborhood quarrels.

Social exchange activities always occurred between households or individuals as members of certain household units. Some activities such as coffee-visits created social bonds and obligations between households mainly through women and thus integrated the community through women; others, like communal or voluntary work, through men; still others, like evening gatherings (*sijelo*), engaged both women and men. The site for these activities was either one of the participants' households or a more public place. Since people acted as individuals as well as on behalf of their household unit this could create conflicts of interest or accentuate already-existing conflicts between members of a household. Hospitality is closely related to the reputation of individual households; indeed the verb for offering hospitality (*častiti*) has the same etymology as the word for honor (*čast*). A household, which outsiders always see as a unit and therefore reflecting on men and women equally, gains social standing ("honor") from the way it receives a guest. This link between hospitality and honor has also been pointed out in Greek ethnography. Herzfeld notes that in Crete "social worth [*filotimo*, 'sometimes glossed as honour'] is hospitality" and that the latter is the primary category (1987:87). The serving of food and drink is an important part of treating a guest well. Older informants told me that the first thing one should ask a guest when he or she arrives in one's house, whether a stranger or not, is, "Would you like something to eat or drink?" In the late nineteen eighties the deteriorating economic situation combined with aspirations for new consumer goods often made it difficult (or of lower priority) for people to honor (*častiti*) guests as they believed they should. There was a sense of shame and inadequacy in not being able to offer guests much in the way of food, as people pride themselves in treating guests lavishly. The more prominent and rare the guest (in terms of being from "outside" the village), the more lavishly was s/he treated, and the greater was the effort made by a household to try and surpass a neighbor or covillager in generosity in relation to the same event or guest—as when the *hodža* (or priest, in the case of the Catholics) visited or when hosting a religious gathering (see chapter six). Lavish hospitality is thus an expression both of the moral superiority of the host (who attempts to leave his guest with future obligations that cannot easily be reciprocated) and of the political potential of the guest (who is now indebted to his host) (Herzfeld 1987).

Voluntary work done by neighbors for individual households was another form of social exchange between households and neighbors which involved hospitality. People were much readier to undertake this kind of voluntary work than to do communal work such as building a road through the village. The latter was initiated by the village council, which represented the local administrative council and was part of the communist party structure. There were two reasons for this. First, the giver may expect to have his help reciprocated, and second, there was the promise of sociability, and food and drink at the end of the work. This kind of help includes the building of a house, work on the fields, and/or any other major operation that a household needs to have carried out quickly. The host or head of the household will feed the workers (his neighbors), who will bring the necessary tools. Such voluntary work was traditionally called *moba*, but the most common term was *akcija*, a word used by the state to mean communal work, particularly the voluntary mass physical labor performed by young people under the auspices of the communist youth organization.[20] Stojaković suggests that the *moba* is understood as a one-way transaction, which means that reciprocity is not expected (1987). This is, however, an idealized model which equates the notion of reciprocity with "direct exchange." I found that reciprocity was an important, though unspecified, aspect of the endeavor and provided the incentive to lend a neighbor a hand. On several occasions I heard wives encouraging their husbands to contribute at a work-party because the person hosting it had helped them with similar work and it would therefore have been shameful not to reciprocate. Thus while it would in any case be shameful for a man not to give a close neighbor a helping hand in the construction of his house, the disgrace would be the greater if the same neighbor had once helped him. So, in fact, there was a strong moral obligation to help all those who had once helped you, particularly for major construction work when people remembered who came along to help and who did not.

During the last ten years the most common form of *akcija* involved the building of a house. Collective work projects for this purpose were frequent, because most households could afford to build as a result of their earnings from migrant work abroad, but also because values were changing. Ideas about individualism had contributed to the splitting up of the communal household and the core family's desire to live alone, and had redirected resources previously spent on communal celebrations, especially life-cycle rituals, into the building of houses. The person hosting the house-building *akcija* would announce it a week or two beforehand to his neighbors, relatives, and friends in the village; sometimes in-laws or work colleagues arrived from outside the village.

6. A house-building *akcija*.

Muslims and Catholics who were friends or neighbors would give each other a helping hand during the construction. The day the roof was laid and the ridge-pole raised a major "building-party" was held, and everyone who had been involved in the construction was invited. A "building-party" was one of the few communal events which involved both Muslim and Catholic communities (although there were a couple of Muslim and Catholic households in the village which would not invite or receive help from neighbors belonging to a *nacija* other than their own). When the ridge-pole is raised—an event called *sljeme* (meaning ridge-pole)—it is customary for neighboring households ("those who wish") to give presents to the sponsoring household. While the voluntary workers who have arrived in large numbers for the final roof-laying keep working, the craftsman who has been supervising the work will affix all the gifts to a crossbar attached to the ridge-pole. The gifts are thus displayed for neighbors and any passerby to see. Every time the host (*domaćin*) receives a gift, the "maestro" (craftsman) climbs the roof to shout his verses of thanks for everybody to hear. This may go on for hours. Thanks are offered to the household (of the giver) through its male head and good wishes to all its members. The recipient hopes the sons and daughters will marry, have a long and prosperous life, and if Muslim that they will be able to go to Mecca.

7. Taking a break.

Gifts usually consisted of clothes, often a shirt, towels, and money. The following is an example of the kind of verse the craftsman will shout from his place on the roof. In this case the craftsman was Muslim. The wording and Islamic content of the verse also indicate that it could only have been addressed to a Muslim. If the giver's name is not included in the verse, the craftsman announces the name of the person to whom the verse is dedicated.

*Mašalah, mašalah, hvala mu, živio.*
*Evo, doneo je dar na novu kuću.*
*Sinove ženio, kćeri udavao*

*živio sto ljeta imao sto kmeta*
*i na Ćabu otišao.*

Masalah, masalah[21] thank him and wish him good health.
Look, he has brought gifts to the new house.
May his sons marry and his daughters too.
May he live a hundred summers and have a hundred serfs
—and may he go to the Kaaba.

The help neighbors, whether Muslim or Catholic, lent each other in connection with the construction of a new house is particularly significant as the house specifically symbolizes the ambiguity implied in belonging to one village and one neighborhood, but two communities, and in expressing similarities and unity, differences and separateness at the same time. The house is at once the physical demarcation of the household, the locus of the unity of interaction in village life, and the embodiment of a separate ethnoreligious identity. As we see from the above poem, this particular house has already been imbued with a specific ethnoreligious identity. In the next chapter we will explore the role of the house as the physical and symbolic demarcation of ethnoreligious identity.

## The Village and the Yugoslav Communist State

In the previous sections we have looked at how unification in terms of a rural Bosnian identification was created locally by the villagers themselves through social exchange and the ethos of hospitality and neighborliness. At another level, however, the Yugoslav state enforced unification through the policies and through its various institutions which penetrated village life. Until 1991 this village was part of a larger federal Yugoslav state system. The integrative mechanism of this state was a Titoist communist ideology and state apparatus. In chapter one I noted that, except for a short period during the 1950s, the policy of this state toward its constituent republics and "peoples" was not based on the notion of a unified Yugoslav national identity, but directed rather at the various state-defined *narod*s and other "nationalities" which were nevertheless united through the state's communist ideology.

People in the village also participated in social spheres defined by this Yugoslavism. They were part of this environment as viewers and listeners of state-controlled television and radio, as members of the self-managing economic system at the workplace, as clients in the bureaucracy, and as the recipients of various social benefits. The young generations were particularly important participants as consumers in the education system, some as members of communist youth clubs or folk-dance groups, and the young men as conscripts in the Yugoslav People's Army (JNA) as described in chapter three.

The Yugoslav communist state administration was present in the village through the village committee (*seoski odbor*) of the smallest local administrative unit called the *mjesna Zajednica* (local community). This committee encompassed both the Muslim and the Catholic communities. It had four members, two Muslims and two Catholics (although Muslims were in a majority in the village, "nationality" balance was always attempted, as at the state level). Candidates for councils at both the village and higher administrative levels, namely the *skupština opština*, the "municipal assembly" or local council, often referred to locally simply as *opština* (the municipality) were elected by the communist party at the various levels and then by the general public in local elections. Members of the village committee were appointed for a period of two years. The committee mediated between the villagers and the assembly of the larger regional *opština*, situated in the nearest market town. It was responsible for all issues concerning the village community covered by legal statutes. Any building projects, such as the building of a new house, had to be reported to the committee, which would seek approval from all the relevant administrative bodies involved, such as the water and health authorities. The committee also mobilized villagers (manpower and money—minimum payment was based on the individual household's known income) for the building of community projects such as a road or bus stop for the commuter bus to one of the Sarajevo factories.

The village committee's mandate was limited to being a bureaucratic link between the village and the local council, and its influence on the village was very limited as people could opt out of its activities if they so chose. It had no authority beyond implementing municipal decisions, and initiating communal work for the benefit of the village community and applying for public funds. Thus, the committee and its members never mediated in conflicts between villagers. The lack of any clear authority in the village to deal with intravillage conflicts left the villagers no choice but to bring in the police. This was done to deal both with more serious conflicts between households and with violent scenes within the household. The villagers, usually wary of officialdom whether secular or religious, considered the police to be the only body with any legal authority. Such authority was recognized as external and was therefore considered impartial. As indicated in the previous section, community projects organized by the village commitee did not have the political potential from a household's point of view of generalized reciprocity; that is, expectations of reciprocity were indefinite and unspecified (Sahlins, 1974:194) in contrast to the social exchange between households. People were still grumbling about the amount of money some had to pay toward the building of the road through the village two years earlier. Many Muslim villagers seemed to feel that the committee was there only when it needed people's money for different projects and that its demands often came on top of those already made by the mosque council and the Islamic Association.[22]

As part of the communist state structure, the members of the village committee had to be communist party members, and could not therefore be elected to the other administrative body in the village, the mosque council. (The Catholics belonged to a church parish with its seat outside the village, but had representatives in the parish council.) The mosque council (an administrative link with the central Islamic Association in Sarajevo) would mobilize money and labor for the building or maintenance of the mosque. Its authority was limited to religious affairs. Since this council only concerned the Muslim community it will be dealt with in more detail in chapter five. However, although the mosque council only represented the Muslim community and dealt with mosque affairs alone, villagers emphasized that Catholics had also contributed money to the building of a new mosque, while Muslims had contributed toward the building of a new church. Such contributions were based on the idea of *sevap* (religious merit, for Muslims) and generalized reciprocity. I never managed to establish how many Muslims or Catholics actually contributed to the building of churches or mosques respectively. Although both Muslims and Catholics took pride in telling me that this had happened, I suspect not everyone did contribute to the building of the other group's mosque or church. However, a sufficient number did for this idealized solidarity model to be perpetually reinforced and thus effectively sustained.

The educational system was perhaps the most powerful agent of Yugoslav state communism. The following section on education is dealt with entirely from the perspective of the Muslim community. When children started at school they extended their sociogeographical knowledge beyond the village and started to participate in a "Yugoslav" identity. Primary school was situated locally (albeit outside the village), while secondary school was in one of the market towns and recruited children from a wide region. Here children also came into contact with children from an urban background, and because intermarriages across *nacije* were more common in urban areas, such categorization was more blurred and therefore apparently less of an issue than in rural areas. However, these small market towns were sufficiently small-scale for the parental and grandparental generations to be informed about the ethnoreligious affiliations of its various families, and they would supply their children and grandchildren with information about the ethnoreligious and kinship ties of specific families. As chapter four will show, such information was vital when choosing a marriage partner. The oldest generation was a particularly rich source of information about family ties and the network of interconnected families throughout the region. (We should keep in mind that Bosnia-Hercegovina was a relatively small-scale society: before the war it consisted of 51.129 square kilometers and four million inhabitants.) Some religiously devout parents and especially older grandparents felt that their children and grandchildren were taught "not to believe" at school. Those parents who were concerned to bring up their children as good (practicing) Muslims might keep them away from school when there were special events highlighting the children's Yugoslav communist (and by extension, atheist) identity.

During their first years at school pupils had to learn patriotic songs and poems in which Yugoslavia's deceased leader Tito was honored as the great father who loved all Yugoslav children. When they had learned these the children got a diploma, a red scarf, and a bright blue beret with the Yugoslav red star in front; they had now become Tito's "pioneers." (At mosque school Muslim children learned songs and poems revering Islam and its Prophet Mohammad.) On the days commemorating the independence of the Republic of Bosnia and Hercegovina and the foundation of the Socialist Federal Republic of Yugoslavia, the schools celebrated by putting on a show in which the children (as young pioneers) performed the kinds of songs and poems described above. The youngest children wore their pioneer outfits.

One Muslim mother did not approve of her son's wearing the pioneer beret in particular and did not take good care of it. On one occasion she refused to allow her son to wear his beret at a school performance. This upset him very much and he said that in that case he could not go at all. To this his mother responded by telling him to stay at home. It seems likely that the pioneer beret was particularly frowned on because Bosnian men wear a dark blue beret as a sign (the only outward one, and a powerful symbol, therefore) of their Muslim identity. The pioneer beret was clearly seen as a challenge to the Muslim beret. However, in spite of her ambivalence about the school and her concern for the possible damage its ideology might cause to her children's Muslim identity, this mother, like most villagers, considered education a very important value for its own sake and for its job potential. (For a separate discussion of Muslim girls and their education, see chapter three.)

In prewar, socialist Yugoslavia there were two institutionally sanctioned dimensions and definitions of a Bosnian Muslim identity: that of the Yugoslav federal state, which saw the Muslims primarily as secular Yugoslav nationals (with the emphasis on Yugoslav), and that of the Islamic Association (the state-authorized *Islamska Zajednica*), which saw the Bosnian Muslims primarily as an Islamic "Yugoslav" community (part of a "Yugoslav" society but also members of the larger community of believers in the Islamic world). As if to accentuate these two official definitions, Muslim village children between the ages of seven and four-teen participated in two different educational systems: one religious (the *mekteb*), the other secular (the state school). While Muslim children were taught at *mekteb* that to be a Bosnian Muslim was first and fore-most to be a Muslim in the religious sense, in the state school they learned that to be a Muslim was first and foremost to be a member of a Yugoslav *narod*, a category which was politically and historically rather than religiously defined and thus in accordance with the official Titoist doctrine.

After 1990 (that is, after the dissolution of the Yugoslav communist one-party system) it transpired that some of my Muslim contacts had been uncomfortable not only with the areligious teachings in school, but also with what they perceived as its anti-Muslim bias. (This was true for believers and nonbelievers alike.) During my visits to postcommunist Bosnia in 1990 and 1993 several of my Muslim friends referred to the "history we did not learn" and when I asked Senad, a Muslim from Dolina what they had learned in the history lessons in school (he was born in 1953), he told me that during some of these lessons he and his Muslim classmates had felt ashamed because Muslims had been por-trayed as the losers throughout twentieth-century Yugoslav history. Fur-thermore, particular Muslim cultural characteristics (such as modes of dress and speech) were branded old-fashioned. So the message inherent in the socialist progressive Yugoslav education system was that "muslim-ness" belonged to the past (although the "Yugoslav Muslim *narod*" did not) and needed to be modernized or changed through education. For instance, two Catholic teenage schoolgirls told me that when their Mus-lim neighbors and schoolfriends talked differently from them (using words of Turkish rather than Slavonic origin which most people consid-ered old-fashioned, and putting the stress on the second syllable of words instead of giving them an even stress, as in *došao*),[23] "We immedi-ately knew that s/he was a Muslim and a villager (*seljak*)." At school they said children who spoke like that were taunted with comments like: "How do you talk?" "Where did you learn that?" And then they ex-plained: "You see they learn one thing at school, but when they arrive home their parents talk to them in their way and the kids learn it and carry it on."[24] We will return to a discussion of the role of the house as the repository for distinct Muslim values in the next chapter.

The "orientalism" of the views and attitudes of the non-Muslim ma-jority cultures in the former Yugoslavia were reflected in education and in popular attitudes generally. In the 1990s some Bosnian Muslim scholars saw this as part of the assimilation pressure brought to bear on Muslims by both Serb and Croat cultural activists and nationalists throughout Bosnia-Hercegovina's post-Ottoman history.[25]

## Contrasting Identities

In the preceding we looked at social contexts in which closeness between the Muslim and Catholic communities in the village was manifested, as well as some ways in which unity was created. In this section we will focus specifically on how social distance was expressed and separateness constructed. Symbolic boundaries of separateness were initially established by referring to "our customs" or "among us" Muslims or Catholics respectively, or "ours" and "theirs," "we" and "they." These markers are best understood as contextually fluid, indicating boundaries for social intimacy as part of a discourse about inclusion and exclusion (Herzfeld 1986). Differences were talked about in terms of what people as members of the two communities did ("we do this," "they do that," or "we do not do that"). But there is a parallelism here in the way the two communities constructed their otherness since differences were structured as parallel opposites, that is, the practices chosen to represent difference were of the same kind. Thus, while the Catholics from Dolina went annually on a pilgrimage to Medjugorije in Hercegovina, the Muslims went annually on a pilgrimage to a sufi shrine in Blagaj on the other side of the Neretva river in Hercegovina.[26] The religious practices followed by members of the other community, to the extent that they were known (Muslims would know when the Christian festivals took place, but not always what was being celebrated, and vice versa), would provide not so much a comparison as a contrast which provided a justification for one's own practices (by way of differentiation).

At Easter it is the custom for Catholics to paint eggs and give them to those Muslim children who are their immediate neighbors. The children used to get excited about this and once two Muslim children told me, "We do it like this," while showing me how they knocked two eggs against each other to see which one was the strongest. The father of the two Muslim children overheard this and got very annoyed, saying, "We have never done that until now." I suspect that his reaction was provoked less by the fact that his children had knocked eggs together than by their comment that "we do this," since this is not what Muslims do but what Catholics do. Their mistake was particularly serious since they were giving the outsider and student of "Muslim customs" the wrong lesson. To the father it was important to tell both his children and me who they were and to whom they belonged. But by telling his children who they were, he was implicitly also telling them who they were not. They knew that their Catholic friends next door would knock eggs and be able to say "we do this" without being corrected.

In this little episode (which is illustrative of similar ones) the Muslim children were reminded of who they were and by implication who they were not and who they were different from. Yet who they were different from was not an absolute, for there would be occasions when they were put in the same category as their Catholic neighbors (e.g., as school-children). Indeed what defines who "we are" and who "they are" changes with context and over time. The knocking of eggs was an example of a particularly inappropriate mix of metaphors as the act was related to a Catholic religious festival. However, the main point to be drawn from this story is that each religious community needs the presence of the other in order to construct an ethnoreligious (and village) identity, since it is mainly through this presence that a person is taught to be aware (by way of contrast) of his or her own identity.

The separate identities of the Muslim and Catholic communities are ultimately maintained by the disapproval of intermarriage between members of the two communities. A mother with a marriageable daughter explained her reluctance to see her daughter married to a Catholic by saying, "We respect their [Catholic] holidays, their churches, their prayers and we see it as a sin to blaspheme against their sacred symbols, but we do not marry them." The men and especially the women who grew up in Dolina next to Catholic families interacted more frequently with their former Catholic neighbors (and as a result knew more about their customs than is usually the case). Women in the village who had no experience of interacting with members of the other group, either because they came from an all-Muslim village or because there were no Catholics in their immediate neighborhood, often felt uncomfortable visiting Catholic households.

I knew one woman who rarely went to visit Catholics even though her close neighbors were friendly with some Catholic neighbors. She had married into the village from a mixed Muslim/Serb village to the east. Her experience of the Bosnian "other" was therefore of the Orthodox Serbs; never having had Catholic neighbors before, they were unfamiliar. However, she explained that she did not like to go "in those houses" because they cooked in lard (Muslims use vegetable oil). She feared it might be used to cook something they served her, such as cakes, or that a residue might have been left on plates or cups. The food in Catholic houses was clearly a major problem for Muslims and was often what made them uncomfortable visiting them. On the one hand, food which had been in touch with pork was *haram* (illicit); on the other hand, by Bosnian standards it was rude to refuse any food offered by the hostess.

Although there were among some Muslims clear perceptions about pollution in connection with food which had a non-Muslim source and therefore might be unclean, this was not generally an obstacle to interaction. The problem of food was, however, cited as an obstacle to intermarriage between a Muslim and a Catholic, as the following case illustrates.

A Catholic had brought home a Muslim bride, but the man's mother refused to share the house with her and the bride had to leave. This was the second time his mother had refused to accept his chosen bride. On an earlier occasion her son had brought home a Serb woman, whom his mother had also rejected because "they cross themselves with three fingers and we with five." She would only accept a daughter-in-law from the same faith. I expressed my surprise at this woman's tenacious opposition to a Muslim daughter-in-law, since she was particularly friendly with Muslim women in the village. Yes, they agreed: "We get along well and we have a good time together, but this is one thing. It is another to have somebody from a different religion together with you in the kitchen. When two who prepare different foods and keep different holy days share the same house many problems arise." In rural Bosnia at the time, villagers saw the household as the only safe sphere for the expression of an exclusive, unaccommodated ethnoreligious identity. They feared that the presence of a non-member would threaten this exclusivity.

Although differences between the two communities were mainly perceived in terms of religious practice, differences were constructed and constantly reinvented beyond the religious domain to serve as markers of membership (and to create a sense of belonging) to different religious traditions and communities. When secular symbols through which difference has been expressed disappear, new ones take their place. To cite an example: In the previous section I noted that *dimije* was worn by Muslim women and sometimes by girls in the house or village, but that Muslims and Catholics shared a dress code when they went outside their neighborhood. Despite this, Catholic girls wanted me to know that there were still differences. On one occasion when some Catholic girls were commenting on the Muslim Saturday dance, they asked, "Have you noticed how they dress?" They assured me that there were obvious differences: "You can see them wearing socks and high heels. Would you ever wear socks with your high heels? They go over the top in dressing up and adorning themselves. We like to dress more sportily." However, the discourse on difference also inspired jokes between good neighbors and friends from the two communities to whom what mattered was who you were, not what you were (in terms of *nacija*).

When the Catholic shepherd in the village brought his sheep back from the pastures in the mountains in the evening, his next-door neighbors, who were Muslim, could sometimes hear him shout to his animals not to trespass on to neighboring Muslim land: "Come back, do not go over there, it is Muslim." This amused his Muslim neighbors greatly. The shepherd was invoking an invisible and symbolic boundary between Muslims and Catholics, a boundary which in his daily interaction with them nevertheless had no relevance. The Catholic shepherd was well-liked by the Muslims and his best friend was a Muslim. He used to joke that he was a Catholic with a Muslim heart, while his friend with whom he would share a glass of brandy, was a Muslim with a Catholic heart. He also claimed he wanted to marry a Muslim woman for Muslim women kept their homes cleaner and were more hardworking than Catholic women. Making a joke through the paradox of pointing out differences to creatures who could not possibly perceive of them, he was also emphasizing the contextual character of differences between Muslims and Catholics.

In differentiating between themselves and the Catholics, Muslims would emphasize practice or "custom" (*običaj/adet*). "Custom" ("ours" or "theirs") was a category much invoked in village discourse. It was used to contrast groups of people who had grown up in what were assumed to be different environments: people from the city, Muslims from villages in other regions, or Catholics within their own village.[27] Or, as one Muslim woman put it to me when I asked her to tell me what she saw as the difference between Muslims and Catholics: "The difference between Muslims and Catholics is in the way we pray and what we eat." It is, in other words, primarily what people do that defines their membership in a particular *nacija*. (This is a Muslim view of identity, and need not apply to, say, Serb perceptions of their collective identity, but see chapter one.) These practices which defined Muslims as different from non-Muslims were largely religiously and morally based, although as discussed in chapters five and six, Islamic leaders did not always agree with the villagers that all of these were "Muslim" (according to their Islamic understanding of Muslim). For instance, the Muslims in the village celebrated *Jurjevdan* (St. George's day), as did Muslims in other mixed Muslim and Catholic/Croat villages, but I was told that such festivities were not observed by Muslims in villages with a mixed Muslim and Orthodox/Serb population to the east. The Catholics in Dolina saw *Jurjevdan* (Serbian, *Đurđevdan*) as a Serb "custom" and they did not celebrate it. Muslims from eastern Bosnia told me the same. Although some Muslims in Dolina also said it was not Muslim but gypsy, overall it was seen as a day celebrated by the Muslims—contrary

to the local Catholics (see also chapter six). Indeed, this tradition was
seen as part of this particular Muslim community's *adet*. (*Adet*, a word
of Turkish origin, was regarded as a traditional Muslim word used by
older people. Young Muslims and Catholics would use the standard
"Serbo-Croat" *običaj*.) *Adet* is specific to the Muslim community, it is
what defines this community as distinct from the local non-Muslim
community and therefore what defines a person and the community of
which he or she is a part. An old Muslim in the village with whom I used
to discuss "Muslim customs" once summed up our discussion with a
well-known proverb: "Better that the village should die than our customs" (*Bolje je da selo propadne nego adeta*). Traditions and customs are
critical to the survival of a people; whatever else changes, their customs
must remain. Customs, like culture, are, however, the result of a "con-
tinual activity, coincident with ongoing social life itself" (Fox 1990:10).
To insist on "our customs" as if they were the unchanging essence of a
community's identity, is to express resistance to change, but under specific circumstances it can also express resistance to assimilation pressures
from a dominant culture. Many Muslims and Bosnians perceive the ongoing war in Bosnia-Hercegovina not only as a war for territory, but also
as a war against a people and their traditions, their essence and their
community's very being. The systematic attacks not only on people, but
on their cultural heritage (mosques, libraries, gravestones, houses, etc.),
is understood as an attempt to completely annihilate a people and their
way of life. "Our customs" are thus critical to a meaningful social life.
The village depends for its existence on "our customs," but while they
cannot persist without the village, the reverse is neither desirable nor
possible. The village often consists of different groups of people with
partly contrasting, partly overlapping sets of traditions or customs.

> I wish everybody was one *nacija*, that
> everybody was either Croat, Muslim, or Serb.
> It does not matter what. It would have been so
> much simpler if we were all the same.

The above quotation is from a young Dolina girl who happened to be
Catholic and had fallen in love with a young Muslim, but thought that
marrying him would cause too many problems (see also chapter four). I
think her words sum up beautifully some of what this chapter has attempted to convey, namely the tension between and simultaneous presence of similarities and difference, unity and distance between the two
Bosnian communities in the village, one Muslim and the other Catholic.
This ambiguity created by the constant enactment of both similarities
and differences in the social life of the village is recognized by people

themselves, but it is also the case that one community cannot sustain itself without the other. To most Bosnians (and particularly to the post–World War II generations) difference in ethnoreligious affiliation was one of the many differences between people, like differences between men and women, villager and city dweller. It was acknowledged and often joked about but it never precluded friendship. Indeed, for these Bosnians being Bosnian (*bosanac*) meant growing up in a multicultural and multireligious environment, an environment where cultural pluralism was intrinsic to the social order. Dealing with cultural differences was part of people's most immediate experience of social life outside the confines of their home, and it was therefore an essential part of their identity. In the village mutual acknowledgment of cultural diversity and coexistence was an intrinsic quality of life and of people's everyday experience, and therefore an important element in the process of individual identity formation.

In this chapter we have moved between the various contexts within which the household and its members participated. In discussing village life in terms of the household, neighborhood, village, and the world outside the village, I have explained relations which intersect these different spheres and contribute to identity formation, at times to unify, at others to create differences. I have shown that the expression of identiy (that is, of belonging to one specific community) varies according to whether relations are enacted in the household, neighborhood, village, or outside the village, and that a Bosnian Muslim identity both includes and excludes communality with non-Muslim Bosnians. We have seen that a person's social and moral worlds consisted of several partly separate, partly overlapping social environments: the ethnoreligous community which was exclusively Muslim, the village which was a mixed Muslim and Catholic community space, and which we could call the Bosnian environment, and the city, which was a nonreligiously and nonethnically defined space or the "Yugoslav" social environment. (Furthermore, there were the religious [Islamic] contexts which will be dealt with in chapters five and six where the Muslims in the village and beyond came together not only as members of a collective distinguishing itself from other Bosnian non-Muslim collectives, but also as one identifying with a larger non-Bosnian Islamic community of believers.)

Thus, in different social environments different dimensions of a person's identity came into play. Through the household, family, and sometimes the neighborhood, they entered a Muslim social space. Through the village, friendships, and social life generally they entered a Bosnian (Muslim and Catholic) space. And through the education system, the Yugoslav People's Army, and employment, Bosnians entered a "Yugoslav" social space. This account revolves around the village and the household and therefore primarily around women. The village men, in other words, maintained links with the unifying Yugoslav state more than village women did, since they spent more time socializing in an environment defined as "Yugoslav" and establishing a network of "Yugoslav" colleagues, through further education, work, labor migration, and the "Yugoslav People's Army," and were more involved in the public sector and officialdom. Most women, on the other hand, were more closely involved with activities in the household and the village neighborhood, social space which was ethnoreligiously defined.

The ethnoreligious dimension of the villagers' Bosnian identity was thus physically and morally demarcated by women. The primary domain within which identity is formed is the household. The house as the physical demarcation of the household is also the symbol through which ethnoreligious identity is expressed. This is the topic of the next chapter.

# *Three*

## Men, Women, and the House

IN THE PREVIOUS CHAPTER we saw that during the last decades there was a radical change in the composition and organization of the household in the village, due to wage labor and a junior couple's increased independence from their parents and parents-in-law. Socioeconomic changes had strengthened the position of junior women and encouraged a preference for smaller household units. It was also noted that the most frequent form of work parties and cooperation and help between neighbors was connected with the building of a new house. *Kuća* is the name both for the house as a building and for the household: the one represents the other and is at the same time both a moral unity and the unit of interaction in the village.

Finishing a new house could take years of hard work and careful economizing. Building materials were expensive in the eighties (new houses were built of mortar blocks), and even more difficult to purchase because of the very high inflation rate in Yugoslavia at the time (in 1988 it ran at 250 percent, while in the previous year it had been at 120 percent). A young couple who decided to move out of a communal household with the young man's parents, would either be given a piece of land by the old man as part of the inheritance next to his house or somewhere else in the village, or they would purchase communal land from the local municipality (*opština*). Then they would work and save money to buy building materials, which would be bought bit by bit over a period of months and often several years. The couple would do most of the building themselves with help from neighbors. For specialized work such as installing electricity they would bring in and pay a craftsman. They would construct the house floor by floor and room by room, often moving in before the house was completed, living on one floor and then adding others over the years as they managed to save the money for bricks, windows, and doors. Some building materials were particularly expensive, and sometimes although the floor had been finished it could take another couple of years before the couple could afford to buy the windows. For many (if not most) people building a new house was a life project. This was what men (and women) worked for years to obtain, working long, hard shifts locally, in Sarajevo, or by migrating abroad to central Europe or the Middle East. It often took ten to twenty years to

finish a modern house. Only when we realize the amount and length of
the hard work and effort which families have invested in the building of
their house (and home), can we fully understand the tragedy of the systematic burning of homes in rural Bosnia in the war and the devastating
effect it has on people. When they lose their house, they lose all they
have worked for in the past and much of what they would have lived for
in the future. Particularly for the man as husband and father, the house
he managed to build symbolized his social worth; it was the proof of his
hard work and commitment to his family and their future well-being.
But the house or *kuća* also represented the moral unity of the household
and the moral quality of its members, and while men were the builders
of the house, women were the guardians of its moral values. In this
chapter I will argue that this unity and moral quality were ultimately
embodied in the women of the household, indeed that the house and its
women were symbolic mirror images. They both embodied moral values
and unity and delineated the boundaries for social intimacy.

The critical role of women in sustaining the *kuća* is acknowledged in
the saying that the woman makes the three poles (*ćošak*, corner) of the
house, and the man only one. Men are the constructors of the *kuća*,
women its sustainers. Men provide the material substance for the *kuća*,
while women are critical in determining the moral environment within
which new members are given their Muslim identity. As argued in chapter one Muslim identity is not only ethnic (about origins) but is also
understood in moral terms as it is anchored in a religious system. Within
this ideal system although men are seen as the ultimate moral guardians,
it is women who literally embody this morality. Women's bodies and
movement in space are symbolically defined and protected. The morality
at the center of *nacija* identity (in the cultural and religious sense) is
seen to be determined by what is referred to as the social environment
or *sredina* (captured by the expression, "We are the way our surroundings are"). The center of any individual's social environment is the *kuća*.
A social space primarily occupied by women, this is where children are
initially socialized. Later in a child's life, school (and state education)
becomes an important part of his or her moral environment, and sometimes (as described in chapter two) it represents itself as in opposition or
competition to the *kuća*.

This chapter will examine the *kuća* as a moral unit, and in particular
some of the ways in which women embody and express its morality and
the ethnoreligious identity of its members. I will examine the socialization of girls and what is implied both symbolically and practically in their
transformation from unmarried girls to married women. This means discussing the social activities of girls and women, and the value judgments

made in relation to such activities, particularly of girls' and women's movements in social and geographical space. The transformation in a person's status from unmarried to married, from being *momak* (boy) or *cura* (girl) to becoming *čovjek* or *žena*, is crucial to creating and sustaining a new household unit, by directing productive forces toward this end, but above all by reproducing household members. It will be argued that a girl's transformation from *cura* to *žena* is more critical to this process than a boy's from *momak* to *čovjek*. There are two aspects to the reproduction of household members. First, channeling and therefore controlling sexuality, and second, socialising new and young members within a Muslim-defined space. Indeed, it will be argued that a young girl's successful transition from *cura* to *žena* is seen as critical to the maintenance of a distinct Muslim collective identity.

## The House Embodied

The modern house typically had two or three rooms of which the central one was the combined kitchen, lounge, and bedroom. This was where the stove was located and in older houses the *banjica* (a small space in the corner with a cemented drain for washing by pouring water from a jug) as well. In traditional houses there were mattresses and pillows along the walls which served as beds during the night and sofas during the day. In new houses there were sofas and chairs, and in the room where guests were received every house had a cabinet. On its shelves were displayed elaborately crocheted small tablecloths, and beautifully arranged cups and glasses, serving trays, porcelain figures, and the miniature ceramic mugs made locally. Most homes had a television set but everybody seemed to prefer listening to popular Bosnian folk music on the radio. What a guest entering a house for the first time saw was the fruit of years of hard labor: The building itself represented men's hard labor while the interior of the house was the expression of the woman's moral worth. It told a visitor that the hostess was *vrijedna* (worthy, also meaning industrious) and *čista* (clean, but meaning a woman who kept her house and its members clean and tidy). The kitchen was where the wife would prepare her pastry and bake her bread. The space in the house was dominated by different members and activities at different times of the day.

A wife's busiest time was in the morning when she did the cleaning and the baking. She would then go out in the neighborhood on coffee-visits and be back in time to prepare lunch. If a neighbor dropped by while she was working she would continue to work, but might take a break when she had finished to sit down with her guest and drink the coffee she had prepared. They would chat, exchange the latest gossip, then return home to do their own work. Women who sat too long would gain a reputation for being lazy and for engaging in activities considered damaging to the unity and reputation of the household, such as gossip. Guests were always received in the kitchen. Other rooms served as bedrooms for the bigger children. In some houses the living quarters were above the cellar and the stable, while others had separate buildings for this purpose.

Women's daily routines, including the coffee-visits, were structured around the timetables of husband and children; the week changed character according to what hours husbands worked and when children went to school. From an early age a daughter was brought up to assist her mother with household chores, and a mother who had a teenage daughter would usually delegate major tasks to her. A woman's workload during the day was therefore to some extent dependent on whether her daughter was at school or not. However, a married woman's daily routine was also affected by the presence or absence of her mother-in-law (or that of her daughter-in-law if she was a mother-in-law) but most importantly by the presence or absence of her husband. Most men commuted daily to work at one of the factories in the industrial suburbs of Sarajevo. They worked three shifts: the morning shift, called *prva smjena* (first shift); the afternoon shift, called *druga smjena* (second shift); and the night shift, called *treća smjena* (third shift). Most women preferred to have their husbands away during the day; they felt quite constrained in their activities if he was around. Women would often ask one another what shift their husbands were working to find out when they could expect to receive a visit or when best to visit another woman. A woman who wanted to decline an invitation to come and have coffee with her women friends and neighbors could easily excuse herself by referring to her husband's presence at home, or his imminent return from work. What shift a woman's husband or grown-up sons worked determined when she was free to go "coffee-visiting" (*ide na kafu*). He would expect her to be at home whenever he was there and ideally also when he was not there. She, however, felt that what she did in his absence was not really his concern so long as she fulfilled her duties toward him.

Some husbands described coffee-visits as "going about in the village" (*hodati po selo*), of which they disapproved. Both men and women often judged a woman by whether she liked to "go about a lot" (*puno hoda*) or whether she liked working. The word *hodati* (to walk) came up repeatedly in conversations when certain women and their behavior were talked about. In everyday speech in the village this concept harbored a whole set of moral values. (To express the neutral action of "walking" they would use the expression *ići pješke*, go by foot.) To say about a woman that she "goes about a lot" (*ona puno hoda*) is a negative assessment and entails moral condemnation; "to like working" (*vole raditi*), obviously enough, has positive connotations. *Puno hodati* and *vole raditi* were often presented as mutually exclusive opposites. Wives might walk around alone, but girls should ask a female relative or, failing that, a child to accompany them. For a *cura*, therefore, "going about" may imply that she is not honorable, while for a wife it implies that she goes visiting a lot (the men would say, "goes around gossiping a lot") and therefore that she is not industrious (*vole raditi*). Industriousness is one of the ideals for a woman, for "moral untidiness and an untidy house go hand in hand" (Dubisch 1986a:200). Furthermore, a woman who "goes about" probably knows more about what is going on in the village, which makes people wary of her. (The same opposition and moral ideal have been noted in several Greek communities; see, e.g., du Boulay 1976; Hirschon 1978.)

One woman in the neighborhood was considered by most villagers, both men and women, to spend too much time "going about the village," and was often characterized as "devilish" because of her "talk." However most people tolerated her; her conspicuousness made her a welcome scapegoat. Because she went around a lot visiting people's houses, she was probably the most important source of information about household events in the village. Villagers' feelings about her were ambivalent; her company was feared, but also sought out since she was a source of information and gossip about others. Indeed, any unfavorable rumors about other people would almost inevitably be traced back to her, whether she was the actual source or not.

The villagers' judgment of her should be understood in relation to their general moral condemnation of "going about a lot," which is closely connected to the ethos of household loyalty and the fear of women's gossip. However, there is another aspect to this, namely men's fear of and wish to control the possibility of illicit sexual activity by women. (For a similar symbolic construction between women, the house, and sexuality in a Greek village, see Dubisch 1986a.) The term *hodati*, to walk, conveys two important ideas. First it implies that a woman is going about beyond the household and immediate neighborhood, and is thus outside the moral control of her household, neighbors, and relatives, and a potential danger to the reputation of her household. Second, it suggests that the action is aimless, in the sense that it is not *kuća* directed.[1] Since the *kuća* is seen as a moral unity and one member's behavior will ultimately reflect on the household as a whole, the central issue is whether a person is acting in the interests of the household, or pursuing individual interests.

When women who comply with social expectations of their role morally condemn other women for "going about a lot," this may be understood as a reflection of their internalization of men's control of female sexuality. Although a classical "Mediterranean ethnographic" theme ("the honor and shame complex") this argument falls into the trap of seeing women as defining themselves through men. Furthermore, this argument depicts women solely as reactive rather than active and as re-creative rather than creative. I suggest that this analytically biased and, indeed, ethnographically incorrect presentation can be challenged by also looking at women's control of men and the moral restrictions women place on men's behavior. Indeed, it turns out that the moral condemnation of "going about a lot" applies equally to married men. Since in this respect women condemn married men, and there are men (as there are women) who comply with behavior which women see as being in the interest of the household (working and being a responsible provider rather than "spending" [*trošiti*] money and visiting coffee-bars), it may just as plausibly be argued that married men have internalized women's control of their labor, time, and ultimately of their sexuality.

It is significant, however, that this is only true for married men, as bachelors are expected to "go about a lot." (As we will soon see, they will go to coffee-bars, dances, and fairs, meet friends, and date girls. This is their privilege, because they must seek potential marriage partners.) Upon marriage, a man's life-style is expected to change. From the woman's point of view it is undesirable for him to continue behaving like a *momak*—just as a *cura* should change her behavior to be like a wife's, so too should he change his to be like a husband's. This point was particularly clear on one occasion. A young man had married, and now it was the bride's parents' turn to visit their daughter's household with presents (*dar*). The date for the visit had been set and the hosts had invited all their relatives in the village to attend the event. When we arrived we were met with embarrassed apologies; the daughter-in-law had gone back to her parents, who therefore had no reason to turn up with presents for their new in-laws. We were served coffee and cakes and the event was discussed in a very low-key manner. The "bridegroom" was out on his usual round of coffee-bars. In the presence of their hosts, my company expressed the view that the "bride's" behavior was no good (*ne valja*), but on our way back the same women, who were relatives, through their husbands, of the young man's household, criticized the young man for still "running about a lot" like a *momak*, leaving his wife at home. The young man's mother was also criticized for seeming to accept her son's behavior.

A married man who was "going about a lot" would not be acting in the interests of his household, as he would spend household money on drinks at *kafana*s, money that should have been spent for the household's common good. Likewise, a husband who was unfaithful would be condemned if he was having an affair with a woman in the village as he would be risking good neighborhood relations and the reputation of the household.[2] Furthermore, a husband who placed too many restrictions on his wife was disapproved of by both women and by men (at least in public and in the presence of women). In fact there was one particular settlement where the men were notorious for what was considered their restrictive attitude toward their wives and womenfolk. They were said in this respect to be like *Šiptar*s (Kosovo Albanians).

In interactions which linked the household and the community, women's behavior was particularly crucial, as (postmarital residence being patrilocal) all married women had initially arrived as strangers in the household they were now representing. Their loyalty could therefore not be taken for granted by men and senior members, but had to be reinforced through moral injunctions. On the other hand, as initial outsiders women were able to link their households with other households throughout the region in a network of affinal relations. Although this made women in Dolina potentially powerful, their freedom to draw on this pool of people and resources was controlled to various degrees by moral injunctions expressed by senior members of their household and community. Women were indeed at the same time both of the household and extrinsic to it. We may say that the vulnerability of the household as a unit was literally embodied in the woman who was at once the outsider to and the main reproducer of the unit. In the next section we look in more detail at the role of women in maintaining neighborhood relations and a sense of community through social visits on behalf of their respective households.

## Women and the Neighborhood

Usually twice every day, my hostess would say to me: "Come on, let's go and have coffee!" (*Hajdemo na kafu*) On a day-to-day basis the most sustained informal interaction between households was through women and the coffee-visits by which they frequently and visibly represented their households in the village community.[3] Since men spent most of their time outside the village they relied on women both to inform them about the latest village events and to express and maintain Muslim community values which they, as proletarianized workers in a "Yugoslav" environment, could express only rarely. This did not mean that men were completely absent from daily socializing between neighbors. On winter evenings particularly, villagers, whether men, women, or children, socialized at *sijelo*: several household members, often together with members of other households, went together to visit a neighboring household. They spent the long evenings drinking coffee, exchanging the latest news about life in the village, and talking about the tasks that lay ahead next spring and summer in the fields and at home.

We would visit close neighbors more frequently than those living further away. A woman was obliged to go and see all her immediate neighbors in turn during the week, while other visits further away had to come second. Frequent visits were seen to reaffirm friendship. If for some reason she went several times to visit one house consecutively without visiting another, people would start to talk, and in the household passed over the women in particular would wonder if they had upset their neighbor in some way. On special occasions when there was some sort of celebration, it was shameful for one of the closest neighbors not to be among the first to visit. But coffee-visits between close neighbors were generally more frequent and had precedence over others. On one occasion when the senior woman in one household felt ignored by one of her closest neighbors she told her: "I am your closest neighbor (*prva komšija*, first neighbor) and therefore your most important one." On being asked, members of both households involved agreed that this was the way it was: when you needed help in everyday life, or if you got ill, it was your first neighbors who would be the easiest to reach, while your kin may live in a different hamlet or village.

The importance of friendship and mutual help between close neighbors was particularly valuable to women who could find personal support and understanding that they would not find among members of their husband's family. However, in discussing matters internal to the household there had to be a fine balance between seeking personal support on the one hand and not betraying the household as a unit on the other. Indeed, men often held women responsible for starting quarrels between neighboring households with their "gossip." (Women's precarious role in this respect has also been noted in Greece; see, e.g., du Boulay 1974; Dubisch 1986a; Hirschon 1978.)

All major events in a person's life (which involved a change of status and would therefore affect the structure of his/her household) were recognized by the community in the form of a visit by at least one representative, usually the married woman who acted as the household manager. Such visits were made by each household in the hamlet as also by many from further afield in other hamlets within the larger village. On happy occasions in a household, such as the arrival of a new bride, the birth of a child, or a son returning from the army, neighbors and covillagers were expected to come and visit *na slatko* (for sweets) during the day for as long as a week after the event had taken place. Some who had not had the opportunity may have to wait longer to visit. The wife of the household did not usually need to invite people, as the rumor that something had happened traveled fast. The female head of the household would have prepared sweet cakes to be served in addition to sweet fruit juice and coffee. The guest would usually bring a small present of something sweet, such as a packet of biscuits. The wrapped packet would be left discreetly on a table or shelf. On occasions such as a son leaving for the army, the birth of a child, or the arrival of a bride, it was customary to give a small sum of money to the individual at the center of the event. Sometimes a woman prepared cakes and invited her best neighbors and friends to come *na slatko* to celebrate a major purchase like that of a cow, but this would be more for fun and an excuse for getting together.

The "sweet visit" may also be called *na radost* (for joy). This was different from the visit *na žalost* (for sorrow) which took place after the death of a household member, when neighbors and relatives came to show sympathy with the bereaved. Old villagers would also call the visits which took place immediately after a daughter had left her native household to marry *na žalost*; others, however, would call this *na slatko* or *na radost*. When confronted with this confusion of terms a man in his thirties was quick to answer: "Before, parents were sad when their daughter left them, but today they all mean trouble and parents are happy to get rid of them." (He said literally that they were corrupted, *pokvarene*). Sometimes men would join their wives on a *sijelo* in the evening to pay respect or share in joy; men were particularly expected to visit a household when a son had returned from his national service in the army.

For a boy who had finished secondary school, a major event in his life was his call to service in the Yugoslav People's Army at the age of eighteen. Just as a girl was not considered ready for marriage until she had finished her primary education (and increasingly her secondary education too), a boy should ideally marry after he had finished his army service. For a village boy this meant leaving home—and usually his republic (Bosnia-Hercegovina) as well—for the first time. For many boys this was their first experience of a truly Yugoslav environment, where they shared a room with young men from all six Yugoslav republics. For the boy's family it was a sad moment when their son left home for the first time. The atmosphere in the household was much the same as when a daughter left to marry. In both cases neighbors would visit to comfort the mother, bring something sweet as a present or some money for the young man. The hostess would serve cakes and coffee. The mother would often express her anxiety about her son's well-being away from home. But in the late 1980s there were additional worries because of the politically unstable situation in Serbia, and particularly in the province of Kosovo. It was every parent's hope that their son not be sent there. When Neđad left to do his military service in Kosovo in 1988, the situation there was very tense as there had been clashes between native Albanians and local Serbian police. At the coffee-visit, his mother not only expressed her sadness at her son's departure from home, but was also clearly scared at the thought of where her son was going. She was worried for his life, but above all that he would be ordered by the army to shoot at fellow Muslims and "Yugoslavs." Even though Neđad's father had constantly pressured the authorities, he had not succeeded in having his son transferred to a different region (although some months later Neđad was transferred). On his return, neighbors would again call in for a "sweet visit": this time the atmosphere would be one of celebration and happiness, as the son had become a man and it was now expected that he would marry. Three years later, in 1991, Neđad's cousin Almir was brought back by his father (at great risk) when he happened to be doing his military service as the war in Croatia started. He was determined that his son not be used by the Yugoslav People's Army to fight his neighbors and then fellow Yugoslavs. The circumstances of his return, however, gave no cause for celebration nor a "sweet visit."

The two most frequent visits for joy were those celebrating the birth of a child and the arrival of a bride, respectively. The first was also referred to by the more specific term, to go *na babine*, and the second was called to go *na šerbe*. Both were occasions for women to come together to share their experiences and to encourage the newly arrived bride or the new mother. Close neighbors and friends of the household were expected to visit sooner or later; first neighbors were expected to be the first to pay a visit. People would remember and comment on who came and who did not, who came quickly and who was slow to react. Women would visit on the day immediately following the bride's arrival or the return of a mother from hospital with her newborn child. Some would come in the course of the week or even three weeks later if the relationship was distant or if there had been no earlier opportunity to visit. A woman who did not have a particularly close relationship with the household in question was relatively free to come whenever it suited her without upsetting the host, who would be pleased and honored by the visit in any case. Women would usually go during the day, whenever they found it convenient, but they would never go alone. Groups of sisters-in-law or close neighbors and friends would decide to go together. Men might also go, but never during the day. They would go with their wives in the evening after getting back from work, and when they knew that the male head of the household would be at home.

The importance women obviously attached to paying a visit on these occasions underscored the significance of these two major status changes in a woman's life, her marriage, and her becoming a mother.[4] Men who did not go to drink *šerbe* were not reproached, whereas women would be. As a household was seen to act collectively in ritual contexts, it was sufficient that one member went on behalf of the whole unit. But since the primary function of the *šerbe* was to welcome the bride to the village social network, and since her network would mainly consist of women, her incorporation into the village community was the responsibility of women. It was different when a household invited *na slatko* on a son's arrival from the army; this was a celebration to some extent for the mothers, as a son had returned home, but mainly for the men: their junior member had now been initiated into their ranks (although he was not considered to have attained full manhood if he was still unmarried). It was an experience that could only be shared by those who had been through it, namely, other men. By the same token, to go to *babine* was mostly the affair of women, as only they could understand or share the young mother's experience of birth at the hospital in Sarajevo.

*Šerbe* (sherbet) takes its name from the sweet drink—either water sweetened and flavored (usually with rosewater) or sweet fruit juice— which is offered to guests as a refreshment before the coffee at religious or secular celebrations. The *šerbe* played a significant role when women visited a household to welcome a new bride to the village. The bride would serve the *šerbe*, which had to be drunk immediately. When she came to collect the empty glasses the guests were expected to leave some money for her on the tray. When women went on these visits they satisfied their own curiosity about the new bride, but they also welcomed her to the neighborhood and the village, and showed their desire to integrate the new member in the community. In the absence of a more public and ritualized marriage feast, the *šerbe* marked the change in status of the individuals concerned (and therefore the resulting changes in the household to which they belonged), but above all it established a relationship between the stranger (the bride) and the community of women.

## Including New Village Members

At *šerbe* the first greetings exchanged between the bride and her new covillagers consisted of good-humored questions: "Have you got used to this place?" "Do you get along" [with the other household members, but particularly the mother-in-law]?" "Do you obey?" The shy young girl could only answer in the affirmative while concentrating on doing everything (especially the serving) right, as she knew that all present were observing her critically. However, they gently advised her in her task as hostess, and were quick to minimize the impact of any mistakes. During their visit they made her feel welcome and often showed their sympathy and support by referring to their own experiences when they had first arrived in an unfamiliar household. In fact, to go to *šerbe* was an opportunity for women to reminisce about their own arrival in a strange village and household. Memories of this event were rarely rosy: older woman who had married twenty to thirty years earlier in the poor post–World War II Yugoslavia, would recall the poverty they had had to endure as young brides, how they had lacked in everything, including food and clothing, how strict and sometimes unpleasant their mother-in-law had been, and how their husband in some cases had arrived home drunk and had never supported them against their mother-in-law. There was much humor and laughter during this exchange of experiences; the humiliation (especially as junior women) and the struggle they had often coped with were never elaborated on, though these were nevertheless implicit in the women's short, factual statements.

As some guests arrived others would be leaving, and the bride would be busy washing glasses and coffee-cups, mixing the *šerbe* and making and serving the coffee. All of this was discreetly supervised and organized by her mother-in-law. Whenever she had to leave the room to wash dishes or fetch drinks, the women visiting would take the opportunity to ask her mother-in-law whether she got along with the new member. The mother-in-law would either respond positively, or she would already start complaining that the young bride got up too late in the morning, was lazy, and did not work as required. The guests would ask the mother-in-law questions like, "Whose is she?" "Where is she from?" Or, referring to the girl's relatives, "Who has she got?" Those who knew people in the village or area she was from would ask for news about them. "Does she know A?" or "Is she related to B?" The question could be about people as peripheral as a brother's wife's aunt who had married someone in that particular village. In all their questions the visitors sought to place the new woman into an already existing network of neighbors, relatives, in-laws, thereby aptly illustrating the importance of women as links between households and social networks beyond the village.

*Babine* is the name both for the woman's forty days' "lying-in" period after childbirth, and for the gifts presented to her, usually sweets, or some material to be stitched into clothes for the child. (Some also leave money underneath the baby's pillow. I was told by women in Dolina that this was a custom more rigorously observed in other villages in central Bosnia.) As soon as the forty days of confinement had passed, the new mother was expected to drop in on those neighbors, family, and friends who had visited her at *babine*. She was expected in turn to give presents to (*darovati*) the households she visited. The woman, who often lived with her mother-in-law, would usually have one of her own female relatives, such as an unmarried sister, to come and stay for a month or more while she was recovering. This female relative would take on the responsibility for all the household chores, serve guests, and help to look after the newborn baby.

The visit at *babine* was an occasion for women to come together to remember and nowadays, increasingly, to share their experiences at the hospital in Sarajevo. A hospital stay provided one of the few opportunities for Bosnian village women to experience a close community with women from completely different social and religious backgrounds. (In this respect women's sharing of hospital memories was akin to men reliving their Yugoslav army days when visiting to celebrate the return of a young man from the service.) If the husband and father was present the women would often teasingly ask him how he would manage during his forty days of abstinence. The Islamic prohibition against sex between man and wife during her period or until forty days after she has given birth is not understood in terms of the woman being polluting, but rather as a health insurance for women. Thus, I was told that a villager now in his eighties had buried three wives because he had never respected the commandment to abstain. Although men may construct Islamic tenets about what is believed to be women's physical vulnerability as women's moral inferiority (associated with their sexuality and reproductive functions), women themselves saw these commandments more in terms of their own health and well-being. Similar commandments prevent women from observing religious practices at certain times, when they are considered (in the women's own words) "not clean." When menstruating, or until forty days after having given birth, or just after having had sexual intercourse and before ablutions (the latter is also true for men), a woman should not touch the Qur'an, enter the mosque, or enter a saint's grave lest the saint get angry.[5]

Having given birth the young wife has become a mother and thereby fully a woman of the house. It is believed that a mother should not leave her house before the days of confinement are over as both she and the child are particularly vulnerable to bewitchment (*sihir*; newborn babies are also considered particularly vulnerable to attacks by the evil eye, see chapter six) and attack from evil spirits (*džin*s). She should make sure she brings any of her own or her child's towels, bed linen or clothes into the house before dark as, I was told, "something may gather on it and enter her or the baby that way." The time around *akšam* (sunset) is considered particularly critical. It is believed that "something" may enter a person through the openings of his or her body, thereby causing minor paralysis, for example, of the mouth or parts of the face.

Because a person is attacked through the openings of her or his body, women are seen to be particularly vulnerable: what is sometimes referred to as "devilish brew" may enter a woman through her vagina. She is more vulnerable immediately after childbirth when her vagina is considered more open. Furthermore, a woman is taught by older women never to urinate outside after dark; if she absolutely has to, she should keep her hand in front of her vagina. Before the forty days of confinement have passed she should not leave her house, or at least not her courtyard. If she has to go further, for instance to see a doctor, she should take the key to her house or a *tespih* (rosary) from the house with her. I suggest that these two items are specific and powerful symbols of the woman's status and identity, being intimately associated with the house. The key opens and locks the door to the house. With the key in her hand the mother controls who may enter, but it also places the responsibility for drawing the boundary for intimacy between her, her house, and the outside on her. The *tespih* is for saying prayers which she as a Muslim will say, and which will protect her; but above all the *tespih* has been used by her and other household members to say prayers with many times over in the house, and it ensures the well-being of its members. It is therefore imbued with a spiritual power linked to the house. By carrying either of these items, the key or the *tespih*, the young mother expresses who she is: a member of a particular *kuća*, a Muslim, and a mother. Knowledge of her identity gives her moral power and protection.

## Socializing the Bride

As a rule postmarital residence is patrilocal, with few exceptions. Bosnian Muslims have a taboo on marriage between kin, and marriage between neighbors (within the village) is rare today, since most of those born in the village can trace a kin relationship between them (see chapter four). Married women are thus usually strangers in the village, a fact which made older male informants agree that "Where women are born does not mean anything to them, their native village is not important to them. Women can, contrary to men, go anywhere and be at home." In this way men justified a patrilocal residence pattern.

Women I spoke to, on the other hand, did not agree with these men, and younger men tended to agree with the women. Although they accepted having to move to a strange village as their destiny, they often referred to their native village, saying that theirs was a strange life, since

at one point in their lives they had to change both village and "mother."
Even older women who had lived in Dolina for more than thirty years
would still refer to the "customs" in their native village (which would be
different from those in Dolina) as the "customs among us where I am
from." Men's assumptions about women's easy adaptability and lack of
any solid roots were repeatedly contradicted by women's expression of
their own feelings and experiences about their native village and the
often traumatic move to a new village and home when they married. A
woman's life cycle consisted of several stages moving toward the senior
status of a mature wife, with daughters-in-law under her control.
Having achieved the status of wife, a woman became powerful, and in
charge of her own and other household members' lives. She had earned
her reputation, and needed to worry less about how her subsequent acts
may affect it negatively. And while being a *žena* (wife) was defined by
what she should do, being a Muslim *cura* was defined largely in terms of
what she should not do.

Although the main transition from an unmarried girl to a married
woman and wife occurs when consummation of the marriage has taken
place, a *cura* does not become a *žena* as soon as she has married, but has
to pass through the liminal period of being a bride or *mlada. Mlada*
means young woman, but also denotes bride. She obtains this status as
soon as she goes and lives with a *momak* (unmarried boy) and his family
in his home and her status reflects her position in her new household.
Her husband's family and immediate neighbors in the village will now
frequently refer to her as "our bride." But while the young man is referred to as the bridegroom only on the day of the wedding, and perhaps
as a joke for some days after, the bride is referred to as such for a long
period after her arrival in the new household and neighborhood. It
often took me a long time to actually learn the name of a new bride in
the village as everybody referred to her and addressed her as *mlada*.
When it was not clear from the context "whose" *mlada* she was, her
husband's name or sometimes (depending on who was talking) her
mother-in-law's would be added in the possessive form. Thus, for instance, Sanella married to Salim would be referred to as "Salim's bride."
Later as a wife she would often be referred to as "Salimovica" (the possessive form of Salim combined with the female diminutive "ica"). Thus
while almost everybody refers to the young bride in terms of her status
from the collective viewpoint of the members of her new household,
they refer to her husband in terms of his individual relationship with
each member: son, brother, or by his personal name. (For the bridegroom to continue in seriousness to refer to his wife as bride would be
terribly old-fashioned. When addressing her directly and usually also

when referring to her in the third person he will use her personal name,
although he may say *mlada* partly as a joke and partly as an affectionate
form of address.)

The bride occupies an intermittent status between a girl and a
woman. She only becomes a woman when she has proven herself as a
wife and above all as a mother. This means that she is often addressed as
*mlada* until she gives birth to her first child. Village women will then
start calling her by her first name as an acknowledgment of her status as
a wife. Since she has not undergone the same natural socialization processes a child born into the household would have, symbolically the new
bride is made to change allegiance from her parents' to her husband's
parents' household. One manifestation of this change is in the form of
address used for household members. Upon marriage it is considered
good practice for the bride to address her husband's closest relatives,
including lateral ones, by the same terms as he uses.[6] He may address her
relatives the same way, but there is less moral pressure on him to do this:
I never came across any examples of the practice, and I certainly never
heard anybody complaining about a man not using his wife's terms for
her relatives. He will generally address her parents as *pun/punica* (fa-
ther-in-law/mother-in-law), while a woman when talking in the third
person about her parents-in-law will call them *svekr/svekrva* (when addressing them directly she uses the word for mother and father). More
generally, he addresses her relatives either by their first names or by specific terms for in-laws.

Nevertheless, even if it is desirable and honorable for a bride to address her husband's relatives by his terms for them, for instance calling
his mother *mater* and his aunt *tetka*, I found that not many women actually did this nor did they expect their daughters to do so. When Faketa
visited her native neighborhood for the first time after she had married,
she referred to her husband's aunt as *tetka* during a conversation with
three of her mother's neighbors and friends. But the women smiled and
commented, somewhat surprised, "You say *tetka*?" The bride answered
that she did this to show respect (*poštovanje*), whereupon the women
reassured her that this was fine and the way it ought to be.

Elsewhere, particularly in Yugoslav ethnography, this practice has
been explained by the presence of a patriarchal ideology. But in chapter
four we will see that even though the Bosnian Muslims are mainly patrilineal and patrilocal, the role of a married woman's (wife and mother)
kin is also very important in the overall kinship network. There is thus a
fairly strong bilateral tendency among Bosnian Muslim families (Filipović 1982). I believe it would be more fruitful to center our analysis on
the primary social unit, the household, and on the strict code of loyalty
demanded of all its members, but particularly of members recruited

from the outside, in other words women. This point is illustrated by the following case history.

Dina, a seventeen-year-old wife, worked in the kitchen of a cafe in one of the market towns. Some days she traveled home quite late in the evening by bus, and then walked for about fifty minutes to reach her house. The women closest to her (her immediate neighbors and in-laws) had given her instructions in how to behave. They had told her to come straight home and not to hang around talking to customers, and whenever possible to walk home with a male relative of her husband's if one was traveling on the same bus. One night, however, she had walked home chatting to a neighbor who had also been her neighbor in her native village (he was renting a house in Dolina). Her husband's father's brother had also been on the same bus, but instead of traveling with him she had chatted happily with her neighbor. Her husband's and husband's uncle's household were terribly upset with her. Her case was aggravated by the fact that the particular neighbor in question and her husband's uncle were not on speaking terms at the time. Her husband's uncle felt insulted, and his wife, mother, and sister-in-law all condemned her behavior. In conversations with neighbors they kept repeating that Dina was behaving and thinking like a *cura*, even though she was now a wife.

In other words, a wife should not behave independently of other household and extended family members but represent the moral unity of her household. Even if married men and women generally are less suspicious of a woman's whereabouts after she has married, as a stranger to the village, the new bride is continuously assessed by neighboring women on the daily coffee-visits which the bride attends together with her mother-in-law. The young woman is always under the control of her mother-in-law when interacting with other women. She keeps her eyes and her mind on her needlework while her mother-in-law answers most questions on her behalf. Thus the mother-in-law controls all information about the household and its members. I suggest that the often strong control by a mother-in-law of her daughter-in-law is related not so much to the fact that the latter is a junior woman within the household, as with the fact that she is a stranger whose loyalty has hitherto lain elsewhere. This makes her a threat to the ideal of loyalty between household members which is a prerequisite for the formation and representation of the household as a moral unity.[7] Loyalty is about the integrity (and ultimately the ethnoreligious identity) of the household, and is embodied in women through their behavior, speech, and dress (see previous chapter).

At least in the old and more traditional part of the village, the transition from *cura* to *žena* was marked by a change in style of dress. When consummation of the marriage had taken place, a woman was no longer considered to be ignorant about her own sexuality and was consequently expected to be aware of the possible sexual undertones in her interactions with men. Even if most mothers had their own idea about how a decent *cura* should dress (for example, that she should not wear shorts or "revealing" T-shirts), she had a greater choice of clothing than married women (see chapter two). There was a kind of humorous tolerance toward a *cura* on the part of older women. After all, she should be attractive to men, even if she should not openly be seen to be seeking contact or initiating conversations with them. All this changed when a girl married and became a woman. She would have to be more careful about how she dressed.[8]

How the different roles of *cura* and *žena* should ideally be expressed in the way you dress was brought to the fore when Emina, who was newly-wed, came to visit her mother for the first time after she had left. As she walked up the path toward her house neighboring women greeted her heartily with the following words: "Are you wearing jeans? But you are not a *cura* any more." "And where is your headscarf?" But by then they were laughing. These women were simultaneously commenting on Emina's new status whereby she had joined their ranks, and through their good humored remarks, indicating that although she had become more like them (since she could no longer be assumed to be ignorant about sex) they did not really expect her to dress like them. They knew that Emina specifically, who was working in town, and her generation of women generally, thought differently about matters of dress and what was appropriate behavior for both a *cura* and a *žena*.

But the woman's change in status from *cura* to *žena* was not only supposed to be followed by a change in style of clothing; it was also expected to change her general behavior and "way of thinking." This was something the younger generation of women were more ready to accept. Their own experiences had taught them as much. Although socialism, industrialization, and modernization had provided these girls with new role models as members of the wider society, as soon as they married and went to share a house with their husband's family, more traditional household and family structures took precedence in defining their new roles as responsible household members who would soon also have the responsibility of bringing up new members. As soon as Emina sat down to drink coffee with her mother and mother's sister-in-law, they started to advise her about how to behave in her new role: "Remember, you are a *žena* now, you are no longer a *cura*, so be clever. You may no longer joke and have fun with the men at work like before, when you were a *cura*. Men are angry as only men can be (*muškarci su ljuti kao ljudi*), and jealous. So you must be serious and shut up and just do your job. Don't give anybody a pretext to gossip about you or hint that you are not honorable." I suggested that maybe standards of behavior were not as strict as when they had been young and that things had changed, but they rejected this completely, because "men are always the same, they never change." Then it was Emina's turn to advise the daughter of the house, a fourteen-year-old girl. She told her to take her secondary school seriously, and not to run around in cafés. "If you do not intend to take it seriously from the start, you make your parents spend money for no use." The girl, her cousin, said: "You are saying this to me, you who never cared about school." Then Emina showed that not only had her status changed, but so also had her way of thinking. She answered: "Yes, this is true, but I was a fool. I did not understand then and I had nobody to tell me how to conduct myself, but now I know better."

## Women and Sexuality

The women agreed that after having married they had immediately changed their behavior and way of thinking from that of *cura* to that of *žena*. A wife should take care to establish her reputation as someone who is *fina* early. For a woman to be *fina* means that she works for the good of the household (that she is hardworking, clean, does not gossip or walk about a lot, dresses decently, and behaves seriously when interacting with men). The women emphasized that if you obtain a good reputation from the start when you first arrive in the village as a wife, it will stick to you for the rest of your life. Likewise a bad reputation will also endure all your life. However, becoming a woman also implies acquiring the subtle skills whereby what you appear to have done or said is more significant than it really is. A woman will learn to deny fiercely any unfavorable gossip about herself or any of her household members, and to take any opportunity to present herself as hardworking (*vrijedna*), good (*fina*), clean (*čista*) and honorable (*poštena*). Her experience and knowledge of sexuality are now stressed; more or less direct references are made to this effect among equals (i.e., wives). Jokes about mens' and women's sexuality were common currency when some of the liveliest women met at coffee-visits. (This is one of the most important reasons why women forbade their unmarried daughters to attend wives' gatherings.[9])

One of the rituals a woman should perform is particularly essential to defining her womanhood as a Muslim. The *gusul* or ritual washing after sexual intercourse is one of the key rituals distinguishing girls from wives. Significantly, however, it also distinguishes Muslim wives from Catholic ones. Performing *gusul* is an assertion of sexual activity and is thus a statement about womanhood, and about Muslim womanhood in particular. Little wonder, then, that this was one of the favorite topics in more humorous conversations among married women. In fact "to take a bath" (done by pouring water over your body from a jug), had become a metaphor for having had sexual intercourse. The physical structure of a house in a settlement made it difficult for a woman to take a bath in secret. Her closest neighbors would make loaded remarks, the frequency of bathing being commented on as an allusion to the frequency of sexual intercourse.

Although women appeared outspoken and open about sexuality in their jokes and humorous chats, they rarely talked about contraception or abortion. They usually knew about artificial methods of contraception, including the pill (which they had heard about from female relatives living in the city or from doctors at the health center in town), but they were hesitant about using them. Instead they practiced withdrawal, the unreliable character of which was only too clearly demonstrated in the high rate of abortions. If a woman became pregnant when more children were not wanted, she always blamed the man for not taking more care. It was his responsibility, and a man who "had no control" was ridiculed. Thus every time the neighbors observed the man who had five children from the ages of one to five passing by on the road, they (particularly the women) would joke and sometimes make disapproving comments about his apparent lack of sexual control. Remarks were made by women and men alike and everybody would join in the laughter. Women complained that they became pregnant when the husband had been drinking and "had no control." Contrary to the common attitude in northern European societies where women are considered primarily responsible for birth control, here it is seen mainly as the man's responsibility. To have no control is seen as unmanly. On the other hand, this implies that ideally men, not women, should have control over reproduction and thus ultimately over women.

Women did not wish to have many children because, they said, many children meant increased poverty. Most women preferred to limit themselves to two or three children in order to be able to maintain a certain standard of living. Counting the number of children of twenty couples heading their own household (ten of the pre-1945 and ten of the post-1945 generation), I found that the pre-1945 generation had five children on average while the post-1945 generation had three. Abortion was common and many women had several during their reproductive years; it was legal and carried out at the hospital in Sarajevo. Although the young idealistic Muslim religious instructors preached to village women about the sinfulness of having abortions, and women were aware of the health hazards of having one, they still preferred this as the ultimate method of birth control when withdrawal failed. They had not taken on board the "sinfulness of abortion"; rather they found this "rule" quite out of touch with the realities of life. In fact, women were not ashamed of having an abortion nor did they feel it was sinful in any way. On the contrary, a woman often included her abortions among her pregnancies in conversations with other women. Discussing her pregnancies with a visiting pregnant woman, I heard one woman say, "I have two children but have been pregnant seven times." Her abortions and her children were all part of her fertility record and also proof of how desired she was by her husband.[10]

When a woman married, her social network changed far more radically than her husband's, which was merely extended. This was also true for her social activities. In addition to the household chores of cooking, cleaning, and waiting on guests (and later also looking after children), she would participate in wives' social activities, neighborhood visiting, and religious ritual events such as *tevhids* (see chapter five). These were focused on the village and the house to a much greater degree than when she was a *cura*, when usually both school and courtship venues would have been situated outside the village. As a wife a woman's behavior was judged in relation to her behavior within the neighborhood and village, and in terms of her critical role as representative of the moral standing of her household on a daily basis.

## Gendering Young Household Members

The word *cura* (pl. *cure*, girl) underscores a girl's or young woman's unmarried status, but carries the meaning of an unmarried virgin. A *cura*'s status was radically different from that of all other women, whether wives, divorcees, or widows, the chief distinguishing factor being her assumed ignorance of sexuality. Above all, her status was contrasted to that of a *žena* (pl. *žene*), which means both "woman" and "wife." I have chosen to translate this word as "wife" because in the rural context it has to be understood in its opposition to *cura*.

A girl becomes a *cura* in her early teens at the age of sexual maturity. Before this she is called a *curica* (little girl). Increasingly in recent years, however, maturity was related more to educational level than to sexual maturity. Since most parents wanted their daughters to finish at least eight years of compulsory school, they did not allow them to go to places outside school (such as fairs or the Saturday dance) where they would meet boys. This would change after the age of fourteen, when a girl would have finished her eighth year. Being allowed to the dance meant that parents considered their daughter to have reached marriageable age. Some parents extended these restrictions well into secondary school. But by then parental control was becoming increasingly difficult since their daughters had to travel to one of the market towns to attend secondary school.

A girl remained a *cura* until she married. If she married late or not at all, she would be referred to as a *stara cura* (old girl), and likewise an "old" unmarried male would be referred to as an old *momak*. Among the girls in the village some married very young before the legal age of eighteen, at seventeen or even earlier, while others married in their late twenties. However, the most common age was between the age of eighteen and the early twenties. If a girl's unmarried status continues beyond the age when it is seen as natural for her to start her own family (into her late twenties), her status is ill-defined. An unmarried woman who had reached this age was invariably described as "being alone," a state to be pitied for a woman should not be alone. It is a sad and dangerous state for her to be in, dangerous because she is not protected from untrustworthy strangers (men), and sad because a woman acquires status by being married and having children, which is the true fulfilment of her life. For an adult female not to be married means that she has not yet fully become a woman. Her status is ambiguous, since according to her age she should be a *žena* but in terms of marital status (i.e., sexual experience) she is a *cura*. On the other hand, married women would reassure unmarried friends that it was never too late to marry, and point out that their own situation was not to be envied. In their usual articulate and good-humored way women in my neighborhood would describe their own married lives as dreary, with boring work and limited opportunities to experience anything outside the village. As one neighbor put it laughingly, "Look at us. We only wait for the bread to come out of the oven and the children to be born." But their main message of comfort was often that "as long as you stay unmarried there won't be any man to mess you around."

Already as a *curica*, the Muslim girl was taught about her role as a female. From early on she was expected to help her mother with household chores, and was encouraged with words like, "You are a real little girl" (*ti si prava curica*) whenever she performed typical female tasks like knitting or serving coffee. Her younger and older brothers were neither encouraged nor expected to do much work for the household. They were served by their mother and sisters and spent most of the time playing and walking about in the neighbourhood and village.

A *cura* could often be heard saying, "I am not allowed" (*ne smijem*) when explaining why she could not do things like coming along to *kafić* from school, or visiting somebody after dark, when women and particularly girls are thought to be vulnerable to attacks from evil spirits (*džin*s)

8. Girls cleaning the entrance to the mosque.

and other possessive powers. Even when the prohibition was not explic-
itly linked to a girl's gender, there were several contexts in which gender
was the reason given for certain moral commands. A girl would soon
learn that her younger brothers had privileges which she had to respect
because they were male. This inequality was most typically expressed in
comments like, "Do not upset him, he is male" (*nemoj ga sekirati, on je
muško*), and "Shut up, you are female" (*šuti ti si žensko*)—a girl was not
to speak unless spoken to. Thus boys and girls were clearly socialized
differently.

Some mothers were stricter than others, frequently telling their
daughters to "be silent," "work," and "be honorable" (*šuti, radi*, and
*budi poštena*). As they grew into puberty and started going to the dance
and the summer fairs, flirting with and dating boys, mothers controlled
their movements by keeping up the pressure to work harder and requir-
ing them to conform to their ideas about decent behavior. This was the
time when girls experienced the greatest conflict and frustration on account of the opposing pulls of two different value systems and codes of
behavior, between the traditional Muslim *kuća* and village neighborhood on the one hand, and the wider, urban, consumer society encountered through the media, school, and friends with a different sociocultural background on the other. This was particularly the case if they
went on to secondary school and had to travel into one of the market

towns. It is worth noting that married women (mothers and female relatives as well as neighbors) rather than fathers and brothers were the ones who often controlled and disciplined unmarried girls.

Teenage boys, men, and fathers usually show great affection toward children; they cuddle and play with babies and small children around them, their own as well as other family members' and neighbors'. At the social gatherings in the neighborhoods in the evenings, small children would literally crawl on their father, uncles, or older male cousins. Indeed, mothers and women were more ready to tell the children off while the men would be more tolerant or instruct the children more mildly. It should not be forgotten that women dealt with the children most of the day while the men were away at work, so that the evening was the only time the women could hope to have some time to themselves while the men interacted with their children. Although in principle authority in a household is invested in the male role and nurture is invested in the female role, this does not preclude men from also being caring and nurturing (or women from exercising authority).

A father's attitude toward his own children seemed to change, however, as they grew into their teens. While tension between father and son might arise as a result of the son trying to assert his own identity and establish his independence of the father, a father's relationship with his daughter was often characterized by an ever-increasing assertion of control and authority over her freedom of movement. Some fathers were not as strict as others but most were under pressure (not untypically from their wives or their own mothers) to guard the moral reputation of their daughters and make sure they did not shame the household by inappropriate behavior, which in most cases meant inappropriate sexual behavior. They worried that their daughter would get pregnant before marriage, that she would run off with a boy before she had finished her education, or that she would run off with someone who was unacceptable to the family for various reasons ranging from a reputation among men for untrustworthiness or promiscuity to poor economic prospects and lack of financial security, to his not being a Muslim.

Girls, then, grew up with clearly defined rules about what was allowed and what was not. They internalized the prohibitions at an early age: any offence would be punished, sometimes by caning. For boys rules were less clearly defined. Although they too might at a younger age be punished by caning, mothers in particular were more lenient toward their sons, and what was not allowed at one point might be allowed at the next. Boys thus were less worried about "correct behavior"; they found that other people (particularly women) adapted to them and their needs, and that any external constraints could be ignored without severe consequences. Girls, however, learned that they had to negotiate conflict-ridden situations to create some freedom of movement and choice for themselves. These were skills they could later apply in their daily negotiation between the expectations and moral values of their Muslim village on the one hand and of the then "Yugoslav," secular, and westernized public world on the other. Often articulate women, they expressed such skills through an aptness at switching between different cultural codes, at handling different cultural contexts and concomitant role behavior expectations. One evening the girls and young women would be dressed for mosque attendance in traditional *dimije* and headscarf, while the next they would be dressed up in the latest fashion to attend a dance or go to the district coffee-bar. While most girls did not perceive a dilemma in moving between these different social and moral spheres, devout religious parents might. Social contexts outside the village involving non-villagers represented a moral space apart from—and often perceived by senior villagers as in conflict with—the moral space of the house. School was an important part of children's lives, but many senior villagers perceived it as a potential threat to the moral sphere of the house and the traditional Muslim community.

## Muslim Girls and State Education

In chapter two I pointed out that school and state education was a social space defined as "Yugoslav." Because this meant that it was nonreligiously defined, for some it represented a different and competing non-Islamic definition of what it meant to be a Muslim. Nevertheless, in recent years rural families increasingly encouraged and wanted their daughters to continue with school after the compulsory eight years. Among the fourteen-year-old girls in the village, two categories had crystallized: On the one hand the "modern" (*kulturne*) girls who were getting a secondary education and were the most numerous, and on the other the more traditional girls who finished school after eight years. When a girl finished her eighth school year, her family would decide whether she should go on to secondary education or stay at home. Some parents did not send their daughters to secondary school because they could not afford the books, clothing, and bus fares. Some mothers simply preferred to have their daughter stay at home and help them. Others were worried about their diminished control over their daughters, who would have to go to one of the market towns to get a secondary education. Those who did send their daughters to secondary school thought that education was an important end in itself (which, one mother told me, would enable her daughter to conduct more intelligent conversations than the uneducated wives in the villages) and also that it would teach their daughters a trade and increase their possibility of getting a job. Under the extremely difficult high inflationary economic situation of the 1980s most parents saw the value and necessity of their daughters finding employment.

When Amra started at secondary school I asked her where her classmates from the village school had gone. I was particularly struck by one girl who had not gone on to secondary school. Her parents were relatively prosperous and she was bright. They were also devout Muslims. Amra told me that her parents would not let her, but she was unable to tell me the reason. Her parents, however, explained that it was because they were worried that she would get married. The answer puzzled me, as my data showed clearly that those girls who did not attend secondary school, and/or got a paid job instead, married at a younger age than those who did. It was generally accepted that a girl should not marry before she had finished primary school. Furthermore, the boredom of working at home for their mother made the girls see marriage as the only way of getting away from home and experiencing something new. I was later told more reluctantly that the parents were not so worried that their daughter would marry, as that she would marry a non-Muslim (Catholic Croat or Orthodox Serb).

In the school context, a girl was more likely to interact with non-Muslim boys. State education tended to deemphasize religion and highlight instead the common "Yugoslav" identity of the children. As women were generally left with the primary responsibility for perpetuating Muslim customs and values, some families preferred to shield their daughters (and women generally) from exposure to the state-sponsored areligious ideology which they saw as anti-Muslim. As believers they experienced their Muslim identity above all as a religious identity and not as a nonreligious "ethnic" and "national" one, in the sense defined by the communist state. Not only was school an environment where children were exposed to the official communist areligious ideology, and where they met primarily as fellow "Yugoslavs" and not as in the village as Muslim or Catholics, but their common loyalty as "Yugoslav" citizens was emphasized. Thus the boundaries for social intimacy valid in the village were redefined to the extent that love, and possibly marriage, between two people of different ethnoreligious backgrounds became conceivable. This may explain why some Muslim girls, and Amra's friend in particular, were discouraged from attending secondary school, even if their parents could afford it. (This was less true for Catholic girls, and my impression was that the Catholic, Croat *kuća* did not consider state education as hostile toward a Catholic and Croat identity as Muslims did.)

## *Cure* and *Momci*

The main arena for a *cura* to meet other young people if she did not attend school would be the Saturday dance or summer fairs, all of which were attended almost entirely by young Muslims. Most Muslim parents did not allow their daughters to go to either of the two types of coffee-bars, *kafana* (the traditional café) or *kafić* (the modern, central European version), even if the two were perceived as different by many, particularly female villagers.[11] While *kafana*s in this particular region were seen as a meeting place for young Muslims, a *kafić* was regarded as a modern urban phenomenon, and believed to be predominantly attended by Catholics (Croats). To a certain extent, however, both young Muslim and young Catholic men would frequent both kinds of places freely and often, but since there were fewer Muslim girls at the *kafiće*, Muslim village boys tended to attend the dances whenever they took place. At *kafiće*, they played recorded pop music, both Yugoslav and Anglo-American. In *kafana*s the music was often live, and the style was what is called *novo-kompovano*, that is, traditional Bosnian folk music modernized with synthesizers.

All parents allowed their daughters to go to the local dance every Saturday, and some parents allowed their daughters to go to *kafana*s if they had trusted male company, but most parents did not approve of them going to *kafiće*. Some girls who were only allowed to the dance told me that the reason for this was that in cafés there were usually young men from other faiths, but that this was specifically the case at *kafiće* (the modern coffee-bars). A couple of Catholic girls who did go to *kafiće* confirmed this and added that they and "their young people" (i.e., Catholic Croats) preferred the more "Western style" ones. This style, as they saw it, included Anglo-American pop music and coffees like espresso and cappuccino (rather then traditional "Turkish coffee") and discos. (Until the early 1970s the Catholics, too, had their dance which was held on Fridays, while the Muslims then as now held theirs on Saturdays. In both cases the organizers were from the communist youth organization. I was told that in those days young unmarried Catholics and Muslims were not supposed either to speak to or to greet each other.)

In the village there were two seventeen-year-old girls who were close friends and neighbors. One of them went to *kafana*s twice a week with her boyfriend, while the other had never entered a coffee-bar and used to go to the dance every Saturday. The first girl was a Catholic, the other a Muslim. When I asked the latter why her friend was allowed to go to coffee-bars when she was not, she said: "Their girls are freer than ours, they may go to coffee-bars." (But see the comment made by a Catholic girl in the next chapter to the effect that Muslim girls had more freedom when it came to marriage and divorce.)

Those girls who did not go on to secondary school also tended to be the ones not allowed to go to coffee-bars. Girls who went to secondary school were more familiar with coffee-bars. Another Muslim girl who was allowed to coffee-bars by her parents told me that mothers made up such prohibitions because they did not know what coffee-bars were, since they themselves had never been to one. She told me: "They haven't got a clue, they maybe went to a dance and a fair a couple of times and then they married at fifteen or sixteen, so what do they know? What have they seen? Besides, they are stupid to have fears about coffee-bars; much more can happen at the dance. At a coffee-bar you sit nicely at a table and everybody can see who you talk to and where you go, while at the dance people are constantly moving in and out and it is always crowded, so it is easy to leave the dance for somewhere else with a boyfriend and come back later without being noticed." Most girls were under strict orders from their mothers to refuse any offers to go to a *kafana* by car or to go somewhere with her boyfriend on her own. Yet few girls complied with this. The few girls who were obedient were often criticized by their more experienced friends of the same age for the way they were conducting their courtships. One girl I knew well who had particularly strict parents was reproached by her best friend for always sitting and waiting for her boyfriend in the dance hall every Saturday for a year. "You do not know anything about him, his behavior or whether he likes to go around to *kafana*s and run around with women," she said. The nineteen-year-old girl, however, said shyly that her parents did not allow her to do otherwise.

Girls often expressed their discontent with the many restrictions their parents imposed on their behavior which reduced their range of experience. But these restrictions were particularly embodied in their mothers. One girl told me: "If we had listened to our mothers and all their prohibitions, we would never have experienced anything. There are so many things I would like to do: for instance, to go to Sarajevo, go out more . . . , but my mother stops me." Mothers thus embodied the moral and social control over girls. But even if a mother considered it to be shameful for a *cura* to go to coffee-bars, her daughter soon learned that the act was shameful only when it came to the knowledge of her family and neighbors in the village. The point was, in other words, not so much to avoid "shameful" behavior as to prevent one's behavior becoming an excuse for village talk.

While a *cura* who "was around a lot" or frequented coffee-bars (*hoda po kafanama*) was condemned by older, married women and some men as morally corrupted, a *momak* was expected to be out and about a lot to spend time with his friends, enjoy himself, flirting with and courting girls (*ašikovati*). He was not taken seriously, and his behavior was expected to be irresponsible with much of his time spent away from the house and village. The young people from Dolina mixed socially with people within a central Bosnian region which stretched to the borough of Fojnica to the west, the borough of Kiseljak to the south, to Visoko to the east, and to Busovača to the north. This being a geographical territory of an estimated 740 square kilometers with 115,000 inhabitants altogether, boys clearly moved over a larger area than girls, although not all girls were equally restricted. In summer boys and girls would travel to fairs around the countryside in their region and in winter they would go to community dances. Girls would also travel to fairs and dances if they had trusted company and access to a car. The young men could visit any fair or dance in the region. Like their fathers and grandfathers before them they could "walk around a lot," having fun and courting girls while searching for a bride. For the young the annual gatherings at the sufi lodges (*tekija*) had a similar function. Consequently, the young men would get to know their region very well. With access to a car their trips could be more frequent than their fathers' had been.

For *cure* and *momci* (girls and boys) the main point of going to these venues where young people met was to *ašikovati*. This word comes from the Turkish *ašik* (lover) and to the ears of urban people is a rather old-fashioned word best translated as "courting." It refers to affectionate talk between an unmarried girl (*cura*) and an unmarried boy (*momak*). It was not uncommon for either girls or boys to *ašikovati* with more than one suitor at a time. The rivals were usually from different villages and therefore might not know about each other. Eighteen-year-old Mirsada explained: "Take for instance Asima, she is now quarreling with the boy you last saw her with, and she is now flirting with somebody else whom she has been flirting with on and off for three years; he, however, has somebody else. You see, we usually flirt with several boys at a time, then there is quarreling, then a break, then someone else and so it goes. . . ."

*Ašikovanje* used to be a ritualized and very romantic undertaking in Bosnia, praised in numerous Bosnian folktales, epic folk songs and particularly in *sevdalinke* (love songs; *sevdah* is from the Turkish *sevda* and means love).[12] Marriageable boys would court their girls below the windows of their rooms (in town they would go to the door leading to the courtyard, where there was a special wooden window called a *pendžer*). Muslims usually courted on Fridays and during holidays (Lockwood 1983). The stories women in the village told me about their own youthful courtships often merged with the spirit and romanticism of Bosnian folklore, woven into some of their dearest and most popular *sevdalinke*.

The etiquette of courtship had changed considerably over the last forty years or so. Villagers in their sixties would talk of how as young unmarried teenagers they were never allowed to interact directly with the opposite sex; there was always a mediating agent—a friend, cousin, or neighbor—who would act as a go-between in initial conversations between the two. They were never supposed to be left on their own, so that when a girl married there would be no doubt about her status as a *cura*. In contrast, when young, independent, and fashionable Almira was getting married, a married woman and relative of the girl confided to me that she was not sure Almira was a *cura*. Although she had not asked her and did not intend to either, she thought it quite possible that she was not. However, had she learned that she was not a *cura* this would in no way have changed the girl's public status nor, therefore, the term of address. The change in status is only acknowledged as such when it is part of a ritualized (more or less public) marriage procedure in which a sexual relationship is formalized and properly established within the framework of a household (see chapter four).

The way Almira conducted her courtships and eventually married was different from her mother's experiences thirty years previously in two major aspects: the degree of physical closeness allowed before marriage, and the involvement of a third party and the patrigroup in the marriage and during the phase leading up to it. For Almira and her friends there were many opportunities to meet their peers away from their elders and relatives. They rarely met at *sijelo* gatherings at houses in the village, like their mothers had done (although this was still happening in more remote mountain villages). The village dance, the coffeehouse (*kafana*) and modern coffee-bars (*kafiće*) outside the village had superseded the *sijelo*. For some, the dance had already become old-fashioned (it was started in the fifties), and the new coffee-bars were preferred. The weekly dance was frequented chiefly by the youngest (fourteen- to eighteen-year-olds), but was still the main arena for most Muslim village girls, since their parents did not usually allow them to go to coffee-bars. The dance (*igranka*) took place throughout the year except for the summer, when most teenage children were busy helping their parents on the fields and there are other events like fairs (*teferić*) taking place.

Every Saturday at around eight the young Muslims of Dolina met their counterparts from other villages in the region at the community center next to the municipality school. The community center or *zadruga* was a low concrete building with a dance floor and small stage.[13] The Saturday dance was organized by the youth organization in the municipality, which was part of the ruling communist party structure. There were also dances held on Fridays and Sundays in other villages in the municipality, but usually only Dolina boys attended these. Each place always held its dances on the same day of the week. This meant that young men often came from far away to attend the only dance in the region on Saturdays. The community center was near the main road to Sarajevo and was therefore easily accessible by bus, car (if you were lucky enough to have access to one) or foot (if you did not live too far away). Most young people walked there.

The dance was an important event which village girls planned and looked forward to for the whole week. As Saturday approached their excitement increased. A couple of hours or so before they had to leave, some of the girls would come together and help each other with advice about what to wear and put on makeup. The mood would be upbeat and cheerful and the girls would express their hopes as to who would turn up, and would lay strategies and plans for how to cover for each other if needed. Every Saturday evening throughout winter you could hear village girls shouting a girl's name, stopping outside her house and asking her to join them as they proceeded through the village on their way to the dance. As winter proceeded and spring approached the number of girls decreased as they were married off. Next winter a new peer group would join the ranks of those who remained. The latter, however, were sad to have been left behind by their friends to face a winter going to the dances with girls of a younger age group. However, throughout the summer there were also the fairs, and more chances to meet a boy and marry. As they walked through the village, the girls' shouts let everybody know they were off to the dance. This symbolised the public and acknowledged role of courtship.

Married people often teased the girls and boys about courtship and getting married. The boys would walk to the dance too, in their own group either in front of or behind the girls. When walking back in the evening, however, the girls would usually make sure they walked together with a couple of boys, their cousins, or neighbors. The dance itself, called *kolo*, was a traditional circular one in which anybody, male or female, could participate at any time. Particularly for the girls this might be the only time in the week they had time off and could meet with friends or a boyfriend. The fact that the Saturday dance was where most young people in the village eventually found a marriage partner endowed it with a ceremonial importance.

## Choosing a Marriage Partner

During the period of courtship, which might last from a couple of weeks to several years, the two young people would use their meeting (which generally took place only once a week, for reasons of distance and cost) to assess each others' qualities as marriage partners. My data show that a greater number of women in the parental and especially the grand-parental generation had married within the village, albeit usually into a different *mahala*. However, most girls in present times would marry out of the village. There are two main reasons for this pattern. First, the reason given by the villagers themselves was that it is difficult to find anybody from one's own generation who was not a cousin; marrying within the village for two or three generations had created extensive kinship ties throughout Dolina for most of today's youth. Second, the younger generation was more mobile than their parents and grand-parents had been. Some had cars, there were buses; the young men trav-eled to dances and fairs outside the village. There was thus a larger pool of potential marriage partners spread over a larger geographical area. It was also my impression that girls were more calculating and aware of their own demands and requirements than their mothers had been. On the other hand, a marriageable girl often had to devise sophisticated ways of getting information about a boy, his family, and background in order to know what she could expect from an eventual marriage. This was information to which her grandparents, most of whom had married within the village, would have had easy access. A girl would never visit a boy in his home before she married him. Since, as a rule, he was not from her native village, she had to rely on information from a third party about his family's social and economic standing. She would ask: "Is he good?" (*Da li on valja*) A youth would ask his friends the same question: "What do you know about her family? What family does she come from?"

In choosing a marriage partner there were certain aspects a girl would take into consideration. It was preferable for the boy to have built his own house separate from his parents'. A girl was reluctant to share a house with her mother-in-law, and would prefer to run her own house-hold from the beginning of the marriage. Earlier, when material stan-dards had been lower, and sons had no income of their own, or at any rate not enough to build a house, the young bride would have had no choice in the matter. Another preference was for a boy who lived in a more urban area, or at least in a village which was close, in terms both of distance and of accessibility, to a market town and to her native vil-lage. If a boy lived in the hills (*žive na strani*), his marriage prospects among the girls in Dolina were slim. It would also be counted against him if he and his family owned much land or livestock,[14] as this implied that the potential daughter-in-law would have to work very hard, both on the land, milking and looking after the livestock, and in the house, cooking and cleaning for her husband and in-laws. This last factor might be particularly influential if the girl had a hard agricultural workload in her parents' house. Even those men who owned much land were seldom actually full-time farmers. They usually held jobs as skilled or semiskilled workers; some were officials in the market town. This left the women with most of the responsibility for agricultural work.

The priorities were such that if a potential marriage partner did not possess the preferred characteristics, he would usually be ditched for someone else who did, even if the girl said she loved the former more than the latter. (Girls who insisted on marrying for love were criticized for being ignorant, especially by older women, who had learned the importance of material standards and the relationship with the mother-in-law.) The story of Aida, a nineteen-year-old girl, was typical. She had been "courting" a certain boy for two years. She was very much in love with him, but as she obtained more information about his background, she became increasingly doubtful about his eligibility. He had a good and steady job, and owned a car. (Owning a car usually made a marriageable youth more eligible; it gave the impression of one who was hardworking and steady (*solidan*), and who could provide a wife with the means to "get around a bit.") However, the fact that he lived "in the hills", had much land and livestock, and shared a house with his parents all went against him. When Aida made enquiries about his mother through a third person who knew his family, she was told that her potential mother-in-law had a reputation for being a troublemaker. By now she was very skeptical indeed. In addition to her own reservations she now had to put up with those of her mother, who made a scene every Saturday when Aida went off to the dance to see the young man. Aida was getting very tired of struggling against her doubts and handling all the problems at home. So when she eventually met somebody else who lived in one of the market towns and had a house of his own, she married him after a short acquaintance, but without telling her first boyfriend, who she feared would be "blind with rage." Even if Aida did not love the one she finally married, she was sure that she had her priorities right and that she would learn to love her husband. She was happy living in a modern house, with hot and cold running water and a bathroom, and without a mother or mother-in-law to boss her around. She and her husband would often go on trips in his car, and she was happy to have seen more places within a year of her marriage than she had seen in her entire life in the village.

Most girls who sought a marriage partner with good material prospects—which usually meant that he had a secondary education—had in return to accept that these boys sought a potential wife with the same qualities. A young female informant put it this way: "When our mothers were young, boys would ask them if they knew how to milk, but today they will ask how much schooling we have had."

In rural Bosnia modernity had particularly influenced the young female population. What was acceptable behavior for unmarried girls had become open to negotiation and as I hope some of the above examples have shown, there were wide variations in actual behavior among girls (parental control of their movements, dress, education, and so forth) and their aspirations. For boys the main impact of modernity had been in terms of more readily available education, paid work and travel, but also stronger pressure to offer a future marriage partner higher living standards, preferably a house separate from his parents. However, boys did not have to deal with tensions between the demands of their seniors within the household in respect to their behavior, freedom of movement, choice of dress, and their own desire to participate in a more urban, consumerist (and Western) youth culture to the same extent as the girls did.

By the late 1980s Bosnia-Hercegovina and the former Yugoslavia had experienced rapid social change caused by industrialization and urbanization over the relatively short period of twenty years. That there would be a marked disparity in moral values between the older and younger generations was to be expected. Although the disparity in values between married women and unmarried girls was partly a generational one, which reflected an overall reorientation in women's roles, these differences were also a reflection of the different roles of *žene* and *cure*. Women and girls represented the morality of their households, but girls were seen as the more vulnerable since they were not yet married and were neither wives nor mothers.

One woman told me that when she had first arrived in the village fifteen years earlier (to what she considered a very traditional village compared to her own more urban one) she used to put on her miniskirt under her *dimije* when she wanted to travel on the bus to her native home. Before she boarded the bus outside the village she would take off her *dimije* and headscarf. Fifteen years later, however, the same woman, now a mother, refused to allow her teenage daughter to wear bermuda shorts (fashionable at the time). When her daughter pointed out the obvious discrepancy in her mother's attitude, she laughed and told her it was different then and besides she never wore it in the village. What had changed was not the dress code (if anything it had become more liberal) but that the woman who had once worn a miniskirt had become a mother with the responsibility for the moral education and therefore the shaping of the Muslim identity of her children. Daughters had to be taught that they were expected to reproduce and sustain the sexual boundaries which set this specific Muslim identity, mainly expressed and defined through women, apart. This did not mean that Muslim women should not socialize with Catholic women, quite to the contrary. Muslim unmarried girls, however, should not socialize with marriageable non-Muslim boys.

# Four

## Marriage and Marriage Procedures

IN BOSNIA and particularly in rural areas the change in a person's status from being unmarried to married is the major event in his or her life. Indeed, only through marriage does an individual obtain full personhood in the sense of becoming a responsible member of a household. Likewise it marks a crucial change and critical point in a household's cycle. Marriage and death are the two stages in the life cycle most fully elaborated on in ritual. While death was marked by a series of religious rituals, marriage was only rarely confirmed through a religious ceremony. In the late eighties it was in most cases the occasion for an entirely secular celebration.

Through marriage people of both sexes are expected to become socially and morally responsible members of society. This implies channeling one's sexuality into the reproduction of household members and directing one's productive forces into sustaining the household unit. Only by putting reproductive and productive forces to the task of creating and sustaining a household does an individual obtain full personhood. This is reflected in the local terminology. In the village the terms for man and woman (*čovjek* and *žena*) are used in opposition to those terms for unmarried male and female (*momak* and *cura*), and also denote husband and wife respectively. (There are also words for a man, *muškarac*, and husband, *muž*; but *čovjek* is used in opposition to *momak* to mean a married man. A woman and wife also refers to her husband as her "*čovjek*.") In other words, being a man or woman implies being a husband or wife.

Nevertheless, the change in status from being unmarried to married is more radical for the young woman than for the young man. This is true both on a personal and a structural level. First, there is a difference in experience and status before marriage between *cure* and *momci*; and second, the young woman—not the man—has to adopt a new social network and accommodate herself to new surroundings since upon marriage she moves to her husband's household, and usually also to a new village. Indeed, even the verb "to marry" reflects this, as a young man *oženi se*, literally "gets/takes himself a woman/wife" while a young woman *uda se*, literally "gives herself away," an expression which derives from the verb *dati*, "to give." The morphology reflects the fact that postmarital residence is patrilocal and that a girl gives herself in marriage while a boy gains a wife. This meaning is quite explicit and consistent. Indeed, a young man who had gone to live in his wife's native village after his marriage told me jokingly that he had "*udao se*," using the male gender of the female verb for marrying to indicate that he had relinquished his native village and household and joined someone else's, in other words that he had "given himself away."[1] Furthermore, while a *momak* becomes a husband and man when he marries, a *cura* has to go through the intermediate status of *mlada* (bride) and is not considered fully a woman and wife (*žena*) before she has given birth and becomes a mother. Indeed, as was noted in the previous chapter, she is usually addressed as *mlada* (the young one) by senior household members and neighbors until she has had her first child (although her husband would call her by her personal name).

This chapter focuses on two aspects of marriage and marriage procedures in the village. First, we will look at the change in marriage procedures over the last two or three generations, and see how these changes reflect the reduced influence of the extended kinship group and of local community ties as individual choice and economic considerations take precedence. I discuss all this from the point of view of the bride, since this is the perspective which was accessible to me as a female, unmarried anthropologist. It should therefore be kept in mind that the young man and bridegroom's perspective is, unfortunately, more or less absent. Second, I examine restrictions on choice of marriage partner, in terms of kinship ties and of ethnoreligious affiliation. By not allowing marriages between relatives until the ninth degree, Dolina villagers secured an expanding network of affines ("friends") and kin, turning strangers into "friends" and eventually into kin. Furthermore, by not approving of marriages between members of different ethnoreligious communities, the continuity and exclusive identity of such communities were preserved.

## Marriage Procedures

A public marriage procedure ensures that a sexual relationship and the social transformation of a girl into a woman and of a boy into a man is formalized and properly established within the framework of a household. These procedures vary according to the wishes and financial status of the couple and families involved, and have changed significantly in form and content over the last two to three generations. In Dolina young people wishing to marry pursued one of three alternatives. The first of these, which is presented as the ideal, is to have a "proper wedding feast" (*prava svadba*) with a "wedding procession" (*svatovi*). This is a public, planned wedding, which the households involved as well as the wider village know about. The second is marriage by elopement. This is elopement agreed upon by the couple without their parents' knowledge. The third, which is closely related to the second, is what we could call fictive elopement.[2] This happens when a daughter's imminent marriage by elopement is known to her parents, but they pretend not to know, even if the village is buzzing with rumors. This strategy is a mixture of the first and second options. It includes secrecy on the part of the bride's household, but a quiet wedding procession to fetch the bride and bring her to the bridegroom's home.

## Public Wedding Feast

After a period of courtship (see chapter three), the ideal scenario is for the couple and their respective households to start preparing for what the villagers would call a real wedding feast, the *svadba*. This is a big wedding feast with many guests (sometimes including the whole village), food and drink, music and dance. The approximate date of the wedding celebrations are known to the villagers weeks beforehand. The feast, which will be held in the bridegroom's village and sponsored by his household, will be attended by at least one representative from each household in the village.[3] Although older informants held it up as "the marriage custom" which was predominant in their youth, the *svadba* was actually a rather rare occurrence in the village during my stay. When I asked old Vasvija—who had just given me an account of her own wedding and was expecting her granddaughter to be married quite soon— what the wedding customs consisted of nowadays, she commented on the sad state of affairs by telling me, "We have no customs any more." To her, a marriage with a proper wedding feast and guests, the way she was married, was the custom, while its absence represented the absence of "customs."[4] Furthermore, there were several possible approaches in the 1980s and the young couple could decide for themselves about the lavishness of the public celebrations and level of involvement by relatives and neighbors. Indeed, in many cases marriage was no longer an occasion for a communal feast, but was limited to a celebration focused around the bride, bridegroom, and close friends. To Vasvija a marriage was an exciting and festive occasion and the opportunity for a cheerful village party with music, dance, and food. She found that many of the contemporary marriage procedures were not only unfamiliar, but also less inclusive and more unpredictable. Yet my data on actual marriage procedures thirty to fifty years ago show clearly that a real *svadba* was a rare event even then. In effect, it was the privilege of the more wealthy families, as it is today. Presenting the big *svadba* as "the traditional wedding custom" was thus an expression of villagers' aspirations, and indirectly a comment on inequality among the village population.

A wedding with *svatovi* (wedding guests, but also used to mean a wedding procession), is a wedding in which the bridegroom accompanied by some of his wedding guests arrives to pick the bride up from her home. The groom's guests would be close friends of his, such as a brother and brother's wife or a married sister. Thus no one from the parents' generation would accompany the bridal couple. This amounts to a public statement that the marriage is an event involving primarily the couple rather than their respective patrigroups. A *svadba* in the groom's home would always imply the presence of *svatovi* to fetch the bride from her home. However, the groom would be accompanied by *svatovi* even in cases of "fictive elopement," although they would not enter the bride's house as is the custom at a public *svadba*. The reason for this, I was told, was that "the bride had not been asked for." However, this is not as crucial an issue (today few brides would be asked for in marriage anyway) as is the wish to make it appear that way, that is to say to treat it publicly as a marriage by elopement choosing a certain set of procedures.

I was told that the major difference between a prearranged marriage (one that included a big marriage feast) and an elopement was that in the former the gifts would be given and displayed immediately. Although there are other differences as we have just noted, the immediate display of gifts was particularly singled out by people when I asked how they differed. Villagers greatly appreciated the value of the *svadba* as a marker of a household's socioeconomic standing. The *svadba* was the wedding custom of the financially resourceful, who used the occasion for a blunt display of economic status. In a later chapter, we will discuss other, religious rituals, which likewise offer an opportunity for displaying a household's socioeconomic status.

I have noted that there were obvious socioeconomic inequalities in the village. Such inequalities were brought to the fore in the choice of marriage procedures, and were more generally reflected in the scale of hospitality a household managed to shoulder. While *svadba* may be considered the procedure of the wealthy few, elopement was often the procedure of the poorest since it involved the lowest level of hospitality, although this is not to say that elopement did not occur in more prosperous households as well. However, the third strategy which I have called fictive elopement was the most common procedure. It was a face-saving solution for those who did not want to spend all their household resources on a big wedding feast, yet wanted some degree of public display.

## Marriage by Elopement

The most common form of marriage during my stay in the village and I believe over the last thirty years was marriage by elopement. To describe this kind of marriage people would say that the girl *ukrala se*, a reflexive form of the verb *ukrasti*, "to steal." This conveys the idea that the girl "stole away" (as in the expression "to steal out of the house"). This expression indicates the active participation of the girl, which therefore makes it distinctively different from *otmica* (abduction). Given that people themselves clearly make this distinction I believe it is unfortunate to refer to marriage by elopement as "fictive abduction," as the Sarajevo-based ethnographer Kajmaković (1963) has done. Abduction, albeit "fictive," conveys the idea of a passive bride, which is not at all the case in marriage by elopement. When I use the term marriage by elopement it should be understood that I adopt the perspective of the bride, since it is always the girl who elopes.

Marriage by elopement had changed significantly over the last thirty years. To older women, particularly those who themselves eloped, much of the excitement and courage of the "old way" had disappeared. They were mildly disapproving of how seemingly uneventful a girl's marriage had become while remembering with some pride their own departure for a new home. But they never talked about it lightheartedly, and often avoided the emotional details. (In contrast they would remember the period of courtship fondly, and were particularly happy to share with me their memories of "courtship in the old way," some of which I have conveyed in the preceding chapter.) Yet, despite their popularity, some elopements invited adverse comments particularly from members of the older generation. Commenting on a neighbor's marriage, sixty-year-old Nasiha said critically: "They say she eloped, but half the village knew about it. They only pretended not to know to avoid having to spend money on a wedding feast."[5] Puzzled by these comments I asked three of my female neighbors, all in their late fifties, to tell me what marriage by elopement was like when they were girls. They told me first of all that courtship happened "in the old way," with the boy standing outside the girl's bedroom window. Most marriages, they added, would take place in winter, when there was less work to do. Then one night he might propose and if the girl accepted, they would agree on a day that he should come and fetch her. On the appointed day he would arrive with wedding guests (*svatovi*), girls and boys from the village, his neighbors, and relatives.

Alternatively, if they wanted to get married "straight away," she would simply escape through the window and leave with her suitor for his home to become his wife. This would take place entirely without the knowledge of her parents. Next morning the mother would find her daughter's bed empty, and later in the afternoon male relatives of the bridegroom would come to visit the bride's parents *na mir* (for peace). The first time the daughter came to visit her mother after eloping through the window, she would ceremonially enter through the window but leave through the door. Indeed, Zahida who herself had eloped said about her own marriage that she had "left through the window." "I left through the window" was a euphemism for "I eloped." Similarly, women would say, "I left through the door" if they had married publicly with a wedding procession.[6] Since household members were likely to discover a girl's departure through the window sooner or later anyway, leaving through the window was less an act of secrecy to avoid being seen by one's parents than it was an act symbolizing the breaking of the normal rules of behavior. The marriage could only be accepted and normal relations between the bride and her family, and between the families of the groom and bride, restored and established after the bride had returned to her home through the window and made a new departure, this time through the door in the approved way.

Only this, I was told, was "real elopement."[7] Real elopement had to fulfill two criteria: first, the marriage had to be secret and known only to the girl and the young man who had agreed to get married, and second, the girl should have left her home through the window. During my stay in the village, these criteria were seldom met by the bride and her groom. In many cases a girl was said to have eloped (*ukrala se*) even though the bride and bridegroom's households knew about their imminent marriage.

Indeed, in the late 1980s, there were two slightly different elopement procedures. A girl either eloped directly during a dance or fair, or the groom came to fetch her from her house, and she left through the door in full view of parents and neighbors. The first method may be seen as an extension of the traditional custom, inasmuch as the girl still elopes in secret. Although she does not leave through her bedroom window, she still leaves with her boyfriend from the arena where the courtship has taken place; her bedroom window has been replaced by the dance and the fairs. The second, however, is an elopement only in name. The bride's departure is not secret and she leaves from her home, through the door; furthermore the bridegroom is accompanied by some of his wedding guests, who, however, do not enter the bride's house. Although the bride is said to have eloped (*ukrala se*) in both cases, older villagers told me that the second procedure was not a real elopement, "since everybody knew." It is this second, fictive elopement that had become the most common marriage procedure in Dolina during my research, although it did not have the status of the social and economically prestigious *svadba*.

## True Elopement

As already mentioned, the couple often engage in a period of courthip that may last from several months to a year or two before they get married publicly. It is not uncommon, however, for some girls to go off with a boy after only a short acquaintance, believing that he will eventually marry her officially. This is often done directly from the Saturday dance, and is the modern version of real elopement. These elopements take place without the knowledge of the bride's parents and in most cases of the bridegroom's parents either, as they are more or less impulsive decisions. Such marriages seldom last long, and usually the girl decides to leave and return to her parents.

Some of the girls in the village told me that they thought some boys would exploit girls who wanted to get married. They suggested that some boys would use the low degree of initial commitment of a modern marriage by elopement as a strategy for having a sexual relationship with a girl. It also seemed to have been a game among some boys, teasing and challenging each other into trying to persuade the girl to marry one of them that night, "marrying" being a euphemism for "having sexual intercourse with." Older girls and women, themselves very suspicious of men, their claims, and intentions, described the often very young girls who got married like this without any prior knowledge of the boy they had agreed to marry, as very naive. As an educated village girl put it: "Some girls are naive and only think about getting married. A boy may take advantage of this and ask 'Would you like to marry me?' and the girl, who the first evening finds him attractive, and the second finds that he has a car [a symbol of relative wealth and a steady job] will go along with him." She may have a strong desire to get married, and may hope to improve her status and perhaps gain more freedom for herself in a new household as a wife. To her it may be an invitation to change her status and life situation, while for him it does not necessarily mean taking on any commitments through an elaborate ritual involving the two families or households concerned.

Once the girl is in his home he then leaves the responsibility for her well-being to his mother. He may continue his life the same way as before, going to coffee-bars (*kafanas*) and seeing other women. If the young wife is ignored, she will soon feel unhappy and homesick, and sooner or later she will return to her own parents. In some cases when the girl was really young or the family she had arrived in as a bride was considered unacceptable, her father came and fetched her. However, regardless of the circumstances of her arrival, the village women would treat her as they would any newly arrived bride (see chapter three).

But not all girls who marry according to this pattern have been fooled into it by an uncommitted and more or less unknown boy; it may be a conscious strategy pursued by the girl herself. First, she may see marriage as an attractive alternative to the hardships, poverty, and lack of freedom in her parents' home. She might want to spend more time with her boyfriend and friends and believe that when she is married she will always be able to do this, as her parents will no longer be around to refuse her. Yet, in most cases she quickly realizes that far from winning more freedom of movement, she has less, as she must put up with a mother-in-law who may be even stricter with her than her own mother, and more often than not she will find no support in her husband. However, at least these young brides can more easily get out of their marriages than their mothers were able to do.

Second, many of my young female friends assumed that most of these girls were sexually experienced, and that some may have agreed to marry their boyfriend because they thought they were pregnant. It should be noted that girls who marry in the above fashion are very often under age (a minor between the ages of fourteen and eighteen may enter into marriage only with the permission of her parents or legal guardian and the court). In such cases, her husband (if above eighteen) becomes her legal guardian until she turns eighteen. Furthermore, a girl has no legal right to have an abortion without the consent of her guardian if she is under eighteen. She cannot therefore have a legal abortion without involving a senior person such as her mother or father (unless she chooses to circumvent official institutions). It is often easier for a girl to ask permission to marry after she has already eloped than to ask permission for an abortion.

There were two clear marriages by real elopement in the village during my stay there. In both cases, and in other cases I have heard of secondhand, the girls came from and arrived in households that were poor in every sense.

### Fictive Elopement

In contrast to the elopement just described, what I have called fictive elopement is decided on beforehand and is typically the result of a courtship which has lasted for a longer period of time and is known to most villagers. The groom would have told his parents in time for them to buy the presents they are required to give the bride when she arrives, and the food that the bridegroom's wedding guests (*svatovi*) and others will be served after the bride arrives at the groom's house. In its early stages, when no one but the couple knows about it, and they keep it secret, the marriage retains some of the characteristics of elopement.

Not surprisingly, this state of affairs rarely lasts in a village community. All three fictive elopements I observed were talked about weeks before they actually took place, and after the marriage the bride and groom complained that it was impossible to keep anything secret these days. But in fact the behavior of those most closely involved is ambivalent. Hints may be openly dropped by the bride's mother; some may have seen the bride-to-be in town with her boyfriend buying rings; others may have noticed her buying new shoes or at the hairdresser's. All these scarcely concealed clues, added to the fact that the girl has been dating a certain boy over several months, would have led people to conclude that she is getting married. In addition, her sisters or girlfriends usually know and are secretive in a way that is also interpreted as preparation for marriage. Nineteen-year-old Refika's marriage was typical.

All winter my friend Refika had met up with one particular young man at the Saturday dance. Over the last couple of weeks he had also come to visit her at home. For the last two months rumors about Refika's imminent marriage had been rife. But since they had decided not to have a wedding feast, the day of her marriage and her departure had been kept secret. Some said they thought she would elope directly from the Saturday dance. Every Saturday rumors were about that Refika would get married that day. Some had seen her in a nearby market town buying a gold ring, others had observed her at the hairdresser. Every Saturday I worried that she would not return, that the house would be empty without her. I got her to promise to tell me when she planned to leave, which she did. Earlier that winter two other girls in our neighborhood had married, and Refika was worried she would not have anybody to accompany her next winter to the dances. Would she marry her friend if he asked her? I inquired. Yes, she thought she would. He had a good job, he was treating her with respect, he did not mind her continuing her job, and she could trust him. They had fun together, and besides, what else was there for her to do.

Finally, one Saturday she agreed with her boyfriend that he should come and fetch her that evening. She had spent the day packing her trousseau (*ruho*), which she would come and fetch at a later point, and those clothes she would need in the coming weeks. She had dressed up in a nice skirt and blouse, had her hair done and put on makeup. The clock was approaching eight. Refika was constantly looking out of her window. She was getting worried that he might have changed his mind. He arrived some minutes later. There were two cars, as the bridegroom was accompanied by his two brothers and his sister-in-law. Everything went very fast there on. Refika's mother invited the wedding guests (*svatovi*) into her house, but they refused. This was because the procedure was supposed to be an elopement, albeit with *svatovi*. The bridegroom was in a hurry. In the meantime neighbors had gathered outside the house to bid Refika farewell; she embraced all the women, who were crying. She told her mother firmly to stop crying as it made things more difficult for her. Refika's sister-in-law accompanied her in the car to lend moral support when she arrived in her new home. On leaving the hamlet, the drivers hooted in farewell (the "modern" 1980s equivalent of firing a gun from horseback when the wedding procession leaves with the bride). After Refika had left, women gathered in the house of her mother *na žalost* (for sorrow) to comfort her and share her unhappiness. Her mother seemed to sum up all the women's and mothers' feelings when she said: "What else can we do, as females we have to marry."

Refika's marriage is typical of fictive elopement in that it combines elements of true elopement and the public wedding feast. On the one hand, rumor had it that the bride's mother was grumpy and angry because people in the village had been discussing her daughter's imminent marriage weeks before it took place. I was told that the mother wanted to insist on it being an elopement because the bride's household did not want to spend what it took for a proper wedding, with plenty of food and presents. Putting it like this my commentator was being critical. Although she knew very well the costs involved and the limited resources of this particular household, she was basing her judgment on the cultural ideal of conspicuous consumption and a large communal feast which would benefit the whole neighborhood. On the other hand, the parents on both sides had been informed about what was going to happen, and the bridegroom's parents had already been to visit the bride's closest kin (without, however, mentioning their son and his relationship with the daughter). And although there was no intention of giving a wedding feast, there would be a wedding procession accompanying the bridegroom when he went to fetch the bride and bring her home.

Refika's mother had got married in much the same way, while her grandmother was asked for in marriage by the groom's father (any other close male relative, such as the father's brother, could also have filled this role). In the grandmother's case, since the bride had been asked for in marriage, the groom, his father, and those accompanying them entered her house, otherwise they would not have. Like Refika, when her mother (who had married in the 1960s) left home, a senior female relative from her native village went with her to instruct and support her in her new home. When her grandmother arrived in the groom's house as a bride, she first had her hands colored with henna, and was then left in *budžak*. (This literally means corner, but is used in particular to denote the corner made up of two sofas where the bride would sit.) She was required to sit, completely veiled, on "display," easily seen by anybody, whether members of her new household, or neighbors who came by out of curiosity. This seclusion of the bride would last for about three days, the duration of the wedding celebrations.[8] The viewing was certainly less significant when the bride was from the village and already known. Women who had married before World War II and who had been through this procedure would nevertheless recall this part of their experience with embarrassed laughter, not least because of the complete veiling, which was an unusual and awkward state for the young girl to be in. While the bride was sitting on display, the wedding guests would be enjoying the music and dancing.

However, the way elements from "traditional" wedding procedures were being combined in new ways by young couples sometimes created confusion among other members of the village community. They wanted to participate but were often excluded, since the wedding was limited to the two households. This was illustrated in my neighbor Semka's case.

Semka's marriage had been talked about for months, and the villagers had expected it to take place every Saturday night for some time. One Saturday afternoon the rumors became increasingly convincing. Somebody knew that Semka had been to the hairdresser to get her hair done the day before. Women were debating whether there would be *svatovi* in the bride's home or nothing at all, or whether she would leave directly from the Saturday dance. Some neighbors of Semka's were called *na sijelo* later that evening to a household in another neighborhood, where I was also a guest. People began to assume that she was not going to get married that night, since she had returned from the dance. Later in the evening however, a young girl came running to tell us that there were cars on the way to Semka's and that she was going to marry that evening after all. I left with some of the guests to go and have a look. On our way we saw five cars driving up toward the bride's house. We noticed that the drivers were not using their horns.

The question the onlookers asked themselves when the bridegroom and his guests arrived in the village was: Will they enter the house? If they stayed outside, the marriage would be classified as an elopement, and the neighbors would have to keep away. If, however, the wedding procession did enter her house it would imply that this was a marriage by *svatovi* rather than by elopement, to which neighbors and relatives were traditionally invited *na sijelo* to celebrate (albeit in a more modest

fashion than in the bridegroom's home later that evening). When some
of the onlookers realized that the bridegroom and his company had entered the bride's house, they wanted to go over and participate, but an
older woman thought this might not be right, since we had not been
invited. Besides, she thought it was customary for a guest to bring a gift
(*dar*) to a wedding, and she had nothing to give. Others disagreed: two
women from the neighborhood had already gone over, so why could we
not go as well? However, while this discussion was taking place and people were trying to decide what to do, we heard the cars honk on their
way out of the village. There was a short silence before one of the
women commented: "She has left." The wedding procession had lasted
less than an hour and we had all missed it. The bride had now left with
her groom to his home in a village across the mountains. Some weeks
later Semka "legalized" her marriage by registering it at the mayor's office in the regional council office. So did her friend and contemporary
Refika, who also went through a religious wedding ceremony.

The combination of elements from the two kinds of marriage—true
elopement and public wedding feast in fictive elopement—means in
general that the events in the bride's village and household are marked
by quasi secrecy and lack of celebration (as is the case with real elopement), while those in the bridegroom's household when he arrives with
the bride are similar to those at a "proper wedding," albeit on a smaller
scale. Individual couples "combined" elements according to preference,
practicality, and resources. As a result, some older villagers disapproved
of what they perceived as a lack of predictability in the marriage celebrations. I would assume that social life in the village never proceeded according to a ritual recipe book, and that there always were disparities in
ritual procedures generally and wedding procedures specifically. However, the increasing "privatization" of rituals which had once been communal, involving whole neighborhoods, had left the community feeling
unsure about corporate actions. The impact of transport facilities, com-
munications, and the media (television in particular), had led people to
change their own priorities which might indeed conflict with a set of
ideal communal values.

Whenever a couple's marriage plans were known to the household
concerned, the broadcasting of that knowledge and the consequent
wedding feast were seen as the traditional, obligatory next steps. Con-
versely, a public wedding without conspicuous communal consumption
would be considered shameful. But a real wedding feast cost more than
most villagers were able or willing to spend. The obvious face-saving
solution was simply to pretend that the marriage was an elopement, entirely without the prior knowledge of the immediate families. By this
manoeuvre the event is conveniently pigeonholed into the other tra-

ditional category of marriage, "elopement"; events are officially taken out of the parents' hands, and they are absolved of all financial responsibility. This reading of the situation is confirmed by Kajmaković (1963), who points out that "fictive abduction" is becoming increasingly common, and suggests that this is the result of economic factors, namely the wish to avoid the obligations and great expense of gift-giving and hospitality.

It is significant that fictive elopement, motivated by the desire to economize resources, should have first appeared in the sixties during a time of rapid industrialization, rising living standards, work migration to northern Europe, and the massive introduction of consumer goods. The trend toward a less public wedding ritual reflected among other things a change in individual households' priorities in the way they spent their household resources. Such changes were the result of increased access to wage labor, work migration, and education. This had reduced the importance of extended kin groups and the local neighborhood as a source of mutual obligations and help. The wedding feast was designed to enhance the internal cohesion of the extended kin group and facilitate the coming together of two kin groups in "friendship" (*prijateljstvo*). It was an event when hospitality was extended to all households in the community, which gave all members a heightened sense of belonging to a community bound together by mutual obligations, common interests, and understandings. The prevalence of marriage by elopement (whether fictive or not) in the 1980s was above all a reflection of how households preferred to manage their resources. Households were redirecting resources away from hospitality and conspicuous consumption shared by the community as a whole toward consumer goods and improved housing for the core family. As explored in chapter two, such changes had also affected the structure and development of the household.

## The Marriage Ceremony

The marriage ceremony or *vjenčanje* is the official, bureaucratic, or religious confirmation of a marriage. The civil marriage ceremony took place at the nearest town hall and, if the couple wished, might be followed by a religious ceremony conducted by a *hodža* according to Islamic law (or, for Catholics, by a priest according to cannon law). The latter, however, can only take place after a marriage contract has been signed at a civil ceremony. The civil marriage ceremony may take place a week to a year (or even several years) after the wedding. If in the meantime the bride returns to her home, she is said to have been married and is referred to as a divorcee. The social marriage contract, thus, is important primarily in a sexual and reproductive rather than legal sense. A girl's legal married status is irrelevant to her social status as a married woman. When a *cura* has had sexual intercourse with a *momak* in his home, a reproductive rather than a legal contract is established. Although a young woman who later leaves and returns to her home may have to pay a social cost in terms of lower status in the eyes of the village moral community, I have no evidence that it would be more difficult for her to remarry. Young unmarried men did not seem to mind, although the girls' married elders always warned them that they would. It was not uncommon to postpone registering the marriage until the first child was born, as a trip must be made to the town hall to register the child anyway. This was particularly common a couple of decades ago when communication was more difficult, before the road to the village had been built and when private cars were rare. In more remote mountain villages it was still common.

A Bosnian ethnographer with whom I discussed this particular marriage procedure likened it half-jokingly to "trial marriages" and the common north European practice of living in "paperless"(common law) marriages. There is a basic difference between the two, though, in that their conceptualizations of marriage as such are different. Marriage in rural Bosnia is seen primarily as an exchange and contract between households (and not as one between the two individuals and the state/church). It establishes the right of one household and patrigroup to the productive and above all the reproductive forces of a young woman from a different household and kingroup. This lax attitude toward legal confirmation (or any public or third party recognition, whether by a local state official, priest, or *hodža*) of a marriage is, it should be noted, associated with class and socioeconomic rather than ethnoreligious background (or *nacija*). Although some Catholics in the village claimed that the procedure of elopement was a peculiar Muslim custom, and that Muslim girls "just go off like that," Mirjana's case proves that Catholic girls also elope.

Mirjana grew up in the old part of the village described earlier in the book. She eloped in exactly the same way as her Muslim friend Semka did, but like her other Muslim friend Refika, she also had a religious wedding ceremony, a Catholic one in church two weeks after she had arrived at the groom's house as a bride. As it turned out she was going to regret this. She was very unhappy with her mother-in-law and her husband did not treat her well. She decided to return home, but since she had married in church according to Catholic law, the marriage could not be dissolved. Her Muslim friends felt really sorry for her because she could not just divorce her husband by leaving him the way they could (even when they married according to Islamic law, they could still seek a divorce). Mirjana and her Muslim friends told me how much easier marriage was for Muslim girls because if they did not like it or their husband turned out to be violent like hers, or their mother-in-law horrible, they could get out. But poor Mirjana, one of her friends told me later, could not get divorced or if she did she could not marry again. When I asked why she had chosen to marry in church, she told me she had to because his family wanted it that way, and her Muslim friends explained, "You see they [the Catholics] are more religious than we [Muslims] are, and their laws are really strict." Mirjana tried to go back to her husband but he treated her even worse and finally she left him for good. She was very unhappy for a long time, but eventually after two years she married someone else. She had a civil service, circumventing Catholic law, as according to the secular laws of the then Yugoslavia only the secular marriage ceremony carried any legal implications.

### Secular Marriage Ceremony

The legal ceremony in the town hall required two witnesses (usually friends or cousins of the couple). The couple might or might not dress up for the occasion. When the ceremony was held a few weeks before the wedding it was often treated as a festive event. The couple and their witnesses (the *kum* and *kuma*) would dress up, and after the ceremony they would go out for a meal. It might be a low-key event with only close friends attending, or a big party with relatives and friends of both the bride and the bridegroom. The celebration was taken out of the village, and invitations were limited to the bridegroom's and bride's close family and household members.

### Religious Marriage Ceremony

Should the couple want a religious ceremony, this should take place within two weeks of the wedding, that is, after the bride has moved to the bridegroom's house. As already mentioned, it will take place in the bridegroom's home and will be led by the local *hodža*. The two or three witnesses required will be the groom's closest male patrikin. After it is over, the participants will be joined by close male and female relatives of the groom's father for supper.

During the period between the secular wedding and the religious ceremony, the young couple were not supposed to have sexual relations and were given separate rooms. Seeking to get one of the older women in the village to confirm this, I was told that: "Well, such was the law, but when I think of it I believe few actually followed the rule." The main difference between Refika's mother's wedding in the 1960s and her grandmother's in the 1930s was in the official marriage ceremony. In the thirties marriage ceremonies undertaken by religious officials and according to the prescriptions of the religious community (either Catholic, Orthodox, or Muslim) were accepted as legal without a civil ceremony. When Vasvija married in 1931, her husband went to see the Islamic legal officer (*kadija*) in the market town with two witnesses and drew up a marriage contract according to Islamic law. Refika's mother, who got married in 1962, however, had to sign a secular marriage contract before she could marry "in front of a *hodža*." But she was only seventeen when she arrived as a bride in her husband's home, and, according to state law, she had to wait until she was eighteen to have a secular wedding ceremony, and by implication the religious one also. The procedure for the religious wedding ceremony was the same for mother and daughter. Refika's religious wedding ceremony took place in her husband's and in-laws home with two male witnesses, in this case the groom's father and his brother, herself and her husband. After the ceremony about ten people from among the husband's closest relatives on his father's side, who had been especially invited, had supper together.

The *vjenčanje* is surrounded by less excitement and receives less attention from the bride's neighbors and family than the wedding—which, as we have seen, does engage the bride's family and neighbors. The *vjenčanje* as civil ceremony is an event (and a bureaucratic necessity) involving mainly and often exclusively the young couple and their two witnesses. The religious ceremony involves the couple and the bridegroom's close relatives on his father's side. Public accessibility to both ceremonies is restricted; unlike the wedding itself, the bride's relatives and neighbors are less concerned with either of them. While the secular part of the marriage has become less ritualized, leaving more options and decisions to the individual couple, Islamic law sets unchanging parameters for the religious ceremony. As far as the bride is concerned there is, however, one difference. Unlike earlier generations of Bosnian Muslim brides, she will not wear a full veil, but only a headscarf. This change is not related to change in wedding procedures as such but to a change in the dress code for Muslim women generally. At any religious ceremony and when reading the Qur'an women will cover their heads with a headscarf, but veiling has not been practiced since before World War II. When Refika married in front of the *hodža* she did not wear a veil, instead she wore the headscarf as she would in the mosque when saying prayers. The couple and the *hodža* agreed on a sum of money which the groom would pay the bride in the event of a divorce. It was all settled between the couple with no interference from the groom's family. Since the bride had her own income she disputed the necessity of setting an amount at all. (When the *hodža* reminded her that this was the law they agreed on a "symbolic" sum since religious law did not carry any jurisdiction.) The religious ceremony was held at the request of the groom's family who were more devout Muslims. But neither the bride nor groom were devout and both treated the ceremony rather light-heartedly.

However, the marriage process is not complete until a proper relationship has been established between affines which acknowledges the intimate interconnectedness between the bride's and groom's patrigroups through the future children of the couple, that is, the two families' equal contribution toward the new household unit. The quality of this relationship is expressed symbolically through the particular kinds of gifts exchanged in a series of ritual gift-exchanges between the two patrigroups involved. It is to these exchanges that we now turn.

## Establishing Affinal Relations

In Bosnia gift-giving and ritual gift-exchange are common in the context of both secular and religious ritual events, but are particularly salient in the secular sphere. Such exchange is occasioned by any change in status by a member of the community and the attendant necessary re-ordering of statuses and reconstruction of relations of mutual obligations. The gifts presented on occasions such as marriage, the birth of a child, and when a household finishes the construction of a new house, are called *dar* (pl. *darovi*).[9] Gift-giving and gift-exchange are particularly conspicuous between in-laws in connection with marriage. We have seen in the preceding section that the institutional importance of marriage has changed character over time. There are indications that marriage involves the two patrigroups less than before, being more centered on the conjugal couple and their individual relationship with each of the households. Yet, in spite of the reduced influence of the patrigroups in the initial stages of the marriage procedures and indeed during the wedding itself, the importance of marriage as an alliance between two households and two families (understood in a wide sense) is still ritually emphasized in the pattern of visits and gift-exchange between the bride's and bridegroom's patrigroups. A marriage is only fully acknowledged and established when the gift-exchange obligations, which are conducted according to a set of rules fixing the order and amount of the exchange, have been fulfilled. The particular visits called *pohod* (the dictionary translation of this word is "visit" but in the village it was used to denote ritualized visits between affines in connection with marriage) and the associated exchange of gifts establish a relationship between the bridegroom's household and family, of which the bride is now a member, and the bride's family, which usually belongs to another village community. In addition to marking the beginning of a new household unit and establishing an alliance between two households, the marriage of a household member also means that its social network outside the village is extended, a network which may be a source of access to new resources.

All known relatives of a son or daughter-in-law are called *prijatelji* (friends), but this term has an even wider application, since any two people who have relations connected through marriage will call each other "friends" (*prija* is used for a woman, *prijatelj* for a man). Both one's own affines and those of one's agnates are referred to as *prijatelji* and this is not only restricted to ego's own generation. (For instance: ego's father's brother's affines are also ego's affines.) "Friendship" is not automatically established upon marriage but has to be confirmed and strengthened through gift-exchange and reciprocal visits. The main visits are the *na mir* and the *pohod*.

In a marriage by elopement, representatives of the bridegroom's household go and visit the bride's family as soon as possible, preferably the day after her departure, "for peace" (*na mir*). Going *na mir* is required only in those cases where the daughter has left to be married without her parents' knowledge. The bridegroom is accompanied not by his parents, but by male representatives of the family, usually an uncle or brother.[10] For the girl's parents receiving this first visit from their new in-laws, their immediate questions are about where their daughter is, with which family, and in what village. The bridegroom's household will bring presents, usually coffee, sugar, and cigarettes, and exchange news and wishes for a good "friendship." These items will later be offered to neighbors and relatives who come to visit *na slatko* (for sweets) to offer good wishes for the marriage and the new "friendship." When offering cigarettes, the host or hostess will remark on who brought the gift and guests will make approving comments about the in-laws and wish them well. These gifts enable the bride's household to offer and display hospitality and therefore to state its social worth in the local community, but the event also reflects on the reputation of the bridegroom's household and name (patrigroup). Through their visit and gifts they show their respect for their bride's parents, good intentions, and willingness to honor their obligations which are a prerequisite for a "good friendship."

At the same time, however, their behavior reflects on the reputation and social worth of the bride's household. Indeed, the social standing and reputation of the bride's and bridegroom's households have become interconnected. This is symbolized by the fact that guests who come to the bride's household consume what has been provided by the groom's household. However, this has an even wider meaning. By consuming the gifts the guests, that is, the neighbors and relatives of the bride, are implicated too. They are part of a network connected by mutual obligations where collectivities of individuals—be it a household, a family, a neighborhood, or a village—are at risk of being insulted by or losing face in front of another party if all members do not honor their obligations.

If the bride did not elope, but was accompanied by wedding guests or had a wedding feast (*svatovi* or *svadba*), her bridegroom and his attendants will present her household with coffee, cigarettes, and sugar on the day they come to fetch her. The personal gifts to each household member and other close relatives are presented at the main gift-giving event, the *pohod*. A few weeks to a few months after the wedding, depending on how long it takes for the household to acquire all the gifts, the bride, bridegroom, his parents, and close relatives visit the bride's parents' household with gifts, and a few weeks or months later the bride's parents and close relatives reciprocate with a visit and gifts of their own.[11] Neighbors too are welcome to attend the *pohod* as it is a festive event and an occasion to display the gifts and draw judgment from the community about the social standing of the in-laws and to assess how well their daughter or son has done in choice of marriage partner, and their parents in gaining new in-laws. Indeed, the first time the parents of the newly married meet officially in their new status as *prijatelji* is at the first *pohod* (when the bride, bridegroom, and his parents and close relatives visit the bride's parents' household).

The date for the visit is agreed on beforehand, and the hosts (the bride's parents) are therefore given the opportunity to invite relatives and neighbors to an evening gathering (*sijelo*) in honor of their new in-laws. The bridegroom's parents bring *dar* to the household's members. In addition to clothes and material, they also bring food which will be offered to the guests. The household members who receive *dar* are usually the bride's parents and grandparents. However, some may also extend the gift-giving to collaterals who would traditionally have been members of the extended household but today form separate households, such as the bride's father's brothers and their wives. The number of family members included in the gift-exchange depends on the social and economic standing of the two gift-giving households. An example of how two families of unequal economic means and family size negotiated the lines for inclusion and exclusion of family members in the gift-exchange is given below. For the bride's parents to postpone the reciprocal *pohod* for too long without acceptable economic reasons is seen as

shameful, but may be less so if the *dar* is considerable. As soon as the
bride's parents have managed to collect the gifts for their new in-laws,
they return the visit.

In addition to the gifts to household members and close family (as we
shall see, who constitutes "close family" is open to negotiation) the
bride's parents also have to provide an *oprema*. The *oprema* may consist
of furniture and kitchenware. It is separate from the *ruho* (trousseau)
which the girl herself brings to the house (embroidered and crocheted
pillowcases, tablecloths which she has made or, increasingly, if she has
paid work, decorative items and linen that she has bought). In the villagers' usage *oprema* may also refer to both what the bride brings herself and what her parents give toward her household. In other words it
covers the sense of both a "trousseau" and a "dowry."[12] Larger items
like furniture are not displayed and are not given at the same time as the
personal *dar* given at the main gift-giving visit (the *pohod*). Unlike the
*dar*, the *oprema* is outside the realm of public gift-exchanges between
in-laws. It is given to the bride by her parents toward her future household, and not to her in-laws.[13] Nevertheless, there are usually rumors
about what has been given and villagers will comment about how well
certain parents have equipped their daughter in marriage. The word that
parents have equipped their daughter well (*oni su nju dobro opremili*)
travels fast in the village. Rheubottom (1980:247–48) has argued con-
vincingly that the "bridal furniture" is not displayed because it is associated with the bride's productive and reproductive capacities. The bride's
future role as a mother is seen as ambiguous as it represents both a threat
to the stability and unity of her new household as well as hope for the
continuity of the lineage.

As Rheubottom has suggested, the *oprema* may be seen as the bride's
parents' way of compensating her for her labor and assistance, and ward-
ing off any claims she may make for shelter and support in the future. In
so doing, they are redefining the boundaries of membership to the
bride's native household (Rheubottom 1980:234). However, as we saw
in chapter two, this redefinition and "exclusion" of the married daughter is not necessarily final. Should her marriage not work out, she will be
able to return to her parents' house.

The gift-exchanges which have to take place when a son or daughter
marries are a major economic burden on most households. This is especially true for the bride's household, since the *dar* is in addition to the
*oprema*. Less prosperous households may spend months and maybe
years saving money and buying *dar* and *oprema*, while others may
choose to be less ambitious and prestige-seeking in the quality and number of gifts given. The bridegroom's household, which visits first, sets
the standard: the most important principle in these exchanges is that the

gift given be equivalent in value to that received. When all the gifts to a daughter- or son-in-law's family have been bought and prepared, the mother will go through them, checking that the content of each corresponds to the relative status of the person to whom it is to be given and that people of equal kinship status receive gifts of identical value and prestige. A mistake would shame the giving household: when received, the gift will be examined in detail by visiting neighbors and any unfairness or flaw will soon be detected and commented on in public; and the report will soon reach the gift-givers. If the two households now connected by marriage are economically unequal, the recipients must deal with the problem of matching the givers when it is their turn to give. If the standard set by the bridegroom's family cannot be met by the bride's, they will do their best to attain a standard within their means which will not shame them. In reciprocating the gifts, the bride's parents have to consider not only what they received from the groom's household, but also what the bride has received separately. At the time of this study, it was becoming increasingly common for the bridegroom's relatives to give the bride jewelery, usually gold. This was a move away from giving her clothing and linen (associated with fertility) toward "display items" which would be worn in public. The bride's parents would acknowledge this special gift by adding something extra to that person's *dar*. In one observed case bed linen was added. Otherwise, the people who are most closely related to the bride or bridegroom, the parents and grandparents, should as a rule receive more valuable gifts than kin further removed. Grandparents will usually receive old-fashioned underwear and shirts, made of thick, handwoven cotton, sewn and embroidered by hand. These would not normally have been bought, but would have been given in *dar* to older members of the household, perhaps at the marriage of another of their grandchildren.[14] In addition to relatives of the groom, the bride's parents should also reciprocate gifts to the *kum* and *kuma*, the ritual sponsors and witnesses at the marriage ceremony, who will both usually have given the bride a gold ring.

The rules for the content of the *dar* are more or less fixed and known, but highly dependent on the standard set by the household which initiates the gift-exchange, that is, the bridegroom's parents' household. The women (the mother of the bride or bridegroom), who are generally in charge of putting together the gifts, are nevertheless uncertain about the correct course of action. They will often ask female neighbors and in-laws for advice. This insecurity has a very real base, inasmuch as customs vary from region to region, and as earlier noted the women in the village were originally outsiders. Even if the main components are generally the same, there was a strong feeling among women who once

women's gifts are a sign of wife's fertility

came from other villages that things were done differently in Dolina, and that they had to take care to get things right.

The *dar* typically consists of underwear, nightgown, and material for *dimije* (baggy trousers) for a woman, and underwear, shirt, and material for trousers or pajamas for a man. Rheubottom suggests that underwear symbolizes sexuality and fertility and that this is strengthened by the fact that these kinds of gifts are exchanged within the bride's new household (clothing is thus a symbol of kinship). In Dolina, however, such gifts are exchanged between in-laws and we could therefore argue that contrary to the Macedonian case (Rheubottom 1980) the emphasis is rather more on the exchange of fertility between the two groups rather than an exclusive preoccupation with the "fertility" of the groom's group through the new bride. Some clothes like a shirt (for a man) and head-scarf (for a married woman) or *dimije* cannot be directly associated with sexuality and fertility. They do, however, symbolize intimacy as they are clothes that should not be taken off in public. Moreover, being usually made of better material than everyday clothes they are also "display items" such as those worn on religious public occasions. Furthermore, the *dimije* and headscarf which married women receive are Muslim identity markers, a point to which I shall return.

A similar concept of equal contribution is at work in the exchange of food, as both the bride's and groom's mother carry food to their respective *pohod*s. In addition to clothes and material, the relatives by marriage (*prijatelji*) will bring all the food which will be consumed by the guests: sweet and savory dishes, fruit juice, coffee, and cigarettes. This food has been prepared by the senior woman in the household and is brought to be consumed by her affines. A household is a unit of production, consumption, and reproduction; the food and clothing which are exchanged between affines, that is, the household of the bride and bridegroom respectively, represent all of this. The offering of food is furthermore the epitome of hospitality and therefore essential to the reputation of a household.

But perhaps even more important in this context is the fact that sharing food is an act of inclusion and symbolizes social intimacy. Indeed it has been argued that sharing food in someone's household is a symbolic act of kinship (Filipović 1982). The offering of food in the bride's or groom's parents' house which has been prepared and brought by their affines symbolizes a merging of the two families and households through the bride and groom, which the latter's children will render into kinship. From now on the reputations and future well-being of the two households are inextricably linked to each other. When the gifts have been presented and displayed and the food consumed by *prijatelji* and neighbors at the last *pohod*, the bride's parents' gift-giving obligations will have been fulfilled. A good "friendship" will now have been established and the marriage process may be said to have come to an end.

When my friend Amela married into a household of higher socioeconomic standing than her own, I had the opportunity to learn how her mother—as the manager of her household's resources but also as the one most responsible for the reputation of her household—struggled to reciprocate the gifts received from their in-laws in a way which would gain her, her daughter, and her household the respect of her new in-laws and indeed of the community. This was even more important as her daughter had married within the village, albeit into a different hamlet. The difference in economic status between the two households was an acknowledged fact in the village. While the mother struggled to save up for the *dar* and worried that she still had to provide her daughter with the *oprema*, her neighbors showed their sympathy by telling her to be happy that her daughter had not married the man from across the mountains in Hercegovina, where they said the customary gift-giving included buying the daughter and son-in-law furniture and gifts to fill a whole house. They depicted the struggles and worries of a certain woman whose daughter had married in that region with much compassion. Amela married in April by fictive elopement. In July the bridegroom and his immediate family, that is, his parents and his brother, came to visit (*došli su u pohode*) on a day chosen by prior agreement with the bride and her family. Negotiations between the two households as to the date and extent of the gift-giving had been carried on through the bride.

Amela's mother-in-law, conscious of the more difficult economic situation of Amela's parents, wanted to make sure that her household did not intimidate them by bringing gifts of a value that they would find difficult to reciprocate. The main problem in this case was the question of the exclusion or inclusion of aunts (*tetke*, father's brothers' wives), since the bridegroom had many more aunts than the bride. As one of the bride's aunts was sharing a household with her grandparents, the bride and her in-laws felt it would be wrong to give a present to the grandparents (which was considered compulsory, even if they were not sharing a house with the bride's parents), and ignore the aunt (their daughter-in-law). But in that case the bride's other aunts, living in different hamlets of Dolina, would also have to be included. This in turn had repercussions for Amela's parents, as they would then have to give gifts to all their daughter's husband's aunts. The bride's mother-in-law suggested that they should give each of Amela's aunts a gift separately and at a later time, through a visit by Amela, but that the aunt sharing a household with her grandparents would receive her gift at the *pohod*.

The other aunts would be told of this arrangement to preclude their getting upset and jealous and spreading a bad reputation about their *prijatelji* in the village. Since this *dar* would not be included in the *pohod* and its handing over would therefore not be ritualized or public, this solution would free Amela's parents of the obligation to give each of their son-in-law's many aunts a gift.

However, it became a matter of pride for Amela's parents to match their in-laws' "prestations," and in the end they did not accept any special arrangement. They made it clear that they would need more time to prepare the gifts, but that they would eventually fulfill their obligations. This would include planning and economizing and might not be possible immediately after the bridegroom and his parents had visited. Not until four months after the *pohod* of the bridegroom and his immediate family were his in-laws able to make a return visit.

During this period, the bride's mother had been putting money aside to buy gifts. In the intense heat of summer, she picked berries in the forest and sold them at the local cooperative. She knitted sweaters for a firm in one of the market towns, and sent her husband to chop wood for the local forestry authorities. Whenever a fellow villager returning from a visit to one of the market towns reported a sale or special offer of material or clothes, Amela's mother would travel by foot and bus to the town in question and shop for her collection of gifts. Some of the necessary items Amela bought herself with the money she was earning as a shop assistant. Her mother's friends and neighbors engaged in the project with moral support: advice about where to make purchases, what to give whom, what would still be needed and how she could best economize on the gift-giving without shaming herself and her household. They would also encourage her with praise when they saw the purchases. On the day of Amela's parents' *pohod*, her mother went through all the gifts for the last time with her sister-in-law to check that everything was as it should be. The gifts were wrapped individually for each in-law in a towel. A close neighbor and friend of Amela's mother, herself born and married in Dolina, recollected her own wedding while admiring the gifts. She remembered that she [in fact her parents] had carried gifts only to the household (*u kuci*), and not, as she said, "to the sides (*na strani*), like they do now."

This remark might at first glance convey the impression that gift-giving has been extended to relatives who were not earlier included. However, it is important to remember that earlier this century the household was a much larger unit, usually consisting of brothers with their wives and children, and parents. (Brothers who were not living in the household would not receive gifts.) Eligibility for receipt of gifts was clearly defined by membership of the household. In the late 1980s,

9. The gifts ready for the *pohod*.

however, only parents, unmarried children, and possibly grandparents made up the household. To include the father's brothers in the gift-giving exchange was therefore merely to include those who used to be part of the bride's or groom's household. The problem seemed to be to know where to draw the line with those relatives who lived outside the primary household. Social and economic changes in Bosnia had affected the social organization and membership of households as well, such that close patrilineal kin did not necessarily share a household (as by living in *zajednica*) any more. As the case of gift-exchange between Amela's natal and parents-in-law's households illustrates, the lines for defining "close family" and therefore social intimacy had to be renegotiated in the absence of a clear overlap between close patrilineal kin and household membership.

## Restrictions on the Choice of Marriage Partner

Endogamy, a preference for marrying within the group, has been widely reported in Middle Eastern ethnography. The ideal rule of patrilateral parallel cousin marriage, or marriage between a father's brother's son and a father's brother's daughter (FBS-FBD), has received particular attention as a phenomenon which challenges classical anthropological theories of alliance groups and exchange (Bourdieu 1977) or as the epitome of endogamy in strongly patrilineal societies (Delaney 1991). Islamic law does not prescribe who its followers should marry, only those they should not. Endogamy, as expressed in a preference for parallel cousin marriages, has nevertheless often been perceived as a Muslim practice particularly since this preference is also found among peoples outside the Arabian Peninsula, as in Anatolian Turkey (Stirling 1965; Delaney 1991). However, since there are both Christian communities in the Middle East where FBS-FBD marriages are the preferred ideal, and Muslim communities outside the Middle East where the practice is condemned, such endogamous marriages are not per se Islamic.[15]

In the Turkish village which Delaney (1991) describes, endogamous marriages were the rule. Among these there were also some parallel cousin marriages. However, according to Delaney, endogamy by itself is significant, as women are seen as perpetuators of the family group, both because they inherit land and produce new family members. To Delaney, all endogamy rules satisfy the same practical and symbolic demands, namely to "keep the seeds and the fields, both human and earthy of the group circulating within the group" (1991:103). The group in this case is the patrigroup and the endogamy rule reflects a strong patrilineal ideology. The Muslims in Bosnia and Hercegovina, by contrast, are exogamous. They would consider any form of first cousin marriage to be incestuous, and although they too are primarily patrilineal (and patrilocal), a wife's and mother's kin have an important role in a person's kinship network. Indeed, their kinship reckoning is bilateral.[16]

The Bosnian Muslims, like their Bosnian Christian neighbors, have a taboo against marrying relatives (collaterally) within the ninth "generation" (koljeno).[17] "Generations" are counted from ego or alter up to an apical ancestor. If ego and alter are not of the same formal generation, the longer of the two descent lines is used to establish the degree of relationship.[18] Among the Muslims as among their Christian compatriots genealogical reckoning is primarily agnatic, but uterine kin are also included in the exogamy rule. This therefore requires that individuals have some knowledge of their network of relatives through their mother. Nevertheless, knowledge about uterine links is more scanty, not least because relatives through the mother are usually scattered over an area outside ego's native village. Based on his research in Montenegro, Hammel notes that there is no separate term for uterine kin since *familija* (a general term for "family") usually refers to agnatic kin. This is not so in our case, where the term *familija* clearly includes uterine kin. It is a general term used to refer to all known relatives, including more distant cousins (as opposed to affines), to whom one is related through male and female links. I would contest the perhaps more obvious conclusion that the weaker knowledge of uterine kin reflects the relatively dominant role of agnatic kin and the patrigroup. I would argue instead that the weaker knowledge is a function not primarily of the fact that these ties are uterine, but that they are extra-village. Indeed, in cases where a woman has married within her native village her children have a more thorough knowledge of their uterine kin.

The "ninth-generation" taboo, however, is often broken. First, many Muslims within a cluster of neighboring villages are usually related in some way or another.[19] Second, most people, especially those of the younger generation, have merely a sketchy knowledge of their genealogies and of who their cousins are (and this, in line with my argument above, is particularly true of uterine extra-village links). Most know about their first, second, and even third cousins if they live in the same village, but knowledge about relatedness that goes further back is rare.[20] Although seniors usually try to tell younger relatives about their kinship ties with those of the opposite sex they are likely to meet, two young people often find out by chance that they are related. When asking each other questions upon the first encounter to establish common friends or acquaintances, they may well discover family bonds. Some couples go out together without knowing that they are related, but as soon as family ties are established, often by an older member of the family, the parents usually forbid the two from having any further contact. Some only discover kinship ties after they are married, because older family members who could have traced the family tree may not have been told of the courtship. An eighty-year-old grandfather of a man who had married his second cousin without knowing it complained: "Nobody asked me, and when I learned about the marriage it was already too late." The old man was also referring to what has become a diminished influence (if not complete absence) of elders in their sons' or grandsons' choice of marriage partner (although they still seem to be able to block a daughter's choice). The choice of marriage partner has increasingly become an individual matter, though as we saw at the end of the previous chapter, parents do still interfere and try to exercise some influence if they do not approve of a potential marriage partner for their son or daughter.

On one occasion I overheard three girls discussing a young couple who were in love with each other. During the conversation it transpired that the girl's mother had forbidden her daughter from continuing with the relationship because the two families were related. One of the girls was very surprised to hear this. The other two could only reiterate that the two were actually related (*familija*) and even "close family" (*fina familija*, which implies that the connection is easily traceable, as second or third cousins). The girl who was surprised about the family connection—because she herself was related to the boy in question and did not know about his connection to the girl's family—claimed that she would not be able to find a single marriageable boy in the village to whom she was not related, both of her parents being natives of the village and both agnatic and uterine kinship ties known and easily traceable. The girls then concluded that they were all related, but one of them emphasized that this was particularly the case with her and one of the other girls because her father was related both to the other girl's father and to her mother. (The two girls were second cousins through both parents.) As already suggested, this indicates that even if genealogies tend to emphasize agnatic ties they include all collateral kin (father's and mother's side) particularly in cases where the mother's kin are part of the patrilocal context, that is, where ego's relatives on both the mother's and father's side are neighbors in the same village. Furthermore, when a person's maternal relatives are also the father's affines more distant relatives are more likely to be known. This in turn becomes an important restriction on choice of marriage partner. A kinship pattern whereby a person's maternal relatives are also her paternal affines will be generated in succeeding generations if, for instance, two female first cousins through their fathers marry two brothers. But while the exogamy rule encompasses both uterine and agnatic kin, there is a preference for marrying agnatic affines.

The strict exogamy rule whereby strangers are turned into relatives is contradicted by the desire to strengthen already existing ties between families established through one marriage. This desire is expressed in the preference for marrying one's *prijatelji* or affines, primarily through the agnatic line, so that affines in one generation are turned into agnatic kin in the next, or alternatively through the marriage by two brothers in one family to two sisters in another. In both cases affinal ties are strengthened. Such ties are seen as an important extension of a household's social network. As we just saw, mutual obligations are established through extensive gift-exchange and ritual visiting immediately following a marriage.

I noted that the taboo on marriage between people related until the ninth generation is a rule which the Muslim and Christian Bosnians share. Muslims, however, have an additional restriction on choice of marriage partner. Marriage between those related "through milk" (*po mlijeku*) is as serious a taboo as marrying kin. This means that a person who was nursed by a woman other than his or her mother may not marry a person who was nursed by the same woman. Persons nursed by the same woman call each other sister or brother "through milk." Holy, discussing the Berti of Darfur, has noted that "the belief about milk as creating the child's substance is supported by reference to the Qur'anic notion of a special relationship [rid'a] between a child and a woman, other than its own mother, who nursed it, which creates a bar to marriage between those related through milk" (1988:481). Delaney notes the same practice for her Turkish village and furthermore notes that "milk represents the closest physical tie, surpassing even that of blood since it constitutes siblingship even between children born of different mothers" (1991:73). All these ethnographic examples, including the Bosnian one, refer to "relationship through milk" and to the fact that this "creates a bar to marriage between those related through milk."

However, contrary to what Holy seems to suggest, the Qur'an does not refer to milk as such or to those who share milk; rather it refers to those who share the breast. In other words, it is not the sharing of milk as a substance which is at issue, since this would have affected relationships more widely than the *rid'a* actually does. It is the sharing of the breast and the juxtaposition of the woman's breast as an object of pleasure and of food. Indeed, the meaning implicit in *rid'a* is not milk, but to suck. It is, in other words, a fictive kinship not based on shared substance but on sharing a part of a woman's body. These two functions should be kept strictly apart, so that we may see that sharing of the same breast creates in essence a bar not to marriage, but to having sex with.[21] Understanding *rid'a* as a "relationship through milk" is a folk conceptualization of Islam, and should not be mistaken for the actual Qur'anic prescription. In the Bosnian case, Filipović (1982) informs us that the Serbs in some regions in Bosnia talked about kinship through the father (patrilateral) as "through blood" and kinship through the mother (matrilateral) as kinship "through milk." It is possible that the local understanding of *rid'a* in Bosnia has been influenced by a Serbian and strongly patrilineal understanding of kinship as the sharing of blood, and thus of substance. (Among the Bosnian Muslims, however, it is ultimately "morality," and not "blood" which binds people together in a collectivity.)

Today, the practice of nursing other women's children has virtually disappeared with the availability of baby formula and bottles. In the village I knew of only one instance of "milk-relatives." Altorki (1980) notes that although the four major schools of Islamic jurisprudence agree on the principal legal aspects of what she too calls milk-kinship, different Muslim peoples have interpreted the law to include various degrees of kinship "through milk" and have even extended the rule beyond the range stipulated in Islamic law.[22] While in Dolina only those who had actually been nursed by the same woman at the same time were considered siblings "through milk," in Bosnia too there were differing interpretations of who was to be included as kin "through milk," although the most common understanding was the same as in Dolina. Filipović mentions that among the Muslim population in one particular region "milk-kinship" was passed on to posterity, creating cousins "through milk" (Filipović, 1982:133).

Perhaps the most fascinating aspect of Filipović's account of "milk-kinship" in Bosnia-Hercegovina is his thorough ethnographic documentation of "milk-kinship" existing within all three religious communities, Muslim, Catholic, and Orthodox, and it might even exist between people of different faiths. He gives several examples of this in mixed communities where such relations strengthened friendly relations and established a form of fictive kinship, the overwhelming number of them being between Muslim and Orthodox (Serb) or Muslim and Catholic (Croat). Although "milk-kinship" also existed in Croatia, Serbia, and Montenegro, Bosnia-Hercegovina was, according to the same source, considered "the classic areas of kinship by milk." A significant difference between the communities, however, was that while among the Muslims, Islam defined this type of kinship and considered it an obstacle to marriage (that is, to a sexual relationship), the Christian church neither acknowledged it nor considered it a barrier to marriage. (Filipović 1982:127). Although shared between all three groups it was a practice pursued more consistently by the Muslims (according to Filipović's account it was also common among the Orthodox but less so among Catholics). It is unlikely that "milk-kinship" in Bosnia constituted a conscious strategy for managing interfamily relations as described by Altorki for Arab Muslim societies. First, polygamy was extremely rare in Bosnia and second, since parallel or cross-cousin marriages were taboo anyway, "milk-kinship" was not needed as a strategy to prevent such marriages. Rather, in Bosnia it was an act of friendship and neighborliness between women helping each other out in times of crisis, and a way of strengthening ties of friendship.

The rules, then, about who ideally a person may or may not marry are largely shared by the Bosnian Muslims and their Christian neighbors. Indeed it is a system to which both the Christian (Orthodox and Catholic) and Islamic religious traditions have contributed. And while the ninth-generation rule clearly sets the Muslim Bosnians apart from their coreligionists to the south and east, the prohibition against marrying "kin through milk" sets the Catholic Croats and Orthodox Serbs apart from their coreligionists to the north and east (although it was also practiced in Bulgaria[23]). In his article on "milk-kinship," Filipović inquires whether this was introduced to the South Slavs through the influence of

Islam or whether it antedates it. Although he adds that this is not established, he concludes by saying that it was also present in the Balkans in
antiquity and thus predates the South Slavs' contact with Islam
(1982:146). His claim is an interesting one and entirely in line with a
common western assumption in this area that practices shared between
the Muslims and the Christians must either be "Christian" practices
picked up by the Muslims or, if not Christian, must be pre-Christian. I
have yet to come across a scholar who argues for the equally plausible
explanation that Christians in this area have picked up an Islamic practice. After all Islamic philosophy, religion, and practices dominated this
region for more than five hundred years.

## Interethnic Marriages

We have already established that the Bosnian Muslims are exogamous.
Consequently they do not demonstrate a concern with keeping the
"seeds and the fields" (Delaney's phrase) within the patrigroup, as many
other Muslim patrilineal societies do. However, although the Bosnians
are exogamous in kinship terms, they are nevertheless endogamous in
ethnoreligious terms. To Antoun, marriage with the "closest in blood"
is a guarantee of loyalty, ethical behavior, modesty, and thereby the
"honor of the group" (1968:693). So while in Delaney's Turkish case
this group is the patrilineal group, in the Bosnian case it is the ethnoreligious group. However, I would dispute the aptness of the metaphor
"closest in blood" in the Bosnian Muslim case since morality takes precedence over "blood." Although we have also seen that a Muslim child
inherits its father's last name and thereby usually also his or her father's
ethnoreligious identity, this does not invalidate my argument. It merely
tells us that in creating and determining membership in the Bosnian
Muslim ethnoreligious collectivity, "morality" can exclude "blood" but
"blood" cannot exclude "morality" (see chapter one).
    By examining attitudes toward mixed marriages, we can learn about
notions of identity and particularly the interplay between ethnoreligious
identity and gender.

### Opposing Mixed Marriages

In rural areas in central Bosnia, marriages between members of different
religious communities were rare, as the social costs in terms of opposition from the respective families and the general community were often
adjudged too high. Although the villagers were clearly aware that the

attitude toward such marriages was more liberal in urban settings, they emphasized that the social environment in villages and in towns is different, and that rules for expected behavior which apply in the village do not apply in town. The difference is mainly understood in terms of the weaker role of religion in cities and therefore of religious identity, and ultimately of *nacija* membership (or what some scholars would call ethnic identity, and others would call national identity). By marrying across ethnoreligious communities a person shows by implication a lack of concern for the unambiguous identity of his or her children. Since, according to village perceptions of identity, religious affiliation and *nacija* are one and the same, someone who does not have a religion does not have a determined *nacija* either.

Urban areas are not only more secularized but also more influenced by Western notions of individualism. A young couple who are economically independent may more easily act independently of their parents' wishes. Indeed, the reduced importance of ethnoreligious ties and loyalties in urban areas relative to rural ones is parallelled by the diminished influence of kinship loyalties. We have seen that there were different attitudes toward mixed marriages in town and the country. The villagers felt that such marriages had negative implications in the village as everyone perceived himself as a member of a *najica*. A mixed marriage therefore would produce a child with no firm *nacija* identity. Or as one woman put it: "The children from mixed marriages, who will they be? Who will be their friends? They will be neither Catholics nor Muslims."

The opposition to mixed marriages is typically explained in terms of possible everyday practical conflicts. Women in particular worry about getting a daughter-in-law from a "different religion" and the consequences this may entail for the everyday running of her household (see chapter two). That the negative attitude toward mixed marriages is understood in terms of problems in the daily running of the household reinforces the argument already put forward, namely that the *kuća* is seen as the primary environment where ethnoreligious membership and identity are formed.

## Attitudes to Actual Cases of Mixed Marriages

Because marriage across ethnoreligious communities is generally not approved of (neither by Muslims nor by Catholics), parents particularly discourage their young daughters from marrying someone of a different ethnoreligious background. In this respect rural Bosnia offered a contrast to urban Bosnia and Hercegovina (cities and larger towns), where *nacija* generally and intermarriage specifically seemed to be much less of a concern to most people. (Although the number of mixed marriages is difficult to document, it has been suggested that 27 percent of all marriages in Bosnia-Hercegovina before the war were between people of different *nacije* [Thompson 1992:91].) As far as I have been able to establish there were only a few instances of marriage across ethnoreligious communities in mixed villages. In Dolina, there were three such marriages in the late eighties. In all three cases a Muslim man married a non-Muslim woman, who was in all three instances an Orthodox Serb. This is worth noting, since the village is in an area which is mainly mixed Muslim and Catholic Croat. In other words, the bride was from the only ethnoreligious category not part of this village community. (In 1993 the Muslim men married to Serb women were being particularly targeted for acts of terror by Bosnian Croat soldiers.)

While some older men and women in the village thought it was a pity that these men had married non-Muslim women (though they did not react with the same outrage as an old man felt when his own granddaughter married a non-Muslim), other, younger people did not think it made any difference. Women would welcome the bride into their neighborhood in the customary way by going to visit, though they would feel more insecure than when the bride was Muslim. Nevertheless, the initial distance would decrease as the young woman proved willing to live up to the ideals Muslim women set for themselves: to be hardworking, clean, and loyal to her household.

On one occasion I was discussing one of our neighbors with a friend. We both agreed that he was a good man, but my friend added, "It's a pity he is married to a Serb." I remembered this when two years later I again visited the village; the same friend now had a Serb neighbor married to a Muslim man. They had become very good friends and had a lot of fun together. I said I thought she was really nice. My friend agreed and gave me a balanced view of her Serb friend's positive and negative sides: "We like each other's company, we have fun, she is a really good person, but you know I like to tease her because she gets upset very easily, but she's better now at standing up for herself." In contrast to the Serb wife of her Muslim neighbor two years earlier whom she did not know very well, and whose personality I suspect she did not even like, my friend did not regret or mention a word about her neighbor's *nacija*. She liked her new friend and neighbor well; personality, not *nacija*, was what mattered. I am relating this story because I think it illustrates rather well the relatively arbitrary use of *nacija* categorization in actual social interaction in Bosnia prior to the war. As this case illustrates, ethnoreligious categories and labels were often used to negotiate social distance with people with whom one did not want close social contact.

Yet young women (both Muslim and Catholic) generally expressed stronger misgivings about mixed marriages than young men. Unmarried girls in particular had reflected on the possibility of marrying someone of a "different religion" but thought it would cause too many problems. They worried about what names they would give their children, what holidays they would celebrate, the negative attitudes of parents. One Catholic friend, marriageable and in her twenties, echoed these views during a discussion of such marriages, saying: "You may be good friends with those from other religions, but you do not marry them. It is better not to because so many problems occur. He wants you to take his religion and you want him to take yours; and when children arrive, the problem is what name to give them, etc., and then the respective families interfere. This is why it is better to marry somebody from your own religion."

It is not surprising that girls should pay more attention to such issues than boys. After all it is the girl, not the boy, who as a rule must adapt to new ways when she goes to join her husband in his parents' household. Although women are seen as guardians of moral and religious values in their role as educators of the children, when a non-Muslim woman joins a Muslim household (or a Muslim woman joins a non-Muslim household) the children will grow up in an environment where the traditions and values of that particular household, the household of the father, prevails. (Postmarital residence is, as we remember, usually patrilocal.)

According to Islamic law it is *haram* (forbidden) for a Muslim woman to marry a non-Muslim man. A Muslim man, however, is allowed to marry a non-Muslim woman. Indeed, Muslims in the village told me that the latter was *sevap* (a good deed).[24] This law is the logical consequence of the belief that the man is more reasonable and better able to control his "natural" drives than a woman who is governed by her instincts. The man is therefore also considered the morally stronger. Although the role of the mother as educator of her children is underlined in Islam, the father's influence is seen as the stronger one, not only because the woman is under his influence and that of his family but also because men are perceived to be morally stronger.

Indeed, a child is thought to belong to its father's patrigroup, to the environment in which it has been nurtured. This was brought home to me through an episode discussed in chapter two, when a young mother decided to leave her husband's household and return to her mother's because she was having great difficulties with her mother-in-law. Neighboring women told her to leave her baby son behind because, they said, after all the child was "theirs," meaning her husband's and his family's.

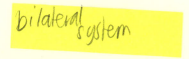
bilateral system

(However, they also hoped that this would strengthen the young woman's bargaining position and eventually bring her back to the village.) Yet it is not uncommon in Bosnia for children to remain with their father after the divorce of their parents (divorce, too, is not uncommon in villages and even less so in towns). I knew of two such instances in the village, and of three divorced mothers with children.

Because ethnoreligious and social identity are believed to be formed by the child's environment, villagers aver that a mother from a different ethnoreligious background will inevitably bring with her the knowledge of her own religious traditions. Furthermore, a non-Muslim mother (or a non-Catholic one, in reverse cases) cannot teach her children religious and cultural values she never learned herself. Since religious rituals and values are the main distinguishing factor between the three Bosnian "peoples," this is obviously less of an issue for nonpracticing Muslims (Catholics or Orthodox). She thereby brings an element of insecurity and ambiguity into the household. This is true for any bride who arrives as a stranger to her husband's household, but is much more pronounced when the bride is from a different religious background. The degree to which this does create problems in the household and immediate families varies. Religiously devout families of all denominations may find this more of an obstacle than nonreligious families.

The three mixed marriages in the village all seemed to work well. All men came from nondevout households and the women came to be well regarded by their Muslim neighbors. For any new bride it is important that she prove her loyalty to the household of which she has become a member. For non-Muslim women this is even more so since their loyalty is expected to be less genuine than a Muslim woman's. The children of these marriages were in all cases given nonethnic or so-called *narodni* (folk) names.

In this section we have seen that young people looking for a marriage partner have to identify first the ethnoreligious affiliation of the person they are attracted to and second, this person's kinship network. The first is in most instances a much easier task than the latter. As already noted, a person's name usually conveys sufficient information to determine ethnoreligious affiliation, while kinship ties when distant are more difficult to establish. It is therefore rarely necessary to ask about a person's *nacija* directly, though it is necessary to ask about that person's relatives. Hence one of the first questions a young couple asked each other was not "what are you?" (in terms of *nacija* membership) but rather "whose are you?" (who are your parents?). For the young unmarried people in Dolina both who you were in terms of your kinship ties and who you were in terms of ethnoreligious affiliation defined who you could or could not marry. This was true for both ethnoreligious communities in the village. Ideally, then, Bosnians are exogamous within the network of kin and endogamous within the ethnoreligious community.

## Conclusion

I have argued that the equal and amicable gift-exchange in connection with marriage emphasizes the equal contribution of the bride's and bridegroom's households (and families) to the creation of a new unit of production, consumption, and reproduction. In addition, gift-exchange between the members of the two families who come together through marriage also bespeaks of the conversion of a stranger via "friend" to kin. Ultimately, their equal contribution to the creation of a new household unit also symbolizes their common membership of the wider ethnoreligious community. The gifts exchanged between affines symbolize their commonality relating to the household as a unit of reproduction, production, and commensality, and thus a high degree of intimacy. I suggest that the gift-exchange which takes place between affines highlights the common interests of the bride's and bridegroom's households and their equal contribution to the formation of a new productive and reproductive unit.[25] Eventually, this unit will contribute to the continuation of the patrilineage since any children born to the couple will be considered the children of the husband and his family. As we have seen, the marriage of a daughter and the accompanying giving of *oprema* means relinquishing any rights to her productive, and more importantly, her reproductive forces. Nevertheless, the relationship between any children and their maternal kin, particularly the mother's brother, is often warm and close. It should also be remembered that all in-laws become relatives (*familija*) of the children of the couple whose marriage established affinal relations between their two families. Marriage, then, is not only, as symbolized by the *oprema*, about one household relinquishing (and losing) its rights in a daughter's work and her future children, and another household gaining the same through the marriage of a son. It is also about the exchange and, ultimately, the sharing of identity, as symbolized by the *dar*, the equal and amicable exchange of gifts. This is thus the other, and I believe paramount, aspect of marriage.

The political mobilizing potential of kinship networks implies that in addition to its ethnoreligious aspect this identity also has an ethnopolitical one. The gift is a mode of nonmonetary exchange which both derives from and creates relationships (Humphrey and Hugh-Jones 1992:17). Relationships are about identity. The relationships a person is part of give to that person a sense of who he or she is and tell other people through association who he or she is. People form relationships on the basis of "having something in common." What this common ground may be varies greatly, but it does imply a sense of "something shared," whether this be other people such as relatives, or an interest in music, a particular experience, or the idea of a shared past, present, or future. In a sense we are the people we form relationships with.

So if the gift both derives from and creates relationships, it is also an expression of the quality of that relationship, the degree of intimacy, and a sense of what is shared. To Strathern "the gift realises two sets of relationships, namely a past origin and a present cause, or what makes it part of a person and what makes it detachable" (1992:186). However, in this present study a third aspect is also crucial, namely what makes the gift attachable to the receiver.

In chapter two I noted that a central aspect of the day-to-day interaction which integrates the community is social exchange. Gift-giving is part of this social exchange. Such exchanges create bonds of alliance and commonality. The strength and intimacy of these bonds are reflected in the types of gifts given on different occasions. However, these gifts also establish a common identity between their giver and the recipient. Earlier I noted that in the exchanges at marriage, married female relatives receive pieces of clothing (or material for such clothing) which are part of the traditional dress code for Muslim women. (In mixed marriages these items will be replaced by material for a shirt or suit, which is also often what young, "modern" women will be given.) It has already been pointed out that Catholics are only to a limited extent part of Muslims' social exchange. The gift-exchange pattern between Catholic affines is similar to that described for Muslims, but since intermarriage between Muslims and Catholics is not common, the particular exchanges which take place at marriage are rare between Catholic and Muslim households. This is crucial, as these exchanges in particular highlight the intimacy of shared identity expressed in terms of a common interest in preserving the continuity of the ethnoreligious community. Indeed, I would argue that rather than emphasizing clan boundaries as suggested by Rheubottom (1980), the prestations exchanged between affines emphasize the equality and common identity of those who marry each other, that is, their membership in a single ethnoreligious community.

In this chapter I have discussed the different stages in the process of marriage. We have seen that individuals choose different strategies according to their economic means. It is clear that the young act more individualistically than their parents' generation did. Nevertheless the

continued cohesive power of the family, household, and kinship network more generally, is reflected first in the continued importance of
gift-exchange between "friends" (affines) in connection with the establishment of a good "friendship," and second in the reluctance of most
young villagers to marry across ethnoreligious communities (and the
continued low number of mixed marriages in rural areas). On the other
hand, while such marriages may have been unthinkable in village communities thirty years ago, they were conceivable in the late eighties, and
the skepticism of young people about such marriages, particularly when
lived outside the village context, was decreasing. The emphasis on good
"friendship" is furthermore an indirect acknowledgment that women
(or wives) are the vital links between the household and a wider social
network of relationships entailing mutual obligations.

At the beginning of this chapter two restrictions on the choice of marriage partner (which amount to prohibitions) were mentioned, that on
marrying relatives (whether matrilineal are patrilineal) within the ninth
degree, and that on marrying members of another ethnoreligious community. The first rule may be seen as a strategy for a household to continuously expand its network of "friends," or people who are under a
mutual obligation to offer and receive favors. It is part of a wider pattern
of networking, sustained by gift-exchange. The second restriction, on
the other hand, ensures a contained and exclusively defined ethnoreligious community. Marilyn Strathern has suggested that "the exogamic
rule, which defines both a clan's identity and its partibility, ensures that
the clan will detach from itself an out-marrying category of persons
who carry its identity—the quality of its being—into other places"
(1992:179). However, since in Bosnia this identity is based on religious
adherence and therefore primarily on morality (not necessarily on descent) it is believed to be adversely affected by the influence of a different religious/moral environment. In theoretical religious/Islamic
terms, this idea is reflected in the rule that Muslim men are allowed to
marry non-Muslim women as men are morally superior to women. Yet
in practice people in the village also opposed such marriages (although
some did take place). I argue that this can be explained by reference to
the important role of "friends" (affines) in the social support network,
and by the notion that the bride's and bridegroom's households contribute equally to the formation of a new household unit, the continuation of both groups, and the preservation of their common ethnoreligious identity.

Although Bosnians of all three religious affiliations share a preference
for marrying non-kin, this preference does not apply to members of
a different ethnoreligious community. The ethnoreligious community
would reinforce its internal cohesion by pursuing an ideal rule of ethno-

religious endogamy on the one hand and an ideal rule of kinship exogamy extended to the "ninth generation" on the other. The preferred ethnoreligious exclusivity of networks between kin and affines will have consequences for the kind of integration and bonds of mutual obligations found between different ethnoreligious communities within a village or region where non-kin are potential marriage partners.

# Five

## Caring for the Living and
## the Souls of the Dead

WHEN THE BRIDE ARRIVES on the doorstep of her husband's parents' house on her wedding day she will carry two items under her arms as she crosses the threshold into her new household: a loaf of bread (*pogača*) under her right arm, and the Qur'an (*musaf*) under her left. Significantly, the two items are placed under her arms by her mother-in-law. These items are symbolic of a woman's primary roles as nurturer and embodiment of a *kuća*'s moral and religious values as a future wife, mother, and new member of the *kuća*, and the expression of the hope that she will fulfill them.[1] The loaf of bread symbolizes fertility, and thus a woman's reproductive powers. (In some areas instead of the loaf of bread the bride is given grain which she is supposed to disperse around herself and in front of the house.) When the bride has entered the house, a child is placed in her lap. It is desirable that the child be male, since it is believed that in that case the bride will give birth to a male child, but if there is no male child present a female child will be placed in her lap instead.

Several anthropologists working in southern and southeastern Europe have made a symbolic connection between the making of bread and the household's capacity for reproduction. According to Pina-Cabral (1986:42–44) in rural Portugal bread is food par excellence, the very source of life. It is both a symbol of community created through the unity of commensality (which in this case is physical as well as spiritual since a parallel is made to the Holy communion) and of the household's capacity to reproduce itself. Delaney sees bread making in her Turkish village as "analogous to the process of procreation" and although it is not a sacred activity, the creative engendering process is. The live germ, she argues, is transmitted from batch to batch as seed from generation to generation (1991:95).

In Dolina bread making is part of women's daily work. Bread is made in a big round pan (*tepsija*) and accompanies every meal (except when the meal consists of *pita*, a savory filled pastry dish). Indeed people in the village felt they had not eaten if they had not had bread. The wife cuts pieces off the loaf and hands them out to those gathered around the *sofra-bošča* or *sinija* (a cloth laid on the floor on which the meal is served or a low round table), then sets the bread down next to herself within easy reach. After making sure everybody has got their share she puts it away, only to bring it out again when a person wants more. In this way she looks after the physical well-being of her family and household members. Likewise as wife and mother she is often the person in the house who feels responsible for the spiritual well-being of household members. She encourages her husband to go to the mosque on Fridays if he does not work that day, and it is her responsibility to make sure the children go to mosque school. She is also active in ritual and devotional practices which provide spiritual support to dead relatives, as well as others who seek to provide for the health and well-being of her family and household members.

In chapter three I noted that if a mother has to leave her house before the end of her forty days of confinement after she has given birth, she should bring with her a *tespih* (rosary) from the house to protect her from malevolent spirits or *sihir* (sorcery). The *tespih* is imbued with the spiritual power of an endless number of prayers by members of the house, and is therefore a powerful symbol of her belonging to the moral and Muslim community of the house. When the bride carries the Qur'an which belongs to the *kuća* and is used by its members, into her new household the symbolism is the same: it serves as a reminder of her moral and spiritual responsibilities as future wife and mother, and the hope that she will represent the morality of the *kuća*. Although most brides only see the act as "one of those traditions" it nevertheless reminds them of who they are, namely Muslims, and that the source of this identity is Islam. In other words it is a potent symbol of the Islamic heritage of the *kuća*. The Qur'an should be the moral foundation of the *kuća* and ensure its members' happiness and prosperity.

This chapter will discuss the Islamic dimension in the lives of Dolina's Muslims from the point of view of the *kuća* and focus, in particular, on the role of women. It will examine some aspects of the role Islam played in everyday life prior to the war as the main constitutive element in a Bosnian Muslim identity of which women were the custodians. It will discuss how Islam was practiced and how its moral content was interpreted and expressed in rural central Bosnia. The last chapter of the book will focus on who communicated Islamic doctrines and knowledge locally and how this was received and made use of locally by the Muslims in Dolina.

Different members of the *kuća* are involved in different kinds of religious activities and devotional practices. Some of these involve the mosque, others take place in the house, while others again are focused around sufi lodges or Muslim shrines. Householders' involvement and practice also vary greatly both within the *kuća* and between different *kućas*. Although I was told that "in villages everybody believes" (that is, unlike cities where "atheists," a term villagers used as synonymous with communists, were believed to be dominant), the degree of devotion and religiosity varies from family to family and from individual to individual. People judged others' devotion in terms of how dutifully they fulfilled prescribed Islamic practices. The emphasis was thus on practice rather than on personal conviction and belief. After having spent some time in the village it also became clear to me that women were generally more dutiful than men in their observance of religious festivals (although this was not true for older men). Indeed, in this chapter I hope to show that the woman as wife and mother plays an important role in caring for both the living and the dead, and that the most frequently performed religious ritual other than the daily prayers, namely the *tevhid* (prayers for the dead), attended and performed by women, takes place in the house. Muslims in the village understood religious practices mainly in terms of acts that please God. They were less concerned with the categorization of religious acts according to *shari'at*.

## Seeking Blessing and Earning Merit

In the anthropological literature on Islam, it has been noted that Islam is better described as a religion of "orthopraxy" than of "orthodoxy," that authoritative uniform practice is more important than authoritative uniform interpretation of the texts, since interpretations of the texts vary greatly. However, the term "orthopraxy" is problematic too, for again there are significant differences among Muslims in the practice of Islam (Eickelman and Piscatori 1990:19). According to the Hanafi school of Sunni Islam (to which Bosnian Muslims belong), there are seven categories of ritual action varying from *farz* (practices that God has commanded and that all believers must therefore perform, as for example the fast, one of the "five pillars") to *haram* (that which is forbidden). Of these categories, Dolina Muslims would know about the first and the last, *farz* and *haram*; a few would also know about *sunnet* (what the Prophet said and did, which provides an example for all Muslims) and *mekruh* (hated by God, but not forbidden, such as divorce).

However, a different categorization was used in Dolina (not only by the villagers, but also by Islamic instructors when talking to Muslims in the village). Muslims in Bosnia divide Islamic practices into two broad categories. They distinguish that which is *propisano* (prescribed, according to the law) and *obavezno* (obligatory) on the one hand and that which is *lijep* (beautiful) and of *dobra volja* (goodwill) on the other. In trying to help me make sense of practiced Islam in Bosnia a learned local *hodža* pointed out: "In Islam you have a set of rules about what you must do, what is prescribed (*propisano*); customs that come in addition are voluntary (*dobrovoljan*, of goodwill) and these are the ones which vary and which Muslims disagree about." The *dženaza* or burial ceremony and the month-long fast are examples of the former, while *tevhid* and prayers for the souls of the dead are examples of the latter.

The categorization of some practices, however, was the subject of debate among the Muslims. *Sevap* (a Turkish word) is widely used to describe any act which is considered meritorious because it pleases God. *Sevap* is religious merit which will be counted on the day of judgment at a person's death. Some of the acts which earn *sevap* have not been specified and formally evaluated within Islam and it is thus left to people themselves to decide what they are and whether to perform them. Picking up pebbles from the path and throwing them to the side, helping an old woman to carry a heavy load, or cleaning the mosque are some examples of actions which were considered *sevap* by Muslims in Dolina. Nevertheless, many Muslims also thought of prescribed acts such as the month-long fast in terms of *sevap*. While the *obavezna-dobra volja* distinction can only categorize ritual actions performed by Muslims, Christians too can perform some acts of *sevap*, although Dolina Muslims disagreed about whether such acts would help a Christian in the afterlife. Thus, when I expressed a wish to fast during Ramadan I was told that it was not "obligatory" for me but that it would be *sevap*. I was told too that it was *sevap* for me when I joined the women in cleaning the mosque. Thus, to a limited extent a non-Muslim can also partake in the Muslim moral community, without converting, by earning *sevap*.

Performing acts which earn *sevap* is believed to increase the chances of a good life in the other world. A person can also earn *sevap* on behalf of someone else and thereby also for him—or herself (for instance by saying prayers at *tevhid*). Other devotional acts were performed for divine blessing or *berićet* (often known by the Arabic term *baraka* in the literature on Islam) in this life (such as *mevlud* and praying at Muslim shrines). Blessing can be actively sought, as for instance by visiting Muslim shrines, or it may be an aspect of regular devotional practices. Blessing was understood as rewards in this life (as opposed to rewards in the afterlife). However, there was often a semantic overlap between earning religious merit for the afterlife (*sevap*) and seeking blessing in this life (*berićet*). Sometimes the two were thought of as aspects of the same act. Seeking blessing and earning religious merit, in other words, were not

mutually exclusive motivations. An act such as lighting a candle at a
Muslim shrine was thought of both in terms of earning *sevap* and of
increasing one's good fortune in this life.

In the village, people often saw success (especially material) as proof
and result of a *kuća*'s devoutness (demonstrated in the frequency of
devotional practices and prayers). Thus, the people in Dolina often ascribed their poverty to generally weak "faith" in the village (which comment when made by women was also an implicit criticism of men wast-
ing money on alcohol and feasting). A comparison was sometimes
drawn with villages north of Dolina where peoples' material living standards were considered higher, which some villagers believed to be the
result of their devoutness. (Others, however, would make the point that
people there worked more, had more money, and thus could "display"
their religiosity through lavish rituals such as *mevlud*.) To illustrate this
point further: on one occasion a woman who had been to Germany to
visit her Bosnian Muslim brother-in-law told women at a coffee-visit
about the prosperity she had seen (exemplified for her by the ten different kinds of bread in the shops). There, she explained, everybody believes in God. (It is interesting to note that the perceived connection
between faith, prayers, and good fortune, or blessing, was to this speaker
also valid for Christians.)

Generally, when things went wrong in the village they were explained
by lack of faith and devotion assessed on the basis of observed practice.
Thus, the women assessed the drought and consequent bad harvest one
year as follows: "The harvest has become as damaged (*pokvaren*) [a
word which has the connotation of being morally corrupt] as people
have; nowhere is there prayer to God." Traditionally, when there was a
drought women held prayers (*dove*) at the three holy graves in Dolina.
They had not yet held prayers for rain and when I asked why, they said
they were unsure whether it would work or not because "here people
have weak faith." In other words, the Muslim community in the village
had not earned enough religious merit for itself to be deserving of divine
blessing.

The intensity of religious activities in the village was not constant, but
changed according to the ritual calendar. In addition to the prescribed
five daily prayers, there were some major annual ceremonies, of which
the most important are *Ramazan* (Ramadan), *Ramazanski-bajram* (celebrating the end of Ramadan), *Kurban-bajram* (or *Hadžijski-bajram*)
two months and ten days later, and the autumn *mevlud* celebrating the
birth of the Prophet Mohammad. The Muslim new year was not celebrated in the village (but I did hear of some urban, devout families who
celebrated it); nor was the *hašure* (a celebration on the tenth of
*Muharem*, the first month of the Islamic calendar), which most villagers

did not consider a part of their traditional or ritual calendar.[2] Other rituals which occurred at various times throughout the year were *tevhid* (congregational prayers for the dead), *dženaza* (burial ceremony), and *mevlud* (in connection with life-cycle celebrations, or other happy events such as the opening of a new mosque). Most of these rituals required services in the mosque, although the most frequently held rituals were *tevhid*s and *mevlud*s which were typically held in private homes.

In both the literature on Islam and Christianity ritual religious practices have often been classified into those performed by women and those performed by men, the former being private and nonofficial, the latter formal, public, and official. However, this division has been challenged both by anthropologists focusing on Christian societies and those studying Islamic ones (Stewart 1991; Tapper and Tapper 1987). This study of Islam in Bosnia is another critique of such rigid categorization and understanding of how religious practices relate to gender. Ritual activities in Dolina can be divided analytically into those activities or rituals that are performed by both men and women, those performed exclusively by men, and those performed exclusively by women. Such categorization will cut across other dimensions as well, so that rituals performed by men are not necessarily concomitant with rituals that are more "orthodox" and "official" in form (Tapper and Tapper 1987).

During my stay in the village some of the prescribed key Islamic rituals, such as Ramadan, were mainly performed and observed by the women. However, some Islamic rituals are "obligatory" for men only and these are all associated with the mosque. Men's obligations include attending the Friday prayers (džuma), any burial ceremony or *dženaza*, and the morning prayer at Bajram marking the end of the month of fasting. In addition they should attend the organizational meetings of the village mosque council. The younger men and women who did not observe daily prayers or the Ramadan fast, might occasionally attend a special religious celebration (such as a *mevlud*) and would never eat pork (although my Catholic friends in the village liked to refer to one young Muslim man who they claimed liked pork and ate it in secret). In the village nonobservance did not, however, imply that people were nonbelievers (and communists).

State officials from outside the village were, however, perceived differently. Their position in the state apparatus implied that they were communist party members. Villagers therefore also assumed that they were atheists. The relationship between being a Muslim and a communist (and atheist) was problematic to many of the Muslims in Dolina despite the official "Yugoslav" definition of Muslim according to which the Muslim *narod* was a nonreligious category and a member of such a *narod* could call him- or herself a "Muslim" and be both a communist and an atheist. Indeed, to most of the Muslim villagers I knew a Muslim was necessarily a believer, although he or she did not have to be devout or regularly observant. To be a communist and a nonbeliever was therefore in some ways to be like a member of a fourth Bosnian nationality (in addition to Serb, Croat, and Muslim).[3]

An incident which took place in a nearby village may be related to emphasize this point. When a local woman, a lawyer at court in town, attended the burial ceremony of a neighbor and colleague at the mosque during a visit to her village, there was strong resentment among some of the locals. First a woman should not be attending a Muslim burial, as only men do so (unless she is a Christian honoring a dead relative, neighbor, or friend in accordance with her own customs). Second, it appeared, most importantly, that she was a communist party member and therefore supposedly an atheist whose presence was not only blasphemous to the Muslims, but also disapproved of by the state. From the villagers' point of view this woman was seen to be breaking two kinds of laws: that of the state which she represented, and God's. Their message was clear: this woman could not both hold a respected job within the state apparatus which a believer could not hold, and attend a ceremony given by believers who may have had to relinquish privileges which she as a member of the party enjoyed.

However, this did not mean that individuals from Muslim families and with Muslim names who were declared communists were not perceived as "Muslim." But in the village they were at least understood as belonging to a different category of "Muslim." Early on during my stay in the village, I asked one of my neighbors whether the head of the village committee (appointed by the council, part of the state administration and therefore of the party structure) was a Muslim. Yes, she answered, but added disapprovingly, he is a communist. Even this so-called communist, however, occasionally wrote charms with Qur'anic verses in Arabic for his Muslim neighbors. Her disapproval, related perhaps not primarily to the fact that he was a nonbeliever (which he was obviously not) but to the fact that he was a representative of the state, and of the kind of administrative authorities villagers usually hoped to avoid, unless there was some benefit to be drawn from such contact. Within the village itself some Muslims were seen as more devout (*pobožni*) than others, but there was no categorization of people as believer or nonbeliever. "Not praying" did not imply "not believing," since not to be praying was not necessarily a constant in people's lives but only true for certain periods in their lives, often connected to their life cycle.

Men typically became more observant as they grew old and retired from work. This was partly as a preparation for death, making up for the lack of observance in younger years, but also related to the fact that with retirement men could observe the prayer times and attend services in the mosque regularly, which was impossible for them as long as they were participants in the secular (and "Yugoslav") public workplace. As men retired they became more like women, walking around the village, visiting neighbors, and observing the fast and the daily prayers.

Ramadan, the month-long fast (called *ramazan* in Bosnian), is considered the main event in the Muslim ritual calendar. As one of the codified rituals in Islam, the fast is both an individual statement of one's personal commitment (as a believer, *vjernik*), and an affirmation of Muslim unity and identity. It is also a period of the most intense devotional activity centered in the mosque, and of socializing in people's houses. It is believed that any good deed performed during Ramadan earns the person double *sevap*. Keeping the fast in itself is, however, thought of in terms of both *berićet* and *sevap*.

In Dolina the fast was kept mainly by the women. While a man who did not fast was readily excused by the women who did (for example, by referring to how hard he was working), a woman who did not keep it was criticized on moral grounds (unless she was menstruating, ill, or pregnant). A commonly held opinion among Muslim men in the village was that the fast was for those (i.e., women and old retired men) who had the time and did not have to work so hard. Women often found it upsetting that while they were fasting, they still had to cook for their husbands and sons and were also expected to work next to them on the land if Ramadan fell at a time of year when agricultural work had to be done. Even then they would hear the men say: "Let those fast who have got time for it." Many *hodžas* criticized this attitude ("many of our people think fasting is only the responsibility of those who do not have to work so hard"), and challenged it by voicing their admiration for the Muslims in the Middle East who fast in the heat and still work.

Despite their own problems, women would often excuse their husbands by explaining that they did not fast because they had to go to work in the factory or firm, and "they cannot manage to go hungry." One evening a couple had a rather typical dispute during Ramadan. The quarrel started when the wife urged her husband to come along for evening prayers in the mosque. It then developed into a row about past events during their twenty-year-old marriage, the husband asking his wife angrily why she had not married a *hodža* if that was what she wanted. He then summed up his miseries: "I am in pain, I am cold, I have had no coffee all day, and it is Ramadan and I may not drink brandy."[4] The women widely acknowledge that Ramadan is a particularly difficult time for men. Women with legitimate reason, do not meet their demands as usual (for instance, the men are not served coffee whenever they want) since they are fasting and have less energy. Furthermore, because the women are fasting they hold the moral high ground. During Ramadan I found that relations between spouses deteriorated. Nevertheless, some women would insist that men could also fast if they really wanted to, and that the point was rather that in Dolina the men are "no good" (*ne valjaju*). Some women referred to men they knew who worked and still fasted through the whole of Ramadan. Often these were men who worked in private firms where the adjustments for fasting were less complicated to make than for men who worked in public firms. In a public workplace like a factory, the facilities for somebody who fasts (and prays) were poor.[5]

Despite its hardships the fasting month may nevertheless be a period the women look forward to; the usual routines of cooking and work are broken and they are entitled to more rest. They attend congregational prayers in the mosque more often: a legitimate activity away from household chores and the demands of grumbling men. During this month people also socialize more intensely. For all households where at least one member is fasting it is indeed an extraordinary month. After sunset when the fast is broken neighbors invite each other *na iftar* (the evening meal with which the fast is broken). When the lights are turned on in the mosque everybody sits down to eat; the food is better and richer than usual, and there is always a dessert (which is uncommon at daily meals). Those families who do not have a view of the minaret from their house will send a child out to where the lights can be seen and he will report back. Others may follow the *takvim* (the lunar calendar which shows the times for prayer and for sunset and dawn throughout the year) and the announcements on the radio. The last fifteen minutes or so before the fast may be broken are often tense. When the lights are eventually turned on, there is a sigh of relief both from those who fast and those who do not: the latter will have had to wait a long day for a proper meal.

The keeping of the fast distinguishes not only "those who have time" from "those who do not," but also those Muslims who are devout or believers (*pobožni, vjernici*) from those who are not. (We remember that according to a Bosnian notion of "Muslim," a person may well be a "Muslim" as indicated by his name but may not adhere to the Islamic faith or practice his religion.) A nineteen-year-old girl gave this explanation for fasting: "I fast because it is a *sevap*.[6] I believe in God, and I believe he will love me more if I fast, because he likes it. It is a good thing to do. But there are those who never fast, for instance my next-door neighbor: she has never fasted or done anything which shows that she believes in God." (This girl was one of the few girls who fasted, as the fast was mainly kept by married women.) A woman in her mid-thirties commented: "I believe in God, as you must have noticed, and this belief comes from the heart. Look at how sick I felt yesterday because of fasting, and today my body feels heavy and I have difficulty in walking. But if anybody told me that it is not possible to fast, I would say that it is a load of rubbish; it all depends on your wish and your will, and I wish very strongly to fast."

We see from both these comments that the strength of belief is confirmed through visible religious acts and other Muslims' judgment of these acts. The girl also mentioned that the fast was an act seen by God as well as covillagers. It often seemed, however, at least in the short term, that it was more important that the act (here the fast) be seen by covillagers, both fellow Muslims and non-Muslims. It is nevertheless accepted that some find the fasting physically and mentally unbearable. One older woman said that she never fasted, though she had tried several times. She had always cried and cried, and in the end had gone to see the doctor who had given her legitimate medical reasons for not fasting. It was not uncommon for women who found the fast difficult to sustain to visit the doctor and then take a couple of days' break, allegedly on the doctor's advice, while still officially fasting. An old, devout Muslim would say that there are two categories of Muslims: "those who cannot [like the woman who cried all the time] and those who will not." To him the show of will was the essential factor.

In addition to being a way in which a person could express her devoutness and earn *sevap*, the fast was also a collective ritual for expressing the unity of the Muslim community vis-à-vis non-Muslims. This aspect was particularly stressed by many *hodžas* throughout Ramadan. In Bosnia displaying the moral unity of the Muslim community at Ramadan took on an added dimension as a statement of Muslim *nacija* identity vis-à-vis the other non-Muslim Bosnian *nacije*. This was made quite explicit in a speech by one *hodža* at the collective prayers in the mosque during Ramadan (*teravija*). At these prayers which were very well attended compared to prayers at other times through the year, it was customary for the *hodža* to give a sermon on a moral issue. One evening, he told a story to illustrate the importance of keeping the fast. It was a story about two neighbors. The first man was a very rich Serb who had a beautiful daughter, the other was a poor Muslim. One day the Serb offered the Muslim his daughter and as many possessions as the Muslim wanted, if only the Muslim would convert to the Serbian faith. But the Muslim replied proudly: "One minute of my Ramadan fast is more valuable than your daughter and all your possessions put together." The story is an allegory which says that Muslim identity, seen as spiritual possession, is more valuable than material possessions and the economic advantage implied in giving up this identity. This statement is particularly mean-

ingful in the context of the communist Yugoslav state where membership of the ruling communist party, which was considered to be Serb-
dominated and which implicitly required a denial of one's Islam-based
Muslim identity, was in practice a prerequisite for career and material
advancement.

However, there is yet another aspect of moral unity displayed at another level by observing the fast, which sums up the importance of at
least one member of a household (usually the woman) observing the fast
and other prescribed Islamic practices. I started this chapter by pointing
out the symbolism in the bride being given the Qur'an by her mother-
in-law to carry over the threshold into her new *kuća*. While it was rare
for all members of the *kuća* to keep the fast, it was nevertheless important that the moral unity of the *kuća* be presented to the outside world
(beyond family and immediate neighbors, although what was defined as
"outside" varied with context). It was often more important to display
such unity to Muslims than to non-Muslims since only the former could
judge a Muslim household according to their common value system,
and appreciate the moral implications of observance. It is in line with an
argument I made earlier that it was the woman and wife who often felt
responsible for presenting the moral unity of the *kuća* to the outside
world, that she kept the fast not only for her own *sevap* but for that of
her household as whole. In addition, by observing prescribed Islamic
duties such as the fast and thereby honoring what is uniquely Muslim,
the household gains the respect of fellow Muslim friends, neighbors,
and others.

The following story illustrates this point: In one household the
daughter-in-law had returned from hospital with her newborn son, and
I had gone to visit with a neighbor. The young mother and her parents-
in-law were present. Since it was Ramadan, coffee and cakes were not
automatically served, as would normally be done to celebrate the happy
event. However, the hostess (who was fasting) asked me if I would like
coffee. When I said that was not necessary, she suggested that I have a
cup with her husband (who was retired), thus implying that he was not
fasting. Instead, she made lemonade and served her husband and me.
Soon we heard a car stop outside the house, whereupon the hostess hur-
riedly removed the empty glasses from the table and the husband went
out to greet the guests. He returned with a young man (the best man
[*kum*] of the oldest son in the house) and his three-year-old son. The
new guest was asked if he would like lemonade, but the hostess added,
"Maybe you are fasting?" The young man answered: "For the little one,
but not for me, thank you." She again asked him if he was fasting, but
he only smiled without saying a word. The hostess told him she would
make him one as well and that there was no reason to be ashamed: "If

you do not fast, you do not fast and that is all." She then decided to make coffee as well, which she served the guest and me, but not her husband! It was apparently important to give the outside guest the impression that everybody in the household was fasting. It would have been shameful for the host and senior representative of the household to disclose his (and thereby the *kuća*'s) nonobservance to the guest.

As one of the five pillars and a key event in the Islamic ritual calendar, Ramadan sums up the role of practiced Islam in Muslim identity formation in Bosnia. First, it is an individual expression of faith and devoutness; second, it is concerned with earning *sevap* and seeking blessing for oneself and one's household members; third, it serves to display the moral unity of the household; and fourth, as a practice which is uniquely Muslim it serves as a vehicle for the expression of a distinctive Muslim *nacija* identity vis-à-vis other non-Muslim Bosnians.

## Caring for the Living

One of the most prestigious devotional rituals which is not "obligatory" but was described as "beautiful" and of "goodwill" by the local *hodža* is *mevlud*. A *mevlud* is specifically held in celebration of the birth of the Prophet Mohammad. However, it is also held in association with other happy events which celebrate life and for blessing. By hosting this ritual a household gains religious merit primarily in terms of blessing, though women also referred to *mevlud* as giving *sevap*. In addition, however, hosting a *mevlud* raises one's prestige in the local community. When held in private homes, the *mevlud* is given both in the spirit of Islam and in the spirit of Bosnian hospitality (which among other things means lavish meals). It is an occasion when a *kuća* can display its socioeconomic status and gain both moral and material standing in the eyes of others. There are two kinds of *mevlud*: the annual celebration of the birth of the Prophet Mohammad (on the twelfth of *Rebiul-Evvela* on the Islamic calendar) held in the mosque, and those held throughout the year in private homes. A *mevlud* consists of prayers and the chanting of specific *mevlud* poems praising the birth and life of the Prophet. A *hodža* put it this way: "People decide that instead of having a big feast where there is a lot of drinking, they will do something that pleases God." By phrasing it like this, the *hodža* was implicitly drawing a contrast to the way non-believers and non-devout Muslims customarily celebrate similar events.

A household may decide to hold a *mevlud* for various reasons: to celebrate the birth of a new family member, whether a son or a daughter; when moving into a new house, so that Allah will bless it; in connection with a marriage ceremony conducted according to Islamic law or *shari'at* (*šerijatsko vjenčanje*); or when a son is leaving for the army (I had the impression that this was the most common reason for holding *mevlud*s in the region during my stay). A *mevlud* may also be given in conjunction with a *tevhid* on the fortieth day after death (when the soul is believed to leave the body, therefore a celebratory event). This is clearly different from what Tapper and Tapper (1987) report for Turkish Islam, where the *mevlud* (especially the one for and by women) held on an occasion associated with death seems to display more of the traits characteristic of the women's *tevhid* in Bosnia.

*Mevlud* is usually attended by both men and women and is led by one or more *hodža*s. The exceptions are those held within the dervish milieu attended exclusively by men (dervishes and *hodža*s). However, I also attended a *mevlud* in one of the market towns which was for and by women and sponsored by a well-known Muslim family of the devout urban elite. It was attended by several *bula*s (female religious instructor), including one from Sarajevo who was leading it. The *bula*s are female relatives of the household and members of other spiritual elite families. This *mevlud* distinguished itself markedly in form from the women's *tevhid*s and a *mevlud* I had earlier attended in a village. In fact it displayed several of the traits the Tappers describe for the *mevlud* in a Turkish market town; there was an emphasis on didactics and on preaching and the *bula* leading it was overtly emotional during the performance. My companions from the village felt awkward and embarrassed at this *mevlud*, in part because of the apparent socioeconomic distance between them and most of the other guests, but most significantly because of the display of such religiosity. A *hodža* familiar with the region told me there were no particular rules for *mevlud* and that "everybody has their own traditions" (for example, the dervishes shout more and louder *Allah illalah*s). He claimed, furthermore, that there was no difference between the texts used in men's and women's *mevlud*, and that women's *mevlud*s do not have any particular characteristics that distinguish them from men's. It became clear, however, that although there was no difference in the specific texts used (as reported for *mevlud* in Turkey, see Tapper and Tapper 1987), there was more emphasis on didactics and emotional preaching in this urban style *mevlud* than in mixed village *mevlud*s and those by and for men where the emphasis is on the performance of texts.

More prosperous households or members of the Muslim religious elite often give a *mevlud* annually. Prestige is gained by inviting a large number of guests, especially if some of them are well-known Islamic reciters and leaders, and also by being able to pay for several *hodža*s (or *bula*s) to recite. Those who were invited from the major towns in the region would be of higher status than ordinary village *hodža*s (or *bula*s).

The amount and quality of food is a final source of prestige. A couple of families in the region were famous in the village for their sumptuous annual *mevlud*s. (One local family was trying very hard to be included in the elite. It had a high living standard based on money earned in Germany, but did not belong to the traditional elite, and was possibly still not quite accepted by them, although covillagers considered it more "cultured.")

Compared to the *mevlud*s given by religious families of the urban elite, a village *mevlud* was a more modest affair; the participants would be local *hodža*s and the guests and relatives of the host household. A private *mevlud* was never held during my stay in the village (though there was a children's *mevlud* in the mosque), but I had the opportunity to attend one in a neighboring village given by the family of a relative by marriage of the household in which I was staying. This was a combined *tevhid* and *mevlud* held in honor of the deceased male head of the household. *Tevhid* was held first, with *mevlud* following immediately afterward. Three *hodža*s recited as well as a number of lay people. This was a relatively small *mevlud*, reflecting the economic situation of the family. Well-to-do families may invite ten or more *hodža*s to recite, and a large number of guests. *Mevlud*s seem to have been held more rarely in the village where I was staying than in other villages like it, though this may have been mere coincidence, as I did hear about *mevlud*s that had been held before my arrival. I suspect, however, that the picture I received is representative. To hold a *mevlud* is an expensive affair: food should be abundant, and the *hodža*s who are invited to recite should receive their *sergija* (donation of money). A *mevlud* needs to be planned a long time in advance, maybe as much as a year, and it is crucial to save money. As already mentioned, *mevlud* is characterized as a "voluntary" and "beautiful" devotional practice sponsored by a household for blessing, though at the same time it is a social event which allows a household to offer and display hospitality and gain the acknowledgment of neighbors and fellow Muslims. Members of a household may, however, also seek blessing for the living through other more personal venues by visiting Muslim shrines. Such visits are usually motivated by the need for blessing and help in connection with specific personal events or problems.

## Prayers at Muslim Shrines

The specific tradition in practiced and lived Islam whereby a person's prayers to God via a mediator (a *šehit*, *hodža*, or *bula*) are believed to be more powerful than his or her direct prayers is found throughout the Islamic world and is particularly pronounced in what has been glossed as "saints' cults" in much of the literature.[7] The "cult of saints" is a pan-

Islamic phenomenon but as Gaborieau notes, "The cult of the saints . . . forms part of those non-obligatory devotions in which a great freedom of choice is left to individuals or groups" (1983:305). In Bosnia this cult has its own coloring.

Through the annual *dova* for rain, when women pray collectively to ensure a fertile soil and a rich crop, they seek blessing not only for their own households, but for the village community as a whole. (In Bosnian *dova* is usually a generic term for "prayers," but it also means prayers other than the obligatory *namaz* where the wording is prescribed and in Arabic.) The prayers for rain are said at the same site as the annual *tevhid* (see below), by the *turbe* (a small mausoleum of a *šehit* or Muslim martyr; a *turbe* can also be the mausoleum of an *evlija* or Muslim saint), as well as at two other *šehit*s' graves in the village. Prayers for rain are said throughout Bosnia-Hercegovina and are often held at a *turbe* or at *šehit*s' graves which may happen to be near what are believed to be Bogomil tombs (see chapter one).[8]

Every spring in Dolina there were prayers for rain at the three different *šehit*s' graves in the village. It was usually said that the event took place only in cases of severe drought, but in practice it seems to have been held annually anyway, to prevent drought later on in the summer. It should be held on the seventh Tuesday after *Jurjev* (a traditional spring celebration described in chapter six). In Dolina it was attended exclusively by women and the prayers were led by the local *bula*.[9] While the *bula* recites and says prayers, the participants hold their hands flat out toward the ground to illustrate rain falling. It is significant that the prayers for rain, which are clearly a fertility ritual, should be the concern of women.

The annual *dova* for the dead or *tevhid* (which will be dealt with at length in a later section) was also held at the same site, on a Tuesday, four weeks after *Jurjev* (while the *dova* for rain was held on the seventh Tuesday after *Jurjev*). This annual *dova* (like the prayers for rain) was attended and organized by women only. Unlike individual worship at the *turbe* on other occasions, these prayers were specifically devoted to the dead. The *šehit* (from the Arabic *shahid*) was seen to mediate between the women, their dead relatives, and God. Women came from surrounding villages, but also from further away. If they had relatives in Dolina they would stay the night. It was an occasion for which women prepared lots of food and expected to play host to many visiting relatives, in-laws, and friends.

On the day of the *dova* women gathered in great numbers at the small hill near the *turbe*. Several *bula*s would lead groups of women in prayers around the large *tespih* (prayer beads) typical of female *tevhid*s. At one stage women also entered the *turbe* to pray individually for blessing. On

10. Women gathered for *dova* at the *turbe*.

their way out they would leave money in the *turbe* for its maintenance; this is believed to be *sevap*. Later in the evening there was a fair with dance, food, and music on a field not far from the *turbe*. Both this *turbe* and the two other *šehits*' graves are close to the so-called Bogomil burial grounds and their *stećak* (see chapter one). At the *dova* some women would go to the most well-known *stećak* in Dolina "for *fajda*" (benefit; note that this is different from the word *berićet*, also of Turkish origin, used in connection with seeking help or "blessing" from Islamic shrines). They would stroke the stone and then touch their faces while saying prayers. Dolina women did not believe that this had any beneficial effect. An old woman born in Dolina said that she had never seen any of their women doing it; she was from the place and knew that there was no point to the practice.

The *turbe* in the village was visited individually at other times when no collective prayers were taking place. There are many such holy tombs throughout Bosnia-Hercegovina and they are all visited by people who need help and strength to tackle particular life crises, such as infertility or an illness in the family. The *turbe* is a place to pray to gain strength and perhaps increase the chances of a favorable outcome by asking the pious dead to mediate on a person's behalf. Because of their piety during their lifetimes (in the case of *evlije*) and their heroic deaths and martyrdom (in the case of *šehits*) the dead are believed to be closer to God and in a position to mediate on behalf of the living. This particular role of the *šehit* is characteristic of the sufi-influenced region of central Bosnia but in this respect the holy graves are clearly comparable with saints' shrines of North Africa, the Middle East, and South Asia (see, among others, Gellner 1969; Eickelman 1976; Gaborieau 1983). Although the visiting is done primarily by women, they often do so on behalf of other members of the family.

In Islam a *šehit* is defined as a man (or woman) who died "innocently" in the fight for his or her religion; a Muslim martyr whose death is considered heroic. His/her identity is often unknown. Because of his heroic death "for the faith" a *šehit* is secured a place in heaven. The villagers seemed to define *šehit* more broadly as any Muslim who had been innocently killed or had suffered a violent or tragic death. They told me that a *šehit* is a particularly "good man" or *evlija* (from the Arabic *waliyya*, saint), and that the corpse of a *šehit* does not decompose. There are also other shrines of "good men" or *evlija* who are not referred to as *šehit*s and there are *šehit*s who are not necessarily considered *evlija*. Some people therefore prefer to pray at what they consider to be the even more powerful tombs of the pious men and known *evlija*. The most popular and supposedly the most powerful of these are buried at a sufi lodge in a nearby village. All such shrines are visited "for blessing" (*berićet*). There are several *šehit*s' graves in or near Dolina, three of them in the village itself. Most of them are fenced and have a headstone (*niša*) at both ends of the grave. (This is what distinguishes a *šehit*'s grave from an ordinary one. In recent years some wealthy men had evinced a desire to have a grave with a headstone at each end, resembling a *šehit*'s grave, but many villagers dismissed this as pretentious and "no good.") The stone at the head of the grave has a carved stone turban on its top. One of the Dolina graves, moreover, has a small square house built on top of it. This is called a *turbe* (mausoleum). The house is built of concrete and is painted white, resembling a miniature Bosnian Muslim dwelling. The miniature house used to be of wood, like the traditional *čardaklija* and the mosque, until it started to fall apart. Concrete was then used to replace it.

Inside the mausoleum is a sarcophagus covered with a green felt cloth and with headstones at each end. Unlike the headstones of most mens' graves, this one does not have a carved turban, but instead has cloth wrapped round it in the shape of a turban. The popular explanation for this is that this *šehit* was beheaded; it is said that he came walking with his head in his hands and asked to be buried in this particular spot. (Both the absence of a carved turban and this particular mythical explanation for it are common to several Muslim shrines throughout Bosnia-Hercegovina, as for instance the one at Buna in Hercegovina.) There are also prayer mats and *tespih*s in the *turbe* available for anybody who comes to pray. On the wall is a framed scripture which, I was told, somebody from Sarajevo once tried to interpret, but apparently without success.

This *turbe* was being looked after by a woman who lived nearby and who had inherited her duty from her mother-in-law. (She would eventually have handed it down to her daughter-in-law had the family not been expelled during the war.) In theory, the caretaking duties were passed down through the male line of the family who owned the land where the *šehit* died; in practice, however, they went from mother-in-law to daughter-in-law. This family claims that three brothers were killed on their land, hence the three graves in Dolina itself; others say there were seven (including the *šehit*s' graves in surrounding villages). However, this myth is typical of all *šehit*s' graves. The popular story is usually that if several *šehit*s are buried within an area, they were brothers. (The original meaning may well be that they were brothers in the faith.)[10] The woman who had been looking after the *turbe* for more than fifty years, explained that it is *sevap* to light a candle every night at the sunset prayers (*akšam*), but that Thursday night (on the eve of Friday, said to be the day the Qur'an was revealed to the Prophet) and Sunday night (on the eve of Monday, said to be the day of the Prophet Mohammad's birth) and all nights during Ramadan are the most important. On those nights, more candles than usual are lit. Sometimes (if the woman was asked), water was carried in a *bardak* (traditional water jug) and left overnight in the *turbe*. This water is believed to have healing properties and is rubbed into the body or drunk during illness. The woman who looked after the *turbe* told me that once a man had come to the *turbe* every day for fifteen days and left water overnight to help his wife who was ill.

Before a person enters the *turbe* s/he prays for health and good fortune; once inside, s/he lights two or three candles while saying prayers. When entering a *turbe*, a person should always enter with the right foot first, and make sure s/he does not turn his or her back toward the tomb when leaving. Some will take the melted wax from the candles home with them, remelt it, and use it for healing.

The other two graves in Dolina belong to "smaller *šehit*s," and have no mausoleum over them. They are nevertheless conspicuous for their headstones at both ends and their fencing, as described above. At one time people were afraid to go to one of them, because the *šehit* was said to be angry. If anybody tried to enter the place where he was buried, a very strong wind would start to blow in the trees surrounding it. Some said he was angry because somebody had entered the place without *abdest* (that is, without ritual ablution before prayers, in which water is poured on parts of the body while reciting verses from the Qur'an) and was therefore unclean, others that an unclean (that is, menstruating) woman had entered. Some *šehit*s are known to be angrier than others, and not to allow "just anybody" (even if they are clean) to enter. This *šehit* only admitted the man who lit the candles. However, his anger only lasted a year and the following spring prayers for rain were said as usual. The other one was regularly seen to by the daughter living in the house closest to it. She explained to me that she went there to light candles, for two reasons: first, because the grave is on its own and nobody saw to him or worried about him (this is an interesting statement, given that Muslims do not attend to the graves of their relatives in the graveyard behind the mosque), and second, because it is *sevap*, and it might bring you happiness and good fortune. In other words, she did it both to earn *sevap* and for blessing in this life.

The local *hodža* explained that people went to pray at *šehit*s' graves because *šehit*s are considered to be closer to God and therefore to be possible mediators between human beings and God. He said: "Some people feel that they cannot always pray directly to God and therefore say their wishes through a *šehit*. They feel that the dead person [who as a *šehit* is secured a place in heaven, *dženet*] is in a better position to ask God for help. At such a grave someone has seen something no one else has seen. It is like a flame. The dead person, who we call *evlija*, possesses a special power which few possess; he sees and knows what you yourself do not realize. Because this is the way it is, is it not; some have the ability to see more than others?" In explaining what a *turbe* is, he drew a parallel with images and symbols of the socialist Yugoslav federal state: a *turbe* was like the memorials for fallen partisans in such places as Sutjeska.[11] *Šehit*s are Muslim heroes who, like the partisan heroes, died fighting for what they believed in (or so "history" claims), the first representing the Muslim and Islamic credo, the second the Yugoslav and Socialist one.

The dervish orders have their own holy graves, belonging to men of religious learning believed to be *evlija* because of extraordinary powers to "see" or to perform "miracles" in their lifetimes as well as after. Many of them were sheikhs, leaders of a sufi sanctuary or *tekija*. In the largest *tekija* in the mountains not far from Dolina are buried all the sheikhs in the history of the *tekija*. They are believed to have extraordinary powers, and people will come there to pray for health and good fortune in the same way as they do at *šehit*s' graves. But unlike the *šehit*s' graves, which are accessible to everybody who wants to pray, the sheikhs' graves can only be entered with special permission from a senior dervish.

Once a year, however, when the annual *mevlud* takes place at the *tekija*, there is general access. The same practice of praying at *šehit*s' tombs for health and good fortune may (before the war) be observed at the annual *mevlud* at the sufi lodge at Buna in Hercegovina (see chapter six). Before and after the recitals in the courtyard of the *tekija*, people enter the *tekija* to file past the tomb of its founding sheik; prayers are said for good fortune and health and money left on the tomb. Some believe that if they say prayers while touching the tomb and then that part of their body where they have pain, they will be healed. However, the organization of the *mevlud* had been taken over by the official Islamic Association in Sarajevo and, although the organization cashed in the money people left at the tomb, it did not approve of what it considered an ignorant healing practice not in the spirit of Islam. During one visit, a *hodža* pointed out an old woman to me who tried to touch it but was told not to by a guard nearby.

Most official Islamic literature explains the belief that special powers reside in a *šehit*'s or *evlija*'s tomb and the custom of praying at such tombs for health and good fortune in terms of pre-Islamic influences (Johnson 1980). Many of the urban Islamic leaders and instructors in Bosnia-Hercegovina were also critical of such practices, seeing them as the legacy of Christian, pre-Christian, or Bogomil influence (Hadžijahić 1977:84–86). However, the local *hodža* made it clear that while the custom of praying at *šehits*' graves is not prescribed (*propisano*), it is not against Islamic law either. But not all Islamic scholars agree with him. Many official *hodža*s condemn the use of intermediaries, together with the idea that the dead can be helped through prayers, as being of Christian inspiration. They argue that it is against Islam to assume that anyone can intervene between God and anyone dead or alive, since there is no hierarchy in Islam and no one can be assumed to be closer to God than anyone else. As already mentioned, however, visiting Muslim shrines for blessing is common throughout the Islamic world. Furthermore, when a person visits a *šehit*'s tomb for health or to ensure a happy outcome to a personal problem, the visit and the specific prayers have often been recommended or prescribed by one of several faith healers or diviners active in central Bosnia. These faith healers are seen as carriers of Islamic knowledge and therefore as mediators of religious power and blessing. Such carriers of a particular kind of Islamic knowledge will be dealt with in the next chapter which is concerned with those representatives of Islamic knowledge with whom Muslims in Dolina were in contact.

## Counteracting Negative Influences

Personal problems for which solutions were sought through divination and faith healing were commonly explained by "something having upset the person." Women explained a good many physical afflictions by saying "she has been upset" (*ona je se sekirala*). In so doing they made an explicit connection between mental and physical health. If women feel worn out they will complain that they are ill from worry (*od sekiranje*), or that they have been upset and are therefore not feeling well. These, they know, are afflictions which doctors at the health center cannot cure, and they are therefore the most common reason for seeking faith healers. The idea that physical discomfort or pain that doctors cannot diagnose is caused by some sort of psychological imbalance or lack of peace of mind is reflected in several popular beliefs which seek to identify how the pain was inflicted in cases where this is not immediately obvious. What causes a person to be upset (often expressed through headaches, fever, or similar pains) may have a less obvious and sinister source, since it may be the result of attacks by malevolent spirits, the casting of the evil eye, or *sihir* (sorcery).

I will deal with all three sources in turn. Some of the ways in which people (and particularly women) could be attacked by malevolent spirits were noted in chapter three. In the next sections we will look in more detail at the possible result of such attacks, and more specifically at the casting of spells. It is often a faith healer or *hodža* who identifies the source of a person's affliction. Sometimes people may identify it themselves, as most malevolent forces and the precautions to be taken against them are common knowledge.[12]

People are believed to be particularly vulnerable to attacks from malevolent spirits (called by the Arabic term *džin*) between sunset and dawn, when the cock crows, the most critical period being just at sunset. This is when bad spirits are roaming about, and they may enter a person in different ways. There are several different expressions used to describe the fact that a person has become ill as the result of an attack by malevolent spirits. When describing this phenomenon, informants used many different words, all of which translate as "malevolent spirit" or "devil." If they were asked to be more specific, the answer would usually be, "Who knows what it is?" People were always understandably vague or even contradictory when explaining the cause of events or the nature of the spiritual power. Nevertheless, two main expressions were used: *ograjisati* and *uhvatiti*. The latter means to seize or to take hold of, as in the phrase "something may take hold of you." The words were used as a warning against doing certain things: for instance, a woman or girl would be told not to go out after dark on her own or into the forest as something might seize hold of her. Only a *hodža*'s *zapis* (amulet) can protect a person against attacks by malevolent spirits.

The other expression, *ograjisati*, has no simple literal translation and requires some explanation. The villagers use it to express the bewitching of a person as a result of certain acts performed by him or her. It is a

word which does not exist in any dictionary, and my Sarajevan informants did not understand it. They suggested it was supposed to be *na-
gaziti* (*na urok*), which means to be bewitched, or alternatively *nagra-
jisati*, which means to get into trouble or to fare badly. It is believed that
a person may be "bewitched" by what most informants referred to as
"something," or more rarely as a "devilish brew," which may attach itself to breadcrumbs, nails, blood, wood chips, or rubbish which has
been left outdoors by humans. This stuff is believed to be used by sorcerers when making *sihir*. This devilish brew containing malevolent spirits may thus be transferred deliberately by sorcerers to people who are
thereby "poisoned." Again, a person is most vulnerable to such attacks
at *akšam* (sunset). If going out after sunset he or she should always say
*bismillah*,[13] as he or she may unknowingly step over rubbish of the type
described, left by humans on the ground where "agents of the devil"
gather. The best protection, however, is to wear a *zapis*.

Another source of physical and mental disequilibrium and pain is the
evil eye. This is a specific type of spell which in most cases is believed to
be unpremeditated. Beliefs about the evil eye are well known and documented throughout the whole of southern and southeastern Europe and
"the Mediterranean area" (both in Christian regions; see, for example,
Campbell 1964; du Boulay 1974; Herzfeld 1981; Stewart 1991 on
Greece, and the Islamic parts of these regions; see Delaney 1991 on
Turkey), the Middle and Near East and much of South Asia (for a review, see Maloney 1976). Such beliefs were also present in Dolina, even
if informants were initially reluctant to talk about them. Although most
of my material was collected in rural Bosnia, I also consulted informants
in Sarajevo about popular beliefs there and discovered that belief in the
evil eye and knowledge about different protective measures are also
found among Sarajevans. The more educated people in Sarajevo dismiss
such ideas as superstition, however.[14]

The villagers use several different terms for the "evil eye," the most
common being *grdne oči* (ugly eyes); others are *urokljive oči* (bewitching
eyes) or *pogane oči* (filthy or evil eyes). I was told that you cannot know
if someone has an evil eye or not, and even the possessor does not know.
A person may not know that s/he has been bewitched by the evil eye
until s/he gets ill with a splitting headache and fever.

If someone looks at another person and says that he or she is beautiful
without saying *mašalah*, the first person may unintentionally cast a spell
on the second person. *Mašalah* (see the poem in connection with the
building of a house in chapter two) expresses wonder at and pleasure in
what a person sees. In the original Arabic it means something like "what
God wants will be" (that is, everything is dependent on God's will).
Beautiful girls and babies are thought to be particularly vulnerable. A

warning sign that a girl may be a potential victim of the evil eye is the reddening of her face: it is believed that the red color causes a headache, and that it is the result of many people staring at her, and since "not all people's eyes are the same," she may be bewitched.

The word *mašalah* also refers to an amulet worn by a small child to protect him or her from spells, primarily the evil eye. Children are considered to be the most vulnerable of all, particularly if they cry a lot or are very beautiful. The original *mašalah* is a golden medallion on which is written *mašalah* in Arabic. But as these are expensive most villagers will attach small colorful plastic figures on the front of a baby's cap, or alternatively a red thread around his or her right leg and left wrist (or the other way around). Some people attach the small silver plate which is part of a horse's bridle to the front of the baby's cap. Whatever is used as a *mašalah*, it should be conspicuous in order to draw people's attention away from the child's eyes so that the "child's harmony is not upset." (The concept of personal harmony is an Islamic theme to which I shall return in a moment.)

To ease the discomfort of a child that cries a lot and is therefore suspected of reacting to the evil eye, the mother recites a verse while blowing air onto its face and then creating a star pattern by symbolically licking its face in three lines. The verse is in Turkish and means: "Dark, black eyes, blue and green eyes, spells fly back!" Thus no particular eye color is especially suspect, unlike other areas where blue and green eyes are particularly so. (Herzfeld argues for instance that that eye color which is uncommon in a region is particularly suspect as the "evil eye." This underscores his argument that evil eye accusations are indicative of the social marginality of the accused [1981:570]. In Bosnia, however, all three eye colors are common; evil eye accusations cannot therefore be indicative of social marginality.) The verse is repeated three times. There are also others, some in Bosnian, which express the same idea, telling the spells to go away and return to where they came from. One particular verse asks the spells to return to Romanija, a mountain area east of Sarajevo known as a Serbian nationalist stronghold.

The idea that babies, and those who are beautiful (particularly young girls) and fortunate are prone to attack by the evil eye is widely reported, as is the belief that casting the evil eye is often unintentional (see, e.g., Stewart 1991:233; Delaney 1991:65), in contrast to spells through sorcery which are premeditated. Although the different anthropological explanations also reflect the fact that people emphasize different symbolic aspects of belief in the evil eye in each ethnographic case, many anthropological analyses of the phenomenon focus mainly on explaining who and why people are accused of casting the evil eye (see, for instance, Herzfeld 1981). I suggest that this one-sided concern with the kind of person that casts the evil eye is misleading as it implies that beliefs about the evil eye are more or less the same phenomenon as sorcery. Important aspects of beliefs about the evil eye are therefore lost.

Herzfeld suggests that beliefs about the evil eye in a Rhodian village are one of many symbols of social marginality, as people accused of the evil eye are often incapable of conforming to the village's norms of social interaction (1981:570). In the Bosnian village of Dolina, I did not see evil eye accusations as a means of enforcing social control and conformity. Instead, the concern was with the person who was at risk from the evil eye, and with this person's power to attract another person's attention because of her beauty rather than with accusing someone of having "bewitching eyes" (since that person had probably cast the evil eye unintentionally). I have no information about actual people accused of having cast the evil eye, but was repeatedly told that there was no way of knowing who had. This is reflected among other things in the fact that the verb for casting spells, *ureći*, was never used actively in the third person to describe the agency, but only passively to describe the person who had been the victim of the evil eye, as in "the child has been cast spells on" (*djete je ureknuto*). The people most concerned about such spells are those closest to the person or object believed vulnerable to the evil eye, such as the mother of a newborn baby. I suggest that beliefs about the evil eye are primarily an expression of one's own fear of losing someone or something which one highly desires and which is therefore very precious. But because it is highly desired, the person who has it knows that others might desire it too. Scholars discussing evil eye beliefs stress that they express the fear of envy (and through envy jealousy) and its destructive powers (Maloney 1976; Campbell 1964; Stewart 1991:234). In Bosnia allusion was never made to the envy (or jealousy) of the potential possessor of the evil eye (although accusations of jealousy are often made to explain hostile and uncooperative behavior in other contexts), and envy was not seen as problematic as it was common and assumed from the knowledge and experience of one's own feelings. Of course, the attention paid for example to a beautiful girl may in itself arouse jealousy in others and present her with the problem of having to protect herself from such envy. More importantly, however, beliefs about the evil eye can tell us something about what individuals in a certain society value and desire as objects of social worth.

In the literature on Islamic mysticism, religious activities such as divination, healing, magic spells, and so forth are all labeled *sihr*. However, in Bosnia, *sihir*, which is the Bosnian spelling of the Arabic *sihr*, is only used for magic performed for an evil purpose. A *hodža* told me that *sihir* is knowledge which is not from God: it is evil and comes from hostility, and therefore God does not permit it. (By the same token, I was told that the various mystic activities performed by the sufis are never intended to cause anybody ill fortune.) The Muslim *hodžas* themselves are known to cast only love spells. (This is also what Catholics and Orthodox Serbs visited them for, as they have their own healing practices and remedies.) I was told that you could go to a certain *hodža* and ask him to make the person of your choice fall in love with you, or to influence a sweetheart or spouse to return if s/he had abandoned you. One informant told me that when she first arrived in her husband's home, her mother-in-law accused her of having had a *hodža* "*nešto napraviti*" (cast a spell on her son to make him fall in love with her). The mother-in-law was obviously concerned that her power to influence her son had weakened since he was now listening to his wife. Sexual attraction and love between a man and a woman were thus feared for their potential to subvert properly organized domestic relations. The alleged power of a *hodža* to cast love spells is the most talked about and is surrounded with the most myths.

The casting of spells may cause the victim suffering which only a *hodža* may remedy with a *zapis* (a charm with Qur'anic verses written in Arabic). *Sihir* is believed to be caused mainly by Serbian, especially female, sorcerers. Muslims believe they have the power to cast spells or use evil sorcery (*učiniti/napraviti sihir*). Several Muslims told me that they were wearing a *zapis* so that nobody would be able to "make something against" them. When I asked what this meant they said, "So that nobody can cause you evil." It took me a long time to find out who they thought would do this. When a good friend finally indicated to me that Serbian sorcerers were known to cast evil spells on people, including Muslims, I was intrigued. My informants stressed that Muslim sorcerers, on the other hand, would very rarely make *sihir*; if they did, they would not be real *hodžas*. A *hodža* (or *bula* through *saljevati stravu*) with knowledge of the Qur'an is the only person believed to have the powers to undo evil spells. One logical explanation as to why Serb sorcerers in particular (rather than Muslim or Catholic ones) are believed to cast evil spells could be that Muslims were more ambivalent about Orthodox Serbs than about Catholic Croats. This in turn is mainly due to historical factors: first, the Serbian orthodox church's close identification with the Serbian nationalist cause and its fervent anti-Islamic and anti-Muslim content and, second, Serbian nationalists' atrocities toward Bosnian Muslims during World War II, which had left the Muslims fearful of the Serbs' capacity for evil.

It is significant therefore that Muslims believe that their personal names may protect them from *sihir*. After I had been in the village for some time one of my neighbors told me: "You know, they call me Latifa, but my real name is Fatima." She then explained that not many knew this, but officially she was Fatima since this was the name under which her father had registered her at the local council after her birth. Some time after this, I was repeatedly confused about a village girl's identity as two different names were used to refer to her. The daughter in the house where I was staying, who was also the girl's classmate, gave me an explanation which was later verified by the girl's mother. The girl, who was thirteen, became ill. All my informants were vague about her symptoms other than to say that she would not eat and had become very weak. Her parents took her to several doctors, but she did not get better. Finally, they decided to go and see one of the sufi *hodžas* in the region (see chapter six). He suggested that her first name was somewhat difficult (*teško*) for her and that she should adopt a different name. The one he suggested had a meaning which he thought more in harmony with her personality. After this she would only respond to her new name and gradually she got better. Her schoolmates admitted that they found her change of name awkward, because whenever they forgot and addressed her by her former name she would just walk straight on without taking any notice. Later, I learned that the official name on the identity card of quite a few people I knew (especially of the older generation) was different from the name I knew them by. They all explained that as children they had been ill a lot and their fathers had therefore changed their names to something "easier" on the advice of a *hodža*.[15]

Muslim first names are of Turkish and Arabic origin. They may be the names of Islamic prophets or connected with religious values and they may describe personality traits. Thus, Čazim means someone who calms anger, Hazim means dependable, Remzija means allegoric speech, and so on. The villagers seldom know the meanings of the names. However, the sufi *hodža*s do, and they are also able to assess the appropriateness of a certain name to a certain personality, and how it fits with a child or person's astrological requirements at birth. When necessary, they can therefore suggest a new name more appropriate than the current one.

On a more general level we can explain the practice of changing names by the positive psychological effect that an implicit identity shift may have on an unhappy person. Not responding to his or her original name, after the change of name s/he is no longer the anxious or ill person s/he was before. More specifically, however, this practice should be seen as part of the concept of harmony in Islam and above all in the harmony of body and soul as part of a larger whole in time and space. The centrality of this idea is reflected among other things in the bodily movements during prayers and in architecture (where the mosque is the prime example). The idea of harmony is particularly emphasized in sufism and pursued by the dervishes in their sanctuaries (*tekija*). In Islam a person's name carries strong spiritual power, often referred to as *baraka* in Islamic literature, though I never heard the equivalent Bosnian term *berićet* used in this context. Instead a person's name was said to possess *sila*.[16] A *hodža* explained that a person's aim or strength (*sila*) is decided by the stars at birth but that no one knows what it is. If, however, a person's *sila* does not fit with the *sila* of his or her name, that person becomes ill. The only remedy then is to change the name to a different one so that there will be better correlation between the *sila* in the name and the *sila* in the person.

But a name should not only reflect the strength of the person who carries it; it should also hide a person's weaknesses and protect him or her from *sihir*. A child's original name (given at birth by the parents) is not a good one if it makes him or her vulnerable to *sihir*. When the original name of a person (which exposes the disharmony between person and name; weakness and strength; body and soul) is not generally known because it has been changed, he or she is protected from sorcery, as the sorcerer cannot attack someone without knowing his or her real identity.

From the above it is clear that Muslims believe that only Islamic knowledge and those who possess such knowledge—whom they therefore see as agents of divine power—can counteract malevolent influences, whether these are premeditated such as *sihir* (sorcery/casting of spells) or the evil eye (where a person is used as an agent by malevolent powers).

## Caring for the Souls of the Dead

It has already been noted that the most elaborate rituals among the Muslims in Dolina related to marriage and death. In chapter four I discussed marriage procedures and rituals and how they reflect certain ideas about identity and the formation of a *kuća*. In the next sections I will look at ritual and belief associated with death. In particular, I discuss the various forms of congregational prayer for the dead, in which the women's *tevhid* occupies a central place.

At death there are certain obligatory rituals (prescribed in *shari'at*) which are performed by men (except for the ritual washing of a female corpse, which must be done by a woman). In addition there are some rituals which Muslims considered "voluntary" and "beautiful" such as the *tevhid*, which are performed mainly by women. The obligatory rituals at death are the ritual washing of the corpse by a *hodža* (for a male deceased) and a *bula* (for a female deceased) and the *dženaza* prayers and burial according to *shari'at* rules. Only men attend the burial ceremony in the mosque (this is one of the ritual obligations for men). After the *hodža* or the *bula* has performed the ritual washing of the corpse, it is wrapped in a white shroud and placed in a *tabut* (lidless coffin) covered by a large green cloth with the Islamic profession of faith *lailahe illallah* ("there is no God except for the one Allah") printed on it in Arabic. I was told that in the past only women were placed in a *tabut*. This was so that the men would not have to touch the female body when carrying it to the mosque and to the grave.

After the washing, the husband or wife of the deceased is not allowed to see the dead spouse as he or she may pollute the dead by "thinking of something," in which case the body would have to be washed again. The possible polluting effect of certain thoughts or memories relates in part to the Islamic belief that the soul does not leave the body until the fortieth day after death and that during this time the deceased is still a sentient being. The living, especially those emotionally close to the deceased, should therefore avoid saying, doing, or even thinking anything that may upset the deceased. Crying will upset the soul of the deceased; so will any comments or thoughts (memories) about the physical closeness of a person with his or her deceased spouse. The latter is associated with the polluting properties of sexual relations. (Both men and women are considered "unclean" after sexual intercourse and may be the source of misfortune until they have taken the obligatory bath.)

However, mere physical closeness like a friendly kiss or the shaking of hands is a sufficient metonym for such relations in the context of ritual purity, and must therefore be avoided. Thus, women must sit behind the men in the mosque, because if they could be seen, men might "lose their *abdest*" (the ritual ablution before prayers which symbolizes both a physical and a mental cleansing). For the dead the danger of pollution is particularly great after the ritual washing of the body until the burial (hence the custom of carrying a deceased woman in a *tabut*). The mere eye or even the thought of the spouse is potentially polluting to the dead. This seems to confirm Bloch's thesis (1982) that death needs to be denied to sustain the social order (and more specifically traditional authority), by denying sexuality and birth. However, in this case the denial does not concern women in particular (as he argues generally); men too are associated with sexuality and both men and women must ritually deny any physical and sexual link with their dead spouse. Furthermore, the emphasis is on the possible pollution of the soul rather than the body of the deceased (Tapper and Tapper 1987:87). The notion that the living may pollute the dead by their thoughts and desires is a reversal of the apparently more common idea that the dead are polluting to the living (Bloch and Parry 1982).

Male relatives and covillagers of the deceased walk together to the mosque, taking turns carrying the *tabut*, four at a time. The women remain in the house to hold a *tevhid* (the *žalosni* or sorrow *tevhid*) for the deceased. Close female relatives may express their grief by sobbing, though rarely by loud crying and never by lamentation. Stoicism is the ideal behavior in such a situation for this is considered a sign of one's submission to the will of God, which is the essence of being Muslim. (When someone dies, particularly if it is a child, friends and neighbors comfort the bereaved by saying that "Allah loved him or her even more than we did.") But Muslims also believe that the display of strong emotions may upset the soul of the dead. Furthermore, in striving not to be overtly emotional, and thereby not upsetting the soul of the dead, a Muslim woman is also distinguishing herself from her Christian neighbors, and especially from the Orthodox Serbs who are notorious for lamenting their dead. The Muslim villagers tended to be embarrassed by what they perceived as the excessive crying of Serbian Orthodox women at death rituals.

Even so, women are generally prone to cry when emotional, and a public display is avoided by the custom which forbids women from attending the actual burial ceremony. At least this was the explanation given to me by both women and a *hodža* when I asked why women did not attend. The local *hodža* gave a beautifully argued explanation: "Women never go to the graveyard, only men do. This is a good rule (*propis*) we have, that women should not go to the grave. The moment which is the most difficult is when the body is carried away from the house. And when the journey toward the graveyard starts the women remain. In that most difficult of moments the women are together in the house where they recite prayers for the dead person's soul, and it becomes easier for them to cope. Women do not go to the grave because they cry a lot."

Occasionally, however, when the deceased has Christian in-laws, non-Muslim women attend that part of the *dženaza* which takes place at the grave. A Christian daughter-in-law of the deceased will for instance remain slightly apart from the men, maybe with her Muslim husband, and lay flowers at the grave. (In the large main cemetery in Sarajevo, which consisted of four separate sections, one for Catholics, one for Orthodox Christians, one for Muslims, and one for atheists, in the late eighties you could see flowers next to Muslim gravestones.) In the villages, Muslims have not traditionally tended the graves of their deceased relatives, focusing all their attention instead on spiritually supporting their dead "in the other world." By contrast, they attend to the graves of *šehit*s which, as we have seen, are often the site for various kinds of prayers, including prayers for the souls of the dead, for good fortune, and healing.

Bosnian Muslims pray in the name of their dead on several occasions: at *mukabela* (Qur'an recitation in the mosque, usually by one or more *hafiz*, learned men who know the Qur'an by heart), during the *hatma* (one reading of the Qur'an from beginning to end), during Ramadan, and at the male collective prayer (*džuma*) at Bajram. In the district of which Dolina is a part it is also common for participants at the main burial ceremony (*dženaza*) to recite prayers for the dead at the grave in order to increase the religious merit of the deceased in the eyes of God. For this they will be given money (*sergija*, donation)—as when the *hodža* leads the prayers—by the senior member of the deceased's household. This was, however, criticized by some Islamic teachers. They argued that the Qur'an states unequivocally that there is nobody between man and God, and therefore nobody can mediate or "interfere."

Villagers did not generally talk of the money they handed out to the reciters in terms of "paying" (*platiti*) but of "giving a gift" (*darovati*), as they believed that unless the person who recites is a relative or member of the household of the deceased he does not earn religious merit from the act. The concept of a "gift" is in accordance with the concept of reciprocity and equal exchange described in chapter four. Furthermore, the act of praying or reciting for the dead is referred to as *pokloniti* (to give as a gift). The person or persons who say prayers or *dova*, ask that the *dova* be received on the dead person's behalf, that the recital be counted as his *sevap*. In other words the living family members of the deceased are reciprocating the gift given by the reciter on behalf of the deceased. In Bosnia such prayers are only rarely referred to as prayers for the *souls* of the dead (except by Islamic scholars). Instead they are called "giving as a gift" prayers to the deceased person, referred to by name.

## The Tevhid

*Tevhid* is the most formalized ritual in which congregational prayers are said on behalf of the dead. It comes from the Arabic *tawhid*, which means "faith in one supreme God," but is often translated more freely as "praise of God." Škajlić gives the following two definitions of *tevhid* in his dictionary of Turkish words in the Serbo-Croat language: (1) "commemoration of the dead which consists of the collective recital of religious declarations and prayers"; (2) "collective recital by dervishes of religious declarations which is held while sitting in a circle."[17] In the following paragraphs I shall concentrate on the first kind, since the only dervish ritual which is reasonably publicly accessible, while organized as described above, is nevertheless cast as a *mevlud*.

Softić (1984) mentions two types of *tevhid*: the *tevhid* for sorrow associated with death, and the *tevhid* in praise of life (or the joyous *tevhid*) held during a marriage or the circumcision of male children.[18] However,

I never came across the "joyous *tevhid*" in Dolina or its surrounding region. *Tevhid* was used solely to describe the ritual congregational prayers for the dead, while the religious rituals held in connection with joyous events were *mevlud*s (since *mevlud* was primarily held for blessing in this life; see below). I suspect that rather than a disparity in practice between Sarajevo and rural areas, we are dealing merely with a difference in terminology. The confusion is probably related to the fact that the concepts are Turkish and that learned Islamic literature still operates within the Turkish definitions, failing to recognize that *tevhid* in partic- ular has developed into a Bosnian ritual associated with death (what Softić calls *tevhid* "for sorrow").

Although there is some disagreement between Bosnian Islamic schol- ars concerning the origin of the *tevhid*, it should probably be traced back to dervish practices and rituals in Bosnia. Softić (1984) suggests that is so, based on the evidence that first, it is similar in form to the *tevhid* held by the dervish orders in their *tekija*: one person leads the *tevhid*, while all others present follow; the large rosary (*tespih*) is used collectively during the prayers. Second, *tevhid*s are held mainly in those areas of Bosnia where there were (and to some extent still are) sufi traditions and influences through the presence of an active dervish order and its lodges. How exactly the practice of holding *tevhid* was then taken up by women, Softić does not establish. An old *hodža* from central Bosnia sug- gested to me that the *tevhid* had entered private homes through dervish sheikhs who started to perform *tevhid* in peoples' homes to help finance their *tekije*. It was then taken up by women.[19] The theory about the *tevhid*'s dervish origin is strengthened by the fact that there was no tra- dition of performing *tevhid* in eastern Bosnia until ten or twenty years ago (according to a *hodža* from that part of Bosnia). Instead the dead were cared for spiritually by *hatma* and the saying of the *fatiha* (the opening chapter of the Qur'an), some lines of which Muslims always recite "for the souls" when passing a Muslim cemetery. At the time of my research sponsoring a *tevhid* was becoming increasingly popular throughout Bosnia.

*Tevhid* is held five times following the death of any individual, male or female, usually in the house of the deceased. The first is held on the day the deceased is carried away from the house: while the men attend the *dženaza* (burial ceremony) in the mosque, the women gather in the house of the deceased to say *dova* for his or her soul. The ritual is re- peated on the seventh and fortieth days (on the fortieth day, when the soul is believed to leave the body, some families also give a *mevlud* in conjunction with the *tevhid*), after six months, and after a year.[20] At the first *tevhid* nobody is invited (although those who wish to may attend), and neither coffee nor food is served. At the others relatives and neighbors are invited and food is served.

There are both *muški* and *ženski tevhid*s (*tevhid*s by and for men and by and for women respectively, irrespective of whether the deceased was male or female). The main differences between the men's and the women's rituals are as follows. First, women's *tevhid*s are held at the home of the deceased and are led by a *bula*; men do not attend. *Tevhid*s attended by men, on the other hand, are usually held in the mosque. However, they may also take place in the house, in which case women will also attend; the *tevhid* is then led by a *hodža* while the *bula* is only present in her capacity as relative or neighbor. If such a mixed *tevhid* is small (that is, the guests are neighbors and relatives from within the village), women may recite, but this is rare. At mixed *tevhid*s men and women sit in separate rooms if space permits; otherwise men sit at the front closest to the *hodža* while women sit at the back, as in the mosque. Second, men's *tevhid*s are shorter (with the exception of those within the sufi milieu). Third, more lay people recite at women's *tevhid*s, perhaps because there are fewer *bula*s than *hodža*s in the district. (I have no reason to argue that the wider participation of lay women in the recitals reflects a less formalized "female structure.") Fourth, in women's *tevhid*s a large communal *tespih* (rosary) is used instead of the individual *tespih*; the women sit in a circle and let it pass through their hands. Fifth, at women's *tevhid*s food is served.

Some households (usually fulfilling a wish of the deceased) prefer to give two simultaneous *tevhid*s, one in the mosque attended by the men, and another in the house attended by the women. There are thus several possible combinations of place (mosque or house) and people attending (only men, only women, or both men and women). What particular form of *tevhid* a household chooses depends on three main factors: the devoutness of the family, the stated wish of the deceased, and the economic status of the sponsoring household.

Like the *mevlud*, the women's *tevhid* is an occasion for individuals to strive to impress others and prove their capabilities both in religious matters, as by displaying religious knowledge and reciting well, and in secular activities as by cooking and organizing the event. A woman will also signal the socioeconomic status of her household and earn it prestige by the manner in which she dresses (this is the case for all guests), the number of guests she entertains, the number of Islamic instructors (*hodža*s or *bula*s) called upon to recite, and the amount and quality of the food served.

While the female head of the household sponsoring the *tevhid* organizes the cooking and serving of food, the *bula* leads the prayers, is the

11. Reciting at *tevhid*.

main reciter in the *tevhid* and appoints other women to recite. She always sits in the sofa at the center of the congregation with the Qur'an on the table in front of her. Older women and those renowned for their piety will sit closest to the *bula*. The other women will gather on the floor sitting facing the *bula*; if it is a large *tevhid* (with many guests and a big house), women will also gather in adjacent rooms. The order of recitation is decided according to a strict hierarchy of age and skill. Those closest to the *bula* will be called upon first, although younger women sitting on the floor may also be called upon to recite if they are known to be particularly good. As many as ten different women may recite at the larger *tevhids*.

After every individual recital there are prayers. These prayers, called *namaz*, consist of a standard, prescribed set of prayers accompanied by a set of body movements (one such set is called *rekat*). Having finished all the *rekata* (pl.) of one *namaz*, the congregation recites the *tundžina salavat* (salvation prayer) together. This prayer provides an obvious visual marker between the recitals of *namaz*, since the open hand is placed on the heart at the mention of the name of the Prophet Mohammad while the body is bent slightly forward. This movement, revering the Prophet, is characteristic of this part of Bosnia, and I was told stems from the influence in the region of the local dervish order and its *namaz* practices. (At a *mevlud* I attended in the nearest market town, which was led by a high-ranking *bula* from Sarajevo, this particular motion was not performed because the *bula* did not do it.)

Following a series of *amins*, when the hands are held, palms up, in front of the face, the *tevhid* recitals finish with prayers "as a gift" in the

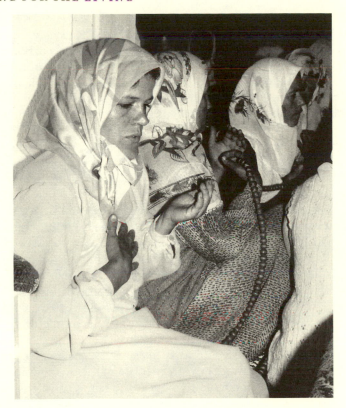

12. Invoking the names of God, revering the prophet (note the large rosary).

name of the deceased (it is requested that the prayers be received on his or her behalf and for his or her benefit). Prayers are then given in the name of other deceased close relatives of the household sponsoring the *tevhid*, and of other participants who ask for it. Finally, prayers are said in the name of "all our deceased." The local *bula* also used to say prayers on behalf of all deceased relatives of the hostess of the *tevhid* up to the "ninth degree." (As we remember from chapter four, this is as far as Bosnian Muslims traditionally go in defining kinship.) This specification was criticized and considered ignorant and non-Islamic by the younger religious instructors in the district. However, the local *bula*'s often detailed knowledge about families and their kinship network, necessary for this practice, is one of the reasons she is well liked in the villages (see also chapter six). If she should happen to omit a particular deceased relative the women will remind her. The *bula* and the women then say a prayer together.

After the recitals and prayers are over, women will engage in relaxed talk until they are invited to the table to eat. Food is usually served only once, except in prosperous households where it is served both before and after the recitals. Now they will meet women from other villages who may have news about relatives or neighbors from their native village. They exchange information about who has married, who has died, and who has had a child. They will also learn about forthcoming rituals and celebrations such as *mevlud*, *tevhid*, or weddings sponsored by other households. Indeed, women's different kinship and neighborhood networks may overlap: a woman may meet another woman unknown to her who passes on a greeting or perhaps a wedding invitation from relatives or neighbors in the first woman's native village.

The women eat in the traditional way from a common pot served at *sofra*. Since only a limited number of people (usually eight to ten) can be seated at the table at any one time the table is usually set several times. A set table is called a *sofra*, and the size of a reception is often described in terms of how many *sofre* there were. As many as seven different dishes may be served at *tevhid*s sponsored by more prosperous households. However, any household sponsoring a *tevhid* aspires to at least five dishes. People usually eat quickly and take only a couple of spoonfuls from each dish. The number of guests may be a problem for some households. Between thirty and forty guests is a respectably large number; most households invite between twenty and thirty, a few above fifty. It may be difficult to limit the number if the family is large, although space and economic resources will necessarily keep the numbers down. Some households restrict their invitations to close relatives out of town, and relatives and close neighbors within the village. Another solution is to avoid the women's *tevhid* altogether and give a men's *tevhid* in the mosque.

Usually, most women attending a *tevhid* were married and middle-aged. Some women were more active in attending than others. In Dolina there was a group of five women, including the *bula*, who were known as the *pobožne* (devout) women in Dolina. They were always present at religious events at which the village was represented, and regularly went to services in the mosque. While most villagers, men as well as women, only attended congregational prayers in the mosque on special occasions like *mevlud*, *tevhid*, or during Ramadan, these women also attended regular evening services during the week when the *hodža* was staying in the village. Young unmarried girls saw the *tevhid* as a gathering for *žene* (wives) and rarely attended, unless the *tevhid* was for a close relative or they were there to help prepare and serve the food, in which case they would not participate in the prayers but would stay in the kitchen for the most part while the recitations took place. Furthermore, young girls usually had obligations at school or work and *tevhid*s often fell on a weekday.

*Tevhid*, like *mevlud*, was an occasion for women to dress up. Urban influences on dress were becoming increasingly apparent at religious gatherings. The current fashion in places like Sarajevo was to wear big, white, embroidered headscarves from Turkey that cover both head and shoulders (called *namazbezama*), though urban women had also recently taken to wearing silk headscarves from the Middle East.[21] In rural areas usually only *bula*s would dress in this "modern" way, although some women who could afford them had started to wear the large white headscarves, together with their newest and finest *dimije* or *kat* (*dimije* and blouse in the same material). A village woman who dressed like this would often be told that she had become "more like a *bula*" (*se pobulila*). (This comment was made half teasingly, half disapprovingly, since dressing like this implied that she was being pretentious.) In the urban areas there was a trend toward women wearing long skirts or even skirts just below the knee rather than the rural "old-fashioned" *dimije*. However, should a woman choose to wear a *dimije*, the most prestigious kind was a *dimije* or *kat* made of privately imported silk from Turkey. Very few of the women in Dolina could actually afford to buy such material. It was therefore rarely seen except at *tevhid*s among a richer elite outside the village. All the women following the urban fashion wore their headscarves in the same way as the *bula*, with the ends tucked in at the cheeks, to signify that they knew how to pray. A few village women tied them as they would everyday with a knot under the chin.[22]

Many of the *hodža*s disapproved of women's *tevhid*s. According to a respected *bula*, this is mainly because they are held in the house and therefore, I suggest, outside the authority of the *hodža*. Instead *hodža*s thought the *tevhid* should always be held in the mosque and led by a *hodža*. Men in rural areas generally tended to belittle female *tevhid* as an occasion for gossiping and eating. Although this opinion is at odds with what Sorabji reports from Sarajevo, it does not in fact contradict her argument that the *tevhid* is valued by the men as a "vehicle for the expression of [Muslim] group identity" (1989:195). On the contrary, such disapproving comments should be seen in relation to the remark that often follows (and that is made particularly by *hodža*s) that all *tevhid*s ought to be held in the mosque. This suggests that men think the *tevhid* is too important to be organized by women and should therefore be under their control in the mosque.

Indeed, since the *tevhid* organized by women in the house persists and even seems to have increased in popularity, a few *hodža*s now lead women's *tevhid* in the house on their own initiative on the grounds that "the *džemat* (local mosque community) has no officially employed *bula.*" Furthermore, the *tevhid* is the most frequently held ritual in the region and, of all religious activities, the one in which a woman most often engages. Indeed, the *tevhid* is the most frequent legitimate occasion for women (or wives) to socialize outside the immediate neighborhood and the village. However, it also means socializing exclusively with and primarily as Muslim women. The *tevhid* in Bosnia thus has a similar position to the *mevlud* in the Turkish town studied by the Tappers (1987), with the significant difference that in Turkey the *mevlud* associated with death are mainly by and for men.

*Tevhid* also highlights the central role of the wife as the link between two kinship and social networks. A wife should attend *tevhid*s given both for her own deceased relatives and for those of her husband. In these contexts she represents the household (or if her mother-in-law also attends, her husband's segment of the patrigroup). If a woman is a good cook she may often be called upon by her own or her husband's relatives sponsoring a *tevhid* to help with the preparations and serving of the food. This may mean traveling to villages a couple of hours' bus ride away. Such invitations are often a welcome break from her usual routine as a wife and a source of prestige both for her and her household. It would be considered shameful for a husband to forbid his wife from accepting the invitation. For the woman herself the most important aspect of the *tevhid* is fulfilling her responsibility to care for the spiritual well-being of deceased persons with whom her household had close social relations, whether they were relatives, neighbors, or friends.

In conclusion, there are several dimensions to a *tevhid* as practiced and understood by women in the village. First, praising the oneness of God and expressing one's membership of a Muslim moral community. Second, the remembrance and honoring of dead relatives and neighbors. And third, the earning of *sevap* on behalf of the dead whereby one assists the deceased in the other world, and increases not only one's own chances of well-being in the afterlife but also those of the other members of one's household. That it is this felt responsibility toward the well-being of members and relations of one's *kuća*, rather than abstract religious doctrines, which is the primary motivation for performing these prayers on behalf of the dead, became clear to me during a discussion I heard and that I relate below.

The *mukabela* is a gathering of several *hafiz* in the mosque to recite the Qur'an aloud from beginning to end. This reading is called a *hatma*. At Ramadan, when the *mukabela* usually takes place, some will pay their *hodža* well to read a *hatma* on behalf of a deceased close relative or relatives; this is believed to earn both the deceased person and the person who recites or sponsors the recitation *sevap* (reciting earns greater *sevap* than sponsoring it, but not all people know how to read the Qur'an). In villages like Dolina a group of Muslims who know how to recite the Qur'an gathered in the mosque every day during Ramadan with the local *hodža* to read a *hatma*. It is prestigious for a devout Muslim to participate in the *mukabela*; in most towns men are the reciters, yet in Dolina the reciters were a group of women led by the *hodža*. There were only a few men in the village who were good reciters, and they were old and not interested in participating. It is likely that women in the village had taken over many of the ritual obligations primarily assigned to men. As participants in a public space defined as communist and Yugoslav, men who were believers had had to compromise their religious beliefs and practices to a larger extent than the women who spent most of their time in the village.

Although many Islamic instructors would give the more scholarly explanation that *mukabela* is held in commemoration of those who have done good works in life, in Dolina it was understood slightly differently. At one meeting in the mosque council the issue of payment for the *hodža* leading the *mukabela* was raised. In other mosques in the municipality it was usual to pay the *hodža* extra for this service. One man, however, refused to pay on the grounds that if payment were made his wife who had participated in the recitation should also receive "compensation." Later the villagers discussed the issue with each other. A woman who had also participated in recitations said she did not want to be paid, since she "had hers at the cemetery"; the *hodža*, however, ought to be compensated as he had nobody buried at the mosque and thus there "was nothing in it for him." She added that, after all, the *hatma* they recite at *mukabela* was for those of their relatives who are buried at the mosque; thus the *hatma* was recited on behalf of the dead relatives so that they could earn *sevap*, but also so that the women who had recited (and their households) could earn *sevap*.

This woman's comment highlights both the personal relationship these prayers are seen to reflect and establish between the deceased person (or persons) and the one who prays, as well as the responsibility women feel for the well-being of close relatives in the world beyond. This relationship is often summed up in the idea that recitation and prayers of this kind are *sevap* not only for the person or persons in whose name they are given, but also for those who perform them. Furthermore, the dead relatives this woman referred to as hers are her husband's kin (his grandparents), in other words former members of her household. Her role as moral nurturer is not limited to the living members of her *kuća* but extends to former, deceased members too. Indeed, the one is an aspect and a continuation of the other.

In this chapter the analysis of the religious practices of members of the *kuća*, and particularly of women, has been organized according to two intersecting concerns: that of seeking blessing in this life and that of earning religious merit, which is primarily directed toward the afterlife. Yet, while the dead are paths to blessing for the living, they in turn need their living family members to sustain them spiritually by earning *sevap* on their behalf. Furthermore, praying in the name of a dead family member increases the *sevap* of the living who performs the prayers. The living and the dead are thus connected in a mutual relationship of spiritual exchange which ensures the continuity and indivisibility of life and death, the world of the living and the world of the dead, and of the past, present, and future. This continuity was expressively enacted through the different devotional practices at the *turbe* in Dolina. At this site both prayers for rain (and fertility) and prayers for the dead were said. It was here also that people prayed for individual blessing in times of special need. In all cases the *šehit*, symbolizing the islamization of Bosnia, was addressed as a powerful intermediary between people, the living, and God. At the same time the *šehit* is also the link between the past and the present.

# Six

## Debating Islam and Muslim Identity

ALTHOUGH the official Titoist understanding and definition of "Muslim" was based on historical Islamic legacies, Bosnian Muslims were discouraged from experiencing the dynamics and relevance of Islam in their everyday lives and as a community. An important aspect of religion, and of Islam in Bosnia, is that it defines Bosnian Muslims in relation to Serbs and Croats. Islam sets them apart. By practicing Islam people become and experience themselves as different.

In Bosnia religious practices and symbols are the constitutive factor in the construction of parallel and competing collective cultural and political entities or *nacije* (Muslim, Croat, or Serb). However, religion also has its own internal dynamics and produces meanings which change with context and over time. Practiced Islam creates a community of Muslims and also communicates differences between Muslims in lifestyle, forms of religiosity, practices, and interpretations of the role of Islam in everyday life.

In Bosnia Islam attaches people to two symbolic communities, each different in content, function, and scale. On the one hand Islam (as cultural heritage, historical legacy, a set of practices and moral values) binds people together in a community of Bosnian Muslims (with the emphasis on Bosnian, as opposed to Serbian, Croatian, and the like, and on Muslim as opposed to Catholic or Orthodox Bosnian). On the other hand it unites them with a community of Muslims worldwide (the Islamic *umma*) as opposed to non-Muslims. During my research in Bosnia the former was the primary identification. The extent to which the latter was meaningful to Bosnian Muslims was dependent on devoutness, style of religiosity, and socioeconomic status. At the time it was an identification made by a small urban-oriented economic and religious elite, or what we might call the Islamic establishment.[1] Typically one member of such a family would have been educated in the Islamic Middle East and the family would have a long tradition of religious instructors and learned men and women.

In the introduction to this book I said that war changes people and that it changes their perceptions of who they are. As a reaction to and part of the process of the war and the politics behind it, many Bosnian Muslims are redefining both the content and function of their collective identities, and identifying with a wider world community of Muslims more than before. To what extent these changes signal a more assertive Islamic identity and an extension of a Muslim-defined identity by expanding the use of Islamic discourse and symbols into new domains (e.g., specific Muslim greetings), or a redefinition of Muslim identity, is a subject for further research. This chapter, like the book itself, contains ethnographic data which are now history.

I suspect, however, that changes since 1987 are salient to my discussion in this chapter which deals with discourses on Islam, since this discourse itself has become more prominent and politicized. I have nevertheless chosen to include the present chapter as I believe it provides an important frame of reference for what has been described in previous chapters, in terms of the various official definitions of "Muslim" available to the Bosnians at the time of my research, and as points of reference for the changes currently taking place. The discourse on Bosnian Muslim identity in war-torn Bosnia-Hercegovina is a response to the redefinition and politicization of the categories Catholic Croat and Orthodox Serb. Because of the attempted genocide against them the Bosnian Muslims have also become a powerful symbol and political badge for Islamic activist organizations around the world, perhaps particularly in the West. These issues, are, however, beyond the scope of this book which deals primarily with the period up to the fall of the communist regime and the disintegration of Yugoslavia in 1990.

The previous chapter examined some aspects of the role of Islam in everyday life in Bosnia prior to the war as the main constitutive element of a Bosnian Muslim identity. It was concerned with how Islam was practiced and its moral content interpreted. Religious life in the village was presented mainly through the eyes of Muslims I observed practicing Islam. Muslims in the village were, however, in constant dialogue with representatives of the Islamic Association headquartered in Sarajevo, which constituted official Islam in Bosnia-Hercegovina (and Yugoslavia) at the time. This is the official body which organizes and supervises Islamic education and instruction, and also to an increasing extent attempts to direct local religious life.

In this chapter we will focus in particular on how and by whom Islamic doctrines and scholarship were communicated, received, and made use of locally, and how the dynamics in this discourse related to the formation of a Muslim identity in Bosnia. The next sections will introduce some of the carriers of these doctrines associated with Islamic learning and show how they were positioned in relation to the village and the Muslims there. The official Islamic authority is dealt with in terms of its influence at the local village level, and primarily as experienced by Muslims in the village. From the villagers' point of view those who were critical of some of their practices all represented the same category: an official and educated authority. Labels such as modernist, traditionalist, fundamentalist, reformist, and orthodox, used in the description of various political trends within the Islamic movement, are accordingly irrelevant to the present analysis.

## Official Administration of Religious Life

The *Islamska Zajednica* ("Islamic Association"), hereafter referred to as I.Z., is the state-approved body responsible for all matters concerning the Muslim community in Bosnia and Hercegovina (and in pre-1990 Croatia and Slovenia). It is a highly bureaucratized, stratified organization which operates on three geo-administrative levels. The I.Z. is led by the *Starješinstvo* (council of elders) in Sarajevo, and its head the *Reisul-ulema*. Below this there are councils representing all the mosques within a *opština* (a secular administrative unit), attended by each mosque's *hodža* and elected lay representatives. Lastly, there is the village mosque council representing one *džemat* (a religious administrative area consisting of one mosque and/or one *hodža*) which is led by the mosque's *hodža*.

During communism, which is the period and framework within which the main body of the data in this book belongs, the *Starješinstvo* was supervised by (the official rhetoric was "in contact with") a government committee for religious affairs. It had to report to this committee every time it held a meeting. The committee would intervene if it felt challenged by delegates who were "too political" in their views. An informant put it this way: "The committee will intervene if young people bring politics into religious affairs, and do or say something which is not good; they will be criticized and then everything will be all right."[2] We see here the delicate balance Islamic instructors had to tread and the extent of their accommodation to political authorities based on terms set by the latter. The state authorities in the socialist republic of Bosnia-Hercegovina were wary of antistate and pan-Islamic ideas propagated by the *ulema*.[3] It is interesting to note that my informant thought that it was the young *hodža*s who were inclined to create problems. Indeed, it was they who challenged the accommodating attitude of the I.Z. The older *hodža*s were understandably more restrained, as they owed their positions to their cautious attitude and/or communist sympathies in the the restrictive postwar years. In effect, the leading Islamic scholars' accommodation to the communist authorities led them to encourage Muslims to put their obligations to the state before their obligations as practicing Muslims. (See Johnson 1980 on similar attitudes in Algeria.)

There was thus a pragmatic coexistence between Islam and the communist ideology of the state. A Muslim's duties and obligations as a citizen of the religiously diverse state had to take precedence over those of the Islamic community. The presiding *Reisul-ulema* was quite clear on this point in a speech he gave at a ceremony to mark the opening of a new mosque in a small Bosnian town.[4] He said that during Ramadan, whenever a person was faced with a choice between fasting or working, s/he should work, because this would benefit the wider society. To illustrate his point about the value of work, the *Reisul-ulema* criticized in sarcastic terms a meditating dervish who allegedly considered work beneath his dignity and was dependent on others for his daily bread.[5]

Representatives of official Islam were opposed to two of the main characteristics of practiced Islam in the region where I did my field research: first, the mystic orders and their nonofficial practices, and second, ideas and practices that they judged as un-Islamic and influenced by Christian concepts, such as praying through intermediaries. The scope of an Islamic discourse was restricted and overt challenge to the state ideology punishable by law. However, the leaders of the I.Z. could also use the socialist state discourse to reinforce their own power base. For instance, they would oppose any groups or individuals who could mobilize a following and thereby threaten the virtual monopoly of their organization on "Muslim ideology." This was expressed in their attitude toward the sufi orders and some of the activities of their members which the I.Z. either condemned or attempted to co-opt or direct (see also Sorabji 1989).

## Dolina Džemat

The village mosque (*džamija*) was the visual focus and potent image of the presence of Islam and a Muslim community in the village. It was at the mosque that devotional obligations and religious practices such as the *namaz* prayers, the *dženaza*, the *mukabela*, the *teravija*, and sometimes *tevhid* or *mevlud* were held. It was here too that the children went to *mekteb* and men held their mosque councils. The mosque was situated in the upper part of the village, but at the time of its construction in the 1960s it was the lowest building in the settlement.[6] It was built in the architectural style typical of Bosnian village mosques (i.e., square, rather than round). In those days there would have been dwellings clustered above the mosque along the river, some opposite it and others on the surrounding hills. In the late eighties, those who lived further down the river could go to a mosque which had recently been built in a nearby village, and was closer. The village was defined in terms of the proximity

of the settlements to the mosque (see chapter two). In addition to defining the village geography, the mosque was also an important institution
integrating the Muslim community in the village.

In most traditional mosques in rural Bosnia both men and women
enter through the same door, and the women sit downstairs with the
men. (The main mosques in larger towns, as well as the ones recently
designed, built and paid for by Middle Eastern countries, are built with
two separate entrances, one for men leading into the main room at
ground level and another for women which leads up to a large room
at the back of the mosque (the *musandara*) overlooking the main area
where the men sit.) However, this does not mean that boundaries are
not marked or expressed; rather, the lack of any clearly defined physical
segregation causes women to be all the more careful not to trespass.
Thus, the men always make up the front rows closest to the *mihrab* (a
niche in the wall at the front of the mosque, facing the *kibla*, from which
the *hodža* leads the prayers), while women sit in the back rows toward
the entrance and always make sure they enter the mosque last (just as the
congregational prayers are about to start), allowing the men to enter
before them. Again, when the prayers are over the women get up hur-
riedly, making sure they leave the mosque before the men. They should
never look at or talk to the men while on their way to or from the
mosque; that would be shameful. One old *hodža* argued that during
prayers in the mosque as well as on other ritual occasions men and
women ought to be separated, but that since the advent of communism
they had been sitting together. The separation of the sexes in the
mosque was adhered to more strictly in the larger mosques in urban
centers. The mosque is primarily the *hodža*'s domain, as only he can lead
the prayers. A *bula* will sometimes lead *tevhid*s but these are held in
the schoolroom, or a young *bula* may give a didactic speech during
Ramadan.

Although Muslim women in Bosnia have access to the mosque to an
extent which would be unusual in most of the Islamic world, there are,
however, some mosque services which women do not attend, such as
the Friday prayers.[7] Although most *hodža*s said that women may attend
since it is not forbidden by the Qur'an, they emphasized that women
were not under a religious obligation to do so, and that it was not customary for them to do so. The *hodža* leads the Friday prayers throughout the year. *Džuma* (Friday noon prayers) can only take place if a minimum of three men are present. Usually no more than one row of men
attended, that is, between five and seven. Most of them were retired, but
some went when they were working a late shift and therefore had the
early afternoon off. The younger men often went only after their wives
had told them that it was shameful not to when they were at home any-

way. Once I asked the village *hodža* whether I could sit in on *džuma* one Friday. He smiled, reflected on the matter, and then said all right. "But," he added, "it has never been done before." My friend, who had just arrived to ask if the *hodža* wanted coffee, suggested that I could sit upstairs where there are no men, on the *musandara* or gallery where women generally sat. But the *hodža* was not very happy with this solution. "Sometimes men sit upstairs as well. You know that it is not our custom." We finally agreed that I should come with my friend and sit in the classroom, which had windows toward the *musandara*. The *hodža* again stressed that it is not that women are not allowed at the *džuma*, but rather that it is not an obligation for them to attend (being a prescribed religious duty for men only). However, at mosque school only the boys learn to pray *džuma*. When I attended the Friday prayers with my friend, she was confused by the order of the movements in the prayer, found she could not follow, and finally decided to perform a normal noon prayer.

Dolina had its own mosque and *hodža* and was therefore defined as a *džemat*, with its own mosque council. Dolina *džemat* was, however, not a strictly defined or constant entity. First, although the local residents together comprise the *džemat*, the geographical borders between two different congregations (*vjerski skup*) may be vague. The question of who belongs to which *džemat* is therefore a matter of personal choice, particularly for those who live close to the border with another *džemat*. The *hodža* mentioned two examples: a man who lived in Dolina wanted to be buried at the new mosque in a neighboring village which had earlier belonged to the Dolina *džemat*, while a resident of the new *džemat* wanted to be buried beside his relatives at the old mosque in Dolina.

The mosque was where both boys and girls in the *džemat* attended *mekteb*, ideally every day, either in the morning or in the afternoon depending on when they went to state school. *Mekteb* ran parallel with primary school, that is, a child started at the age of six or seven and went on until the age of fourteen or fifteen. Most children, however, dropped out much earlier, and some children never attended as their parents did not mind. This was a recurring topic of debate between the *hodža* and the parents of those children that attended *mekteb* regularly. However, the school was better attended by girls than by boys, who also tended to drop out at a much earlier stage than the girls.

During the week, fewer children attended than on Saturdays, when the classroom on the first floor of the mosque was almost always full. About thirty children attended each of the two classes given that day. Children learn to read and recite the Qur'an by heart in Arabic, although most do not understand what they are reading: some younger *hodža*s with better training and a more modern approach to education stressed understanding of the text, rather than rote learning, which is the traditional method. The children also learn the technicalities of prayer: how, what, and at what time of the day, as well as the ritual ablution and recitations before the prayers. At the end of each *mekteb* year, which in this particular village was in May, a children's *mevlud* is held. On this occasion the children sing religious songs in praise of the Prophet Mohammad.[8]

The Christian children in the village have their equivalent to *mekteb* in the Sunday school. But as the name suggests, children only attend on Sundays. Besides, the school is not located in the village. Another difference is that these children read the Bible in their own language. Bosnian scholars explained to me that this was one of the reasons why the Muslims in rural areas had a higher illiteracy rate than the Christians. Before World War II, when education in rural areas was generally taken care of by the religious institutions, Christian children learned to read their own language, while Muslim children learned to read Arabic first and had to learn "Serbo-Croat," written in either Cyrillic or Latin, separately.

Attending *mekteb* was an extra workload for children as it came on top of primary school responsibilities. It could also be rather unpleasant: in winter, when temperatures may be as low as −20°C, the child had to get up at 6 A.M. and go to a freezing cold mosque. Girls in the last years of primary school had a particularly busy time; the older she gets, the more responsibility a girl is expected to take on for the running of the household, cleaning, cooking, and looking after younger siblings. At the same time school becomes more demanding and the pressure to finish with marks high enough to get into an attractive course at secondary school increases. Such pressures are no doubt partly responsible for the high dropout rate from *mekteb* of girls this age. An additional reason may be the old-fashioned and authoritarian teaching methods. Teenage girls who dropped out of *mekteb* before finishing primary school said they hated the Qur'anic school and the *hodža*'s light caning across their fingers, in spite of which, they said, "I still couldn't get all that Arabic into my head." The local *hodža* repeatedly told the children that he wanted them to be as dedicated to *mekteb* as they were to their state school, and that missing *mekteb* was just as serious as missing school. Teachers at school, however, would complain that Muslim children were tired and had less time to spend on homework because of their commitments to the Qur'anic school during weekdays.

The two educational systems clearly saw each other as rivals, and were perceived as such by devout Muslims (as for instance the mother who refused to allow her son to wear the communist pioneer beret, described in chapter two). It could be argued that the two institutions complemented each other (state schools did not have religious instruction).

Nevertheless this is not the way the representatives of the two types of school saw the matter; indeed, in an important sense the schools could not be complementary, as they offered competing definitions of Muslim identity. To the teacher in state school a "Muslim" was a member of a primarily "Yugoslav" *nacija*, that is, communist and nonreligious. To the mosque teacher, on the other hand, Muslim identity was primarily an Islamic one. To some Muslims in Dolina, social context determined which understanding of being "Muslim" was predominant, while to others the two definitions were mutually exclusive.

From the religious instructor's point of view, children's attendance at *mekteb* was often undermined by the demands of state education, and adult (male) attendance at congregational prayers in the mosque was negatively affected by the need for industrial labor. However, both were affected by a third factor, namely the changing political climate toward religion at various periods in post–World War II Yugoslavia. Attendance at mosques was at a low during the restrictive fifties and once more in the eighties, when alleged fears of pan-Islamic demonstrations led to a harsh attitude on the part of the authorities toward all public Islamic activities (see n. 3, this chapter).

Although socialist Yugoslavia allowed free expression of religion (and even sponsored religious institutions), worship was seen as a private matter which should not interfere with whatever role a "Yugoslav" citizen was performing for the state, such as wage labor or national service in the Yugoslav Peoples' Army. Furthermore, an individual could not at the same time hold communist party membership and be a practicing Muslim (or Catholic or Orthodox Christian), and party membership was a prerequisite for making a career as a professional or climbing the hierarchy in the state bureaucracy. Men in Dolina were mostly skilled or unskilled workers to whom the lack of party membership meant a reduced influence in political decision making concerning their situation at work, and a less secure job (nonparty members were the first to be sacked in times of low productivity and economic crisis at the factory). Women on the other hand usually did not hold any state employment and consequently no party membership either and could worship freely in the mosques.[9]

The late 1980s saw a new openness toward religion, reflected, among other things, in the number of new mosques being built. The fall of communism opened the way for the free expression of religious faith and devotion without the fear of being accused of Muslim nationalism or "fundamentalism" (in Bosnia the two labels are often used synonymously). This increased liberalism coincided with a softer political climate in Bosnia-Hercegovina, which had long been known as the most hard-line communist republic in Yugoslavia. Under communism it was difficult for a Bosnian Muslim to combine his or her obligations as a worker in a factory or shop with those of a devout Muslim, as there were no officially recognized times or places for prayer and ritual ablution, and canteens might well serve only pork. Bosnian Muslims had to accept the conflict: having a job and working for the state prevented them from being able to perform all their ritual obligations.

A retired village *hodža* told me in 1988 that mosque attendance had been higher twenty years earlier, an opinion confirmed by other *hodžas* of the same generation. In the sixties more people were working the land, and the young, who either went idle or worked on the fields, would join their seniors when they went off to attend the congregational prayers in the mosque. The *hodža* thought the fall in mosque attendance had occurred not so much because people no longer wanted to go, as because they were increasingly tied up with secular obligations. However, in postcommunist Bosnia-Hercegovina such secular obligations could again be combined with the ritual duties of Islam, and mosque attendance rose sharply, particularly in the cities.

### The Village Mosque Council

The Dolina mosque had its own council consisting of four or five men elected annually by the male household heads in the *džemat* from among their midst. The village mosque council or *džematski odbor* is always led by the *hodža* and is the smallest administrative unit in the hierarchy of the Islamic Association. The authority of the *hodža* and the mosque council is limited to the sphere of religious affairs.[10] Between this village council and the central organization in Sarajevo there is one other level, namely the Islamic council for the *opština* to which the village belongs. The latter is responsible for all the village or mosque councils in that area. It is led by the *hodžas* of the two mosques in the administrative township of the *opština*; members are elected from among the male household heads in the *džemats* just as they are for the village council. The Islamic council for the *opština* decides on matters concerning all the nine mosques or *džemats* under its jurisdiction. More important decisions on religious learning and administration are taken by the *Starješinstvo* in Sarajevo. The role of the Islamic councils at the *opština* and village levels is to implement decisions taken by the Islamic Association in Sarajevo, and to function as a mediator between the local and central levels.

The village mosque council will meet when needed, often to discuss specific cases that have come up and usually at the request of the *hodža*. The village council is responsible for matters concerning the running of the mosque and for organizing its members whenever necessary. Thus the council arranges for the building of a new mosque if the *džemat* has decided on this, and organizes and finances maintenance work. When it has been agreed that a new mosque should be constructed, the council also decides on how much money each household should be encouraged to give. It is responsible for collecting the annual membership fees to the Islamic Association from all the *džemat*'s members, and determines the *hodža*'s wages within the framework laid down by the Islamic Association. It also elects the *muezzin*, the man who calls the faithful to prayer from the mosque's minaret. Furthermore the council is responsible for collecting the annual *zekat* ("alms" given by each household). The money goes to a charitable purpose determined by the Islamic Association in Sarajevo. Formerly it used to be given directly to a needy person in the community, but since the Islamic Association integrated the *zekat* into its bureaucratic procedures and decreed that it should be redistributed through the organization the money has tended to be earmarked for organizational and educational activities within the Islamic community under their jurisdiction. The year of my stay, for instance, the money went to the *medresa* in Sarajevo.[11] Another responsibility of the village mosque council is the daily running of the Qur'anic school (*mekteb*), though the curriculum and general organization of the Qur'anic schools are determined by the *Starješinstvo* in Sarajevo. Finally, the village mosque council is responsible for implementing decisions made at higher levels, that is, by the regional (*opština*) and state (republic) bodies.

## Islamic Instructors

There were two religious instructors for the village, a man or *hodža* and a woman or *bula*. The former was employed by the Islamic Association while the latter was not. This also means that the Association asserted more influence on the Islamic education and religious rituals led by the *hodža* than on the devotional activities presided over by the *bula*. However, there are also female religious instructors employed by the I.Z., a point to which I will return shortly. The duties of both the *hodža* and the *bula* will be discussed in more detail below.

*Hodža* is the local word for the Arabic *imam* and comes from the Turkish *hoca*. However, the term *imam* is becoming increasingly fashionable among the devout Muslim urban elite and among Islamic scholars. A *hodža* will be addressed by his first name and the honorary *efendija* (master) preceding it.

Before World War II (in what older people called "old Yugoslavia"[12]) only young men from families who owned plenty of land could become *hodža*s. First, they needed someone to finance their studies at the *medresa* in Sarajevo. Second, they received no salary when working as a *hodža*, only a token sum from their *džemat*. The teachers at the *medresa* were paid from the income of the *vakuf*s (property belonging to the Muslim religious community). In the eighties the *hodža*s were paid a salary decided on by the local mosque council according to guidelines given by the I.Z., while the head of the community and the teachers at the *medresa* were paid by the secular republic of Bosnia-Hercegovina. Furthermore, the I.Z. had in later years established a system of scholarships and quotas for young men and women from the villages. Sorabji (1989) has argued that this was part of a policy to improve the religious instruction in rural areas. Since the *medresa* is a boarding school it also provides accommodation, meals, and from many parents' point of view, protection. It is therefore an attractive and prestigious option for clever students from rural areas.

In addition to their monthly salary the *hodža*s receive additional voluntary monetary donations from villagers when they take on obligations such as teaching at *mevlud*s or *tevhid*s, and reciting *hatma* (see previous chapter). However, there was some resentment among villagers toward the growing "professionalization" of ritual services, as illustrated by the ever increasing practice of giving money to anyone who recites at them. One *hodža* expressed his disapproval of all the "blue envelopes" (with money) which were handed out at burial ceremonies to the men who recite. "What is the point," he asked, "of poor people handing out their money like that and for what? When a person is dead nobody can help him anyway." This *hodža* was upset by what he saw as the increasing professionalization (and commercialization) of religious knowledge, and by the fact that money and knowledge were being used to bring about an outcome which (in his view) had been determined in the deceased's lifetime. Many younger and more *shari'at*-minded *hodža*s considered these practices un-Islamic and influenced by Christian ideas. Yet, as we saw in chapter five, Muslims in the village did not conceive of the money as "payment" but rather as a gift reciprocating the gift given to the deceased by the reciter at the graveside. In Dolina most villagers were not opposed to lay people reciting at religious ceremonies per se; rather, they resented the ever increasing number of reciters at burials and the resulting pressure to give more gifts. The practice reinforces class distinctions: poorer people will not be able to call upon more than one *hodža*, *bula*, or lay reciter for fear of shaming themselves if they cannot live up to the gift-giving standards. The above-mentioned *hodža*'s criticism was (perhaps primarily) an expression of his solidarity with these poorer villagers among whom he lived and whom he knew so well. As we saw in chapter five class distinctions were already present at *tevhid*s and *mevlud*s, as reflected in the amount and quality of the food served and the number and status of the *hodža*s and *bula*s invited to lead the event.

The *hodža* typically lives in a house next to the mosque (although this was not the case in Dolina) and his (and his wife's) obligations are extensive. He will sound the call for prayer the prescribed five times a day, even if he is the only one attending (this often happened, especially during early morning and afternoon prayers). In addition, he teaches the children every day, and whenever summoned, recites at the various rituals discussed in the previous chapter: *tevhid* (congregational prayers for the dead); *mevlud* (recitals commemorating the Prophet Mohammad's birth); and *dženaza* (burial ceremonies). He also conducts wedding ceremonies for couples who wish to marry according to Islamic law. He and his wife have social duties too: visiting households in the *džemat* and entertaining guests—hospitality is expected to be lavish, and a cooked meal should be offered.

The *hodža* in Dolina did not actually live in the village, but in a village about an hour's drive away. This meant he was not always there to lead all five daily prayers. He would, however, be present for all the prayers during Ramadan, including the important late evening collective prayers (*teravija*), and he would always arrive in the village on Fridays to lead the *džuma* prayer in the mosque. While teaching children at *mekteb* (from September to June), he stayed with different households in the village, at their invitation. He would take Mondays and Tuesdays off, going back to his own village to be with his wife and children. The details—where he would stay, when, and for how long—were usually worked out before he arrived in September. In households where facilities were better he would stay for longer, but in poorer households with few resources he would not stay at all. He started at one end of the village and moved on as the year progressed. As the *hodža* approached a particular neighborhood, his movements became the main topic of conversation among the local residents. They talked about who had invited him to stay lately, who had not invited him and why, and how long it had been since he had last stayed in a particular house.

The *hodža*'s visit was a major event in a household, and the female members had to do a lot of work to get everything ready, including a thorough cleaning of the house and the preparation of food. There had been plans for the *hodža* to move to Dolina on a permanent basis, and a house was under construction as a Muslim community project, but because of the lack of cooperation it had not been possible to finish it.

This abortive attempt at house construction for the *hodža* might indicate that many villagers felt it was just as well that he did not live in Dolina permanently. Even if the *hodža* was very friendly with people, modest, and fairly conservative, he was still a figure of authority, and the villagers felt called upon to moderate their behavior in his presence and make an effort to present themselves as good and upright people.

This was particularly true for the women, who also told their husbands how to behave when the *hodža* was present. The men, however, were fairly relaxed about the matter and were not prepared to pretend. They knew that the *hodža* was aware that they drank alcohol, did not fast, and did not go to the mosque as often as they should. They also seemed to believe that the *hodža* was more tolerant and understanding of their lack of piety than he would be toward the women. (The *hodža* of course got to hear about what was going on when he was not around. He knew and understood his people very well, but because his position in the village was ambiguous, his relations with the villagers had to be conducted with great diplomatic skill.)

While staying with others, the *hodža* was served the best traditional food, and for dessert and coffee there would be sweet pastries (*slatko*), which are only served on special occasions. There is a saying that "*hodža*s like sweet things" (*vole slatko*), and another: "He is not a *hodža* if he does not like sweet things." This saying probably originated in the fact that a *hodža* makes many visits and as a guest of honor is always served sweet cakes and pastries, and has to like what he is served, although some villagers would say that since the *hodža* did not drink alcohol (see chapter five, n. 2), he liked *slatko*. (However, when used in certain humorous contexts the saying also has sexual connotations. Someone who "likes sweet things"—usually said of men—is someone who needs surplus energy because he leads an active sexual life, so that "liking *slatko*" often becomes synonymous with liking sex.)

As a representative of "official" Islam the *hodža* was surprisingly unintrusive and tolerant of local practices. This was because he identified with the local scene himself. But he was under pressure from the regional mosque council which was pushing for the village *hodža*s to intensify their religious activities in the villages. For instance, the *hodža* in Dolina was instructed to extend his teaching year, which normally lasted nine months, by another two. This is only one example of how the representatives of "official" Islam tended to assume greater authority and to direct local religious life.

The *bula* in Dolina was not employed by the official Islamic organization, but there were younger *bula*s in other districts who were. There were two kinds of *bula*s or female religious instructors, distinguished by age and educational background. First, there were *bula*s of the old generation who were generally trained by the village *hodža* (in Qur'an recitation) and by a senior *bula* in the region (in the ritual washing of a female corpse). Such a *bula* was often the daughter or wife of a *hodža*, or a particularly talented reciter and devout student of the Qur'an. Whenever she was called to a household to perform a certain ritual, she would be given a token sum of money (*sergija*) in donation by the person who had summoned her. This kind of *bula* always had an informal status compared to the *hodža*, and was never an employee of the I.Z. Second, there were *bula*s of a younger generation who had been educated at the *medresa* in Sarajevo since 1978 (the first class to graduate was in 1982).

This institution offers both sexes the religious equivalent of a secular education at the secondary level.[13] Yet although a *bula*'s *medresa* education is almost identical to that given to a *hodža*, there are marked differences in the kinds of work the two sexes perform after graduating. Both *hodža*s and *bula*s are qualified to teach at *mekteb*, and I knew about one young *bula* who taught at a village *mekteb*. But only male students will be instructed in leading prayers in the mosque and in chairing the mosque council. Young *bula*s argued that the Qur'an does not prohibit women from leading the prayers. *Hodža*s, however, explained that all prophets (*pejgamber*) since Adam had been men, and there had been no female messenger throughout the history of Islam. An older male informant, who was a member of a mosque council, said that women were never members of an Islamic council because "this is not a religious custom" (that is, the idea of having women as council members was based on a different value system, one pursued by the secular state). His argument was, however, challenged by a young *bula*, who said that a female colleague of hers was a member of the mosque council in the eastern Bosnian town where she was employed. She emphasized that the lack of female representatives on the Islamic council for her own *opština* did not imply that women cannot be members, but rather that the male representatives there were opposed to the idea.

However, the local Islamic council for the area where this particular *bula* worked was not only opposed to the idea of a *bula* and female representative on the council, but also to employing a *medresa*-educated *bula* in its region. There was an obvious candidate for the job, a twenty-one-year-old woman from the area. She was upset that the local village mosque councils refused to issue her a decree (*dekret*), and thereby authorize and formally employ her as the *bula* for the *opština*. (There was an old *bula* already working in this region who was not *medresa*-educated and not formally employed.) Instead, the young *bula* performed individual assignments together with the other, established *bula* in the area (mainly reciting at *tevhid*s), which were paid for directly by the person or household which had called for her.

13. A young *medresa* student and *bula*-to-be giving a sermon in a village mosque at Ramadan.

This particular *bula*'s situation was not unique.[14] Women graduating from the *medresa* often had difficulty in finding a job. While those at the I.Z. headquarters were eager to include women as religious instructors, the problem seemed to be at the individual village level where the mosque council often opposed employing the new generation of *medresa*-educated *bulas*, and attempted to justify its decision on financial grounds. The local *hodžas* and the village mosque councils doubtless perceived these women who refused the marginal status of their female predecessors as a challenge to learned male authority in local religious life.

There was one particular *opština* which, in the opinion of many of these younger *bulas*, introduced an ideal system. Here *hodžas* and *bulas* were employed and paid directly by the Islamic council for the *opština* (which was often more liberal) without going through the more traditionalist village mosque councils. Furthermore, *bula*s of the older generation without a formal education could only perform their tasks in the presence of a *medresa*-educated *bula*.

By 1990, however, only a few *opština* had made the *medresa*-educated *bula*s indispensable by passing a decision which said that official rituals exclusively for women could not take place without a *medresa*-educated *bula*'s presence. Furthermore, the traditional *bula*s were opposing what they perceived as a threat to their own authority within the village community. The young, educated Islamic instructors disapproved of some of the traditional *bula*s for their lack of formal knowledge and especially for their lack of fluency in Arabic when reciting. These older *bula*s in turn disapproved of some of their younger colleagues, who they said were unwilling to wash the dead in preparation for burial, but only too eager to display their knowledge by teaching and recitation at *tevhid*s and *mevlud*s.

The distance between the theoretically-based moral world of the "official" *bula* on the one hand and the practically-based one of the village *bula* on the other was apparent in the way they saw their role as religious instructors for village women. In general the villagers themselves were often skeptical toward the young, *medresa*-educated Islamic instructors who wanted them to change their customs and who made them feel inadequate as Muslims. A traditional *bula* was usually from the village where she lived and worked (this was less often the case with a *hodža*). She knew all the families, their histories, and how they were related. For this reason the villagers trusted and respected her and preferred to have their own *bula*, not a young stranger, recite at a relative's memorial service. Women generally felt that their own *bula* understood and accepted behavior that the younger *bula*s did not. While the young *bula*s instructed women on moral issues, as they had been taught to do at the *medresa*, the traditional village *bula*'s advice was informed by her knowledge of everyday life, without preaching.

Young *bula*s tended to make didactic speeches focusing on issues relevant to women: their role in marriage as mother and wife; abortion; appropriate behavior when ritually impure (when menstruating, after childbirth, and after sex); what to do about husbands who drink or do not go to the mosque; and their responsibility for supervising their children's religious instruction. Abortion in particular was condemned as a great sin. Women were told that contrary to what they may had heard from other sources there is no such thing as equality between the sexes since men are the masters. The women had become accustomed to hearing these arguments from Islamic instructors and scholars and usually took them lightly, knowing well that the reality of their lives was one thing, the repeated moral injunctions another. After attending a talk given by a young female *medresa* student on the usual "women's issues," I asked what the village women thought. Although unwilling to voice an opinion, they finally gave the young *bula* credit for having spoken so openly about these issues and acknowledged that the situation had been awkward since the *bula* was unmarried (and by implication sexually inexperienced). They added: "She has to say what she has to say and that is fine, but we have heard this so many times we are sick of it. You know, we comply with what we can and the rest we leave to be written on the side of the bad deeds."

## Muslim Faith Healers and Diviners

So far we have discussed carriers and agents of Islamic knowledge authorized as representatives of official Islam. However, there were also other carriers of Islamic knowledge who were not accepted by official Islam. Some of these people, from whom villagers sought advice and help in times of personal crisis or when in need of divine protection, participated in official Islam as well as in practices not approved of by the latter. They were thus mediators between official Islam and those practices which are associated with mysticism or with personal support and help in times of crisis. Some of the causes for such problems were described in chapter five.

Seeking the assistance of faith healers on behalf of family or household members was one way in which individuals cared for living members of their family or household. Contrary to the practices described in chapter five, however, people visited faith healers not so as to seek blessing (or earn *sevap*) but rather as a means of avoiding, resisting, or counteracting malevolent influences which may cause (or already have caused) someone physical or psychological disharmony and disequilibrium. When faced with problems that neither a doctor, nor (if appropriate) a psychologist had been able to solve, a person would turn to a faith healer. When it concerned illness the faith healer would always make sure the person had already consulted a doctor; if he or she had not, he would tell him or her to do so.

The diviners and healers in Bosnia may for the purpose of analysis be divided into three different categories, on the basis of their backgrounds and the methods they use. Diviners and healers are valued according to their literacy. The first category consists of people, both men and women, who have no formal religious education, but whom the villagers nevertheless call a *hodža*, if male, and a *bula*, if female, probably because

they know the Qur'an better than the average Muslim and can write a
little Arabic. As this usage suggests, in rural areas "knowledge" (and literacy) has traditionally been associated with Islam and Islamic instructors. As we shall see, however, this does not necessarily mean that all
*hodžas* are believed to "know a lot" merely because they are literate in
Islam. Alternatively, diviners may be called by the more general term of
*sihirbaz*, or *sihirbazica* for a woman (the term derives from *sihir*), although this has the negative connotation of sorcerer, that is, one who
casts evil spells. There are also other less respected forms of divination
which do not require much knowledge or particular powers and are
practiced by many people: gypsies traveling the countryside offering to
read palms, and local women who read the villagers' (usually young
girls') future in ground coffee and white beans. This kind of divination
is dismissed as fortune-telling (*gatanje*) and superstitious rubbish and is
often indulged in for fun when women and girls gather in the winter
evenings.

Although diviners and faith healers work unofficially, people frequently come from afar to seek their help. Clients may also belong to
other ethnoreligious groups. However, all the Muslim faith healers I
spoke to told me that while Catholics were rare, Serbs (Orthodox Christian) were less so; they often went to *hodžas* after having tried their own
diviners and healing practices first.[15] An old Dolina woman who practiced a traditional healing ritual said that Catholics (Croats) would ask
her for help only if absolutely nothing else had worked, as they had their
own remedies. She confirmed that she herself had used "Catholic"
methods ("they have this kind of water which is blessed") once when
her cow was ill. Such cross-religious or "syncretistic practices" are consistent with the pragmatic orientation of this kind of religious activity
(Hasluck 1929).

Individual diviners may be known to specialize in treating particular
kinds of problems. One *hodža* may be known to have healing hands for
children (*sevap ruke za djecu*), another may be particularly good at casting love spells, another again at seeing and finding lost items. People
choose diviners accordingly, but their choice may also depend on who
is closest to where the client lives, or on previous contact and personal
preference. In general, however, if the first diviner does not solve a person's problem, he or she may go and see a different one. In seeking to
help their clients healers mix prayers and recitals from the Qur'an with
their knowledge of traditional folk medicine. They may refer a client either to a doctor or a *hodža*, depending on the problem, or they may
prescribe different magical procedures: visiting holy graves, dispersing
corn in a prescribed place while saying a prayer, or swallowing certain
herbal mixtures.

Among the most common problems healers are asked to remedy are chronic illness, marital difficulties, infertility, prolonged bachelorhood, and mental problems such as anxiety or depression. I knew of three people, two women and a man, who practiced healing as described. They are usually called by their first names and the name of their village. All three lived in remote mountain villages. People came from all over central Bosnia and from Sarajevo to see them. One of the villagers' favorite stories about one of them was that during the Olympic Winter Games in Sarajevo (1984) this "*hodža*" had visitors from distant countries who took the trip all the way from Sarajevo to seek his help. The story was always told to establish this man's importance. However, the "real" *medresa*-educated official *hodža*s dismissed these healers (and diviners) as "illiterate" because they mixed Qur'anic knowledge with what the official *hodža*s considered to be non-Islamic folk beliefs.

The second category consists of *bula*s who do faith healing and divination and *hodža*s who write amulets. I will deal with both in turn. Female faith healers are typically middle-aged, and are *bula*s of the traditional rather than the *medresa*-educated kind. Generally, female healers use fewer written sources and concentrate on reciting Qur'anic verses, praying and divination. They are particularly sought after for *salijevati stravu* (to pour/cast horror) and the "praying of *istihara*," traditional healing practices and divination accompanied by Muslim prayers and teachings from the Qur'an.

Prayers of *istihara* are said specifically to predict the future. People, usually women, will come to the *bula* and ask if she can pray *istihara* on their behalf to find out whether a certain project will succeed, for example. Before going to sleep the *bula* will pray for a dream that will reveal whatever it was the person in question wanted to know about her future. The *bula* will then interpret the dream. The *istihara* is said to demand intense concentration and be mentally very tiring; not every *bula* can do it. While *shari'at*-oriented Islamic scholars consider much of the divination practiced by Muslims in Bosnia to be against the spirit of Islam, the *bula* I spoke to emphasized that the *istihara* is a practice referred to in the Qur'an.

The same was not, however, said about *salijevati stravu* which can also be performed by less religiously educated Muslim women, as it requires less knowledge. The central item in the ritual is a lump of lead which is heated and then thrown into water, where it forms a pattern from which the supplicant's troubles are interpreted. Apart from the local *bula* there was one other woman in the village who performed this ritual. She had learned it from an old *bula* from the district, who decided to stop performing it because of pressure from her children who complained that it was primitive superstition. She taught the woman from

Dolina how to perform it and gave her the lump of lead (which should be handed down from one *bula* to another). I observed *salijevati stravu* on several occasions. It was always performed at the request of women who had either been bereaved by the death of a close relative, or had been upset by other events in the immediate family and were anxious and unable to sleep, though they did not know the reason why. The casting of the lead and the Qur'anic recitation were believed to help define the problem and thereby relieve the anxiety. The ritual could only be performed by devout women who could recite Qur'an verses. The pattern formed by the lump of lead was always interpreted as an indication that something had upset the patient, and suggestions were made as to what this might be and what the patient should do. She may be advised to say specific prayers regularly or perform other religious duties. The lead ritual might be repeated a couple of times over the next week or two, until she felt calmer and less worried.

## The Writing of Amulets

The most common and popular form of help Muslims in the village sought in times of personal stress (particularly when this was believed to have been caused by negative influences such as *sihir*) was an amulet, popularly called *zapis* (note), written by a *hodža*. A *zapis* may more rarely be referred to as *mušema* (the Arabic word which describes the wrapper around the note). The more general term *hamajlija* (from the Arabic term for amulet) is also used. A *zapis* is a small piece of paper with a verse or phrase from the Qur'an written in Arabic and carried as a charm or amulet. Worn for protection against spells and indirectly therefore against illness, it can also be worn as an amulet to secure happiness and good fortune, or to ease anxiety and physical pain (such as headaches). Such problems are not untypically brought on by life-cycle changes, such as marrying and becoming a bride and new member of a household, the birth of a child, or the death or illness of a close family member. The paper is wrapped into a triangle in a small piece of red cloth which has been oiled or waxed to make it more resistant. (The Arabic word *mušema* means oilcloth.) The *zapis* is attached by a safety pin as close to the person's body as possible, usually to the undershirt. Only a trained *hodža* is considered competent to write *zapis*; the few who actually do so are well known in rural areas, especially among Muslims. The *hodžas* who write amulets must know how to write Qur'an verses in Arabic, and to be able to choose verses appropriate to each case. They are often retired religious instructors with long experience and good psychological insight into local life. Some *hodžas*, however, think the practice is not in the spirit of Islam and is immoral (because of the money involved). The official Islamic Association was rigorously against it and would teach young *medresa* students to preach against it if posted to rural areas.

The verses written on the *zapis* are chosen according to the problem it is supposed to remedy. After the *zapis* has been written and wrapped there are several possible procedures: it may be worn immediately without any further measures being taken, or it may be put through various magical treatments. (It is important that the *zapis* not be worn or left in unclean places such as the lavatory if unprotected, that is, not oiled.) The magical treatment also varies with the nature of the problem the *zapis* is supposed to protect the person from.

One of the *hodžas* told me that fewer people asked him to write *zapis* for them today than in his younger days, since "today there are more doctors around, so fewer people come and ask us [*hodžas*] to write *zapis*. Besides, young people nowadays do not believe in praying." Villagers and *hodžas* alike told me that in the late eighties fewer *hodžas* practiced forms of faith healing and divination such as the writing of *zapis*. This was clearly related to the younger *hodžas'* more formalized and more *shari'at*-oriented Islamic training, rendering them critical of such practices. Nevertheless, judging from the number of case histories I collected of people who had sought the help of a *hodža* and who had had a *zapis* written for them at least once, it was still a much-used strategy for coping with misfortune. However, people tended to seek the help of one of the more prestigious sufi *hodžas* rather than a knowledgeable old local *hodža*. The sufi *hodžas*, in contrast to the local ones, reported an increase in the number of people who had come to them with health or personal problems over the last few years. Perhaps this was a reaction to the severe economic and political crisis in the country in the late 1980s and people's increased insecurity and distrust of authority. Seeking help from nonstate-approved sources may thus be interpreted as an expression of popular distrust of state institutions.

## The Sufi Hodžas

The third and most prestigious category of faith healers consists of a group of four *hodžas* who are all related to each other through a common ancestor, the founder of one of the dervish *tekija* in the region of which they are members. They combine being employed as *hodžas* by the official state-approved religious authorities with being active members of a sufi order. I shall call them sufi *hodžas* to distinguish them from other kinds of diviners, healers, and *hodžas*. They are all highly literate men who know several languages, including Turkish and Arabic. They use a range of techniques and sources: sacred books, astrology, palm reading, prayers, and Qur'an recitation.

Since what these sufi *hodžas* do is condemned by part of the official Islamic leadership, and is also said by some to be illegal, they prefer to keep a low profile. My information on their activities is therefore not as detailed and accurate as I would have liked; it comes mainly from villagers who have been to see them. The sufi *hodžas* themselves, unlike the first category of diviners who do straightforward charm writing, are unwilling to talk about their work. Indeed, villagers who had sought their help were also evasive when I asked what the *hodža* had told them. They said the *hodža* had warned them that if they told anybody exactly what had taken place it would lose its effect. The obvious explanation for this is that he does not want people to know that he might get it wrong and is thus protecting the authority of his profession. However, more to the point, the purpose of what these *hodžas* do is usually either to "undo" a spell (*sihir*) or to protect a person from one. Passing on information about what the *hodža* has said, and most importantly what he has said about the person's future, would leave that person vulnerable to *sihir*.

Clients are never asked for a fixed payment, but are advised to pay what they can, and wish to. When the consultation is over the *hodža* leaves the room and the client will leave as much money as s/he feels is appropriate. While the *hodža* likes to define what is given as a gift, most villagers see it as a payment (using the word for payment rather than for gift). Those who feel that they have been greatly helped may continue to give the *hodža* presents. One of the four sufi *hodžas* in the area, known to be particularly good at love spells, is visited by people from all educational backgrounds and socioeconomic strata, Muslims as well as non-Muslims. However, all four of them are visited by people from all over Bosnia.

Islamic scholars and *hodžas* condemn divination as they believe that only God can know a person's future. The divining *hodžas*, however, see themselves merely as interpreters of God's message. When I first started to ask villagers about the *hodžas* who write amulets, they told me that they had books or that "they look in books." However, these books are not accessible to just anybody who knows how to read. I discovered that the books from which the sufi *hodžas* derive their knowledge and authority are central to faith healing as a whole. The books are in Arabic, Persian, and Turkish, and consist of Islamic religious literature including the Hadith and sufi writings, among other things. These books were collected and handed down by the dervishes' forefathers and have been in the family for generations. When villagers need to see such a *hodža* they say they will "go to the *hodža* so that he may write something down." The fact that they emphasize the "writing aspect" of the *hodža*'s activity is significant.[16] Because illiteracy was common in the rural population until quite recently, the ability to read and write was considered both powerful and mystical. With increasing literacy in the population at large the knowledge of reading and writing has lost some of its immediate power and mystique.

But literacy does not affect the power of Qur'anic verses written in Arabic, the divine language of revelation. In the village people referred to the diviner-*hodža* as a "*hodža* who knows a lot." There are also *hodža* who, although literate in Islam, are said not to know anything. Knowledge in this context does not refer to knowledge of the Qur'an but to more esoteric knowledge, as such people are credited with the ability to see and understand things that ordinary people cannot. If a *hodža* wants to be respected as somebody who knows a lot he must have sacred and spiritual learning as well as the esoteric power which enables him "to see what others cannot see." Official Islam puts an emphasis on literacy and knowledge of *shari'at*. Nevertheless, in Dolina the villagers viewed religious knowledge as something which moved beyond Qur'anic literacy and knowledge of *shari'at*. For a Muslim to acquire a reputation as "someone who knows a lot" Islamic literacy is a necessary but not a sufficient condition. In addition the person must possess strong spiritual powers and the power to "see." The villagers' concept of what constitutes Islamic knowledge is therefore closer to that of the dervishes than it is to that propagated by official Islam through the Islamic Association.

Because of their religious knowledge and perceived spiritual power, the sufi *hodža*s are seen as closer to God than other *hodža*s and therefore in a better position to mediate between people and God, or at least to advise them on what devotional practices will bring the most blessing under specific circumstances. However, the diviner cannot be as close as the *šehit* or the deceased *evlija* since he still belongs to this world. He may therefore advise his client to visit the shrine of an *evlija* or *šehit* as an even more powerful intermediary than he. There is thus a hierarchy of intermediaries between people and God. It is significant, however, that intermediaries are mainly sought by those who do not read or understand the Qur'an well and to whom a sufi *hodža*, a *šehit*, or an *evlija* is therefore more accessible as a means of communicating with God than normal prayers which sometimes seem inadequate. For the dervishes themselves communication with God consists of several circles, of which the *shari'at* is the outermost. The different means of communication are therefore not mutually exclusive but complementary. Some of those who know a lot may turn out to be *evlija*s. Although I later learned that there were pious men in Bosnia-Hercegovina who were considered *evlija*, at the time I heard this term used only in reference to a dead person who had been very pious and performed miracles both in life and after death.

In a previous section I noted that the official Islamic Association was critical of practices which it defined as not "according to Islam" or not "prescribed." Interpretation of Islam involving faith healing and the writing of amulets by respected members of a sufi order were among these. It is therefore paradoxical that these learned dervishes are also working *hodžas*, employed by the Islamic Association and consequently also representatives of official Islam. The next section will review the sufi presence in the region where Dolina is situated.

## The Dervishes

Dolina is situated in the heart of a region which is known for its sufi sanctuaries, called *tekije* (sing. *tekija*).[17] The Dolina villagers' tradition of praying at Muslim shrines for a favorable outcome in times of personal crisis, and for dead relatives (or neighbors) at the *tevhid* has been ascribed to the influence of sufism as have some practices connected with the women's *tevhid* such as the use of a large rosary (see chapter five). A legacy of the dervish presence in this region which has yet to be mentioned, however, is the performance of *zikir* (sufi rituals of remembrance in which the names of God are invoked; from Arabic *dhikr*) at *mevlud* and *tevhid* in private homes or in the mosque in Dolina and neighboring villages in this region. When performed by the dervishes of the Naqshibendi order, it consists of chanting the names of God accompanied by violent rhythmic movements and the beating of a drum. This increases in intensity until a climax is reached when somebody falls into a trance. However, when performed by villagers and their *hodža* the ceremony is shorter and less intense and is not (unlike the dervish version) the central element in the sequence of prayers and recitations at a *mevlud* or a *tevhid*.[18] (Practicing Muslims and even *hodžas* from other parts of Bosnia are often unfamiliar with the body movements accompanying the collective chanting at a *mevlud* and *tevhid* in Dolina and surrounding villages. One woman who had moved into the area from east Bosnia had never encountered these practices until she attended a *mevlud* in a village near Dolina. When she asked why they did it, she was told that it was *sevap*.)

The *zikir* is associated with the dervishes and thus with men in general. Although women may perform *zikir* at *mevlud* and *tevhid* when both men and women are present and they are being led by a *hodža*, they tend to react with a mixture of amusement and embarrassment and to either perform a restrained *zikir* or not to participate at all. On their way home from such a ritual some women once commented drily that there had been "a lot of *hukanje*" (roaring). At *tevhid* and *mevlud* led by a *bula* (and attended exclusively by women) the *zikir* is never performed.

In the 1950s the Islamic Association banned the dervish orders and closed their *tekije* with the approval of the political authorities. The Naqshibendi order, which had been the dominant one in central Bosnia, was not dissolved; instead a core of its members went underground and continued to hold *zikir* secretly in private homes. But it lost much of its popular appeal as a result of the ban, as its activities could no longer be part of the religious experience of "ordinary Muslims."[19] Whenever our discussions touched on the dervishes, Dolina men in their seventies and eighties would remember attending *mevlud* at a *tekija* in central Bosnia. (The words "sufism" and "sufi" are rarely used in popular speech; villagers and village *hodžas* will usually talk about the dervishes and their influence.) Their descriptions were vivid with the intensity of the experience: the number of men crowded inside and outside the *tekija*, the mystical authority of the sheikh and in particular what they remembered as the "throwing of knives." Today, saber and skewer piercing do not play a prominent part in the *zikir* (except for those attended exclusively by dervishes). There are two reasons for this. First, the order has few dervishes among its ranks who are able to perform these feats; usually somebody has to be invited from another order elsewhere (such accomplishments are more common among the Kosovo dervishes, particularly those belonging to the Bektashi order; see Čehajić 1986). Second, these practices were prohibited by the I.Z., allegedly on the grounds that somebody might get hurt. However sincere the I.Z. may have been, the ban was also a way of reducing the popular attraction of a cult which they perceived as not *shari'at*.

In the eighties the I.Z. attempted to bring the Naqshibendi order and its members under their influence by sending representatives to every major dervish ritual, among other things. Thus, the popular annual *mevlud*s that the order held at their *tekije* in central Bosnia and in Hercegovina began to be supervised by the I.Z. An Islamic scholar and high-ranking member of the organization would give a sermon to the crowds gathered in and around the *tekija*. They had come to listen to recitation from the Qur'an and the singing of *ilahije* (devotional songs), many of which were written by the first sheikhs of the Naqshibendi *tekije* in central Bosnia.

In the late eighties the I.Z. initiated the pilgrimage to the annual *mevlud* at the *tekija* at Buna (Hercegovina). Each *džemat* in the Dolina region organized buses to take interested villagers to the *mevlud*. While during the first few years only the most devout and older Muslims in Dolina went, in later years it became a popular outing in which the young also took part. In May 1990 there were two buses going from Dolina, for by then the *mevlud* at Buna had become one of the major events on the ritual "calendar" in Dolina.[20] People picnicked in the beautiful hills around the *tekija*, and some tried to squeeze through the dense crowd to get inside the *tekija* to pray, to get a better view of the prominent *hodžas* and sheikhs who sat in the courtyard reciting *mevlud* poems, and to say prayers for health and fortune at the shrine of the sheikh's tomb (see chapter five).

The Buna *mevlud* took place during the day, but the dervishes held their *zikir* the night before the official ritual amidst their circle of adherents and guests from other dervish orders in Kosovo and Macedonia. (These private *zikir*s may well include the saber and skewer piercing already mentioned.) While the I.Z.'s takeover of dervish rituals had provided official Bosnian Islam with some of the mysticism and popular appeal it had lacked, it also watered the rituals down to the extent that the mystics had lost much of their former attraction.

During *mevlud* at a *tekija* in central Bosnia, the audience for which is largely limited to people from surrounding villages because of its physical inaccessibility, a *zikir* for the general public was held on the night of the *mevlud*. Again, however, the dervishes had held a more exclusive *zikir* for special guests the night before. The larger, public *zikir* starts with the rhythmic repetition of *lailahe illallah* ("there is no God except the one Allah") and the invocation of the names of God, accompanied by specific physical movements, mainly of the head, all of which have a symbolic meaning. Later, as the collective invocations intensify, the dervishes sitting in a circle with their sheikh (who faces the congregation, his back to the Kibla) rise to their feet. They stand in a circle, their bodies swaying in response to the rhythmic repetitions of the congregation and the beat of a drum. Their body movements gradually become more vigorous. As the intensity escalates, a dervish may fall into a trance, invoking the name of Allah repeatedly. When he recovers, the repetitive words and tunes will decrease in intensity, and will eventually be replaced by recitation and *illahije*.

Women may also attend the *zikir*, but they do so from behind a latticed gallery at the back of the room. A young woman who was close to the dervish milieu told me that there were also female dervishes, although the sheikh of the *tekija* denied this. The woman claimed that a female dervish has to recite three particular verses (from the Qur'an) seventeen times before morning prayers (*sabah*) throughout her life; it is therefore a major commitment. Female dervishes may not participate in *zikir*, but may watch men's *zikir* from the gallery. In other words, the "female dervish" is not accepted as such by the men, as she cannot be part of the brotherhood or participate in the *zikir* which is the main defining characteristic of the dervishes in Bosnia. For a woman, being a "dervish" is thus an entirely individual experience.

A *hodža* familiar with the dervish milieu told me that because recruitment of new dervishes was difficult, the qualifications for acceptance were far from ideal. He suggested that novices have to read some books, but that they did not need to be particularly pious. It is difficult to estimate how many members the three *tekije* in the Dolina region had during my research. When I asked a sheikh about their numbers, he was reluctant to answer, but indicated in the cryptic manner typical of dervishes that it was somewhere between two and three hundred. Each order has a hierarchical structure with a sheikh at the top (the position usually goes from father to son). I was told that the sheikh accepts new members on the basis of an interview.

The main participants at the sufi *mevlud* at the *tekija* made up the circle of descendants from the second sheikh of the *tekija*, Muhammed Mejli Baba, and their friends. Devout Muslims and *hodžas* in the region who fell outside the circle often considered it an exclusive club and saw these dervishes as a spiritual and socioeconomic elite. Some questioned their sincerity. An old village *hodža* familiar with dervish religious practices and their influence on religious rituals in his region, once summed up his opinion as follows: "The dervishes see themselves as better Muslims and closer to heaven than others, but I say every dervish is not a Muslim." This opinion was representative of the popular view of dervishes as well as that of the Islamic Association. Echoing the old *hodža*, a young *hodža* who was not originally from this region and who claimed to know one of the dervishes famed for performing saber-piercing on himself in a trance from his years at the *medresa* in Sarajevo, said that he was the least devout Muslim there, often skipping his prayers and so on. Another *hodža*, who had just witnessed a *zikir* where a dervish had fallen into trance, compared their ritual to a stimulus like alcohol. He claimed that the more solid a person's faith was, the less was he a dervish.

The view of the dervish as less rather than more Muslim has some supporters, especially among the *ulema* faithful to the I.Z. As I noted earlier in this chapter, the senior representative of the organization gave a speech at the opening of a mosque in the so-called dervish region in which he spoke rather unfavorably about a fictive dervish who spent all his time wrapped in contemplation, while somebody else brought him his daily bread. Thus the senior representative of official Islam dismissed the dervish's religious devotion as socially useless. Furthermore, at the I.Z.-directed *medresa* in Sarajevo, students who train to become *hodžas* or *bulas* are taught that sufism and the practices of the dervish orders (including, as already mentioned, the writing of charms or *zapis* by some prominent members of the order, which as we have seen is very popular

among Muslims in Dolina) are not "according to Islam." Being unfamiliar with the orders themselves, this is the message most of them will pass
on to the members of the *džemat* they are eventually sent to teach and
lead.

However, as already mentioned, most dervishes and sheikhs in Bosnia
are also I.Z.-employed *hodžas* committed to its teachings and bound by
its directives. The two functions are not necessarily contradictory; rather
they represent different but overlapping styles of participation in religious life. Bosnian Muslims esteemed for their religious learning adopt
different styles in different contexts. The I.Z.-employed *hodža* teaches
children at *mekteb*, but later in the evening the same man may receive
people in his home who seek his help for a problem which "school medicine" has not cured; his knowledge of healing is part of the sufi tradition
he shares with other senior dervishes. At the village level sufi traditions manifested themselves in various devotional practices such as
*tevhid*, *zikir*, and the visiting of Muslim shrines, and in later years the
annual *mevlud* at a *tekija* in Hercegovina. However, the Dolina Muslims' most direct contact with the dervishes occurred when they visited
those they considered the most knowledgeable in writing charms, healing, protection, and blessing. Although they thereby contested authoritative Islamic knowledge and meaning, the villagers were motivated to
seek various carriers of and sources for such knowledge as meaningful
paths to spiritual merit, social prestige, and physical well-being.

## Defining Muslim Practice

A young Bosnian *hodža*, here called Vahid, was giving me a ride back to
the village after I had visited his sister, Meliha, a *medresa*-educated religious teacher or *bula*. He knew I had come to Bosnia to study "Muslim
customs" (*Muslimanski običaji*) but was critical of me for staying in this
particular village. He argued I would not learn anything because people
there did not read books and thus did not know anything. What kind of
knowledge was he referring to? He made his point clearer: "They only
do things the way they think it should be and their religion is mixed up
with Christianity and all sorts of things."

Many of the younger *shari'at*-oriented Muslims—as I call them since
they approve of practices which are codified and disapprove of those
which are not—define what is "Muslim" strictly as that which is Islamic.
They make a clear distinction between Muslim customs which are "according to Islam" (*po Islamu*) and those which are not. Vahid, like many
of his devout colleagues, would equate "Muslim customs" with what he
considered to be Islamic practices. However, to many Dolina villagers

"Muslim customs" were the customs and ritual practices that they as opposed to their Croat and Catholic neighbors adhered to. Whether it was Islamic or not did not enter into the discussion. Some ritual practices were obviously Islamic while others were not, yet they were all considered to be the traditions and cultural heritage of the Muslims. Vasvija is a typical representative of this understanding of "Muslim." She is a seventy-year-old woman, who performs all the obligatory rituals (except the pilgrimage to Mecca which she cannot afford) associated with the five pillars. The case history below illustrates the difference between her views and Vahid's about what constituted "Muslim customs."

Spring was approaching in Dolina, the village where Vasvija was born and had married. For weeks I had heard people referring to *Jurjev*. The day of *Jurjev* or *Jurjevdan* (St. George's day; the Orthodox Serbs call it Đurđevdan), is on 6 May according to Orthodox tradition. *Jurjev* turned out to be a significant event on both the ritual and agricultural calendars of the Dolina Muslims. Bosnian Muslims were (and are) familiar with all the holy days celebrated by their Orthodox (*pravoslavni*) and Catholic compatriots. They used both the *hijri* (Islamic) calendar and the Christian one, and often reckoned time according to Christian feast days (Hadžijahić, Traljić, and Šukrić 1977:87). Muslims in some regions still celebrated some of these feast days in 1987. Ritual events were said to take place so and so many weeks after *Jurjev*. The sun is said to be good after *Jurjev*, but before *Jurjev* it is recommended that you not expose yourself to direct sunlight for long, as the sun is "not good" and will give you a headache. Certain crops should be sown before *Jurjev* and others after. The dates for the annual prayers for rain and the Dolina *dova* (prayers for the dead) are reckoned from *Jurjev*. In fact the day marks the traditional celebration of spring and fertility, and although it coincides with a Christian feast day, its origin is probably pre-Christian.

What is significant here, however, is the fact that while Muslims living in mixed Muslim/Catholic villages in central Bosnia celebrated this day, Muslims who lived in Muslim Serb/Orthodox villages in eastern Bosnia (prior to 1992) did not. The Catholic Croats in Dolina do not celebrate what they consider a Serbian Orthodox saint's day. When I asked about the forthcoming celebration of *Jurjev*, some of my women neighbors somewhat reluctantly told me what was happening. This day is regarded as particularly auspicious for various magic spells and divinatory practices. For instance, women may perform different sorts of magic to prevent evil spells being cast. Women agreed, however, that Muslim women from eastern Bosnia (which used to be mixed Muslim and Orthodox Serb) knew much more about such spells than the women from Dolina, and everyone remembered a man, since dead, who used to cast spells on cows on *Jurjev*. On this day girls are supposed to throw their shoes across the roof of their house; from the way the shoe points a girl can predict the direction in which she will marry. Most of the customs associated with the *Jurjev* celebrations involve the young and unmarried and are clearly fertility symbols. Customs associated with this day may vary somewhat throughout Bosnia, but in Dolina there were two main events both of which involved the youth.

On the evening before *Jurjev* the boys made flutes of wood. This used to be done by young, unmarried men and significantly, was made from the wood of a young tree. On the following morning they went around to all the houses and blew their flutes to wake people up (originally, to wake up the girls). On the eve of *Jurjev* the girls went to the water mill to collect water in bottles, which are hidden away from the boys somewhere outside the house overnight. On the following morning the girls washed their faces in the water caught from the mill to look beautiful and get rosy cheeks. Later during the day and in the evening, the boys and girls and other villagers and young people from neighboring villages walked up steep paths to attend the fair (*teferič*), which was held on the highest hill in the village. (This event did take place during my stay in the village.) At a small clearing in the forest a team of Muslim boys from Dolina and another from the village on the other side of the hill competed in a game of football. People had picnics while they watched the game and chatted to neighbors.

As if to explain the lack of enthusiasm for answering my question about the celebration of *Jurjev* day, Vasvija added: "But there is little of that nowadays; some say *Jurjev* day is not a Muslim custom, they say it is 'gypsy' (*ciganski*[21]), and others say it is 'orthodox'" (*pravoslav*, i.e., Serbian Orthodox). "But," she insisted, "it is also ours, we have celebrated it for as long as I can remember." She made it clear that she disapproved of the *hodža* for discouraging them from celebrating the day, and added that the old *hodža* (who had retired) was nicer, as he did not mind ("He never said anything, while this one says we should celebrate the Muslim new year instead.")

Vahid and Vasvija are both local Muslims but they represent different voices in the local discourse on what constitutes "Muslim customs" and therefore the defining characteristics of Muslim identity. The young *hodža* who disapproved of the alleged ignorance and misconceptions of the Dolina Muslims about what constituted Muslim customs, grew up in a village not far from Dolina. He was echoing the view of many of the younger *hodža*s and Islamic scholars who had been educated at least partly at Islamic institutions abroad (such as at the Sunni center and Al-Azhar University in Cairo, or at universities in Saudi Arabia, Iraq, or Turkey). Vahid's statement may immediately be understood as an ex-

pression of what some authors would have labeled "Islamic orthodoxy."
The danger with such labels, however, is that they suggest fixed entities
the content of which is assumed to be known. Further questions into
Vahid's understanding of Islam (and Muslim identity) would therefore
seem superfluous. Add to Vahid's biography the following information
and such a label proves less useful: He is a dervish and a member of a sufi
order and also comes from a family of Islamic scholars. Furthermore, he
was also employed by the official Islamic institution in Bosnia-Hercegovina to instruct young Bosnians in Islam and lead Bosnians in their
prayers. His sister, a *bula*, taught children at *mekteb* and led the prominent and characteristically Bosnian prayers for the dead (*tevhid*). She
married by elopement (*ukrala se*), but later divorced. On Saturdays she
changed her headscarf and *dimije* for fashionable Western clothes and
asked her brother to accompany her to the Saturday dance in a nearby
village. Rigidly labeling someone as "orthodox" would not account for
all the elements which coexist in peoples' understanding and practice of
lived Islam, and might lead one to dismiss Bosnians as "not real Muslims" or, as in Vahid's case, as marginal in relation to an officially defined
*shari'at* Islam. Yet, to a Bosnian Muslim, however *shari'at*-oriented and
however devout, such a statement would not make sense as either he or
she is a Muslim or not (and in Bosnia that means being either a Croat or
a Serb).

To Vahid as well as others to whom I presented myself during my
field research in Bosnia I always explained that I studied *Muslimanski
običaji* (Muslim traditions or customs). Vahid and Vasvija (and many in
the village like her) defined "Muslim customs" differently. I had made a
conscious decision not to say I was studying Islam (or "Islamic customs" for that matter), for this, I had discovered, would have prompted
many Muslims to give the "correct" *shari'at* version of Islamic practices,
rather than explaining to me their own interpretations and practices
through their own everyday lives as Muslim Bosnians. A few villagers
who assumed I was studying Islam, would answer my questions concerning religious practices by handing me their children's *mekteb* books
(written by Islamic scholars and members of the Islamic Association in
Sarajevo). One of the older women in the village who used to tell me
about "old Muslim customs," would almost inevitably add to her description of a certain traditional belief or healing practice: "These are
things we believe in villages, but which others might think is nonsense,
but everything interests you, and you want to know everything, so I tell
you."

When asked about issues concerning the Islamic faith, the response
was markedly different. Unless the person was a learned Islamic instruc-

tor, he would immediately bring out his books. The books would tell me how it is (read, should be) done. As mentioned in chapter five, the discourse on Islam and Islamic practices in Dolina was cast largely in terms of which practices are prescribed (*propisano*) or "according to Islam," that is according to Islamic law (*shari'at*), and which are not, and whether the latter are acceptable or not. In other words, while Vahid in his discussion with me understood "Muslim customs" as Islamic doctrines and practices, Vasvija understood Muslim customs in a broad sense as all the customs, practices, and beliefs she knew as part of her world of experience as a Muslim Bosnian born and raised in this particular village in central Bosnia. Some villagers also referred to practices or "customs" not approved by the Islamic establishment as "not Qur'anic." This expression tells us little about the position of the Islamic instructors on these questions, but it does tell us that to the villagers, the disapproval of some of their practices by Islamic instructors was based on literary and scholarly knowledge of Islam. Many of the Muslims in the village said this with some resignation, commenting: "They say it is not Islamic." Muslims in Dolina did not share in the complete identification made by many Islamic instructors and the Islamic elite between [Bosnian] Muslim as *nacija* identification and Islam as a religious system. In other words, the definitional overlap of the latter did not fit the actual practices and experiences of Dolina's Bosnian Muslims. This created fertile ground for debating "Muslim customs" and cultural identity.

Vahid's comment about the Muslims in Dolina and their understanding of "Muslim customs" (which he considered ignorant), touches on two points which have been central to our discussion. First, there is the general point about the relationship between Islam and Bosnian Muslim identity. We can conclude from his comment that his view of what constitutes Muslim customs may be at variance with what the villagers perceive as such. Second, Vahid's comment also says something about what he considers to be "knowledge." His main criticism of Muslims in this village is that the way they practice their religion is not the "correct" one. Indeed he ascribes this to the influence of Christianity and other non-Islamic ideas and practices. What the young educated *hodža* perceives as Dolina's Muslim villagers' misconceptions about Islam, he explains in terms of their lack of formal knowledge of Islam ("they do not read books").

In the anthropological literature of Islam a whole array of terms has been used to categorize practices and interpretations which some men of Islamic learning do not accept as being in accord with "central" Islamic truths (Eickelman 1989:257). Another parallel set of terms is used

to characterize the practices and interpretations these men of learning
stand for. In the anthropological and sociological literature on Islam
there are thus labels to describe certain practices in Islam, such as
"local," "folk," "illiterate," and "rural," which are perceived to have
been influenced by non-Islamic or pre-Islamic elements and often
equated with female and marginal devotional practice. Representing
their opposites we find terms such as "global," "orthodox," "literate,"
and "urban," which describe an "essentialist" Islam often associated
with men (see Tapper and Tapper 1987).

The problem with these rigid dual oppositions is twofold. First, such
dichotomization reflects the views of people who are in a position to
define what is "correct." It is "a statement about the distribution of
power within society rather than an empirical description of on-the-
ground behaviour and organization" (Johnson 1980:28). Second, what
is defined as "orthodox" or "official" Islam (or any other associated
term) has changed in response to political events through the history of
the Muslim peoples (Waardenburg 1979). I find that these terms ob-
scure more than they explain, since they seem to be used more or less
haphazardly according to the preference of the author. Furthermore, I
will argue that such labels are not very helpful in the Bosnian case, as
illustrated by the young *hodža* Vahid. In Bosnia those who criticized
some local practices did so in terms of a specific opposition which is not
exclusive to Islamic scholars but intrinsic to a collective Muslim identity
construction in Bosnia, where Muslim identity as a *nacija* is constructed
in opposition to what it is not, namely either a Catholic Croat or an
Orthodox Serb identity. Islam means "submission," and a Muslim is
someone who submits to the will of God. To define Islam, then, is to
simultaneously define a Muslim and what it means to be a Muslim. This
becomes particularly salient in the Bosnian case where "Muslim" constitutes both a religious community and a *nacija*. In Bosnia the dynamic
relationship between the particularistic and universalistic elements in
practiced and lived Islam is thus closely linked to the process of Muslim
*nacija* formation.

In his critique of what he calls "essentialist" views of Islam,[22] Eickelman argues that such an approach to the study of Islam "neglects attention to the historical conditions which favor the emergence of particular
institutional arrangements or beliefs over alternative coexisting ones"
(1989:262). This and other more recent anthropological literature on
Islam are concerned to bring out the dynamic relationship between different coexisting devotional styles and interpretations, some of which
may be seen as universalistic by the analyst of practiced Islam and others
as particularistic. Recent anthropological studies of Islam emphasize

that there are numerous combinations of such elements, that they change over time, and that certain combinations are not necessarily associated with one clearly defined sociocultural group. (Tapper 1987; Eickelman 1989; Bowen 1993; Lambek 1993). The particular combination of devotional elements and interpretations is one aspect of Islam which should not be taken for granted, but has to be understood in the historical, geographical, political, and socioeconomic context of lived Islam. Most importantly, the authoritative discourse at any given time in any given place has to be understood in terms of the discussants' perception of their position in the authority structure, and in reference to other discourses against which their discourse defines itself.

It has been noted that Islamic scholars considered some of the devotional activities which took place in the village to be non-Islamic. This being the case we need to examine in respect to what these practices were considered non-Islamic. Many of the devotional practices, customs, and beliefs which representatives of "official" Islam oppose, such as the writing of charms and visiting saints' graves for healing and praying for good fortune, are found throughout the Islamic world. Others, more specific to the Bosnian Muslims, are a product of their historical and cultural background, such as the celebration of *Jurjev*. Within the particular discourse which took place locally in Bosnia the debate was not about theoretical Islamic perspectives and scholarly or political orientations, but about defining some local practices as influenced by Orthodox Christian or Catholic practice. In Bosnia, therefore, the discourse on Islam should be understood in terms of the construction of a Bosnian Muslim identity as opposed to a non-Muslim Bosnian one that is either Catholic or Orthodox Christian (and ultimately either Croat or Serb). There was, however, a key difference in the way Muslim identity was perceived and constructed by Muslims locally and by the Islamic establishment. To the latter, being a Muslim as opposed to being a Christian or non-Muslim, implied observing practices which they themselves considered as being "according to Islam." The former, on the other hand, conceived of being Muslim primarily in contrast to the Bosnian non-Muslim group closest to themselves; in Dolina this meant the Catholics, and they defined being a Bosnian Muslim through both Islamic and non-Islamic practices and customs. The important question was therefore not whether a practice (a tradition or custom) was "according to Islam" (*po islamu*) or prescribed (*propisano*) or not, but rather that it was what Muslims in Dolina did and their next-door Bosnian Catholic neighbors did not do.

Islam is the main distinguishing factor between the Muslims and their Bosnian-Hercegovinian compatriots and the main constitutive factor, either as practical religion or as cultural heritage, in self-ascription and the ascription of collective *nacija* identities. As such, Islam is the key to understanding Muslim identity in Bosnia. Yet, Bosnian Muslim identity cannot be fully understood with reference to Islam only, but has to be considered in terms of a specific Bosnian dimension which for Bosnian Muslims has implied sharing a history and locality with Bosnians of other non-Islamic religious traditions.

# Notes

## Introduction

1. For a critical assessment of the definition of "the Mediterranean area," see Gilmore 1987.

2. The role of Islam in constituting a Bosnian Muslim identity has, however, more recently been addressed by Cornelia Sorabji in her 1989 Ph.D. thesis which examines a Muslim neighborhood in the old town of Sarajevo. For an excellent review and discussion in German of the history and culture of the Bosnian Muslims which does consider the role of Islam, see Balić 1992.

3. In Bulgaria where the late president Živkov was venerated as "father of the nation," as was Tito in Yugoslavia, his picture would not be found in private homes in villages. It was only displayed in public state-related areas. (Deema Kaneff, personal communication.)

4. Malcolm (1994:195) has suggested that as a religion under the Yugoslav communist regime Islam suffered a double disadvantage in the eyes of the rulers since "first, it was seen (correctly) as a type of religion which involved not only private beliefs but also social practices, and secondly it was viewed as backward and Asiatic."

5. According to Irwin, the term designating Bosnian Muslims on the official national census has had different forms: "The 1948 census contained a choice between three categories: 'Moslem-Serbs,' 'Moslem-Croats' and 'Moslems unspecified.'" In the 1953 census "Moslem" was dropped, as "Moslem indicates membership in the Moslem religious faith and has no connection with any kind of national question." The 1953 census admitted the problem by dropping any reference to "Moslem" in favor of the term "Yugoslav unspecified." The 1961 census introduced the term "ethnic Moslems" (Irwin 1984:442–43).

6. From Slobodan Stanković, *Radio Free Europe Research Report* (172), 26 August 1982.

## Chapter One

1. Author's translation from the Serbo-Croat second edition of *Derviš i smrt* published in Belgrade by BIGZ in 1986.

2. Muslims emigrated from Bosnia-Hercegovina in three great waves. First, at the turn of the century when the Habsburgs annexed Bosnia-Hercegovina from Ottoman Turkish control; second, when the newly established Yugoslav kingdom introduced land reforms in 1919 which deprived the Muslim landowning class of its former wealth, and third, during the restrictive Stalinist years in Tito's Yugoslavia immediately following World War II in 1953–58. In all cases those who moved were often the economic, religious, and educated elite who had come under political pressure from the authorities (Petrović 1987). More recently it is worth noting that statistical data on migration in Yugoslavia from

1961 to 1981 show a steady tendency for both Serbs and Croats to move out of Bosnia-Hercegovina to Serbia and Croatia respectively. In fact, in 1981 there were as many as five times more Serbs and Croats who emigrated from Bosnia-Hercegovina than immigrated (thus 48,304 Serbs moved to Bosnia-Hercegovina while 266,637 Serbs moved from it). For the Muslims in Bosnia-Hercegovina, however, there was what is called "a negative migration coefficient," that is, the number of emigrants was equal to that of immigrants (Petrović 1987:74–76).

3. For a discussion of the complex background of the Muslim minority in Bulgaria, see Karpat 1990b; for Albania, see Skendi 1982.

4. The general argument is often made that the gentry in the Balkans converted to keep their privileges. Although this may have been a motivating factor in some instances, it has been pointed out that the Ottoman conquerors often preferred to replace the local elite with their own administrators (whether locally recruited or from other corners of the empire) to prevent "old loyalties" from causing unrest and schism (Karpat 1982:143). In Bosnia there are indications that the local elite was more favored than in other regions. Furthermore, they seem to have had a rather more independent government than has been reported from territories under the Porte. Although Muslim by creed, the governing Bosnian elite reportedly often let their local Bosnian loyalties override their loyalty to the Porte, and during later reformist periods resisted changes that threatened their positions (see Balić 1992; Eliot 1908; Malcolm 1994).

5. The Pope charged the Franciscans with the task of winning the "heretical" Bosnians over to the Catholic Church (and of counteracting so-called Bogomilism). During the fourteenth and fifteenth centuries many Franciscan monasteries were built throughout Bosnia, particularly in central Bosnia. (In the fifteenth century there were about forty monasteries throughout central and northern Bosnia; see Džaja 1984:161.) During the Ottoman occupation of Bosnia-Hercegovina the number of monasteries was radically reduced, although the Franciscans obtained special permission to operate. Only three monasteries in central Bosnia survived the so-called "Turkish wars" of 1683–99. These were the monasteries of Fojnica, Kreševo, and Kraljeva Sutjeska.

6. To Eliot the Bogomils were one of the many sects which arose from a mixture of "Dualistic and other pre-Christian religions with Christian and later with Moslem ideas. The doctrines of Yezidis, Druses, Sabeans, Kizilbashes, and of many dervishes have probably been formed by similar processes" (Eliot 1908: 241). The sect had originated in Central Asia and Asia Minor and flourished in the Balkans from the tenth to fifteenth centuries (in Bulgaria, for instance, it had spearheaded a local Slavic movement aimed at reforming the Bulgarian Orthodox Church). The Bosnian Church has, however, been described primarily as a heretic Catholic sect. It has furthermore been seen as a forerunner to the Protestants and as influenced by Islam, or at least compatible with the main tenets of that faith (*Encyclopaedia Britannica*, 28:918; 15th edition). Some of the characteristics considered significant are that members of the Bosnian Church condemned the worship of images or saints and Mariolatry; they objected to the sign of the cross, and probably did not believe in the crucifixion; they apparently

observed ceremonies analogous to baptism and the Eucharist, but did not believe that the sacramental elements underwent any change. Holding that matter was evil they were naturally inclined to asceticism, and objected to marriage and the use of wine and meat. They appear to have attached great importance to prayer, but are said to have objected to the use of any formula other than the Paternoster, which they repeated five times a day and five times each night (Eliot 1908:240).

7. For a review of claims and counterclaims about the Bosnian Church, see Fine 1975. For a discussion of how these claims have been influenced by Croat and Serb nationalist positions and historiography, see Saltaga 1991:29.

8. Srećko Džaja argues that the Ottomans were able to take advantage of the religious and political battles between the two Christian churches, and that Orthodox Serbs even preferred Ottoman rule to the rule of the Pope (1984:209–10). For further discussion and rich historical documentation of the role of the churches before and under the Ottomans, see Džaja 1984.

9. The scant knowledge of the Bosnian "heretics" and their "national" Bosnian Church is partly due to the fact that what has been written has been written about them by clerics in the established churches. Furthermore, at one point around the time of the Ottoman conquest of the western Balkans the Bosnian Church and its "heretics" seemed to have mysteriously disappeared. This has led many scholars to assume that members of the Bosnian Church formed the backbone of the Bosnian converts to Islam.

10. The multifarious sources of identity and the collective past of the Bosnian Muslims and those other Bosnians with whom they used to share their villages are physically present in the landscape in which they live. Soon after my arrival in Dolina people there were keen to show me three monuments as soon as they learned that I was interested in their "customs" (which many understood as "the past"). Did I know about the "Roman church"? Would I like to see the huge stones that no one was allowed to move? And had I visited the šehit's grave? The "Roman church" was the remains of a basilica. Some villagers also referred to it as a Greek church. The remains were on a hillside, and on the hilltop just above were some huge tombstones which villagers had been told by scholars were those of the Bogomils. To the villagers the stones were part of the mystique of the landscape. They had been told for generations not to move them, for if they did disaster would befall them. Some older people said that in the past people in the village had believed the stones had healing properties. There was a story about two of the stones that a young couple who had eloped against the will of their parents had turned to stone. (Similar stories are attached to such stones or stećci all over Bosnia-Hercegovina.)

The best preserved and concentrated collection of such tombstones is in Hercegovina (and eastern Bosnia), while in central Bosnia they are more scattered and less well-preserved, their decorations usually worn and impossible to interpret. Nevertheless I kept stumbling over them in villages, in gardens, and on roadsides. Adjacent to such stones at two sites in the village there are šehits' graves, one of which is a tomb (turbe). It is believed that a strong spiritual power resides in these graves of Muslims, said either to have been killed in battle or to have been the innocent victims of a tragic and violent death. While the *stećci* were no longer believed to possess healing powers, the *šehit*s' graves were the focus for religious rituals and prayers to which I will return in chapter five.

11. *Aliđun* is from the Turkish *Aligunu*, Alija's day. Although celebrated on 2 August, the same day as the Orthodox Serbs celebrate their *Ilindan*, it has a Muslim and Islamic reference. However, the prophet Elijah also has a central place in popular Islam. (For instance, Gaborieau [1983:301] reports from Nepal that a companion of the prophet Elijah, Khwaja Khizr, is venerated as a legendary saint. In the late eighties Aliđun was not as widely celebrated as I was told it had been twenty years earlier. In the villages there used to be a fair and in some villages *dove* or prayers as well.

12. A Muslim who was a member of the communist party told me that in the ideologically hardline 1950s he received a directive from the ideological watchdog of the party not to give his children typical Muslim names.

13. The largest and most influential of them was the *Millet-i-Rum* (sometimes referred to as "orthodox" or "Greek" after this *millet*'s dominant ethnic group) which had a favored position within the Ottoman empire (Clogg 1982). This *millet* encompassed all Orthodox Christians within the empire whether Greek, Albanian, Serb, or Bulgarian (Clogg 1982; on Albania, see Skendi 1982; on Bulgaria, see Karpat 1990b).

14. For further reading on the *millet* system in the Balkans, see Karpat 1982.

15. Similar experiences are reported by Lockwood 1975a, and Sorabji 1989.

16. Nenad Filipović, "O jednom okusaju "Nacionaliziranja" Bošnjaka," *Islamska Misao*, Godina XII, br., 140, August 1990. Quoted in Saltaga 1991.

17. For an excellent review of the events in Bosnia-Hercegovina during World War II and particularly the effect on and role of Muslims, see Malcolm 1994:174–93.

18. I have chosen to cite the census data for 1981 since the data from the 1991 census—the last national census for SFRY as a whole—have been incomplete and contradictory. In the case of Bosnia-Hercegovina, however, I use data from the 1991 census.

19. The category of *narod* was influenced by Stalin's definition of a "nation." According to his definition a nation is "a historically formed and stable community of people which has emerged on the basis of a common language, territory, economic life and psychological make-up, the latter being manifest in a common shared culture" (Bromley and Kozlov 1989:426).

20. As part of the socialist Yugoslav federal state the Serb constitution declared that the Socialist Republic of Serbia was the "state of the Serbian nation and of sections of other nations and nationalities who live in it." Montenegro's constitution stated the same for the Montenegrin nation, listing only one titular nationality. Macedonia and Croatia were termed the national states of Macedonians and Croatians respectively, Slovenia was said to be a "state based on the sovereignty of the Slovene nation and the people of Slovenia" (Ramet 1992: 184).

21. Statistics printed in *War Report* 1992, 16 (London: Institute for War and Peace Reporting).

22. Quoted by Alija Isaković in *Danas*, 30 January 1990. Mrkonjić-Grad is

the place in central Bosnia north of Jajce where the partisans' "Anti-Fascist Council" was turned into a "National Committee of Liberation" with Tito at its head, and declared the de facto government of the future Socialist Federal Republic of Yugoslavia.

23. These statistical data are from Ramet 1992:180.

24. For detailed studies by Bosnian scholars in "Serbo-Croat" of the political process among the Muslims in Bosnia-Hercegovina, and particularly the role of the JMO (Jugoslav Muslim Organization) which led to official acceptance of a Muslim *narod*, the reader can consult Purivatra 1970 (who was central to the political movement within the Yugoslav communist party); Saltaga 1991; Duraković 1993. This issue is dealt with in English by the following: Banac 1984; Ramet 1985; Malcolm 1994; Dizdarević 1985.

25. Indeed the ethnonym *Musliman* may have weakened the Bosnian Muslims' claim to a separate "national" identity inextricably linked to the territory of Bosnia-Hercegovina, since the ethnonym "Muslim" is conceptually associated solely with a religious community and not, unlike Croat and Serb, with a territorial unit. Under the present circumstances the ethnonym *Bošnjak* (a term which was used both by the Ottoman and the Habsburg administrators) or *Bosanac*, that is, Bosnian (referring to a Bosnian of any creed) may have served the Bosnian Muslims better. For a further discussion of this issue see an interview with Adil Zulfikarpašić, the main promoter of the *Bošnjak* term, in *South Slav Journal*, vol. 6, no. 2, 1983.

26. For reasons of space I will not deal with this question here. The book *Moslems in Yugoslavia* (Dizdarević 1985), which has contributions by Yugoslav sociologists and historians, provides a thorough discussion and analysis of this question.

27. For an argument which claims the Muslims are "ethnically" Croats, see Tvrtković 1993; Tomić 1992.

28. Zoran Đinđić, "Ko je za Jugoslaviju," *Oslobođenje*, 29 July 1990; quoted in Saltaga 1991:16.

29. For a discussion of the theoretical problems and ideological underpinnings of the concept of "nation" generally, and not least its invented or "imagined" quality see, for instance, Anderson 1983 ; Hobsbawm 1983; Shanin 1989; and Smith 1986, 1991.

30. The fundamental difference between the perception of their collective identity by Bosnian Muslims and Serbs is clearly brought out in the horrific example of the mass rape of Muslim women by Serbs in northern and eastern Bosnia. While the Bosnian Serbs argued that the children who were born as a result of these rapes would be Serbs because they had "Serb blood," the head of the Bosnian Islamic community, *reisul-ulema* Mustafa Cerić, declared that the babies, if born to and brought up by these Muslim women, would be Muslims. His argument was based, however, not on "shared blood" but on the moral superiority and strength of the Muslim women in relation to their Serbian rapists. Reis Mustafa Cerić was supported in this by a *fatwa* issued by the Sunni Islamic scholars at Al-Azhar University in Cairo.

31. Eliot, writing of the period 1893–98 when Bosnia was theoretically still under Ottoman rule but governed by the Austro-Hungarian monarchy, refers to

all the inhabitants of this province as Bosnians. He then distinguishes between Christian and "Musulman" Bosnians and makes a further distinction between Orthodox and Catholic Christians (1908:344). In other words, he does not operate with what were official categories during Yugoslav communist rule, that is, Croats, Serbs, and Muslims.

32. The letter was printed in the April 27 issue of *Naši Dani*, a magazine run by the socialist youth organization in Bosnia-Hercegovina. On its front page, interestingly, the issue carried a picture of Tito and the caption "Ten years later."

33. According to Saltaga *Bošnjak* is first mentioned in documents dated 1166. But as a national concept *Bošnjaštvo* did not develop as an alternative to Serbian and Croatian national ideologies until the second half of the nineteenth century. In Ottoman sources the term *Bošnjak* sometimes refers to any inhabitant of the Bosnian *vilajet* (province) and at others to Bosnian Muslims only. The former usage was (until the present war) also in accordance with Bosnian self-definition in relation to non-Bosnians. However, it appears that as Serb and Croat national identification took over in Bosnia in the twentieth century, Muslims (including Sandžak Muslims) particularly referred to themselves as *Bošnjaks* and their language as *Bošnjčaki*. In the nineteenth century *Bošnjastvo* was taken up as an idea by the Bosnian Franciscans who had been influenced by the historical tradition of the Bosnian independent state and wanted to mobilize opposition to the sociopolitical dominance of the Ottoman state. Their idea of *Bošnjastvo* was independent of confession and included Bosnians of Islamic, Catholic, and Orthodox Christian religious background. During Austro-Hungarian rule, however, *Bošnjak* was increasingly applied to the Muslim population (Saltaga 1991: 82–83).

34. Alija Izetbegović, "Mi nismo Turci" ["We are not Turks"], Start, nr 560, 1990, quoted in Saltaga 1991:94. For years the Bošnjastvo concept had been advocated by Adil Zulfikarpašić, a Bosnian intellectual, politician, and president of a party called the "Bošnjačka Muslimanska Stranka" who lived in exile in Switzerland until 1990.

35. Alija Isaković, "Muslimani znaju šta nisu," *Oslobođenje*, February 3, 1991:3 (quoted in Saltaga 1991).

Chapter Two

1. After the attack on the village by the so-called Croat Defence Forces (HVO) in April 1993, most Muslim houses had either been burned, shelled, or vandalized, while all Catholic/Croat houses remained untouched. My choice in use of tenses in this section is meant to reflect this.

2. In addition there was one Muslim family of four who had moved to the village in the 1950s, plus two families which were matrilocal. In one of the cases a woman and her husband settled on land given by her father in Dolina, in another a woman returned to her native village with her son. The son was eventually given land by his mother's father and settled in Dolina with his family.

3. The Catholic priest in a neighboring village had the same last name as a

prominent Muslim family in the village. He claimed that the brother of one of his forefathers had converted to Islam, and that the Muslims in the village with the same last name were this man's descendants. The Muslims themselves did not know this to be true, however.

4. The Official Statistics of the Austrian Government in Bosnia. Copy of the Zemaljski Muzej in Sarajevo.

5. The literature is extensive, but see, for instance, Brink 1987 on Egypt, papers by various authors on Turkey in Peristiany 1976, and several authors on central and southeastern Europe in Byrnes 1976.

6. However, the term *zadruga* was not originally a word used by peasants locally; the terms most commonly used by the people themselves varied from region to region. Indeed the Serbian linguist Vuk Karadžić was the first to use it when introducing it into his dictionary of the Serbian language in 1818. *Zadruga* is thus an academic term which has come to be widely known and used through the influence of schools, literature, and legal documents. Having played a part in nineteenth-century discourse and in arousing Serbian and "South Slav" nationalism and cultural awareness, the term *zadruga* was later adopted by the state and by Marxist academic writers to argue for the inherent cooperative and communal (i.e., communist) attitude of Yugoslav peasants. Both the Serbian pan-Slav nationalist school (represented by the linguist Vuk Karadžić) and the communist-inspired Yugoslav state builders defined the *zadruga* in terms of a particular South Slav social and economic orientation which represented a contrast to western Europe's individualistic philosophy and economy.

7. But see Rheubottom 1976 on the difficulty of assessing household size from informants' reports.

8. They finished their new house in 1990 after years of saving and hard work, spending all their free time during holidays and weekends working on it. The house was subsequently destroyed in the Croat attack in April 1993 and they had to flee the village.

9. In 1993 the young couple from household B were refugees abroad while the young man's parents, together with many other Muslims from this and surrounding villages were, as I wrote this, being held as civilian prisoners in a Croat-controlled detention camp suffering under terrible conditions.

10. According to the historian Noel Malcolm, Muslims had fought on all sides in this war—Ustaša (Croatian nationalist fascists), German, Četnik (Serbian nationalist fascists), Partisan (Tito's communist forces)—and had been killed by all sides. It is claimed that 8.1 percent of the total population of Bosnian Muslims was killed. This represented a greater proportionate loss than that suffered by the Serbs (7.3 percent) or any other group except Jews and Gypsies (Malcolm 1994:192, quoting Balić 1992:7).

11. This phenomenon is well reported by Olga Supek in her article, "Transformacija patriarhalnih odnosa: od zadruge do neo-lokalnosti u Jaskanskom prigorju" [The Transformation of Patriarchal Relationships: From Zadruga to Neo-local Household in Jaskansko Prigorje] in *Etnološki Pregled*, 22 Beograd, 1986.

12. I am grateful to my colleague Maja Povrzanović at the University of Zagreb for providing me with this information.

13. For a similar development in Romania see Kligman 1988:53–54, 255. I shall not enter into a discussion of "feminization" here, but see Moore 1988: 75–80 for a comprehensive discussion and critique of the concept.

14. When urban people talked about people from the country this way they often implied that they were ignorant, and lacked an understanding of the complexities of city life. At the start of the war, many Sarajevans, for instance, claimed that it was being waged by country folk (*seljačine*) who hated the city because they could not understand it.

15. Interestingly, when I asked Muslims in the village in 1993 who was in a majority in the village (now under Croatian military and administrative control) they all told me quietly: "I think there are more of us." However, when I spoke to Catholics (Croats) I was reminded that "We are in a majority here, and the Muslims therefore have to obey us." This was just after the Vance-Owen plan for dividing Bosnia-Hercegovina into "ethnic majority provinces" had been introduced. Dolina's administrative center and market town (with a 51.7 percent Catholic/Croat majority) had been designated as a "Croat province." A discussion of the disastrous effects (particularly in central Bosnia) of the peace negotiators' endorsement of ethnic majority governed provinces in Bosnia-Hercegovina will have to be forgone here.

16. *Dimije* was a Turkish fashion, brought in during the Ottoman empire, which influenced Muslims and Christians alike. Color was not initially a distinguishing factor. Muslims and Christians almost certainly dressed in similar fashion before the advent of the Turks. It has, however, been documented that in 1794 a certain Bosnian vizier introduced measures to ensure that Muslims and Christians could be distinguished by the color of their clothes. Thus green, white, yellow, and red were to be worn by Muslims, black and blue by Christians and Jews. In 1827 the Pasha eliminated blue as an option for the latter group (Balagija 1940).

17. Christian Catholic women generally wear knee-length skirts.

18. Ahmed (1992:166–67) argues that colonialists' and Europeans' focus on the veil worn by Muslim women reflected their perception that an "innate connection exists between the issues of culture and women in Muslim societies," and that "because of the history of struggle around it, the veil is now pregnant with meanings."

19. In a documentary program on Bosnia (in a series called "From Beirut to Bosnia" produced for Channel 4), Robert Fisk, Middle East correspondent for the newspaper *Independent*, was investigating the "rise of fundamentalism" in Bosnia as a result of the war. He was interviewing a young man in hospital who was in great pain and about to have his leg amputated. It was clear that Fisk had already decided what answers he wanted and how he would interpret them. His question reflected this. He asked the young man whether the West was to blame for the war in Bosnia. The young man replied "no" but added that they were guilty of not having tried to stop it. The journalist then asked why he thought this had happened (that is, being wounded and being the only survivor of an attack). The young Bosnian answered: "It's fate." Fisk wanted to know what he meant by this. "Do you mean it was predetermined at birth?" When the young man answered yes, Fisk had got his "Islamic" answer. What he did not realize

was that he might as well have received the same answer from any Bosnian, Muslim or not.

20. There were certain days in the year when members of the youth organization (*Omladinska Organizacija*) would have *akcija*, which would include, for example, clearing a green area. The youth organization had committees in every commune, but had little influence or relevance at the village level.

21. *Mašalah* is of Turkish origin and means "What God wills will be." It is used to express positive surprise, as at the arrival of guests. More specifically, however, it is said by a person when s/he sees somebody beautiful, a child, young man or woman, to guard against the possibility that the seer may have unintentionally cast the evil eye (see chapter five).

22. Complaints were never made with reference to financial contributions to the mosque, for such contributions are of a different order as they are considered *sevap* (meritorious in the eyes of God; see chapters five and six) and thus may be understood in terms of generalized reciprocity between a household (and its members) and the divine.

23. Although this is not a difference restricted to rural areas, Catholics would also point out that Muslims pronounce the letter H more strongly and more often than they do. This impression is probably based on the fact that Muslims use more words of Arabic origin.

24. In rural areas the language which children learned at home and in the village among other Muslims was different from the literate "Serbo-Croat" often aspired to by urban and educated Muslims. The dialectical characteristics which teachers in school branded archaic and incorrect (and often implicitly too Muslim) related to pronunciation and vocabulary, the latter containing more words of Turkish origin. Currently, however, such words are experiencing a revival in the Sarajevo media and literature. This particular vocabulary is gaining new status as part of the revival of a distinct *Bošnjak* identity and language in response to the reinvention of separate Croat and Serb languages.

25. Saltaga argues that communist ideology was negative toward all "religious-cultural" phenomena, but seems to have projected this negative attitude particularly on to Islam which, as the most important attribute of the Muslim *nacija*, was said to be primitive, culturally backward, aggressive, militant, and fundamentalist (Saltaga 1991:18).

26. Interestingly, after having returned from a trip to the sufi sanctuary, a Catholic woman in the village told me she had heard I had been on "a pilgrimage to their [i.e., the Muslims'] place where Fatima [the Prophet's daughter and most popular woman in Islam] had appeared." The Catholic woman was obviously drawing a parallel between the Catholic pilgrimage center, where the Virgin Mary is alleged to have appeared before some teenagers in the early 1980s, and the Muslim sufi sanctuary, where the legendary sheikh Sari Saltuk and his disciple Achik-ash of the Bektashi order are said to be buried. Thus even where complete parallels do not exist they are either assumed or constructed by the other community.

27. I never heard or overheard Muslims pass a value judgment on how Catholics did things as Catholics, although I did often register comments to the opposite effect by Catholics. This has inevitably led me to speculate (after also

having considered the impact my own Christian background might have had) about the greater level of tolerance of Muslims toward other ethnoreligious communities than vice versa.

## Chapter Three

1. I have chosen to translate *hodati* as "going [or walking] about" as this best conveys the ideas contained in the local usage of the term.

2. Some women said that if a man absolutely had to take another woman, he should go to Sarajevo where it would be his own business. (Similar observations have been made in a Greek village; see du Boulay 1986:152.)

3. But they were increasingly extending their activities outside the village: for instance, at parents' meetings at the school.

4. In her 1978 paper Renee Hirschon points to the similarly symbolic character of the status of both bride and mother in her Greek material. Traditionally both the bride and new mother were strictly secluded from life outside the house (as was the custom in Bosnia), as women were most vulnerable at these times and, referring to body symbolism, their "open" (and therefore ambiguous) character was most conspicuous (Hirschon 1978:81).

5. Likewise, women's polluting potential is the reason men give for excluding women from an annual *mevlud* at an old mosque in the mountains (famous for the myths associated with it).

6. A similar pattern is found in Greece for the term of address between the bride and her husband's relatives. Thus Campbell notes: "She follows her husband in his modes of address to all senior relatives, father, mother, uncle, aunt, and so on. The family and kinsmen address the newcomer simply 'bride'" (1964:64).

7. In this respect I was treated very much like a *mlada*. As a stranger, woman, and new member of the household, I was initially seen as a threat to the reputation of the household. My hostess therefore strictly supervised all interactions between me and members of other households, at least until my loyalty to "my household" had been understood and firmly established. I had to work within these restrictions, but I benefited from having the loyalty of fellow household members in return. In any disagreement between villagers concerning the character of my stay or my whereabouts, members of my household would always defend me in order to protect my good reputation which, of course, was ultimately also the reputation of the household of which I was a member.

8. In Dolina there were no "pious girls" who rejected all "modern" clothes and none that I knew of who even aspired toward such an attitude.

9. At such coffee-visits the women would be cautious about talking about sexuality or making rude jokes in my presence. They would often censor each other by referring to the presence of the *cura*. However, their attitude became more lax toward the end of my stay when they acknowledged that I was "grown up," "serious," and, they said jokingly, I needed to learn everything.

10. Morokvašić notes more generally that an ambivalent attitude toward unplanned pregnancies is "deeply rooted in the significance of procreation and maternity for Yugoslav women and their perception of women's sexuality, indeed

femininity, as being closely related to procreation" (1984:200). In their 1991 paper P. Loizos and E. Papataxiarchis offer an explanation for the high rate of abortion in Greece and suggest among other things that "From the women's point of view what makes sex 'natural,' pleasurable, and desirable is that it leaves the door to conception open" and that "sexuality in itself, sealed off from the prospect of pregnancy by contraceptive devices, is seen as undesirable" (1991:225).

11. Cowan (1991) reports a similar distinction between more traditional "coffeehouses" and modern "kafeterias" and the "moral geography" implied, in her study of a small town in Greek Macedonia.

12. For examples and interpretations of some such verses, see Lockwood 1983.

13. The building was a joint community project built in the fifties. The municipality contributed money and building material, villagers their labor. The use of the word *zadruga* indicates that the community center is defined as "social property." See the discussion in chapter two.

14. For a confirmation of this trend in a number of other European countries see Franklin 1969.

## Chapter Four

1. I do not want to argue that this reflects the idea of "the gift of the virgin" as understood in Indian ethnography, on which see, e.g., Fruzetti 1982, but merely that the usage reflects the practice of patrilocal postmarital residence.

2. I prefer the term "fictive elopement" to the "fictive abduction" used by Kajmaković (1963), as first it is clear that the girl herself has agreed to leave her home with the young man and second, the villagers themselves always used the phrase "she stole herself away" (*ukrala se*) rather than the term for abduction (*otmica*).

3. During my stay in the village, I did not have the opportunity to observe a "real" wedding feast. However, one "real wedding" did take place a couple of months before my arrival in the village when the son of one of the wealthiest households married a daughter of wealthy migrant workers. According to my neighbors in the village it had been the first real wedding feast in at least ten years. Describing what a big wedding party this was, they mentioned the number of cars—between twenty-five and thirty—parked opposite the bridegroom's house.

4. Customs is a translation of the indigenous term *običaji*. It was always prefaced by "our." When referring to "our customs" Muslims in the village would usually mean a predictable more or less ritualized practice common among Bosnian Muslims (as opposed to what was common practice among their Catholic neighbors, or among Muslims in that particular village or region rather than Muslims in other parts of Bosnia). Since individual practices, such as those in connection with marriage procedures, may vary in detail (because of economic circumstances, for example) what may be thought of as "our" collective custom is often based on one's own personal experience and there may be differences of opinion about what "our custom" is.

5. To say "they do not like to spend" (*oni ne vole trošiti*) is a negative characterization of a household and is always said in a reproachful tone in contexts where a major communal ritual is at issue. It is obvious that "not liking to spend" is contrary to the ethos of conspicuous consumption underlying major life-cycle rituals.

6. According to older women born and married in the village, the last time a girl had eloped though the window "in the old way" was fifteen years ago. Even though they complained about the way current fictive elopements were carried out, my older women friends still thought the old type of elopement was rather out of touch with the times. In some remote mountain villages girls still eloped in this way in the late 1980s.

7. The older generation's use of the word "real" (which is a translation of *pravo* and may also mean "correct") when referring to certain life-cycle rituals and the way they practiced them as opposed to how they were currently being practised by their children or grandchildren is worth noting.

8. Campbell reports a similar custom of keeping the bride secluded among the Greek Orthodox Sarakatsani in the early sixties. He points out that the seclusion "fits the feelings of shyness and shame which the bride is expected to experience . . ."; but that it also protects her from the dangers of the evil eye and the destructive force of envy (1964:62).

9. The more standard word *poklon*, meaning present, is used in Dolina for the kind of present which does not necessitate ritualized exchange.

10. According to Hangi (1906), the father of the bridegroom would also visit, but in Dolina I found this never to be the case. This may indicate (as suggested at the beginning of this chapter) that today marriage is less the concern of the agnatic group of the household and more a matter between the bridegroom and the bride's household. The same trend is reflected in other marriage procedures: for instance, the bridegroom's father will not accompany his son when he goes to bring the bride home with him. It should be noted, however, that the bride's father still has a role to play, as he is usually the one who brings the bride's trousseau.

11. In the 1960s the Bosnian ethnographer Radmila Kajmaković reported from a neighboring region on several visits which took place between the various members of the bride's and bridegroom's households in the days immediately following the wedding. Each time the guests carried gifts (Kajmaković 1964: 200).

12. The dictionary translation of the word *oprema* is "trousseau," and the word for "dowry" is *miraz*. However, I never heard this latter word used to denote any of the prestations in connection with marriage. It was used, rather, to denote a daughter's inheritance, whether she received this before or after the death of her parents.

13. The same point has been made for Macedonia. In other words the equivalent of dowry is not a prestation from the bride's household to the bridegroom's household, but rather gifts to the bride and therefore to her future household (see Rheubottom 1980).

14. I would follow Jane Schneider in arguing that these handmade objects

represent seclusion and virtue and the properly domesticated within-the-house labor of generations of honorable women (1980:350).

15. For instance, it is not uncommon for Christians in mixed Muslim-Christian villages in Palestine to prefer FBS-FBD marriages (personal communication, Moslih Kanaaneh).

16. An ethnographer collecting data in the 1930s (which were not published in English until much later) in a small town to the east of Dolina reports that "the people in this area . . . considered relatives on the mother's side as the most important." (Filipović 1982:153)

17. See du Boulay (1984:538) for a discussion of a similar system of reckoning in "generations" (*zinaria*) in Greece.

18. Here I am using the definition formulated by Hammel who notes that this is also the method used by the Roman Church and that reckoning relationships through "generation" is common throughout rural Yugoslavia. The pre-1991 family law for Bosnia-Hercegovina states that the prohibition against marriage between a man and a woman related in the lateral line through the fourth degree is inclusive. This is also what younger Christians in the village will say, although the older generation will say that they have the same prohibition as the Muslims until the ninth "generation." Hammel explains that "degrees of relationship between persons is accomplished by tallying the number of intervening births. Thus, a parent and a child stand in the first degree, siblings in the second" and so on (1968:8).

19. Kinship terms, especially those denoting kin of the second generation, are different from those used by Christians in Bosnia. The terms used by the Muslims are derived from Turkish, while those used by Christians are Slav. Both groups, however, distinguish between, say, an uncle through ego's mother and one through ego's father.

20. Girls usually have a warm and close relationship with their male cousins, whom they can naively flirt with and use as sympathetic and loyal companions when going out. A similar observation was made by Lockwood in a Bosnian village in the 1960s (see Lockwood 1975a).

21. I am grateful to Moslih Kanaaneh for explaining this point.

22. For a detailed discussion of Islamic jurisprudence on *rid'a*, or what is here translated as "milk-kinship," see Altorki 1980.

23. Deema Kaneff, personal communication.

24. During Turkish rule in Bosnia, the Christian churches had jurisdiction over all their members' marital and family affairs. There were nevertheless cases where Christians were married voluntarily by a *kadi* (a Muslim magistrate acting according to Islamic law). This happened when circumstances prevented them from being married according to church regulations, as for instance if theirs was a second marriage, or if they wished to marry a relative or an abducted bride. Above all, however, the church, particularly the Catholic Church, was fiercely opposed to mixed marriages. Indeed, individuals of different faiths could only be married by a *kadi*. According to Filipović, the Catholic Church sought the intervention of the Turkish government on this issue, and in 1575 Sultan Murat III issued a proclamation saying that Orthodox Christians in the regions

Klis, Zvornik, and Sarajevo were not to marry anyone of the Catholic faith (1982:158).

25. In contrast, Rheubottom (1980:243) argues on the basis of his Macedonian material that "wedding prestations" symbolize the denial of affinity and the drawing of agnatic clan boundaries since the main gift-exchanges after the *oprema* has been presented by the bride's parents take place within the groom's group. This pattern is significantly different from the one found in Bosnia where gifts are exchanged between the bride's and bridegroom's households after the *oprema* has been handed over to the bride.

## Chapter Five

1. According to Kajmaković (1961:216), the bride carrying the book of her religion over the threshold to her new household is exclusive to the Muslims. Among Serbs and Croats in Bosnia the bride's mother-in-law puts either two loaves of bread or bread and wine under her arms.

2. Again, however, I did learn of devout families in some towns who celebrated *hašure*. The main characteristic of the celebration was the making and eating of a compote (called *hašure*) consisting of many different fruits and seeds. According to Muslim folk belief this custom commemorates the day when the prophet Nuh (Noah) was rescued from the flood and made a thick soup of seeds and other foods stored in the boat.

3. For instance, at the main graveyard in Sarajevo (before the war) there were four main sections: one for Muslims, one for Catholics, one for Orthodox Christians, and one for atheists or communists. The gravestones in the four sections had different symbols too, often resembling those used on the death announcements put up on the walls of public buildings or on electricity poles: a green frame with the crescent and star for Muslims; black frames for Christians, with a cross and an olive branch for Catholics and a cross for Orthodox Christians; a red star above the name of the deceased for anyone who defined him- or herself as a communist and atheist or "Yugoslav."

4. Bosnian Muslims, unless devout, have a generally lax attitude toward the consumption of alcohol. This does not imply, however, that they do not know it is *haram* (a sin) according to Islam, although in Dolina I was told that the injunction in the Qur'an against drinking alcohol concerned wine in particular. Dolina Muslims would never drink wine like the Catholics did, but they would drink plum brandy (*šljivovica*). However, most men in Dolina abstained from brandy during the holy month of Ramadan, as to drink alcohol at this time was considered a particularly grave violation.

5. However, this was improving as a result of the political changes since I left the field in 1988, and more men in Dolina did actually fast during my second visit in April 1990.

6. We see here that the girl describes the fast as *sevap*, although according to orthodox categorization it should, as one of the five pillars of Islam, be classified as *farz*.

7. The term "saint" is problematic as a translation for the terms for various Muslim holy men, such as *marabout* (in Morocco) or *evlija* or *šehit* in Bosnia.

"Saint" is a prominent concept in Christian theology and history. In Christianity there was a lengthy period of canonization and people only became saints after their deaths. In other words an institutionalized body of "orthodoxy" had to confer sainthood. In Islam there is no such body, recognition is local, and varies greatly. Furthermore, the recognition of some Muslims as "pious ones" often occurs during their lifetimes (Eickelman 1989:293).

8. Hadžijahić, Traljić, and Šukrić (1977) argue that the practice of praying and performing certain rituals at graves is a legacy of the Bosnian Bogomils and that in the Middle Ages gatherings and prayers were held at Bogomil cemeteries and tombs. The Bogomils also built wooden burial chapels, similar to the early wooden *turbe*, around tombs. The book refers among other things to the will of a certain Gost Radin in 1466 who left the Bosnian Church 140 ducats for a *hram* (temple or chapel) and a *greb* (grave). The Bogomil *hram* or mausoleum was the small square wooden building referred to above. The authors consider it likely that the Bogomils also performed prayers for rain. They point out that prayers for rain are said in villages throughout the area between the rivers Bosna and Drina (which rivers form the borders of Bosnia), usually on a fixed Tuesday (Tuesday having apotropaic properties) after *Jurjev*, either at cemeteries with Bogomil tombs or at old Muslim graves located close by. They emphasize, however, that although praying at graves may have originated in Bogomil practices, the practice was later integrated into the religious system of Bosnian Islam, and the original Bogomil meaning was gradually lost (1977:84–86).

9. There are, however, ethnographic reports of prayers for rain attended by both sexes and led by the local *hodža*. See Palavestra and Petrić (1964).

10. The Bosnian historian and archaeologist Enver Imamović suggests, however, that in spite of the myths surrounding these graves they may be those of local people (personal communication).

11. At Sutjeska Tito's partisans were encircled by German and Ustaše troops and outnumbered by eight to one in 1943. Seven thousand partisans were killed and Tito himself was wounded. On one particular day in the year "atheists"/ Titoists go to Sutjeska to honor their heroes. People flock in processions as in a pilgrimage. The event is usually organized by the trade unions or by schools (when it is obligatory for everybody to participate). The Muslims have what might be considered a parallel pilgrimage to the *tekija* in Hercegovina, while the Catholics have theirs to Medjugorije.

12. It should be noted, however, that many diviners, particularly the educated *hodža*s, do not acknowledge popular explanations such as *crveni vjetar* (the red wind), an evil spirit believed to attack especially children around the time of sunset. They dismiss it as a children's disease (smallpox) which was common some ten years earlier when there was no vaccination for it.

13. *Bismillah* is the first word which introduces all chapters in the Qur'an but one and means "in the name of God." It is often used on its own in a secular context for protection against danger (as when starting out on a long trip), and may in those instances be translated as "God help us!" The complete line is *bismillah-rahmanir-rahim*, which translates: "In the name of God, the compassionate, the merciful."

14. In her study of a Muslim neighborhood in Sarajevo, Sorabji notes that she did not come across beliefs about the evil eye (1989:86).

15. In another healing custom which is not practiced any more, the mother took her sick child to a crossroads and asked the first person who passed to become the child's *šišano kum* (godparent) by giving the child his or her first haircut.

16. According to Schimmel (1989:72), Islamic names carry a strong blessing or *baraka* and it may therefore be changed if misfortune befalls the child because its name "is too heavy" for it, or if the name does not agree with its disposition or astrological requirements of the hour of birth.

17. In his first definition Škaljić refers to *tevhid* as "commemoration of the dead." This is my translation of *pomen za mrtve*. In "Serbo-Croat" the word *pomen* is used in the sense of mass in expressions such as "requiem mass" or to give a mass for somebody. *Tevhid* is clearly not thought of in this sense. I suspect that Škaljić has used this term ("commemoration") to define *tevhid* in terms understandable to his non-Muslim Christian readers.

18. In Dolina there was no ritual in connection with circumcision. Most male babies were circumcised at the hospital in Sarajevo just after birth. In 1974 a health law was passed which stated that the circumcision of children could only be done by an approved medical doctor and either at hospital, a health center, or at a doctor's surgery. However, for a transitional period those who had the skills and had earlier performed circumcision might do so. This temporary provision allowed for the use of the so-called *berber*. During my stay in the village one family called on a *berber* from a neighboring town to circumcise their baby son. Before circumcising the *berber* said the *namaz* prayer, and afterward he said a *dova* for the future happiness of the boy and his parents. This was a private event to which neither family nor neighbors were invited, nor was there any celebration.

19. *Tevhid* is known to have been led by a dervish outside a *tekija* as far back as 1531 when a *tevhid* was held in the main Gazi-Husrevbeg mosque in Sarajevo. Furthermore, according to a manuscript from 1780, a certain dervish ("who liked the company of women") is supposed to have "recited" *tevhid* with them (Softić 1984:201).

20. I was told that the *tevhid* is held on the same days as the Serbian Orthodox hold their funerary rites. The Tappers report from Turkey that *mevluds* given for death are held immediately after the funeral, on the seventh, fortieth, and fifty-second days after death, and thereafter on the anniversary of the death (1987:77). Mulahalilović reports that it had also been the custom in Bosnia to hold the *tevhid* on the first, third, and seventh day after death (1988:113). Likewise, Bowen reports that the Muslim Gayo of Sumatra recite verses and prayers the merit for which is for the benefit of the deceased, on the first, third, seventh, and forty-fourth days after death (Bowen 1993:30).

21. The veil was prohibited by law in Yugoslavia after World War II. Older women in the village explained that this was so because during the war spies against the partisans had disguised themselves in the *chador* or full veil. The partisans rather diplomatic way of justifying the prohibition was to say that it was

intended to prevent this from happening again. Before the rise to power of Tito's communists the complete veil (*zarovi, ferede*) was customarily worn only in urban areas, or by rural women when leaving the village. While working in the fields rural women would wear headscarves as usual, but no veil. Instead they would pull their big headscarves across their faces if they met strange or Christian men while walking through the village. A woman in her sixties told me proudly that she was the first woman in the village to stop wearing the veil (which she had worn outside her neighborhood). After the veil was prohibited by law the big headscarf superseded it on ritual occasions for urban women as well.

22. I was usually made to wear mine with a knot under the chin, as a little girl who does not yet know how to recite would do. My hostess told me that this was so as to distinguish myself from the others. This was particularly important when we went to other hamlets or villages where people did not know about me. We had already seen that those present could be misled into thinking that I was a Muslim and then get very upset when they realized I did not pray.

## Chapter Six

1. When I talk about the Muslim elite, I refer to those families who have a long tradition of wealth and involvement in major religious ritual events. They are almost without exception based in towns, and have a family tradition of members becoming Islamic instructors or scholars. It is not unusual for them to send their sons or daughters to the Middle East, Turkey and Egypt being the most common countries, for further religious education. For an account which focuses on this milieu see Sorabji (1989).

2. The informant whom I am partly quoting here was very worried about me mentioning any names. This was an attitude I often encountered among older *hodžas*, who were generally cautious about talking to me. They would also express the view that "in the West they often write untrue things about Islam," and were worried that I would do the same.

3. The boundaries of officially acceptable Islamic expression in this one-party, religiously and ethnically mixed republic were logically drawn at the state level, and were opposed to any expression of pan-Islamic sentiments. This is clearly illustrated by the "Sarajevo trials" in 1983, when eleven allegedly "Muslim nationalists" were given sentences ranging from six months to fifteen years for spreading "pan-Islamism" and trying to turn Bosnia-Hercegovina into a "purely Muslim" republic (See *Radio Free Europe Research*, Background Report 210, Sept. 2, 1983). Among the eleven was the current President of the Presidency of Bosnia-Hercegovina, Alija Izetbegović.

4. Also present at the opening ceremony of the mosque were the head of the Catholic Church for Bosnia-Hercegovina and the leader of the Franciscan monastery in the town. They congratulated the Muslims on their new mosque. Their presence was in line with a long tradition of official ecumenism in Bosnia whereby representatives of the clergy from all religious communities in the town

or village were present at larger public events such as the opening of a new church or mosque. This was the practice long before the communists came to power, and is mentioned in Durham (1909).

5. By 1990 this representative had been replaced by someone else, and there were indications that the new leadership would take a less accommodating attitude toward the communist political authorities (which, it should be stressed, by 1990 had become increasingly liberal toward the activities of the Islamic community compared to the early 1980s).

6. The first mosque in Dolina (made of wood but replaced by the present one of concrete in the 1960s), it is believed to date back to the sixteenth century. It was the first mosque to be built in the region.

7. This is apparently not the case in Sarajevo, where some women did attend Friday prayers (Cornelia Sorabji, personal communication).

8. The local *hodža* was criticized by villagers, though not openly, and by younger colleagues of the same *džemat* as well as by the Islamic council in the region, for not continuing with *mekteb* until the summer vacation. He was also criticized for not setting up the traditional *hatma*, a children's examination ceremony in the mosque. The *hodža* became quite bitter about having to put up with the villagers' lack of support on the one hand and his employers' increasing interference on the other, and wanted to leave.

9. According to Malcolm the official party attitude toward Islamic organizations and education was particularly restrictive during the first twenty years of Tito's regime, but was relaxed gradually as Tito started courting oil-producing, nonaligned Islamic states (1994:195–97).

10. Lison-Tolosana notes that in villages in Galicia the teacher or parish priest (being non-natives living in a hamlet or parish) takes on the role of mediator in similar situations. Their role is then to "assume the defense of the priority of communal values when opposed to the private interests of each house" (1973:827).

11. There is an interesting parallel between the way the I.Z. tended to take over and direct religious customs and rituals that had earlier been initiated by the individual household or local community, and the way the regional branch of the communist youth organization was taking over the organization of the traditional *teferić* or fair and, indirectly, the *sijelo* through the Saturday dance (see chapter three).

12. I often heard older people making this distinction between the past and the present and contextualizing the changes that had taken place by using the expressions "old Yugoslavia" (*stara Jugoslavija*) and "socialist Yugoslavia," or just "now," or "today's Yugoslavia" versus "before in old Yugoslavia."

13. Higher religious education for women is supported by representatives of the official Islamic leadership who have been educated at Islamic institutions in Arab countries, and is consistent with the role ascribed to women in both Arab nationalist and Islamicist ideologies. In both a woman's education is seen as desirable because it will raise her quality as mother, educator, and repository of ethical values. (See Haddad 1985).

14. I knew personally of two young *bula*s who could not find employment.

One of them was assisting her father, who is a *hodža*, by teaching at the mosque school after having spent a year instructing at a mosque school in a remote village in her home region. The other had started working as a shopkeeper.

15. Such syncretism has a long tradition in Bosnia and the Balkans and is reported to have been widespread. See Hasluck (1929).

16. The emphasis on the virtue and power of writing in Islamic-influenced areas has been demonstrated by several authors in Goody (1968). See, among others, the papers by M. Bloch, I. Lewis, and J. Goody.

17. Algar (1975) reports that the first Naqshibendi *tekija* in Bosnia, of which nothing remains today, was built in 1463 by the Ottoman governor of Bosnia, Iskender Paša. In the mid-nineteenth century another Naqshibendi *tekija* was founded in Sarajevo; this one was still in use in 1987 after having been closed down by the authorities in 1980 for allegedly holding meetings encouraging fundamentalist and separatist political ideas (Sorabji 1989). Algar notes, however, that it is outside Sarajevo that the traditional life of the Naqshibendi *tekija* continues to flourish. There are three in the region surrounding Dolina: Visoko, Oglavak, and Živčiči, but in 1988 only the last-mentioned, the most active of the three, had a sheikh. For a general discussion of the sufi presence in Bosnia and the Balkans, see Norris 1993.

18. I shall not enter here into elements in the *zikir* specific to the Naqshibendi order, as my account is limited to aspects of the dervish presence in the region relevant to the religious life of the population of Dolina. For an excellent review of the Bosnian Naqshibendi order and their devotional practices, however, see Algar (1975).

19. The influence of the dervish orders in Bosnia has elsewhere been seen as very limited (see, e.g., Popović 1985). Sorabji (1989:169–70) argues that the dervishes did not offer a real alternative to Islam as presented by the *Islamska Zajednica*. However, it is my contention that the dervish orders in Bosnia never aspired to lead the Muslims locally in the region, as sufi sheikhs have done in other Muslim countries (such as Morocco and Bangladesh). The dervish orders in central Bosnia are dominated by the members of the same family, and the position of sheikh goes generally from father to son. This family has to a large extent become the link to inclusion into the sufi milieu.

Although it may be argued that the dervish families therefore have a vested interest in maintaining their exclusivity, it is clear that during certain periods (e.g., the fifties) the orders had to become exclusive in order to survive, and that their "underground" existence made recruitment very difficult from outside their own limited social network. I believe this structure was perpetuated even during the recent more liberal era at the end of the 1980s. There were indications that by 1990 the more liberal attitude toward the orders on the part of the political authorities and the I.Z. had generated a new interest among young, urban Muslims. Furthermore, the difference between the I.Z.-led Bosnian mainstream Islam and the Naqshibendi order's sufi path is not striking enough for the latter to present real opposition and challenge the former. (As already noted, many dervishes, and certainly those in more senior positions, are also I.Z.-employed *hodža*s.)

20. These trips had also become a public expression of Muslim *nacija* identity. This was no less true after the buses on their return from the *mevlud* in 1990 were attacked by young Serb nationalists north of Sarajevo.

21. *Ciganski* is a term used by villagers to denote any practice or "custom" practiced by Muslims themselves which *ne valja* (which has no worth) and which has come to occupy an inferior status either because it is perceived as not "civilized" (*kulturan*) or not Muslim.

22. According to Eickelman, "essentialist" approaches to the study of Islam argue for the "existence of shared fixed beliefs independent of time and place or a set of uniform authoritative practices" (1989:261–62).

# Glossary of Bosnian Terms

*abdest* — ritual ablution before Muslim prayers
*adet* (pl. *adeta*) — custom, tradition
*akcija* — working bee
*akšam* — sunset, evening prayers
*alahemanet* — Muslim greeting when leaving (lit., "Go with Allah")
*ašik* — love
*ašikovanje* — courtship
*ašikovati* — court
*babine* — lying-in after childbirth; gifts presented to a mother during this period
*banjica* — traditional bath
*bardak* — traditional water jug
*bašča* — garden
*berićet* — divine blessing or fortune (from the Arabic *baraka*)
*bezobrazna* — rude (lit., "without honor")
*bijeda* — poor, wretched
*bosanac* — Bosnian
*bošča* — large cloth used to cover floor or table when eating
*Bosna* — Bosnia
*bošnjak* — Bosniak
*budžak* — corner of sofa where the bride would traditionally sit on her wedding day
*bula* — female religious instructor
*čardaklija* — traditional house of wood built for several large extended families
*častiti* — to treat, in connection with hospitality
*čist* — clean
*čovjek* — married man
*cura* — unmarried girl or (unmarried) young woman
*curica* — little girl
*dar* (pl. *darovi*) — gift; in connection with gift-exchange
*darovati* — give gifts
*dimije* — wide, baggy trousers worn by Muslim women
*dobrovoljan* — voluntary, "of good will"
*domaćin* (f. *domaćica*) — host (hostess); head of household
*domaćinstvo* — household
*dova* — nonprescribed prayer; may be said using own words
*džemat* — Islamic organizational unit consisting of a mosque and an *imam*
*dženaza* — Muslim funeral
*dženet* — heaven (only used by Muslims, non-Muslims use the word *raj*)
*džin* — spirit
*džuma* — the Friday noon prayers in the mosque
*evlija* — saint (from Arabic *waliyya*)

*fajda* — benefit, help
*familija* — family (broadly defined)
*fatiha* — the opening chapter of the Qur'an
*fildžan* — small coffee cup without a handle
*fina* — morally good, well behaved
*gatanje* — fortune-telling
*gusul* — the ritual washing after sexual intercourse (menstruation, ejaculation, and childbirth)
*hafiz* (f. *hafiza*) — Islamic scholar who knows the Qur'an by heart
*haram* — what is forbidden by Islamic law
*hatma* — one reading of the Qur'an from beginning to end
*hodati* (*hoda*) — stroll, walk about
*hodža* — Islamic teacher (*imam*)
*ići* (*ide*) — to go (goes)
*iftar* — the evening meal when Muslims break the fast during Ramadan
*igranka* — dance
*ilahija* — religious song of reverence
*islamska* — Islamic
*jadnica* — wretched person
*jurjevdan* — celebration of spring and fertility on 6 May (equivalent to Christian St. George's day)
*kadi* — magistrate acting according to *shari'at* (Islamic law)
*kafana* — coffee house
*kafić* — coffee-bar
*katolik* — Catholic (also Croat)
*kibla* — the direction in which the Kaaba in Mecca is situated from any standpoint in the world, and toward which a Muslim turns when praying
*koljeni* — generation, degree of kinship
*kolo* — a circular, traditional South Slav folk dance which anybody can join at anytime
*komšija* (f. *komšinica*) — neighbor
*komšiluk* — neighborhood
*kuća* — house, household
*kulturan* (pl. *kulturni*) — civilized, cultured
*kum* (f. *kuma*) — a ritual sponsor (at marriage, equivalent of a best man for the groom, also *kuma* for the bride)
*kur'an* — Qur'an
*lijep* — beautiful
*ljudi* — people and men
*lonac* — clay pot used for cooking
*mahala* — settlement or hamlet (in the city, quarter)
*mašalah* — expression of amazement or approval (also an amulet)
*medresa* — secondary school to educate male and female Islamic teachers
*mekteb* — Quar'anic school, running parallel with primary school
*merhaba* — informal Muslim greeting
*mevlud* — Islamic recitations, songs, and poems honoring the birth of the Prophet Mohammad

*mlada* — bride, also used to refer to young wife who has not yet become a mother

*moba* — voluntary cooperative work

*momak* (pl. *momci*) — bachelor, young man

*musaf* — Qur'an

*muškarac* (pl. *muškarci*) — man

*muško* — male

*musliman* (pl. *muslimani*) — Muslim

*muž* — husband

*nacija* (pl. *nacije*) — ethnoreligious group or "nation"

*nacionalnost* — "nationality"

*namaz* — obligatory prayer; the words are in Arabic and prescribed

*narod* (pl. *narodi*) — people, "nation"

*narodni* — folk

*narodnost* (pl. *narodnosti*) — smaller than *narod*, without the same political status and rights

*nekulturan* — uncivilized, without culture, unsophisticated

*niša* — headstone at a Muslim grave

*obavezno* — obligatory

*običaj* (pl. *običaji*) — custom, tradition

*oprema* — a bride's trousseau and dowry

*opremiti* — equip the bride with *oprema*

*opština* — a secular adminstrative unit (municipality)

*otmica* — abduction, bride theft

*oženi se* — to marry (about a man)

*pendžer* — window

*pita* — a type of savory filled pie

*pobozan-na* (pl. *pobozni -e*) — devout

*pogača* — type of bread (flat and round)

*pohod* — visit; the specific mutual visits by "in-laws" immediately following the wedding

*poklon* — present (different from *dar*, which is used of gifts in mutual exchange)

*pokloniti* — give a present to

*pokvaren* — morally corrupt

*porodica* (pl. *porodice*) — elementary family

*pošten* (f. *poštena*) — honest and honorable

*poštovanje* — respect, esteem

*prija* (m. *prijatelj*, pl. *prijatelji*) — relative through marriage

*prijateljstvo* — friendship, but also "in-lawship"

*propis* — rule

*propisano* — prescribed

*prva komšija* — "first" or next-door neighbor

*punac* (f. *punica*) — wife's father (mother)

*radost* — joy

*ruho* — trousseau

*sabah* — dawn, morning, the Islamic morning prayers

*šehit* — Muslim martyr (or a Muslim who died innocently and heroically)

*šejh* — sheikh, leader of a sufi *tekija*
*sekirati* — worry
*selam* — Muslim greeting
*seljačina* — pejorative of *seljak*
*seljak* (pl. *seljači*) — villager
*selo* — village
*šerbe* — sweet drink made of sugar and water, rosewater or fruit juice, also the name of the visit by neighbors to welcome a new bride
*sergija* — donation of money
*sevap* — good deed, religious merit
*sevdah* — love
*sevdalinka* — traditional Bosnian love song
*sihir* — sorcery
*sihirbaz* (f. *sihirbazica*) — sorcerer
*sijelo* — social gatherings in people's houses, particularly during winter evenings
*sinija* — a traditional low, round table
*šljeme* — ridge-pole
*šljivovica* — plum brandy
*sofra* — a *sinija* set for a meal; a seating
*solidan* — steady, reliable
*sramota* — shame
*sredina* — surroundings, environment
*stećak* (pl. *stećci*) — tombstone with specific decorations, found throughout Bosnia-Hercegovina and dating from the Middle Ages
*sudbina* — destiny
*svadba* — wedding
*svašta* — all sorts (also used as an exclamation to express disapproval)
*svatovi* — wedding guests, wedding procession
*svekr* (f. *svekrva*) — husband's father (mother)
*tabut* — lidless coffin used by Muslims for carrying a dead body to the grave (Muslims are buried in a shroud and not in a coffin)
*teferić* — summer fair
*tekija* (pl. *tekije*) — the dervish sanctuary of a sufi order
*teravija* — late evening prayers in the mosque during Ramadan
*tepsija* — large round pan for cooking (traditionally made of copper)
*tespih* — prayer beads used by Muslims (rosary)
*tetka* (pl. *tetke*) — aunt (father's and mother's sister)
*tevhid* — Islamic collective prayers for the souls of the dead
*trošiti* — to spend
*turbe* — a Muslim mausoleum (for a *šehit* or an *evlija*)
*uda se* — to marry (of a woman)
*ukrala se* — marriage by elopement (said of a girl)
*ureći nekoga* —to cast a spell on someone
*vjenčanje* — marriage ceremony
*vjera* — religion, faith
*vjernik* (pl. *vjernici*) — believer
*vjerski* — religious

*vrijedna* — hardworking

*zadruga* — cooperative (workers', peasants', consumers'); in ethnology used to refer to extended family group

*zajednica* — extended family household

*zapis* — amulet

*žena* (pl. *žene*) — woman, wife

*žensko* — female

*zikir* — remembrance of the names of God; dervish recitation and praise of God

# Bibliography

Ahmed, Leila
  1992   *Women and Gender in Islam*. New Haven: Yale University Press.
Alexandre, Stella
  1979   *Church and State in Yugoslavia Since 1945*. Cambridge: Cambridge University Press.
Algar, Hamid
  1975   "Some Notes on the Naqshbandi Tariqat in Bosnia." *Studies in Comparative Religion*, 9(2): 69–96.
  1977   "The Naqshbandi Order: A Preliminary Survey of its History and Significance." *Studia Islamica* (Paris) 44: 123–53.
Althusser, Louis
  1971   *Lenin and Philosophy*, London: Verso.
Altorki, Soraya
  1980   "Milk-Kinship in Arab Society: An Unexplored Problem in the Ethnography of Marriage." *Ethnology* 19 (2): 233–44.
Anderson, Benedict
  1983   *Imagined Communities: Reflections on the Origin and Spread of Nationalism*. London: Verso.
Antoun, Richard T.
  1968   "On the Modesty of Women in Arab Muslim Villages: A Study in the Accommodation of Traditions." *American Anthropologist* 70 (4): 671–97.
  1989   *Muslim Preacher in the Modern World: A Jordanian Case Study in Comparative Perspective*. Princeton: Princeton University Press.
Asboth de, J.
  1890   *An Official Tour Through Bosnia and Hercegovina*. London: Swan Sonnenschein.
Ascher, Abraham, Tibor Halasi-Kun, and Bela K. Kiraly, eds.
  1979   *The Mutual Effects of the Islamic and the Judeo-Christian Worlds: the East European Pattern*. New York: Brooklyn College Press.
Astuti, Rita
  1995   "The Vezo are not a Kind of People: Identity, Difference and 'Ethnicity' among a Fishing People of Western Madagascar." *American Ethnologist* 22 (3): 1–19.
Aswad, Barbara C.
  1974   "Visiting Patterns among Women of the Elite in a Small Turkish City." *Anthropological Quarterly* 47 (1): 9–28.
Atkin, Muriel
  1992   "Religious, National, and Other Identities in Central Asia." In Jo-Ann Gross, ed., *Muslims in Central Asia: Expression of Identity and Change*, 46–72. Durham: Duke University Press.

Babić, Anto
1963   *Bosanski Heretici.* Sarajevo: Svjetlost.
Backer, Berit
1983   "Mother, Sister, Daughter, Wife: The Pillars of the Traditional Albanian Patriarchal Society." In Bo Utas, ed., *Women in Islamic Societies: Social Attitudes and Historical Perspectives*, 48–65. London: Curzon Press.
Balagija, Abduselam
1940   *Les Musulmans Yougoslaves.* Alger: La Maison des Livres.
Balić, Smail
1992   *Das Unbekannte Bosnien: Europas Brücke zur Islamischen Welt.* Cologne: Bohlau Verlag.
Banac, Ivo
1984   *The National Question in Yugoslavia: Origins, History, Politics.* Ithaca: Cornell University Press.
Baric, L.
1967   "Levels of Change in Yugoslav Kinship." In M. Freeman, ed., *Social Organization: Essays Presented to Raymond Firth*, 1–24. Chicago: Aldine.
Barth, Fredrik
1969   "Introduction." In F. Barth, ed., *Ethnic Groups and Boundaries*, 9–38. Oslo: Universitetsforlaget.
Beck, S., and J. W. Cole, eds.
1981   *Ethnicity and Nationalism in Southeastern Europe.* Amsterdam: University of Amsterdam Press.
Bentley, Carter C.
1987   "Ethnicity and Practice." *Comparative Studies in Society and History* 29: 24–56.
Bertsch, Gary K.
1976   *Values and Community in Multi-National Yugoslavia.* Boulder: East European Quarterly.
Blagojević, Borislav T., ed.
1977   *Guide to the Yugoslav Legal System.* Belgrade: Institute of Comparative Law.
Bloch, Maurice
1968   "Astrology and Writing in Madagascar." In J. Goody, ed., *Literacy in Traditional Societies*, 277–97. Cambridge: Cambridge University Press.
1974   "Symbols, Song, Dance and Features of Articulation." *Archives Europeenes de Sociologies* 15: 55–81. Reprinted in *Ritual, History and Power*. London: Athlone Press (1989).
1982   "Death, Women and Power." In M. Bloch and J. Parry, eds., *Death and Regeneration of Life*, 211–31. Cambridge: Cambridge University Press.
Bloch, Maurice, and Jonathan Parry
1982   "Introduction." In M. Bloch and J. Parry, eds., *Death and Regeneration of Life*, 1–45. Cambridge: Cambridge University Press.

Borneman, John
1992   *Belonging in Two Berlins.* Cambridge: Cambridge University Press.
Bosworth, C. E.
1982   "The Concept of *Dhimma* in Early Islam." In B. Braude and B. Lewis, eds., *Christians and Jews in the Ottoman Empire: The Functioning of a Plural Society,* 1: 37–52. New York: Holmes and Meier Publishers.
Bourdieu, Pierre
1977   *Outline of a Theory of Practice.* Cambridge: Cambridge University Press.
Bowen, John R.
1988   "The Transformation of an Indonesian Property System: *Adat,* Islam, and Social Change in the Gayo Highlands." *American Ethnologist* 15: 274–93.
1993   *Muslims through Discourse.* Princeton: Princeton University Press.
Bracette, Williams F.
1989   "A Class Act: Anthropology and the Race to Nation Across Ethnic Terrain." *Annual Review of Anthropology* 18: 401–44.
Bracewell, Wendy
1993   "Nationalist Histories and National Identities among the Serbs and Croats." In Mary Fulbrook, ed., *National Histories and European History,* 141–61. London: UCL Press.
Braude, Benjamin and Bernard Lewis
1982   "Introduction." In B. Braude and B. Lewis, eds., *Christians and Jews in the Ottoman Empire: The Functioning of a Plural Society,* 1: 1–35. New York: Holmes and Meier Publishers.
Brink, Judy H.
1987   "Changing Extended Family Relationships in an Egyptian Village." *Urban Anthropology* 16 (2): 133–49.
Bromley, Julian, and Victor Kozlov
1989   "The Theory of Ethnos and Ethnic Processes in Soviet Social Sciences." *Comparative Studies in Society and History* 3: 425–37.
Brooke, Christopher
1989   *The Medieval Idea of Marriage.* Oxford: Oxford University Press.
Brown, Peter
1981   *The Cult of the Saints: Its Rise and Function in Latin Christianity.* London: SCM Press.
Byrnes, Robert F., ed.
1976   *Communal Families in the Balkans: The Zadruga. Essays by Philip E. Mosely and Essays in his Honour.* London: University of Notre Dame Press.
Campbell, J. K.
1964   *Honour, Family and Patronage: A Study of Institutions and Moral Values in a Greek Mountain Village.* Oxford: Oxford University Press.
Clogg, Richard
1982   "The Greek *Millet* in the Ottoman Empire." In B. Braude and B. Lewis, eds., *Christians and Jews in the Ottoman Empire: The Function-

*ing of a Plural Society*, 1: 185–207. New York: Holmes and Meier Publishers.

Cohen, A. P.
1985 *The Symbolic Construction of Community*. London: Tavistock Publications.

Cohen, L., and P. Warwick
1983 *Political Cohesion in a Fragile Mosaic*. Colorado: Westview Press.

Connor, Walker
1984 *The National Question in Marxist-Leninist Theory and Strategy*. Princeton: Princeton University Press.

Cowan, Jane K.
1991 "Going Out for Coffee? Contesting the Grounds of Gendered Pleasures in Everyday Sociability." In P. Loizos and E. Papataxiarchis, eds., *Contested Identities, Gender and Kinship in Modern Greece*, 180–202. Princeton: Princeton University Press.

Čehajić, Džemal
1986 *Derviski Redovi u Jugoslovenskim Zemljama sa Posebnim Osvrtom na Bosnu i Hercegovinu*. Sarajevo: Orijentalni Institut.

Ćerić, Salim
1968 *Muslimani Srpskohravatskog Jezika*. Sarajavo: Svjetlost.

Chloros, A. G.
1970 *Yugoslav Civil Law*. Oxford: Clarendon Press.

Ćurić, Hajrudin
1960 *Prilozi Bosansko-Hercegovačkoj Istoriji XIX Vijeka*. Sarajevo: Naučno Društvo NR Bosne i Hercegovine.

Davis, J.
1977 *People of the Mediterranean: An Essay in Comparative Social Anthropology*. London: Routledge and Kegan Paul.
1983 "The Sexual Division of Religious Labour in the Mediterranean." In Eric R. Wolf, ed., *Religion, Power and Protest in Local Communities*, 17–51. Berlin: Mouton.

Dekmejian, Hrair R.
1989 "The Anatomy of Islamic Revival: Legitimacy Crisis, Ethnic Conflict and the Search for Islamic Alternatives." *Middle East Journal* 34 (1): 1–12.

Delaney, Carol
1991 *The Seed and the Soil: Gender and Cosmology in Turkish Village Society*. Berkeley: University of California Press.

Denich, Bette
1974 "Sex and Power in the Balkans." In Z. M Rosaldo and L. Lamphere, eds., *Women, Culture and Society*, 243–62. Stanford: Stanford University Press.
1977 "Women, Work and Power in Modern Yugoslavia." In A. Schlegel, ed., *Sexual Stratification: A Cross-Cultural View*, 215–44. New York: Columbia University Press.

Dizdarević, Nijaz, ed.
1985 *Moslems in Yugoslavia*. Belgrade: Review of International Affairs.

Donia, R.
1986   *Islam Under the Double Eagle: the Muslims of Bosnia and Herzegovina, 1878–1914*. New York: Columbia University Press.
Donia, R., and W. Lockwood
1978   "The Bosnian Muslims: Class, Ethnicity and Political Behaviour." In Suad Joseph and Barbara L. K. Pillsbury, eds., *Muslim-Christian Conflicts: Economic, Political and Social Origins*, 185–207. Boulder: Westview Press.
Douglas, Mary
1966   *Purity and Danger: An Analysis of the Concepts of Pollution and Taboo*. London: Routledge and Kegan Paul. Reprinted London: ARK Edition (1984).
Dubisch, Jill
1986a   "Culture Enters Through the Kitchen: Women, Food and Social Boundaries in Rural Greece." In J. Dubisch, ed., *Gender and Power in Rural Greece*, 195–214. Princeton: Princeton University Press.
1986b   "Introduction." In J. Dubisch, ed., *Gender and Power in Rural Greece*, 3–41. Princeton: Princeton University Press.
du Boulay, Juliet
1974   *Portrait of a Greek Mountain Village*. Oxford: Clarendon Press.
1976   "Lies, Mockery and Family Integrity." In J. G. Peristiany, ed., *Mediterranean Family Structures*, 389–406. Cambridge: Cambridge University Press.
1984   "The Blood: Symbolic Relationships Between Descent, Marriage, Incest Prohibitions and Spiritual Kinship in Greece." *Man* (n.s.) 19 (4): 533–57.
1986   "Women—Images of Their Nature and Destiny in Rural Greece." In Jill Dubisch, ed., *Gender and Power in Rural Greece*, 139–68. Princeton: Princeton University Press.
Duraković, Nijaz
1993   *Prokletstvo Muslimana*. Sarajevo: Oslobođenje.
Durham, Edith
[1909] 1985   *High Albania*. London: Virago Press.
Dwyer, Daisy H.
1978   "Women, Sufism, and Decision-Making in Moroccan Islam." In L. Beck and N. Keddie, eds., *Women in the Muslim World*. Cambridge, Mass.: Harvard University Press.
Dyker, David A.
1972   "The Ethnic Muslims of Bosnia—Some Basic Socio-Economic Data." *Slavonic and East European Review* 1 (119): 238–57.
Džaja, Srećko M.
1984   *Konfessionalität und Nationalität Bosniens und der Herzegowina: Voremanizipatorische Phase 1463–1804*. Munich: R. Oldenbourg Verlag.
Eagleton, Terry
1991   *Ideology: An Introduction*. London: Verso.

Eickelman, Dale F.
1976    *Moroccan Islam: Tradition and Society in a Pilgrimage Center.* Austin: University of Texas Press.
1982    "The Study of Islam in Local Contexts." *Contributions to Asian Studies* 17: 1–16.
1989    *The Middle East: An Anthropological Approach.* Englewood Cliffs, N.J.: Prentice Hall.
Eickelman, Dale F., and James Piscatori
1990    "Social Theory in the Study of Muslim Societies." In Dale F. Eickelman and James Piscatori, eds., *Muslim Travellers: Pilgrimage, Migration, and the Religious Imagination,* 3–25. London: Routledge.
El-Awa, Mohammed
1973    "The Place of Custom (*urf*) in Islamic Legal Theory." *Islamic Quarterly* 17: 175–82.
Eliot, Sir Charles
1908    *Turkey in Europe.* London: Frank Cass and Co. Ltd.
Evans-Pritchard, E. E.
1976    *Witchcraft, Oracles and Magic among the Azande.* Oxford: Clarendon Press.
Filipović, Milenko S.
1969    *Prilozi Etnološkom Poznavanju Severoistočne Bosne.* Sarajevo: Akademija Nauka i Umjetnosti Bosne i Hercegovine.
1976    "Zadruga (*kućna zadruga*)." In Robert F. Byrnes, ed., *Communal Families in the Balkans: The Zadruga. Essays by Philip E. Mosely and Essays in His Honour,* 268–79. London: University of Notre Dame Press.
1982    *Among the People: Selected Writings of Milenko S. Filipović.* E. A. Hammel, Robert S. Ehrich, Radmila Fabijanić-Filipović, Joel M. Halpern, and Albert B. Lord, eds. Ann Arbor: University of Michigan.
Fine, John V. A.
1975    *The Bosnian Church: A New Interpretation.* Boulder: East European Quarterly.
Flere, Sergej
1991    "Explaining Ethnic Antagonism in Yugoslavia." *European Sociological Review* 7 (3): 183–93.
Foucault, Michel
1972    *The Archaeology of Knowledge.* London: Routledge.
Fox, Richard G.
1990    "Introduction." In Richard G. Fox, ed., *Nationalist Ideologies and the Production of National Cultures,* 1–14. Washington: American Ethnological Society Monograph Series, 2.
Franklin, S. H.
1969    *The European Peasantry.* London: Methuen.
Fruzetti, Lina
1982    *The Gift of a Virgin: Women, Marriage, and Ritual in a Bengali Society.* New Brunswick, N.J.: Rutgers University Press.

Fuller, C. J.
  1992    *The Camphor Flame: Popular Hinduism and Society in India.* Prince-
          ton: Princeton University Press.
Gaborieau, Marc
  1983    "The Cult of Saints Among the Muslims of Nepal and Northern
          India." In S. Wilson, ed., *Saints and Their Cults: Studies in Religious
          Sociology, Folklore and History,* 291–308. Cambridge: Cambridge
          University Press.
Galaty, John G.
  1982    "Being 'Maasai': Being 'People-of-Cattle': Ethnic Shifters in East Af-
          rica." *American Ethnologist* 9 (1): 1–20.
Geertz, Clifford
  1973    "Ideology as a Cultural System." In *The Interpretation of Cultures,*
          193–233. New York: Basic Books.
  1983    *Local Knowlege: Further Essays in Interpretive Anthropology.* New
          York: Basic Books.
Gellner, Ernest
  1969    *Saints of the Atlas.* London: Weidenfeld and Nicholson.
  1981    *Muslim Society.* Cambridge: Cambridge University Press.
  1983    *Nations and Nationalism.* Oxford: Basil Blackwell.
Gerholm, Tomas, and Yngve G. Lithman, eds.
  1988    *The New Islamic Presence in Western Europe.* London: Mansell.
Giddens, Anthony
  1991    *Modernity and Self-Identity: Self and Society in the Late Modern Age.*
          Cambridge: Polity Press.
Gilmore, David D.
  1982    "Anthropology of the Mediterranean Area." *Annual Review of An-
          thropology* 11: 175–205.
  1987    "Introduction: The Shame of Dishonor." In D. Gilmore, ed., *Honor
          and Shame and the Unity of the Mediterranean,* 2–21. Washington:
          American Anthropological Association.
Gilsenan, Michael
  1976    "Lying, Honor and Contradiction." In Bruce Kapferer, ed., *Transac-
          tions and Meaning: Directions in the Anthropology of Exchange and
          Symbolic Behavior,* 191–230. Philadelphia: ISHI.
  1982    *Recognizing Islam.* London: Croom Helm.
  1987    "Sacred Words." In Ahmed Al-Shahi, ed., *The Diversity of the Muslim
          Community: Anthropological Essays in Memory of Peter Lienhardt,* 92–
          98. London: Ithaca Press.
Gladney, Dru C.
  1990    "The Ethnogenesis of the Uighur." *Central Asian Survey* 9 (1): 1–28.
  1991    *Muslim Chinese: Ethnic Nationalism in the People's Republic.* Cam-
          bridge, Mass.: Harvard University, Council on East Asian Studies.
Goody, Jack
  1983    *The Development of the Family and Marriage in Europe.* Cambridge:
          Cambridge University Press.

Goody, Jack
1987    *The Interface Between the Written and the Oral.* Cambridge: Cambridge University Press.
———, ed.
1968    *Literacy in Traditional Societies.* Cambridge: Cambridge University Press.
Gross, Jo-Ann
1992    "Approaches to the Problem of Identity Formation." In Jo-Ann Gross, ed., *Muslims in Central Asia: Expression of Identity and Change*, 2–23. Durham: Duke University Press.
Gursoy-Naskali, Emine
1983    "Women Mystics in Islam." In Bo Utas, ed., *Women in Islamic Societies: Social Attitudes and Historical Perspectives*, 238–44. London: Curzon Press.
Haddad, Yvonne Yazbeck
1985    "Islam, Women and Revolution in Twentieth-Century Arab Thought." In Y. Y. Haddad and E. B. Findly, eds., *Women, Religion and Social Change*, 275–306. New York: State University of New York Press.
Hadžijahić, Muhamed
1974    *Od Tradicije do Identiteta: Geneza Nacijonalnog Pitanja Bosanskih Muslimana.* Sarajevo: Svjetlost.
1982    "Neki Pojavni Oblici Islamske Civilizacije u Nas." *Argumenti* 2: 212–35.
Hadžijahić, Muhamed, Mahmud Trajić, and Nijaz Šukrić
1977    *Islam i Muslimani u Bosni i Hercegovini.* Sarajevo: Starješinstvo Islamske Zajednice.
Hadžiselimović, Omer
1989    *Na Vratima Istoka.* Sarajevo: Veselin Masleša.
Halpern, Joel M.
1958    *A Serbian Village.* New York: Columbia University Press.
Halpern, Joel M., and D. A. Kideckel
1983    "Anthropology of Eastern Europe." *Annual Review of Anthropology* 12: 377–402.
Hammel, Eugene A.
1968    *Alternative Social Structures and Ritual Relations in the Balkans.* Englewood Cliffs, N.J.: Prentice-Hall.
1972    "The Zadruga as Process." In Peter Laslett, ed., *Household and Family in Past Time*, 335–73. Cambridge: Cambridge University Press.
Hangi, Antun
[1906] 1990    *Život i običaji Muslimana.* Sarajevo: Svjetlost.
Hann, C. M.
1980    *Tazlar: A Village in Hungary.* Cambridge: Cambridge University Press.
Härje, Jan
1983    "The Attitude of Islamic Fundamentalism Towards the Question of Women in Islam." In Bo Utas, ed., *Women in Islamic Societies: So-*

*cial Attitudes and Historical Perspectives*, 12–25. London: Curzon Press.

Harrell, Stevan
1990 "Ethnicity, Local Interests, and the State: Yi Communities in Southwest China." *Comparative Studies in Society and History* 32: 515–48.

Hasluck, F. W.
1929 *Christianity and Islam Under the Sultans.* 2 vols. Oxford: Clarendon Press.

Hauptman, Ferdo
1962 *Borba Muslimana Bosne i Hercegovine za Vjersku i Vakufsko-Mearifsku Autonomiju.* Sarajevo: Svjetlost.

Hayden, Robert M., and Milica Bakić-Hayden
1992 "Orientalist Variations on the Theme 'Balkans': Symbolic Geography in Recent Yugoslav Cultural Politics." *Slavic Review* 51 (1): 1–16.

Heffner, Robert W.
1985 *Tengger Tradition and Islam.* Princeton: Princeton University Press.

Herzfeld, Michael
1981 "Meaning and Morality: A Semiotic Approach to Evil Eye Accusations in a Greek Village." *American Ethnologist* 8 (3): 560–74.
1985 *The Poetics of Manhood: Contest and Identity in a Cretan Mountain Village.* Princeton: Princeton University Press.
1986 "Of Definitions and Boundaries: The Status of Culture in the Culture of the State." In Phyllis Pease Cook and June R. Wyman, eds., *Discourse and the Social Life of Meaning*, 17–94. Washington: Smithsonian Institution Press.
1987 "'As in Your Own House': Hospitality, Ethnography, and the Stereotype of Mediterranean Society." In D. Gilmore, ed., *Honor and Shame and the Unity of the Mediterranean*, 75–89. Washington: American Anthropological Association.

Hirschon, Renée
1978 "Open Body/Closed Space: The Transformation of Female Sexuality." In S. Ardener, ed., *Defining Females*, 66–88. New York: John Wiley and Sons.

Hobsbawm, E. J.
1983 "Introduction: Inventing Traditions." In E. J. Hobsbawm and T. Ranger, eds., *The Invention of Tradition.* Cambridge: Cambridge University Press.
1992 "Ethnicity and Nationalism in Europe Today." *Anthropology Today*, 8 (1): 3–8.

Holden, Pat
1983 "Introduction." In P. Holden, ed., *Women's Religious Experience*, 1–14. London: Croom Helm.

Holy, Ladislav
1988 "Gender and Ritual in Islamic Society: The Berti of Darfur." *Man* (n.s.) 23 (3): 469–88.
1991 *Religion and Custom in a Muslim Society: The Berti of Sudan.* Cambridge: Cambridge University Press.

Humphrey, Caroline, and Stephen Hugh-Jones
1992 "Introduction: Barter, Exchange and Value." In C. Humphrey and S. Hugh-Jones, eds., *Barter, Exchange and Value: An Anthropological Approach.* Cambridge: Cambridge University Press.

Imamović, M., and I. Lovrenović
1992 *Bosnia and Its People: Bosnia and Herzegovina a Millennium of Continuity.* Sarajevo: Oslobođenje.

Irwin, Zachary T.
1984 "The Islamic Revival and the Muslims of Bosnia-Herzegovina." *East European Quarterly* 17 (4): 437–58.

Jancar, Barbara
1985 "The New Feminism in Yugoslavia." In P. Ramet, ed., *Yugoslavia in the 1980s,* 201–23. Boulder: Westview Press.

Jelavich, Barbara
1983 *History of the Balkans.* 2 vols. Cambridge: Cambridge University Press.

Johnson, Pamela Ryden
1980 "A Sufi Shrine in Modern Tunisia." Ph.D. diss., University of California, Berkeley. Ann Arbor: University Microfilms International (1986).

Joseph, Suad
1978 "Muslim-Christian Conflicts: A Theoretical Perspective." In Suad Joseph and Barbara L. K. Pillsbury, eds., *Muslim-Christian Conflicts: Economic, Political, and Social Origins,* 1–59. Boulder: Westview Press.

Kajmaković, Radmila
1961 *Ženidbeni Običaji Stanovništva Livanjskog Polja.* Sarajevo: Glasnik Zemaljskog Muzeja (Etnologija, separate edition).
1963 *Ženidbeni Običaji kod Srba i Hrvata u Bosni i Hercegovina.* Sarajevo: Glasnik Zemaljskog Muzeja (Etnologija, separate edition).
1964 *Narodni Običaji u Žepi.* Sarajevo: Glasnik Zemaljskog Muzeja (Etnologija, separate edition).

Karklins, Rasma
1986 *Ethnic Relations in the USSR: The Perspective from Below.* London: Allen and Unwin.

Karpat, Ivan
1978 "New Guinea Models in the African Savannah." *Africa* 48 (1): 17.

Karpat, Kemal H.
1982 "Millet and Nationality: The Roots of the Incongruity of Nation and State in Post-Ottoman Era." In B. Braude and B. Lewis, eds., *Christian and Jews in the Ottoman Empire: The Functioning of a Plural Society.* New York: Holmes and Meier Publishers.
1985 "The Ethnicity Problem in a Multi-Ethnic Anational State: Continuity and Re-casting of Ethnic Identity in the Ottoman State." In Paul Brass, ed., *Ethnic Groups and the State,* 94–114. London: Croom Helm.
1990a "The *Hijra* from Russia and the Balkans: The Process of Self-defini-

tion in the Late Ottoman State." In D. Eickelman and J. Piscatori, eds., *Muslim Travellers: Pilgrimage, Migration, and the Religious Imagination*, 131–52. London: Routledge.

———, ed.
1990b *The Turks of Bulgaria: The History, Culture, and Political Fate of a Minority*. Istanbul: Isis Press.

Kedourie, Elie
1960 *Nationalism*. London: Hutchinson.

Kerewsky-Halpern, Barbara
1985 "Rakija as a Ritual in Rural Serbia." *East European Quarterly* 18 (4): 481–95.

Kettani, Ali M.
1986 *Muslim Minorities in the World Today*. London: Mansell.

Keyes, Charles F.
1981 "The Dialectics of Ethnic Change." In Charles F. Keyes, ed., *Ethnic Change*, 3–86. Seattle: University of Washington Press.

Kideckel, David A.
1993 *The Solitude of Collectivism: Romanian Villagers to the Revolution and Beyond*. Ithaca: Cornell University Press.

Klein, George, and Patricia V. Klein
1988 "Nationalism vs. Ideology the Pivot of Yugoslav Politics." In Roman Szporluk, ed., *Communism and Nationalism: Karl Marx versus Friedrich List*, 247–79. Oxford: Oxford University Press.

Kligman, Gail
1988 *The Wedding of the Dead: Ritual, Poetics, and Popular Culture in Transylvania*. Berkeley: University of California Press.

Lambek, Michael
1990 "Certain Knowledge, Contestable Authority: Power and Practice on the Islamic Periphery." *American Ethnologist* 17 (1): 23–40.
1993 *Knowledge and Practice in Mayotte: Local Discourse of Islam, Sorcery, and Spirit Possession*. Toronto: University of Toronto Press.

Lederer, Ivo J.
1969 "Nationalism and the Yugoslavs." In Ivo J. Lederer and Peter F. Sugar, eds., *Nationalism in Eastern Europe*, 396–439. Seattle: University of Washington Press.

Levy, Reuben
1957 *The Social Structure of Islam*. Cambridge: Cambridge University Press.

Lewis, Ioan M.
1968 "Literacy in a Nomadic Society: The Somali Case." In Jack Goody, ed., *Literacy in Traditional Societies*, 265–76. Cambridge: Cambridge University Press.
1971 *Ecstatic Religion: A Study of Shamanism and Spirit Possession*. London: Penguin Books.
1986 *Religion in Context: Cults and Charisma*. Cambridge: Cambridge University Press.

Linnekin J., and L. Poyer
1990 "Introduction." In J. Linnekin and L. Poyer, eds., *Cultural Identity and Ethnicity in the Pacific*, 1–16. Honolulu: University of Hawaii.

Lison-Tolosana, C.
1973 "Galician Moral Structure." *American Anthropologist* 75 (3): 826–35.

Lockwood, William G.
1972 "Converts and Consanguinity: The Social Organization of Moslem Slavs in Western Bosnia." *Ethnology* 11 (1): 55–79.
1974 "Bride Theft and Social Maneuverability in Western Bosnia." *Anthropological Quarterly* 47 (3): 253–69.
1975a *European Moslems: Economy and Ethnicity in Eastern Bosnia*. New York: Academic Press.

Lockwood, William G.
1975b "Social Status and Cultural Change in a Bosnian Moslem Village." *East European Quarterly* 9 (2): 123–35.
1979 "Living Legacy of the Ottoman Empire: The Serbo-Croatian Speaking Moslems of Bosnia-Herzegovina." In A. Ascher, T. Halasi-Kun, and B. K. Kiraly, eds., *The Mutual Effects of the Islamic and the Judeo-Christian Worlds: The East European Pattern*, 209–25. New York: Brooklyn College Press.
1981 "Religion and Language as Criteria of Ethnic Identity: An Exploratory Comparison." In S. Beck and J. W. Cole, eds., *Ethnicity and Nationalism in Southeastern Europe*, 85–98. Amsterdam: University of Amsterdam Press.

Lockwood, Yvonne R.
1983 *Text and Context: Folksongs in a Bosnian Muslim Village*. Ohio: Slavica Publishers.

Loizos, Peter
1981 *The Heart Grown Bitter: A Chronicle of Cypriot War Refugees*. Cambridge: Cambridge University Press.

Loizos, Peter, and Evthymios Papataxiarchis
1991 "Gender, Sexuality, and the Person in Greek Culture." In P. Loizos and E. Papataxiarchis, eds., *Contested Identities: Gender and Kinship in Modern Greece*, 221–34. Princeton: Princeton University Press.

Malcolm, Noel
1994 *Bosnia, a Short History*. London: Macmillan.

Maloney, Clarence, ed.
1976 *The Evil Eye*. New York: Columbia University Press.

Mandel, Ruth
1990 "Shifting Centres and Emergent Identities: Turkey and Germany in the Lives of Turkish *Gastarbeiter*." In D. Eickelman and J. Piscatori, eds., *Muslim Travellers: Pilgrimage, Migration, and the Religious Imagination*, 153–71. London: Routledge.

Marcus, Julie
1990 *A World of Difference: Islam and Gender Hierarchy in Turkey*. London: Zed Books.

Mauss, Marcel
[1954]1990   *The Gift: The Form and Reason for Exchange in Archaic Socie-*
             *ties.* London: Routledge.
McDonnell, Mary Byrne
1990   "Patterns of Muslim Pilgrimage from Malaysia." In D. Eickelman and
       J. Piscatori, eds., *Muslim Travellers: Pilgrimage, Migration, and the*
       *Religious Imagination,* 111–30. London: Routledge.
Mernissi, Fatima
1985   *Beyond the Veil: Male-Female Dynamics in Muslim Society.* London: Al
       Saqi Books.
Molyneux, Maxine
1984   "Women in Socialist Societies: Problems of Theory and Practice." In
       K. Young, C. Wolkowitz, and R. McCullagh, eds., *Of Marriage and*
       *the Market: Women's Subordination Internationally and its Lessons,*
       55–90. London: Routledge and Kegan Paul.
Moore, Henrietta L.
1988   *Feminism and Anthropology.* Cambridge: Polity Press.
Morokvašić, Mirjana
1980   "The Changing Role of Women in Yugoslav Society." Paper pre-
       sented at Conference on Social Movements in Southern Europe. May
       24–25. London: University College.
1984   "Sexuality and Control of Procreation." In K. Young, C. Wolkowitz,
       and R. McCullagh, eds., *Of Marriage and the Market: Women's Sub-*
       *ordination Internationally and Its Lessons,* 193–209. London: Rout-
       ledge and Kegan Paul.
1986   "Being a Woman in Yugoslavia: Past, Present and Institutional Equal-
       ity." In M. Gadant, ed., *Women of the Mediterranean,* 120–38. Lon-
       don: Zed Books.
Mortenesen, Lotte B.
1983   "The Influence of Socialisation and Formal Eduaction of Turkish
       Women." In Bo Utas, ed., *Women in Islamic Societies: Social Attitudes*
       *and Historical Perspectives,* 211–26. London: Curzon Press.
Mosley, Philip E.
1976   "The Peasant Family: the Zadruga, or Communal Joint Family in the
       Balkans and Its Recent Evolution." In Robert F. Byrnes, ed., *Commu-*
       *nal Families in the Balkans: The Zadruga. Essays by Philip E. Mosely*
       *and Essays in His Honour,* 19–30. London: University of Notre Dame
       Press.
Mulahalilović, Enver
1988   *Vjerski Običaji Muslimana u Bosni i Hercegovina.* Sarajevo: Starje-
       šinstvo Islamske Zajednice.
Musallam, B. F.
1983   *Sex and Society in Islam.* Cambridge: Cambridge University Press.
Nagata, Judith
1981   "In Defense of Ethnic Boundaries: The Changing Myths and Charters
       of Malay Identity." In Charles F. Keyes, ed., *Ethnic Change,* 87–116.
       Seattle: University of Washington Press.

Nielsen, Jørgen
1992　*Muslims in Western Europe*. Edinburgh: Edinburgh University Press.
Niškanović, Miroslav
1978　*Ilindanski Dernek kod Turbeta Djerzelez Alije u Gerzovu*. Novi Pazar: n.p.
Norris, H. T.
1993　*Islam in the Balkans: Religion and Society between Europe and the Arab World*. Columbia, S.C.: University of South Carolina Press.
Obolenski, D.
1948　*The Bogomils*. Cambridge: Cambridge University Press.
Ortner, Sherry B.
1978　*Sherpas Through Their Rituals*. Cambridge: Cambridge University Press.
Ott, Sandra
1981　*The Circle of Mountains: A Basque Shepherding Community*. Oxford: Clarendon Press.
Palavestra, Veljko, and Mario Petrić
1964　*Srednjovjekovni Nadgrobni Spomenici u Žepi*. Sarajevo: Radovi Naučnog Društva BiH, knj. XXIV, Odjeljenje Istorijsko-Filoloških Nauka, knj. 8.
Parry, Jonathan P.
1979　*Caste and Kinship in Kangra*. London: Routledge and Kegan Paul.
Peristiany, J. G.
1976　*Mediterranean Family Structures*. Cambridge: Cambridge University Press.
——————, ed.
1968　*Contributions to Mediterranean Sociology: Mediterranean Rural Communities and Social Change*. The Hague: Mouton.
Petek-Salom, Gaye, and Pinar Hukum
1986　"Women's Emancipation after the Ataturk Period." In M. Gadant, ed., *Women of the Mediterranean*, 92–109. London: Zed Books.
Petrović, Ruza
1987　*Migracije u Jugoslviji i Etnički Aspekt*. Belgrade: Istraživačko Izdavački Centar.
Petrovich, Michael B.
1972　"Yugoslavia: Religion and the Tensions of a Multi-National State." *East European Quarterly* 6 (1): 118–35.
Pina-Cabral, João de
1986　*Sons of Adam, Daughters of Eve*. Oxford: Clarendon Press.
1989　"The Mediterranean as a Category of Regional Comparison: A Critical View." *Current Anthropology* 30 (3): 339–406.
Piscatori, James
1986　*Islam in a World of Nation-States*. Cambridge: Cambridge University Press.
Popović, Alexandre
1985　"The Contemporary Situation of the Muslim Mystic Orders in Yugo-

slavia." In Ernest Gellner, ed., *Islamic Dilemmas: Reformers, Nationalists and Industrialization. The Southern Shore of the Mediterranean*, 240–54. Berlin: Mouton.

1990   *Les Musulmans Yougoslaves: 1945–1989, Médiateurs et Metaphores*. Lausanne: L'Age d'Homme.

Poulton, Hugh
1991   *The Balkans: Minorities and States in Conflict*. London: Minority Rights Publication.

Purivatra, Atif
1970   *Nacionalni i Politički Razvitak Muslimana*, Sarajevo: Svjetlost.
1974   "The National Phenomenon of the Moslems of Bosnia-Herzegovina." In Nada Dragić, ed., *Nations and Nationalities of Yugoslavia*, 305–27. Belgrade: Medjunarodna Politika.

Ramet, Pedro
1984   "Women, Work and Self-Management in Yugoslavia." *East European Quarterly* 17 (4): 459–68.
———, ed.
1985   *Yugoslavia in the 1980s*. Boulder: Westview Press.

Ramet, Sabrina
1992   *Nationalism and Federalism in Yugoslavia, 1962–1991*. 2d ed. Bloomington: Indiana University Press.

Redfield, Robert
1960   *The Little Community and Peasant Society and Culture*. Chicago: University of Chicago Press.

Redžić, Husref
1983   *Studije o Islamskoj Arhitektonskoj Baštini*. Sarajevo: Veselin Masleša.

Rheubottom, David B.
1976   "The Saint's Feast and Skopska Crna Goran Social Structure." *Man* (n.s.) 11 (1): 18–35.
1980   "Dowry and Wedding Celebrations in Yugoslav Macedonia." In J. L. Comaroff, ed., *The Meaning of Marriage Payments*, 221–50. London: Academic Press.

Rodinson, Maxime
1974   *Islam and Capitalism*. London: Allen Lane.

Rosen, Lawrence
1984   *Bargaining for Reality: The Construction of Social Relations in a Muslim Community*. Chicago: University of Chicago Press.

Rusinow, Dennison I.
1981   "Unfinished Business: The Yugoslav 'National Question'." *American Universities Field Staff Reports* 35. Region: Europe.

Rycault, Paul
1668   *The Present State of the Ottoman Empire*. London: n.p.

Sahlins, Marshall
1974   *Stone Age Economics*. London: Tavistock Publications.

Said, Edward W.
1978   *Orientalism*. London: Penguin Books.

Saltaga, Fuad
1991  *Muslimanska Nacija u Jugoslaviji: Porijeklo, Islam, Kultura, Povijest, Politika*. Sarajevo: Institut za Proučavanje Nacionalnih Odnosa.

Samardžić, Radovan
1971  *Mehmed Sokolović*. Belgrade: Srpska Književna Zadruga.

Schimmel, Annemarie
1989  *Islamic Names*. Edinburgh: Edinburgh University Press.

Schneider, Jane
1980  "Trousseau as Treasure: Some Contradictions of Late Nineteenth-Century Change in Sicily." In Eric Ross, ed., *Beyond the Myths of Culture: Essays in Cultural Materialism*, 323–56. New York: Academic Press.

Shanin, Teodor
1989  "Ethnicity in the Soviet Union: Analytical Perceptions and Political Strategies." *Comparative Studies in Society and History* 3: 409–23.

Shepard, William E.
1987  "Islam and Ideology: Towards a Typology." *International Journal of Middle East Studies* 19: 307–36.

Šidak, Jaroslav
1940  *Crkva Bosanska i Problem Bogumilstva u Bosni*. Zagreb: Matice Hrvatske.

Simic, Andrei
1969  "Management of the Male Image in Yugoslavia." *Anthropological Quarterly* 43 (2): 89–101.
1983  "Urbanization and Modernization in Yugoslavia." In M. Kenny and D. I. Kertzer, eds., *Urban Life in Mediterranean Europe*, 211–24. Chicago: University of Illinois Press.

Singleton, Fred
1985  *A Short History of the Yugoslav Peoples*. Cambridge: Cambridge University Press.

Škaljić, Abdulah
1985  *Turcizmi u Sprskohravatskom-Hrvatskosrpskom Jeziku*. Sarajevo: Svjetlost.

Skendi, Stavro
1982  "The *Millet* System and its Contribution to the Blurring of Orthodox National Identity in Albania." In B. Braude and B. Lewis, eds., *Christians and Jews in the Ottoman Empire: The Functioning of a Plural Society*, 243–55. New York: Holmes and Meier Publishers.

Smajlović, Ahmed
1979  "Muslims in Yugoslavia." *Journal of the Institute of Muslim Minority Affairs* 1 (1): 132–44.

Smith, Anthony D.
1986  *The Ethnic Origin of Nations*. Oxford: Blackwell.
1991  *National Identity*. London. Penguin Books.

Softić, Aiša
1984  *Tevhidi u Sarajevo*. Sarajevo: Glasnik Zemaljskog Muzeja Bosne i Hercegovine, Etnologija, Nova serija, 39 (separate edition).

Sorabji, Cornelia
 1989 "Muslim Identity and Islamic Faith in Socialist Sarajevo." Ph.D. thesis, University of Cambridge.
 1994 "Mixed Motives: Islam, Nationalism and *Mevlud*s in an Unstable Yugoslavia." In Camilla Fawzi El-Solh and Judy Mabro, eds., *Muslim Women's Choices: Religious Belief and Social Reality*, 108–27. Oxford: Berg Publishers.

Starr, June
 1984 "The Legal and Social Transformation of Rural Women in Aegean Turkey." In R. Hirschon, ed., *Women and Property—Women as Property*, 92–116. London: Croom Helm.

St. Erlich, Vera
 1966 *Family in Transition: A Study of 300 Yugoslav Villages.* Princeton: Princeton University Press.
 1976 "The Last Big Zadrugas: Albanian Extended Families in the Kossovo Regions." In Robert F. Byrnes, ed., *Communal Families in the Balkans: The Zadruga. Essays by Philip E. Mosely and Essays in His Honour,* 244–51. London: University of Notre Dame Press.

Stewart, Charles
 1991 *Demons and the Devil.* Princeton: Princeton University Press.

Stirling, Paul
 1963 "The Domestic Cycle and the Distribution of Power in Turkish Villages." In Julian Pitt-Rivers, ed., *Mediterranean Countrymen: Essays in the Social Anthropology of the Mediterranean,* 201–13. Paris: Mouton.
 1965 *Turkish Village.* London: Weidenfeld and Nicholson.

Stojaković, Velibor
 1987 *Društveni Odnosi i Društvene Institucije Stanovnika Tešanjskog Kraja.* Sarajevo: Glasnik Zemaljskog Muzeja Bosne i Hercegovine, Etnologija, Nova serija, 41/42 (separate edition).

Strathern, Marilyn
 1992 "Qualified Value: The Perspective of Gift Exchange." In C. Humphrey and S. Hugh-Jones, eds., *Barter, Exchange and Value: An Anthropological Approach,* 169–91. Cambridge: Cambridge University Press.

Svanberg, Ingvar
 1989 *Kazak Refugees in Turkey: A Study of Cultural Persistence and Social Change.* Uppsala: Acta Universitatis Upsaliensis.

Tambiah, S. J.
 1979 "A Performative Approach to Ritual." *Proceedings of the British Academy* 65: 113–69.

Tapper, Nancy
 1990 "*Ziyaret:* Gender, Movement, and Exchange in a Turkish Community." In D. Eickelman and J. Piscatori, eds., *Muslim Travellers: Pilgrimage, Migration, and the Religious Imagination,* 236–55. London: Routledge.

Tapper, Nancy, and Richard Tapper
   1987   "The Birth of the Prophet: Ritual and Gender in Turkish Islam." *Man*
          (n.s.) 22 (1): 69–92.
Thompson, Mark
   1992   *A Paper House: The Ending of Yugoslavia.* London: Vintage.
Tomasevich, Jozo
   1955   *Peasants, Politics, and Economic Change in Yugoslavia.* Stanford:
          Stanford University Press.
Tomić, Ivan M.
   1992   *Whose is Bosnia-Hercegovina?* London: Zbornik.
Tvrtković, Paul
   1993   *Bosnia Hercegovina Back to the Future.* London: Paul Tvrtković.
Vinogradov, Amal
   1974   "Introduction." *Anthropological Quarterly* 47 (1): 2–9.
Vucinich, Wayne S.
   1949   "Yugoslavs of the Moslem Faith." In Robert J. Kerner, ed., *Yugo-
          slavia,* 261–75. Berkeley: University of California Press.
Waardenburg, Jacques
   1979   "Official and Popular Religion as a Problem in Islamic Studies." In
          P. H. Vrijhof and J. Waardenburg, eds., *Official and Popular Religion:
          Analysis of a Theme for Religious Studies.* The Hague: Mouton.
Watt, W. Montgomery
   1982   "Islam and the West." In Denis MacEoin and Ahmed Al-Shahi, eds.,
          *Islam in the Modern World.* London: Croom Helm.
Wikan, Unni
   1982   *Behind the Veil in Arabia: Women in Oman.* Baltimore: John Hopkins
          University Press.
   1984   "Shame and Honour: A Contestable Pair." *Man* (n.s.) 19 (4): 635–
          52.
Williams, Brackette F.
   1990   "Nationalism, Traditionalism, and the Problem of Cultural Inauthen-
          ticity." In Richard G. Fox, ed., *Nationalist Ideologies and the Produc-
          tion of National Cultures,* 112–29. Washington: American Ethnologi-
          cal Society Monograph Series, 2.

About the Author

TONE BRINGA has a permanent lectureship in Social Anthropology
at the University of Bergen, Norway.

7152